THURSTAN

———

ARCHBISHOP
OF
YORK

THURSTAN

Archbishop of York
(1114 – 1140)

by

Donald Nicholl, M.A. (Oxon)
(Senior Lecturer in History, University of Keele)

THE STONEGATE PRESS
YORK
1964

THE STONEGATE PRESS, 21 STONEGATE, YORK.

© THE STONEGATE PRESS, 1964

Printed in Great Britain
By FREDERICK DUFFIELD & SONS LTD
421, Kirkstall Road
Leeds, 4

CONTENTS

PREFACE

THE present study was begun in response to the observations made by Sir Maurice Powicke in 1950 when he wrote that "the mental atmosphere of the north of England in the middle of the twelfth century has not yet been recaptured. The sympathetic familiarity which alone would make such a study worth while could come only from many years of leisurely untrammelled observation, and would require a rare mastery, not only of the experiences of mind and spirit in the north-west of Europe, and particularly in Durham and York, since the days of Alcuin, but also of the intangibles of history."[1] For anyone wishing to fill in some of the gaps in our understanding of northern England in the twelfth century the conditions set by Sir Maurice Powicke must appear too daunting, especially for someone such as myself who is stationed in a newly established upland university without easy access to the great collections of both printed and manuscript sources. And yet one must begin somewhere. In my own case I decided to see whether a rather tantalizing person who momentarily appears as an actor in many episodes of the time, that is, archbishop Thurstan, could not be brought nearer to the centre of the stage.

I was proceeding on the assumption that we could only recapture the mental atmosphere of the north of England in the middle of the twelfth century after numbers of monographs on particular persons or themes were available. Now I am inclined to doubt whether this assumption is correct : the documentation for the period is so uneven that there is scarcely a person of that age and area who can be seen both in detail and in sufficient depth to take on life. I think that Sir Maurice Powicke's hopes could best be fulfilled if a group of students of the period were to co-operate to describe the society and institutions of the North in much the same way as Cambridge scholars have tackled early British history under the guidance of Mrs. N. K. Chadwick. In other words, we should be better placed

---

(1) *Vita Ailredi*, p. liii.

to gain insight into individuals after a more extended study of their society than we are by attempting to confront individuals directly. And such an extended study is beyond the reach of an isolated scholar.

That there are enough scholars to undertake such an enterprise was convincingly and pleasantly made obvious to me by the help I received whenever I sought it. Not one of those whom I consulted failed to give generously whatever help they could, even though they were sometimes as puzzled as I was. Those whom I taxed in this way included Sir Charles Clay, Fr. G. Culkin, Prof. C. R. Cheney, Prof. A. Musset, Prof. R. du Boulay, Dr. Ian Doyle, and Dr. C. H. Talbot. Mr. Ernest Bailey and Mr. R. M. Beaumont dealt promptly and carefully with queries I put to them about Beverley and Southwell respectively. To all of these I am most grateful, as also to Messrs. Burns and Oates for permission to quote from B. Scott-James's translation of " St. Bernard's Letters," and also to Messrs. Thos. Nelson & Sons for permission to quote from C. Johnson's translation of Hugh the Chantor's "History of the Church of York." My largest debt, however, is to Prof. R. W. Southern, who read my book in typescript and made numerous suggestions for improving it ; the fact that I have not adopted all of these does not prevent me from recognizing, and being glad to acknowledge, that whatever understanding I may have of the Middle Ages I owe to him.

DONALD NICHOLL.

ABBREVIATIONS

E P N S   English Place Name Society publications (1924 ff).

E Y C   *Early Yorkshire Charters*, 10 vols. (1914–55) ed. W. Farrer (Vols. I–III) and C. T. Clay (Vols. IV–X).

H C   *Hugh the Chantor : The History of the Church of York*, 1066–1127. Ed. C. Johnson (1961).

H C Y   *Historians of the Church of York*, ed. J. Raine (*R S*, 71, 3 vols. 1879–94).

H & S   A. W. Haddan and W. Stubbs, *Councils and Ecclesiastical Documents relating to Great Britain and Ireland*, 3 vols. (1869–71).

Jaffé   P. Jaffé, *Regesta Pontificum Romanorum*, I (1885).

Mansi   J. Mansi, ed., *Sacrorum Conciliorum Nova Collectio*, 31 vols. (1757–98).

Monasticon   *Monasticon Anglicanum*, ed. W. Dugdale, 6 vols. (1817–30).

P L   *Patrologiae Latinae Cursus Completus*, ed. J. P. Migne, 222 vols. (1844–64).

Regesta   *Regesta Regum Anglo-Normannorum* II, ed. C. Johnson and H. A. Cronne (1956).

R S   Rolls Series (*Rerum Britannicarum Medii Aevi Scriptores* 1858–96).

S S   Surtees Society Publications.

V C H   Victoria County History.

Y A J   Yorkshire Archaeological Journal.

THURSTAN'S ITINERARY AND

c. 1070		Bayeux : his birthplace.	
?		Cluny ; makes vow to take habit some day.	(p. 9 of this present work)
1103	September 1	London. One of Henry I's chaplains (cf Regesta no. 652 ; first mention of Thurstan).	
1105	January 1	Windsor. Draws up precept for the king in favour of Church of St. Peter, York, and of Beverley.	(Regesta no. 681)
1110	April	Marlborough, with king's court.	(Regesta no. 939)
1111	September	Winchester. Present when Queen Matilda (in Henry's absence) adjudged in favour of the abbot of Abingdon on the basis of Domesday Book.	(Regesta no. 1000)
1114	August 15	At Winchester ; elected to see of York.	(H C pp. 33–4)
	September 13	Westbourne (Sussex).	(Regesta no. 1064)
	December	Ordained deacon by William Giffard, bishop of Winchester.	(H C pp. 34–5)
	December	York ; enthroned by Robert bishop of Chester/Lichfield.	(H C p. 35)
	December	Durham ; consulting Turgot.	(H C p. 35)
	December	Hexham.	(H C p. 35)
	December 25	Crosses to Normandy.	(H C p. 36)
1115	June 6 (Whitsun)	Bayeux ; ordained priest by Ranulf Flambard.	(H C p. 37)
		Returns to England.	(H C p. 37)
	September 16	Westminster ; king's council.	(H C pp. 37–8)
1116	March 19	Salisbury ; king's council ; Thurstan resigns his office.	(H C p. 41)
	April	Normandy ; with the king.	(H C p. 46)

EVENTS RELEVANT TO HIS CAREER

1109	April 21	Death of St. Anselm.
	June 13	At Henry I's Whitsun court in Westminster were messengers from Germany to arrange the Emperors'' marriage to Matilda, daughter of Henry I.
1110	February 23	The bridal party accompanying Matilda to Germany sets off from Dover.
	August	The Emperor Henry V crosses the Alps on his journey towards Rome as a threat to Pope Paschal II.
1111	February 4	The Concordat of Sutri forced upon the Pope by the Emperor.
	February 12	The Emperor crowned in Rome ; the Pope is his captive.
1112	September 16	Church Council at Vienne excommunicates Henry V ; declares lay investiture heresy.
1114	January 7	Marriage of Henry V and Matilda celebrated at Mainz.
	April 26	Ralph d'Escures elected as archbishop of Canterbury.
1116	March 6	Lateran council ; certain cardinals press Pope Paschal to excommunicate the Emperor.

1117	Autumn (?)	Returns to England.	(H C pp. 56-7)

1118	February	Returns to England, reinstated in his office (?).	(Eadmer, p. 244. Eadmer's dates cannot be reconciled with those given by H C)
	Autumn	In Normandy.	(H C p. 57)
	Christmas	Rouen ; with the king.	(H C p. 60)

1119	Lent	In Normandy; interview with the king.	(H C p. 65)
	June	Rouen ; with the king.	(Regesta no. 1204)
	*September 19	Chartres.	
	September 22	Tours ; meets Calixtus II.	
		Blois.	
	October 3	Morigny.	
	October 9	Paris.	
	October 19	Rheims ; consecrated by the Pope the day before the opening of the Council.	
	November 1	Rheims ; receives the pallium.	(H C p. 75)
		Préaux (west of Rouen) ; at bedside of dying Eudo, the dapifer.	(p. 67 of this present work)
	November 20	Beauvais.	
	November 23	Chaumont.	
	November 27	Saint Denis.	
		Corbeil.	
		Melun.	
	November 30	Ferrières ; present at Pope's meeting with king of France.	
	December 4	Sens.	
	December 7-14	Auxerre.	
	December 23	Saulieu ; where the Pope ratified Cistercian constitutions.	
	December 25-29	Autun.	
	December 31	Cluny.	

1120	January 6	Still at Cluny.	
	January 12	Tournus.	
	January 23	Lyons.	
	Feb. 2-10	Vienne.	
	Feb. 13-17	Romans.	
	Feb. 18-27	Valence.	
	March 2	Crest.	
	March 6-11	Gap ; bids farewell to the Pope, who is journeying to Rome.	
		Blois.	(H C p. 91)
		Rheims.	(H C p. 92)
		Soissons.	(H C p. 92)
	April 18	Colombes.	(H C p. 92)
		Marcigny.	(H C p. 93)

* The entries between September 19th, 1119 and March 11th, 1120 are based on the two works of Ulysse Robert, *Bullaire du pape Calixte II*, and *Histoire du pape Calixte II* (see Bibliography).

1117 January   Paschal flees from Rome towards Benevento through
                       fear of Emperor.
                       Henry V enters Rome.

1118 January 21   Death of Paschal II. A few days later, election of
                       Gelasius II.
      February/   Henry I in Normandy attacked by Louis of France and
      March   his allies of Anjou and Flanders.
      March 8   Henry V sets up Burdinus, archbishop of Braga, as anti-
                       Pope with the title Gregory VIII.
      April 7   Gelasius II excommunicates both Emperor and anti-Pope.
      May 1   Death of Matilda, wife of Henry I of England.
      October 7   Council of Rouen ; papal legate delivers sermon against
                       Emperor in presence of English king and prelates.

1119 January 29   Gelasius II dies at Cluny. Election of Calixtus II.
      August/   Running war in Duchy of Normandy between Henry of
      September   England and Louis of France.
      October 20-29   Council of Rheims held by Calixtus II.
      October 22   Calixtus' vain attempt at Monzon (near Rheims) to
                       reconcile Henry V, who had an army of 30,000 at hand.
                       Excommunication of Emperor and anti-Pope.

1120 June 3   Calixtus back in Rome.
      June 29   Eadmer, monk of Canterbury, elected as bishop of St.
                       Andrews, Scotland.
      November 25   Wreck of the White Ship.

1120	May 30	Nemours ; interview with King Henry.	(H C p. 95)
	October	Beauvais ; at the council held by the papal legate, Cuno.	(H C p. 98)
		Gisors.	(H C p. 98)
		Chartres.	(H C p. 99)
1121	January 31	England.	(H C p. 100)
	February	Windsor ; attending court of Henry and his new queen.	(H C p. 100)
	February 20	York.	(H C p. 100)
	April 7	York.	(H C p. 101)
	April (?)	Clarendon ; with the king.	(Regesta no. 1271)
	September 29	(?) ; attending king's council.	(H C p. 106)
1122	January 10	Southern England ; with the king.	(Regesta no. 1312)
	March (?)	Rockingham ; with the king.	(Regesta no. 1320)
	Autumn (?)	Nottingham ; with the king.	(Regesta no. 1328)
	Autumn	York ; with the king.	(Regesta no. 1332)
	December 6	York ; with the king.	(Regesta no. 1337)
1123	February 2	Gloucester ; council to elect a new archbishop of Canterbury.	(H C p. 108)
	March 11	Woodstock.	(H C p. 110)
	May	Rome.	(Jaffé, p. 813)
		Normandy ; with the king.	(H C p. 119)
	Autumn	Returns to England.	(H C p. 119)
1125	January/ March (?)	Normandy ; with the king.	(Regesta no. 1425)
	April 12	England ; at consecration of bishop of Chichester.	(Florence of Worcester p. 79)
	September	London ; council held by papal legate, John of Crema.	(H C p. 121)
	October (?)	Evreux.	(Regesta nos. 1431 1433)
		Rome.	(H C p. 124)
1126	January	Leaves Rome.	(Jaffé p. 828)
	July	York.	(H C p. 128)
	Autumn (?)	Rockingham ; with the king.	(Regesta nos. 1459 1460 1461 1463)
	Christmas	Windsor.	(H C p. 129)
		London.	(H C p. 129)
1127	Spring	York.	(p. 102 of this present work)
	July 17	Roxburgh.	(pp. 102–3 of this present work)
	September (?)	Rouen ; with the king.	(Regesta no. 1547)
	Christmas (?)	Argentan.	(Regesta no. 1557)
1128		Normandy.	(J. H. Round. Calendar of Documents, p. 521)

1121	January 29	King Henry I marries Adeliza, daughter of Geoffrey of Louvain.
	April	Pope's forces capture and imprison the imperialist anti-Pope.
		Trial of Abelard at Soissons.
1122	June	John, bishop of Glasgow, goes to Rome to argue his case against Thurstan.
	August 9	Death of Cuno of Praeneste.
	September 23	Concordat of Worms reconciling Pope and Emperor.
	October 20	Death of Ralph, archbishop of Canterbury.
1123	February 4	William of Corbeil elected as archbishop of Canterbury.
	March 18	Opening of Lateran Council.
1124		The whole of this year the king was heavily engaged fighting in Normandy.
	April 22	David I succeeds to Scottish kingdom.
	August 26	Pope dissolves marriage between William Clito and the daughter of Fulk of Anjou.
	December 13	Death of Calixtus II ; election of Honorius II a week later.
1125	May 23	Death of Emperor Henry V.
1126	Christmas	English barons swear to accept Matilda as their future sovereign.
1127	May 13-16	Council of London held by William of Corbeil as papal legate.
1128	June 17	Matilda marries Geoffrey of Anjou.
	September 5	Death of Ranulf Flambard, bishop of Durham.

1129	pre-June	Rouen.	(Regesta nos. 1577–8)
	August 1	London ; national ecclesiastical council.	(Henry of Huntingdon, pp. 250–1)
1130	March (?)	Winchester.	(Regesta no. 1654)
1131	July/August	Arques ; with the king.	(Regesta no. 1692)
	August (?)	Westbourne ; with the king.	(Regesta no. 1710)
		Waltham ; with the king.	(Regesta no. 1711)
	September 8	Northampton.	(Regesta no. 1713)
1132	April 29	Westminster.	(Regesta no. 1736)
	Summer	York.	(see pp. 164-170 of this present work)
	October 17	York ; exodus from St. Mary's.	(see p. 170 of this present work)
	(?)	Fontevrault (?)	(Gallia Christiana XI. 575)
1133	June (?)	Westminster.	(Regesta no. 1759)
	August 6	York ; consecrates Athelwold as bishop of Carlisle and Geoffrey Rufus as bishop of Durham.	(see p. 149 of this present work)
1136	February	York ; with king Stephen.	(see p. 217 of this present work)
	March 26	London ; at Stephen's court.	(see p. 217 of this present work)
1137	after April 11	Roxburgh ; truce with King David.	(see p. 218 of this present work)
		Northampton ; holds a council along with the bishop of Salisbury.	(see p. 218 of this present work)
1138	April 10	Northampton ; presides over national council.	(see p. 219 of this present work)
	July 27	York ; assembles Yorkshire magnates to fight the Scots.	(see p. 221 of this present work)
		York ; gives banner of St. Peter to the English army.	(see p. 224 of this present work)
1140	January 25	Pontefract.	(see p. 237 of this present work)
	February 6	Pontefract ; dies.	(see p. 237 of this present work)

1130 February 13   Death of Honorius II ; election of Innocent II next
                    day ; schism of Anacletus.
     September/   French recognition of Innocent as Pope.
     October

1131 January   Henry I meets Innocent at Orleans and recognizes him
                    as Pope.
     September 8   English barons renew oath to Matilda.
     October 18   Council of Rheims under Innocent ; Henry I sends
                    representatives.

1132 March 28   Reform meeting at Cluny.

1135 December 1   Death of King Henry I.
     December 22   Coronation of Stephen of Blois as King of England.

1136 November 20   Death of William of Corbeil, archbishop of Canterbury.

1137 June 8   Great fire at York.

1138 January 25   Death of Anacletus and end of schism.
     August 22   The Battle of the Standard.
     December 24   Theobald of Bec elected as archbishop of Canterbury.

1139 April 4   Lateran Council.
     September 30   Matilda lands in England, civil war breaks out.

CHAPTER I.

THE FORMATIVE YEARS.

Normandy in the late eleventh century was a propitious place for the "lad of parts" to be born in, for it was supremely a land of opportunity. Its vigorous people had long been aware of their Scandinavian ancestry as setting them apart from the people in the rest of France, for whom they exhibited a marked disdain[1]. Their self-consciousness as a race apart had been greatly heightened during the century through the conquests made by men of their blood in areas so far afield as England, Apulia and the Holy Land, especially since in each of these areas their rough and earthy ambitions had received the comforting and uplifting sanction of a religious blessing[2]. As a result of these colonizing expeditions, young men of ability brought up in the bracing climate of Normandy could look forward to distinguished careers ruling church and society in the new lands that the prowess of their conquering ancestors had opened up before them.

Such hopes burned particularly bright in the hearts of young men like Thurstan of Bayeux who were thinking of a clerical rather than a military career, for the turn of events in Europe had brought the advance guard of the reforming movement within the church to the Duchy. The great names of Lanfranc and Anselm had won scholars to the centres of learning at Bec and at Caen ; and with them had arrived the new canon law and the new idea of enforcing celibacy on the church's priests, as well as the impulse towards new and more austere forms of monastic life. It was in the latter field, of monastic reform, that Normandy itself was making its own peculiar contribution. The orthodox pattern of monasticism at Bec and Caen owed much to the influx of outsiders, but local inspiration ran into

---

1. *Cf* Raoul de Caen, Historien et écrivain, by H. Glaisner in *Revue d'hist. éccl.*, XLVI, 1951, pp. 5–21

2. *Cf* Henry of Huntingdon, *Historia Anglorum* (*R S*), p. 208 for the Normans' reputation as fierce and cruel warriors. Duke Robert, the Conqueror's father, had made the pilgrimage to Jerusalem in 1035. In 1096, amongst those who followed Duke Robert on the crusade to Jerusalem was Richard de Condé, seemingly one of the first lords of Condé-sur-Seulles, Thurstan's birth-place. (*Mémoirs pour servir a l'état historique et géographique du diocèse de Bayeux* II, p. 186, G. le Hardy.)

more extravagant forms. On the borders of the Duchy, for instance, the hermit Hervé took into his cell the Englishwoman Eva to serve as his spiritual bride, whilst Robert d'Arbrissel's first step towards founding Fontevrault was to provide a community for abandoned wives. Meanwhile Vitalis of Tierceville (near Bayeux) took to converting prostitutes before eventually gathering together a group of hermits who had been leading extremely ascetic lives, and with whom he founded the monastery of Savigny in the forests of Troarn. It was in line with these experiments that the Count of Mortain, for whom Vitalis had served as chaplain, should have interested himself in monastic reform and have later become patron of the Cistercian house situated not far from Savigny.

Yet we must not be misled by the fact that some of the leading spirits in Normandy were being captured by these exciting innovations. One must constantly bear in mind that most contemporaries remained unimpressed by them, and that the general run of clergy in Normandy were amongst the most conservative in Christendom. Over two issues, especially, they proved themselves not only obdurately old-fashioned but also very articulate, these being the related issues of enforced celibacy for the clergy and the drive to prevent clerical offices from becoming hereditary. In fact, "it was customary throughout the whole of Normandy for priests openly to take wives to themselves, to have the marriage rite carried out over them, and to beget sons and daughters to whom they would hand on their churches by hereditary right at death. Often when they were giving away their daughters in marriage and they had no other possessions they would present a church as a dowry. When they were taking wives to themselves, moreover, before marrying them they would swear in the presence of the relatives that they would never abandon them"[3]. Nor are we surprised to learn, from the author of this description, that the ascetic Bernard of Tiron came near to being lynched by the wives of these priests when he went around trying to wean their menfolk from them. Still, at a pinch, Bernard could be laughed off as a slightly mad wandering preacher; it was quite a different matter when the campaign received official backing from church councils; and the clergy of these parts were bitterly stung by Pope Alexander II's

---

3. Vita S. Bernardi abb. Tiron. n. 51. *Acta SS. Apr.* 14, *Vol. II, p.* 234; notice also the Pope's remark to Hugh, Archbishop of Rouen: In provincia Normanniae . . . multa mala, prout accepimus, pullulant, quae in aliis locis vel omnino non fuerunt, vel sunt desuetudine obumbrata. Mansi, t. XXI, col. 421–2.

declaration that sons of priests were not eligible for ordination to the priesthood. Totally unacceptable to the body of the Norman clergy, this declaration provoked uncompromising replies from at least three of their spokesmen. The three were : a canon of Rouen ; the well-known scholar of Caen generally described from his birth-place as Theobald of Étampes ; and the redoubtable Serlo of Bayeux. Many shrewd blows were struck by these stalwarts ; by the canon of Rouen, for instance, when he asked why the sons of criminals should not likewise be barred from the priesthood if the influence of heredity was to be taken so seriously[4] ; and by Theobald when he pointed out that the prohibition on priest's sons was tantamount to declaring that the waters of baptism had been insufficient to cleanse them and set them in the paths of grace[5]. But perhaps the most revealing commentary on the situation came from Serlo, not simply by what he said in his defence of priests' sons, but equally by what he was, his whole career exemplifying all that the reformers found distasteful in the old order.

Serlo was born about 1050[6], the son of a Norman priest, and went for his education to the diocesan city of Bayeux, where he received a first-class training in humane letters. Though no direct description of the school there has come down to us its alumni bear unmistakable witness to its achievements ; men, for instance, such as William de Ros, who was to be the first dean of the cathedral and who gained a reputation as one of the most learned men of his day[7]. Direct and convincing witness to the fostering of letters there is afforded by the skilful verses composed around the year 1100 when the mortuary role of the great Carthusian, Bruno of Cologne, was borne around the country so that all the prominent religious insti-tutions might contribute to it their homage in verse ; as an indica-tion of the Bayeux offering we might quote the lines of the scholars in the cathedral school :—

> Hic dolor, o Bruno, plus quam processit ab uno ;
> Unde dolet, plangit, quam mors tua funditus angit !
> Non lachrymando parum communis turba scholarum

---

4. *Libelli de lite* III, p. 649–655.
5. *Ibid.* 603–7.
6. For the paragraphs on Serlo, *cf* Der sogenannte Serlo von Bayeux by Heinrich Boehmer : *Neues Archiv* 22 (1897), pp. 703–738, and A. Bouté my, Deux poèmes inconnus de Serlon de Bayeux in *Le Moyen Âge*, 3rd Series, Vol. IX, 1938, pp. 241–269.
7. G. le Hardy, *Mémoirs pour servir a l'état historique et géographique du diocèse de Bayeux* I, p. 340.

Atque genu prono tali viduata Patrono
Pro merito dando diffundit vota precando,
Et regem poscit, qui cuncta latentia noscit,
Ut tibi det vitam, te suscipiens eremitam[8].

This revival of letters in Bayeux had largely been made possible by the patronage of the Conqueror's half-brother, the famous bishop Odo of Bayeux, who had enriched the city with wealth and treasures taken from England. It went hand in hand with increasing prosperity, with the widespread practice of money-lending uncurbed by canonical prohibitions[9], and with a great surge of building activity that provided the 10,000 inhabitants with eleven churches to serve them and enabled the cathedral canons to occupy the splendid new row of houses in the precincts of their cathedral. Though to the traveller approaching Bayeux across the Norman plain even the polished elegance of these bright, new towering buildings was outshone by the magnificent cathedral, a blaze of colour set off by its glistening chandelier[10].

It was against this background that Serlo acquired a mastery of those leonine hexameters in which he has incidentally told us much about himself : how his father left him a modest property as well as a country church in a village not far from Caen, which also he regarded as his by hereditary right. We learn that he was not left long in undisturbed possession of these legacies, for the monks of St. Stephen of Caen began to encroach upon the village, taking over land there, refusing to pay the accustomed tithes to the church, and even appropriating the church itself. Apparently Serlo's only resort lay in his pen, with which he castigated the abbot of Caen, Gilbert, for being a sly, arrogant, luxurious character, proud in his fine house and well-stocked table, leading a life in striking and unedifying contrast to the austerity of other brethren in the abbey[11]. But second thoughts led Serlo to a remedy more effective than satire in the person of bishop Odo, to whom he now applied for protection. And not in vain, because the bishop was not one to be

---

8. *Acta Sanctorum*, October, Vol. III (6 October, St. Bruno), p. 757.
9. *Cf* Lucien Musset, A–t–il existé en Normandie au XIe siècle une aristocratie d'argent ? in *Annales de Normandie*, December, 1959, pp. 285–299.
10. For a poetic traveller's description of Normandy at this date *cf* Raoul Tortaire by M. de Certain in *Bibliothèque de l'École des Chartes*, 1855, pp. 489–521.
11. Described as *fratres inclusi* ; *cf* Boutémy's comment, "Il y avait donc, parmis les Bénédictins de Saint-Étienne de Caen des moines cloîtrés : fratres inclusi, et des moines menant une vie large et, en verité, assez séculière," *op. cit.*, p. 255.

deflected from justice by the wiles of monks ; at the synod of Lille-
bonne (Whitsun, 1080) he even went so far as to make general
provisions against monks depriving clerks of their means of sustenance in similar cases[12]. Indeed, the whole episode eventually
turned out well for Serlo, who soon became closely attached to Odo's
circle, acquiring a stall in the cathedral and gratefully writing
poems in praise both of Odo and of his sister, Muriel. It was a happy
climax to a career that illustrates well the difficulties and opportunities facing a gifted cleric of the day.

Disputes between secular priests and monks, the quarrel over
monks paying tithes, over priests' sons and the hereditary trans-
mission of ecclesiastical offices, the bishop's status as a court of
appeal, all these themes must have been in the air that the young
Thurstan breathed. For his own father was a priest named Auger,
married to a lady called Popelina who gave birth around 1070 to
Thurstan at Condé-sur-Seulles, a township some 7 miles south-
eastwards of Bayeux, situated on the river Seulles that runs northwards down from the bocage to the Channel. Of his birth-place little
is known except that the immediate lords of the township provided
one of the crusaders who in 1096 followed Odo of Bayeux on his last
journey, and that it was situated in the serjeantry of Bricquassard—
which gave its name to the family who were soon to become Earls of
Chester. We also know that at a later date the ancient claim on the
part of the monks of Caen to nominate the priests of Condé-sur-
Seulles was recognized as valid. And this gives some plausibility to
the suggestion that Thurstan went to Caen for his schooling[13].

If this were so he would have found himself in a city that had
attracted the favour of William the Conqueror, who had established
there the rich abbey of La Trinité for women and set his own
daughter Matilda as abbess over it. Here also commerce was on the
upgrade, with trade to England bulking large ; hence the diversity
of race and dress in the market which caught the eye of the visitor
almost as sharply as did those quaint pointed bonnets peculiar to
the women of Normandy[14]. And if Bayeux had its cathedral, so

---

12. Mansi, XX, col. 557, c. 12.
13. For a lively discussion of Caen at this time, see Mlle. R. Foreville, *L'école
de Caen au XI siècle et les origines Normande de l'université d'Oxford*,
in Etudes Médiévales Offertes à M. le doyen Augustin Fliche, 1952,
pp. 81–100.
14. Vidi disparium facies habitusque virorum. Femini sexus carbaseos apices.
(Raoul Tortaire, M. de Certain, *op. cit.*, p. 508).

had Caen its centre of learning in the abbey of St. Stephen[15] from which several generations of monks were to go forth to occupy bishoprics and abbeys in the newly-won lands beyond the Channel ; included amongst them were Lanfranc and Ralph d'Escures, each of whom was first prior of Caen and later archbishop of Canterbury[16]. Amongst the personalities Thurstan could have met were that Theobald already referred to as a defender of priests' sons and Theobald's master, William de Bona Anima. He could also have made the acquaintance of the gifted historian and poet, Ralph, who sang the great deeds of Tancred in the Holy Land and whose own master, Arnulf of Roes, was later to achieve renown as the patriarch of Jerusalem (1112–1118)[17].

Altogether Caen was a likely place to have quickened a young man's imagination and equipped him for a career in the service of its Anglo-Norman rulers. No more so, however, than Bayeux itself, and this was the more probable scene of Thurstan's schooling since the flow of men from Bayeux did in fact run more strongly towards those centres in England with which he became identified. The flow had begun under the inspiration of Odo of Bayeux who supplied promising young men with the means to pursue their studies before placing them in positions of power and influence. Men such as Thomas, who was made firstly treasurer of Bayeux and then archbishop of York, and his brother, Samson, who became bishop of Worcester[18] ; men such as Thurstan of Glastonbury and William

---

15. It was even suggested by Heinrich Boehmer (*Kirche und Staat*, pp. 259–60) that the celebrated but elusive and misnamed Anonymous of York came from Caen because he shows great devotion to St. Stephen and might well have been educated in a place dedicated to that saint. His suggestion is plausible enough for the particular tract he is discussing, but since the manuscript attributed to the Anonymous (Corpus Christi, Cambridge 415) is clearly a collection of tracts by various authors it cannot hold of the whole collection.

16. Others who went to England from Caen were Walkelin, bishop of Winchester ; Paul, abbot of St. Albans ; Gundulph, bishop of Rochester ; Ernulph, bishop of Rochester ; Thurstan, abbot of Glastonbury ; Roger, abbot of Cerne ; Henry, abbot of Battle ; Herluin, abbot of Glastonbury.

17. H. Glaisner, Raoul de Caen, in *Rev. d'hist. eccl.*, 1951, p. 49.

18. Samson's career is a particularly good illustration of how deeply knotted into feudal society married clerics could get. He was the son of Muriel and Egbert, the priest, of Bayeux. In 1073, William the Conqueror wished to raise him to the see of Le Mans, but he declined on the ground that his life had been *valde reprehensibilis*. It is probable that Samson had a daughter, Isabella de Douvre, the concubine of Robert of Gloucester (Henry I's illegitimate son) who was the mother of Roger, bishop of Worcester and of Richard, who succeeded his uncle, another Richard, in the see of Bayeux in 1133. Samson was also, of course, father to Thomas the younger, of York (*cf Priory of Hexham*, p. 50n).

de Ros[19]. Whilst there were many others from Bayeux, Gerard, bishop of Angoulême and papal legate, William of Saint-Calais, bishop of Durham, Theulf, bishop of Worcester, and John of Bayeux, the king's chaplain, who may well have owed their advancement to Odo's patronage, though this cannot be proved. Certain secular lords appear likewise to have prospered in the land over the Channel through his favour. Hugh de Port, for instance, and Hugh Bigot[20]. And is it not also possible that Odo's bitter quarrel in Kent with the archbishop of Canterbury and the monks of that cathedral lined up men of Bayeux provenance against those who had identified their fortunes with Canterbury ; and that this in turn contributed to the suspicion entertained by certain groups in Yorkshire towards Canterbury ? For Odo's brother, Robert of Mortain, was the greatest Yorkshire tenant-in-chief at the time of the Domesday Survey, and the Lascy family held a considerable fee of Odo[21], just as the clerics from Bayeux were the most powerful ecclesiastical influence in the city of York itself.

And when Auger and Popelina emigrated about this time to London where the husband had been granted a prebend in St. Paul's Cathedral they were following in the wake of a notorious Bayeux man, Ranulf Flambard, who was dean of the chapter in London[22]. They took their children with them, Audouen, Thurstan and probably a daughter. Auger's was one of the thirty prebends which bishop Maurice (1086–1107) had organized for the service of the cathedral, each prebendal stall in the cathedral having attached to it a stretch of psalms which the holder of the stall was responsible for singing, or for getting sung, each day. Kentish Town was the title of Auger's, and it had assigned to it Psalms 27–31, beginning with the phrase *Dominus illuminatio mea* ; moreover, when Auger died—some time after 1104—the prebend stayed in the family, being passed on to his son, Audouen. Thurstan also acquired a prebend in St. Paul's about the same period to which was assigned the psalm *Confitemini domino*. The title of the prebend was *Consumpta per mare* because the land in Essex which originally belonged to it had mostly been swallowed up by the sea before the

---

19. For Odo's patronage *cf* Ordericus Vitalis, *Ecclesiasticae Historiae* (ed. Prévost and Delisle), III, pp. 265, 266 ; and *The Domesday Monachorum of Christ Church, Canterbury* (ed. D. C. Douglas), p. 30.
20. L. C. Loyd, *The Origins of Some Anglo-Norman Families*, pp. vii–viii.
21. *E Y C*, III, p. 123.
22. For a description of St. Paul's at this date, see C. N. L. Brooke, The Composition of the Chapter of St. Paul's, 1086–1163, *Cambridge Historical Journal*, X, 1951, pp. 111–132.

Conquest, which meant, of course, that it was the poorest prebend of all. Nevertheless the holder of it was unlikely to be depressed on this score since it also served as a stepping-stone to greater things, witness two of Thurstan's predecessors, Robert Losinga and William Giffard, the first of whom became bishop of Hereford and the second bishop of Winchester. It was not long, moreover, before Thurstan himself was made chaplain to William Rufus, and subsequently to Henry I, when his income would be supplemented by the allowance made to chaplains and by the grant of the chapel in the castle of Tickhill[23] as well as the churches of Shorne and Cobham[24].

Thus by the time he came to manhood Thurstan had moved to the very centre of Anglo-Norman society. Through membership of the chapter of St. Paul's he was one of a closely-knit circle of wealthy, distinguished and sophisticated churchmen who by virtue of their wide contacts were saved from the stuffiness normally associated with the narrow world of the cathedral precincts. Just how closely-knit they were is illustrated by the number of them who received their prebends from their fathers or uncles and then passed them on to their own children. We have seen this happen in the case of Auger with Kentish Town, and the same occurred in Thurstan's day with the prebends of Ealdland, Mapesbury, Mora, St. Pancras, Rugmere, Wenlakestarn and Wildland; in addition, Totenhal prebend was held by the dean, Ranulf Flambard, Sneating by his son Elias, and Ealdstrit by his nephew Fulcher[25]. All of them were well provided for by the revenue from their prebends, and if they resided in the canons' row they were each given a chamber and twelve pence, benefits which they owed to the careful planning of a previous dean, Wulman. Some of these families must have shared literary tastes and aspirations if their names—Quintilianus, Cyprianus and Arturus—are any guide, but most of them were intended for high administrative office whether as bishops or king's chaplains, or even, in the case of one Hugh de Bocland, as the sheriff of numerous counties in southern England. Again, most of the canons were of Norman stock, but there was still quite a group of the Old English; and several sons of Lorraine brought to the chapter the flavour of a different world reflected, perhaps, in the

---

23. *E Y C*, III, no. 1428.
24. *Regesta Regum Anglo-Normannorum*, Vol. II, ed. Johnson and Cronne, No. 1021.
25. *Cf* the list of prebends and their occupiers in R. Newcourt, *Repertorium Ecclesiasticum*, pp. 133–224.

influence of Lorraine upon the cathedral statutes[26]. This cosmopolitan group of churchmen, entrusted with the ecclesiastical
administration of London, almost inevitably spent their days in an
atmosphere of worldliness, involved as they were in constant
disputes over lands and churches, rubbing shoulders with their near
neighbours the goldsmiths, the money-lenders and the merchants,
whom we find witnessing deeds for them[27]. Nor were all of them
preserved from the taint of worldliness if we are to believe William
of Malmesbury's story that the bishop himself, Maurice, was over-
fond of women and justified his resort to them on medical grounds[28].
And Flambard's transgressions in these matters are too well known to
require emphasizing. All the more remarkable, then, that Thurstan
and his brother Audouen should so early have acquired reputations
as men of continent and holy living. It may be accounted for in
Thurstan's case by the fact that in his youth he had paid a visit to
Cluny when that abbey was enjoying its period of greatest fame
under Abbot Hugh (1049–1109) ; the community made such an
impact upon him that he pledged himself to take the Cluniac habit
later in life, a vow that he finally fulfilled.

The visit to Cluny is, unfortunately, almost the only incident
in Thurstan's life before 1114 that has been recorded for us, apart
from the several occasions on which he either drew up or witnessed
deeds of his royal master, Henry I[29]. These give us little
definite information beyond what we could aready have confidently
inferred : that Thurstan was acquainted with such royal ministers
as Hamo the dapifer, the count of Meulan, and William of Warelwast, as well as with the leading bishops of the realm ; though the
nature of the deeds does suggest that he was a chaplain with a special
competence in legal problems[30]. In view of this scarcity of information it is worth referring to the most famous of these deeds to
illustrate the sort of people amongst whom Thurstan must have been
working for some fifteen to twenty years. It records the case

---

26. *E.g.* "Albert of Lorraine, a holder of land and churches on a large scale
   and a survivor from the Confessor's Lotharingian circle," C. N. L. Brooke,
   op. cit. p. 122 ; also Hugo, son of Albert and Robert, bishop of Hereford,
   cf J. H. Round, *The Commune of London*, pp. 36–38.
27. *Ninth Report of the Royal Commission on Historical Manuscripts*, 1883,
   Part I, pp. 60–61.
28. William of Malmesbury, *Gesta Pontificum*, p. 145n.
29. *Regesta* II, nos. 652, 681, 817, 939, 1,000, 1,075.
30. As does Hugh the Chantor's description of his accomplishments, *H C*, p. 34,
   his own reply recorded by Hugh, *H C*, p. 42, and the reasons given by the
   York Chapter for trusting Thurstan's judgment : Litteratus erat ; decreta
   legerat ; canones sciebat . . . (*H C*, p. 35).

between the men of the hundred of Pyrton who were trying to claim jurisdiction over the manor of Lewknor (Oxfordshire) and abbot Faritius of Abingdon who was contesting their claim ; it is notable as the first recorded occasion on which the Book of the Treasury, or Domesday Book, was invoked to end a dispute[31]. Since the king was in Normandy at the time (September, 1111) the pleadings took place in the presence of the queen in the treasury at Winchester. She was Henry's first wife, Matilda, daughter of Margaret of Scotland and as pious as her mother, and just as untiring in her benefactions to religious houses ; she afforded particular encouragement to the Austin canons in co-operation with her "spiritual son," Gilbert the sheriff, "perhaps the best loved magnate of the day," who himself founded the Austin priory of Merton where Thurstan's brother Audouen was to retire to die. Also present on this occasion was Roger, bishop of Salisbury, the poor priest from Caen who had risen to the heights through shrewdness rather than goodness ; and Robert Bloet, bishop of Lincoln and brother to the bishop of Bayeux, who had also secured his office through pliancy to the will of Rufus and of Henry. The other bishop was Thurstan's own chief, Richard of London, one of that Belmeis dynasty that dominated St. Paul's for generations. The rest of the witnesses belonged mainly to the class of people who were known as *curiales* because they owed their status to their service in the king's curia ; often of obscure origin, "raised as it were from the dust" to offset the power of the traditional baronage, these men were agents of the king's will. Ralph Basset, Geoffrey Ridel, William of Anisy and William d'Oilly. Less humble, though equally loyal, were William de Courci, the king's dapifer and a friend to abbot Faritius, Herbert the chamberlain, father of St. William of York, and Geoffrey FitzHerbert and Geoffrey de Mandeville. The two remaining witnesses were Adam of Basing, who hailed from Thurstan's native district of the Bessin and owed much to the patronage of bishop Odo[32] ; and that intriguing character Walter, who was a secular canon, married, and lately appointed to be archdeacon of Oxford ; as provost of St. George's-in-the-Castle he was to become protector of many Oxford scholars including the romancer Geoffrey of Monmouth and, it seems, Theobald of Étampes[33].

---

31. *Regesta* II, no. 1,000.
32. *Cf Complete Peerage*, Vol. XI, sub. St. John.
33. Hastings Rashdall, *The Universities of Europe in the Middle Ages* (ed. Powicke and Emden), Vol. III, pp. 10n and 18n.

In addition to all these influential contacts one must also note that Thurstan was a close friend of William Giffard, the bishop of Winchester[34], the man who was later to introduce the Cistercians to England ; it was to him that Thurstan went to receive deacon's orders. He also seems to have been regarded as an intimate friend by the great scholar Hildebert of Le Mans, to judge by the letter he received from him subsequently ; possibly they had met when Hildebert was in exile and enjoying the hospitality of the English court (1099–1100)[35].

But it may well be that the most profound influence on Thurstan's outlook during these years is one that has left no trace in the documents, that is the effect on him of watching Anselm at close quarters as the saint quietly put into operation the reforming principles urged by Rome in spite of the anger and resistance that they met from Henry I. The struggle between the archbishop and the king can hardly have failed to make a deep impression on Thurstan, not only through the archbishop's saintliness but also

---

34. *H C Y*, II, p. 373.
35. Hildebert of Le Mans, *Opera Appendix*, pp. i–iii.
    Turstino Dei gratia venerabili Eboracensi Electo suo carissimo amico Ildebertus humilis Cenomannorum Sacerdos. Non facile de amico diffidere. Sicut Seneca testatur, & omni et nulli credere vitium est ; unde & nonnulla vos respicit culpa, si apposuistis animo vestro sinistrum aliquid de amico prius credere, quam probare ; prius diffidere de eo, quam in eo diffidendi invenire rationem. Mihi siquidem scripsistis in ore multorum esse, quod legationem Cantuariensis ad Domnum Papam susceperim, ut quem flectere ipse non potuit, mea, quae vel nulla vel modica est, auctoritate flecteretur, Qua relatione vos vel leviter esse motum, me non leviter movit. Sic enim significastis quod vel nunquam fuerim quem credebatis amicum, vel turpiter esse destiterim. Caeterum nondum ego hanc assumpsi audaciam, nondum decrevi justitiae sic adversari, nondum ita persequi me ipsum, ut humeros illi supponam oneri, quod portare nec facile est, quia apostolica resistit auctoritas ; nec honestum, quia impedit ratio ; nec utile, quia imminet periculi magnitudo. Quod si nihil horum obstaret, Apostoli tamen memor sum sic dicentis ; Si ea quae destruxi reaedifico, praevaricatorem me constituo. Nolite igitur credere, nolite opinari me esse motum, me, ab eo qui fuerim, dissentire. Veritatem loquor, animum meum loquor. Vivit Deus & Dei filius, & utriusque Spiritus, quia nec Domnus Cantuariensis, nec pro eo aliquis a me postulavit, ut adversus Eboracensem Ecclesiam causam eius vel litteris commendarem, vel pro eo legationem susciperem. Sunt quae ipse nobis indicavit, unde nostrum quaesivit consilium : sed quae nihil omnino vestram vel spectant vel impediunt causam. De legatione quam antecessor eius, sermo mihi et illi fuit, et de aliis quae a vestro procul sunt negotio. Apostolorum limina nequaquam ad praesens visitare disposui. Vicem mihi rependetis, si in nostra perseveratis amicitia. Ego sum enim nunquam amici immemor, numquam desertor esse substinebo. Vale. Epistolas meas mihi mittere nolite differre.
    Though the editor of Hildebert's *Opera* suggests c. 1120 as the date for this letter, it was probably written at the end of 1118, since Hildebert had been in the company of Henry I and archbishop Ralph at Arganchy in the October of this year. (*Regesta* no. 1183).

because Thurstan had grown up in circles that were accustomed to
take an exalted view of the Christian king's position in the hierarchy
of Christendom. During these same years, in fact, an anonymous
Anglo-Norman writer was claiming that through consecration the
king became, in a manner, God, the mediator between almighty God
and the Christian people, endowed with the power to forgive sins
and in the last resort higher within the Christian body than the
Pope himself[36]. Of this writer it has justly been said that "he is a
conduit through which pour ancient Oriental feelings for the
mystery of kingship"[37] ; and that he "threatened the very heart
of Christianity in the measure that he may have been influential in
reducing the Faith to the proportions of a merely ethnic religion,
a religion of the *polis*, whose chief usefulness is to serve as the
cement of society and to provide the latter with the appropriate
solemnities for its own glorification"[38]. Extreme though it sounds,
this statement sums up a powerful influence at work amongst certain
intellectuals of that day and goes far to explain the stubborn stand
taken by St. Anselm against any of the king's claims that counte-
nanced such a usurpation of the priestly and even the papal office.
And it is noteworthy that Anselm brought numbers of his contemporaries to appreciate the danger, men brought up in the royal
service who had perhaps absorbed "ancient Oriental feelings for the
mystery of kingship" in the process, and who after being tugged
this way or that were eventually brought to acknowledge Anselm's
stand as justified. William Giffard was one of these, likewise William
Warelwast, and even Gerard of York.

That the king's chaplain, Thurstan, should also be numbered
with those who had been converted to St. Anselm's assessment of
the situation in the Anglo-Norman realm would not be surprising
in view of the sharply secular policies that Henry I pursued once
Anselm was out of the way. The most obvious instance of the king's
confident secularism was that he kept the see of Canterbury vacant
for five years after Anselm's death, thereby rebuffing the Pope and
allowing the passage of the years to impress upon Paschal II that no
one became archbishop of Canterbury without the consent and good
will of the king of England. Nor should this action of the king's be
dismissed as simply one manoeuvre in the pragmatic business of
politics devoid of any ideological inspiration. During this period of

---

36. G. H. Williams, *The Norman Anonymous of 1100 A.D.*, pp. 127–8.
37. *Ibid.*, pp. 200–201.
38. *Ibid.*, p. 202.

his reign his legal advisers were compiling a corpus of secular law which they hoped would rival canon law in its self-sufficiency and in which the king's will was the source of its power[39] ; the king had already had dedicated to him a treatise on royal and sacerdotal power by a monk of Fleury whose object was "to defend the privilege of royal authority" against those of the Popes who had been trying to whittle it down[40], and his daughter in 1114 had dedicated to her a work by the same monk glorifying their dynasty[41]. Henry knew what he was about in 1109 when he warned the papal legate cardinal Ulric that he would separate England from the Roman church if the Pope tried to have his own way contrary to the will of the king[42]. Above all, Henry showed a close interest in the ideological struggle being fought on the continent between the papacy and the Emperor Henry V[43] ; and he made it abundantly clear where his sympathies lay when in 1110 he betrothed his daughter Matilda to the Emperor. The betrothed couple did not get married immediately because Matilda was so very young, but when the marriage did take place in 1114 it was the occasion of an extraordinary happening that underlines the ideological framework of the Emperor's policies. On the Feast of the Epiphany in Mainz (the day before the marriage ceremony) the Emperor's most dangerous rebel Lothair of Saxony was offered pardon by the Emperor for his misdeeds ; but to secure this pardon he was made to go barefoot and crawl a considerable distance, in the presence of a great crowd, to the base of the Emperor's throne ; only then was he forgiven[44]. Here was being acted out in public the reversal of those papal policies that thirty years previously had forced the reigning Emperor himself towards a similar act of abasement, but that time at the feet of the papacy. In view of his victories since 1110 the Emperor Henry V could be excused for thinking that the wheel had now come full circle, and that he was truly the mediator between God and man in the territories of the Empire.

---

39. See especially the introduction to the *Quadripartitus* by F. Liebermann, pp. 45–58, and the use of such phrases as *augusti domini nostri Caesaris* and *gloriosus Caesar*, as applied to King Henry, in the text.

40. Hugonis Monachi Floriacensis Tractatus De Regis Potestate et Sacerdotali Dignitate, ed. E. Sackur, *Libelli de Lite* II, pp. 465–494.

41. M. Manitius, *Geschichte der Lateinischen Literatur des Mittelalters*, Part III, p. 520.

42. *H C*, p. 28.

43. W. Holtzmann, Zur Geschichte des Investiturstreites in *Neues Archiv* 50, 1935, pp. 246–319.

44. W. Bernhardi, *Lothar von Supplinburg*, p. 15.

That Henry I conceived a similar image of himself bestriding England is a reasonable supposition and would explain why Thurstan's behaviour towards the king was so unyielding from the moment of his election[45]. Thurstan knew that a man of the king's views and temperament was not to be restrained by half-measures[46] ; he had even seen the gentle Anselm forced by the king into exile and into steadily stiffer opposition. Whether he consciously began where Anselm left off cannot be affirmed for lack of direct evidence, but there is one fact that inclines us to think of him as heir to the saint's attitude : it is that Anselm had been spiritual director to that great lady Adela of Blois, and Thurstan later succeeded to this position. He can hardly have failed to think of himself as Anselm's successor in other respects.

45. For an illuminating analysis of Henry's attitude *cf* K. Leyser, England and the Empire in the Early Twelfth Century, *Transactions of the Royal Historical Society*, 10, 1960, pp. 61–83.

46. Significantly, Ivo of Chartres held a similar view of Henry I, as is shown by his letter to Cuno of Praeneste on behalf of Richard of Bayeux, protesting against the tyranny of Henry I : sub alieno enim iure tanquam sub torculari positus dolet et gemit se nihil plus posse quam permittitur. *P L*, Vol. 162, col. 276.

Chapter II.

INTRODUCTION TO THE NORTH.

Henry I's determination to be master in his own house was sufficiently illustrated by the manner of Thurstan's election to the see of York. After travelling to Winchester in 1114, with Thurstan in his train, the king simply appointed his well-tried chaplain to the office on the Feast of the Assumption (August 15th) without any pretence of consulting the chapter at York. Advanced ecclesiastical theory required that the chapter should have a say in the election of their archbishop, but Henry's practice was simply to nominate some trustworthy candidate and expect no demurrers from the churchmen; his expectations were never confounded. Used as he was to the king's ways, Thurstan can scarcely have been surprised to learn of his own nomination; for he was now in his middle forties, a cleric who had proved his ability in that favoured training-ground of bishops, the king's court; in fact, the very type of man the king would be expected to choose. In the last year, moreover, Henry had shown signs of his good will towards Thurstan's family by promoting his brother, Audouen, to the see of Evreux in Normandy; and the stroke of Henry's generosity was apt to fall in the same place twice.

Nevertheless, Thurstan must have harboured certain misgivings at the prospect facing him as he journeyed north from the royal court in the winter of 1114; after all, he was a man with little or no pastoral experience; he had never even received the order of the priesthood but had remained in the lowly rank of sub-deacon. Apart from which the very journey was daunting enough; contemporary travellers have left us a harrowing description of the difficulties and discomforts that beset one on the way to the North, the cold and the winds and the impossibly muddy roads[1]. So

---

1. Ordericus Vitalis (*Ecclesiasticae Historiae*, Vol. IV, p. 435) transmits to us the sense of desolation that might easily descend upon a stranger venturing into the North when he describes the cold, the great storms and the muddy roads through which messengers from the monastery of St. Evroul had to struggle in the winter of 1122. They made their way to York in order to get permission from Henry I for their abbot, Roger of Sap, to resign his office. As successor to Roger they elected Guarinus de Sartis, with the advice of Thurstan and the attestation of Stephen, the abbot of Caen (who in 1128 became Patriarch of Jerusalem).

uninviting were the roads that the king himself avoided them and
chose to go instead by the much-used waterway from Torksey (in
Lincolnshire) to York ; to make the passage beyond Humber
easier for all concerned he even had the canal from Lincoln to
Torksey cleaned out and made navigable at this time[2]. And the
land north of the Humber was still so untamed that the king used
to surround himself with extra troops on the rare occasions he
ventured there ; packs of wolves and birds of prey still found easy
shelter in its thick forests[3], and the strangeness of the territory
was further emphasized by the fact that the inhabitants spoke a
language offensive to the ears of southerners and quite unintelligible
to them[4]. Hence Thurstan had good reason to ask, what sort of
land he could expect to find at the end of his northward journey ?
And what manner of men was he being appointed to rule over ?

No easy answer can be given to the apparently simple question
as to what were the geographical boundaries enclosing the province
of York. At least, it would not have been easy to provide one to
everyone's satisfaction, though doubtless the chapter at York, a
vigorous, self-confident and disputatious body of canons, would
have defined with complete assurance the boundaries of which
they and their archbishop were the happy defenders. Yet even they
had in recent years been forced to recognize certain compromises
over their claims. In 1093, for instance, they had been compelled to
abandon their claim that Lincoln and Lindsey were by rights
subject to the archbishopric of York. They were gainsaid by King
William Rufus, who settled the dispute between York and Lincoln
by asserting Lincoln's independence and assigning to it the town-
ships of Stowe, Louth and Newark. The canons of York grumbled
that all England knew this to be fraudulent and that the bishop of
Lincoln had secured the king's judgment by a bribe of £3,000 ;
but they had to content themselves with the compensation offered
which allowed York jurisdiction over the abbey of Selby (previously
in an anomalous independent position) and over a similar enclave

---

2.   Symeon of Durham, *Opera* (*R S*) II, p. 260.
3.   For the wolves, see Laurence of Durham's account of their killing 500 foals
in Durham during one winter (*Dialogi Laurentii Dunelmensis Monachi*,
Surtees Society, p. 22), and *Mon. Angl.* V, p. 569 ; amongst references to
birds of prey, *The Chartulary of St. John of Pontefract*, ed. R. Holmes,
Yorkshire Archaeological Society, Record Series, XXV, p. 10.
4.   William of Malmesbury *Gesta Pontificum*, p. 209 : Sane tota lingua
Nordanimbrorum, et maxime in Eboraco, ita inconditum stridet, ut nichil
nos australes intelligere possumus. . . . Rex ipse in istis partibus domestico
contentus militum numero, si quando illas partes regni adit, non nisi magno
auxiliatorum comitatu vadit.

in far-away Gloucestershire that was centred around the church of St. Oswald's[5]. Even so the archdiocese at its southernmost tip stretched beyond the shire of Nottingham just into Leicestershire, with strong-points of its influence at Nottingham and Southwell. The church in Nottingham was under the care of an archdeacon who occupied a prebendal stall in the mother church of St. Peter's, the minster at York, whilst St. Mary's church, Southwell, was itself a minster of ancient standing directly under the supervision of the archbishop but boasting its own complement of prebends and enjoying considerable liberties.

Running north-westwards from Nottinghamshire over the bare hills of the sparsely inhabited Peak District the diocese bordered on the territory of Lichfield/Chester. Here it marched with the territory described simply as "between Ribble and Mersey," so little identity had it achieved at the political and seigneurial level. The responsibility for bringing this district into conformity with the law of the lord Christ lay, strictly speaking, with the bishops of Lichfield/Chester, but its customs allied it closely to Yorkshire as did its fiscal structure, for like Yorkshire it paid geld at the distinctive rate of 4d. to the carucate[6]. It was an area where Thurstan's influence was to be felt.

But if the southern and western limits of the province afforded frequent occasions for dispute with neighbouring bishops they were clarity itself compared with the ambiguity of Thurstan's status northwards of the Ribble, where his claims led him into territory claimed by the Scots. Thus William Rufus had ordered the men of this district (*Chaerliolum*) to accept the jurisdiction of the bishop of Durham who was deemed to have succeeded to the rights of his predecessors of Lindisfarne[7]. However, these rights were lost in 1101 when the bishop of Durham, Ranulf Flambard, absconded from the Tower of London[8]; so that in the early years of the twelfth century we find a bishop of Glasgow, Michael, exercising episcopal duties amongst the people there; he had been nominated by David of the Scottish royal family but, like his predecessors, he had been consecrated by the archbishop of York, professed canonical

---

5. *E Y C* I, no. 126 ; and Hugh the Chantor's comment, *H C*, p. 9. Henry of Huntingdon, never a man for understatement, puts the bishop's bribe at £5,000. (*Historia Anglorum* R S., pp. 216–7).

6. *V C H* Lancs. I, pp. 269–283 ; *V C H* Yorks. II, pp. 134–140.

7. Regesta Regum Anglo-Normannorum I (ed. H. W. C. Davis), nos. 463 and 478.

8. *Cf* Symeon of Durham, *Opera* I, p. 139, 561.

obedience to the archbishop, and had therefore acted as his suffragan
up to the time of his death. He was buried in the old church of
Morland[9]. The truth is that one could not even be certain who
was the secular ruler of this land that had once formed the kingdom
of the Strathclyde Britons, where even now Welsh was one of the
several tongues spoken by its various peoples who followed conflicting customs and were hardly to be thought of as Christians at all[10].
Certainly William Rufus had made a determined attempt to fix the
northern border of England on the Solway, driving out that Dolphin,
son of Gospatrick, whose family were by tradition the first in the
neighbourhood of Carlisle[11]. But the interconnexions of Dolphin's
stock were too firmly rooted in the area to be so summarily elimi-
nated ; the inhabitants of the Carlisle region continued to look
towards the exiled Dolphin for aid, and the English kings' hold upon
the area became even more precarious when in Henry I's reign the
figure of Dolphin's protector, Earl David of Lothian, began to loom
large in their affairs. For David was no border forager content to
enjoy the momentary skirmishing triumph but heir to the throne of
Scotland as well as to the traditions of far-sighted, orderly government which he had imbibed in his youth at the court of England.
He must certainly have made the acquaintance there of Thurstan,
and their fates were to be linked together continuously throughout
their lives just as their jurisdictions crossed and intercrossed :
David's great fee of Hallamshire in south Yorkshire lay within the
spiritual lordship of the York archbishop[12], and Thurstan's ecclesiastical territory fell under David's secular lordship at various
points. It was to do so even more decisively in a few years when
David succeeded to the Scottish throne and became temporal lord of
St. Andrews, for the York party claimed that St. Andrews owed
obedience to the archbishop of York and could point to the fact
that Turgot had received consecration at the hands of Thomas in

---

9. *H C*, p. 14.

10. A. C. Lawrie, *Early Scottish Charters*, pp. 44–5, quotes the Inquest into the
     estates of the church of Glasgow (circa 1120) which says of Cumbria : inter
     Angliam et Scociam sita . . . sed dispari genere et dissimili lingua et vario
     more viventes haud facile (inter) sese consentientes gentilitatem potius
     quam fidei cultum tenuere.

11. *The Anglo-Saxon Chronicle*, s.a. 1092 : In this year King William went
     north to Carlisle with great levies, and restored the town and built the
     castle. He drove out Dolphin, who had formerly ruled that district, and
     garrisoned the castle with his men. Thereafter he returned hither south-
     wards, sending very many peasants thither with their wives and livestock
     to settle there and till the soil.

12. *E Y C* III, p. V.

1109 to support their claim[13]; whereas the Scots claimed that Turgot's action was unprecedented and invalid because it attempted to break the independence of the see.

Further north still than St. Andrews, beyond the power of the Scottish king, stretched another outpost of York's ambitions in the Orkney Islands. Though the islands were subject to the kings of Norway its recent bishops had been ordained by the archbishops of York; the latest of them, Ralph Nowell, was a priest of York who had been elected to the post in 1109 by the Orkneymen dwelling in that city. The law of the Church seems to have been observed throughout the whole proceedings, yet Ralph, far from being accepted as bishop of the islands, never so much as glimpsed the diocese committed to his care. In fact, for the next fifty years Orkney's effective spiritual head was a fascinating character named William, or Viljam as native speech had it. An amalgam of wizardry, learning and daring piety, a scholar of Paris and monk of Melrose[14], William appears to have had little or no canonical justification for the position he had taken over. This did not prevent him from whipping up enthusiasm amongst the islanders for their own martyr, Magnus; he set the seal on Magnus' sanctity, and upon his own fame, by importing builders from Durham to construct the magnificent cathedral of Kirkwall as a shrine for Magnus' remains. The climax to his eventful career came when he headed an exhilarating and slightly madcap crusade to the Holy Land (c. 1149–53).

York's claims in the Orkneys, then, were nullified by the remoteness of the area and its rawness in ecclesiastical organization. Nearer home, in the next area of ambiguity facing Thurstan, the bishopric of Durham, the obstacles to smooth relations were quite opposite: here it was age-old custom and well-worn technical legal distinctions that constituted the problem[15]. For behind the customs of Durham stood the person who even in death remained the most dominant character in the north country, none other than St. Cuthbert; from his grave he was believed to have struck terror into the heart of William the Conqueror himself and to have driven the king to respect the privileges of the church at Durham; his

---

13. *H C*, pp. 31, 35.

14. I have taken this description from A. W. Brøgger, *Ancient Emigrants*, p. 157, although the authorities he cites say nothing about Paris and Melrose.

15. *Cf* F. Barlow, *Durham Jurisdictional Peculiars*, pp. 55 ff.

power had been demonstrated anew in 1104 when his body was discovered incorrupt and examined in the presence of an eminent assembly which included two future archbishops of Canterbury (Ralph d'Escures and William of Corbeil) as well as Alexander, the future king of Scotland. Now there was rising on the rock of Durham a vast cathedral in his honour and constructed according to the latest fashions as if to show that his was no outmoded inspiration. The devotion to him that swept through the country at this time also swept material benefits into the lap of the bishops of Durham, for between 1066 and 1085 in Yorkshire alone their property increased from 81 carucates to 243 carucates ; situated in Allertonshire and Howdenshire, most of this property went to constitute enclaves deep into Yorkshire that were for all practical purposes subject to the jurisdiction of the bishops of Durham. This property brought them so frequently on business to Yorkshire that they found it convenient to maintain a house in Crayke, half-way on the road to York, as well as having a house in the city of York itself[16]. Whether the great prestige now accruing to Durham ever suggested to its bishops that they might win complete independence from their metropolitan at York we cannot say, but it is at least significant of their status that both William of St. Calais (1081–1096) and Ranulf Flambard (1099–1128) exercised their charges unimpeded though neither of them ever swore the oath of obedience to their respective archbishops of York[17].

But just as Durham had a foothold in Yorkshire so the York archbishops had a strongpoint of their own influence in what one would naturally have considered to be Durham territory ; this was the Hexham district. Though in this case, as in so many others, the bare facts of physical geography had to give way before the pull of tradition and the centuries, for it was the great bishop of York, St. Wilfrid, who had established the church at Hexham five hundred years previously. Hence it was to Wilfrid's successor at York, Thomas the elder, that the provost of Hexham turned soon after 1071 when he found himself bereft of a protector through a long vacancy in the see of Durham[18]. During the following forty years Hexham was drawn still closer to York by the favours that the York archbishops bestowed on it ; through grants of both land and

---

16. *Cf* Writ of Henry I to Robert de Lascy in *Regesta* II, no. 561, and the comments of H. H. E. Craster in *Archaeologia Aeliana* 1930, VII, p. 47.

17. Symeon of Durham, *Opera* I, p. 138.

18. *The Priory of Hexham*, S S, p. 191, and Illustrative Documents IV.

money they enabled the provosts to transform a derelict site over-grown with weeds and nettles into a flourishing religious centre now manned by a community of regular canons.

The name of yet another seventh century saint graces the last of York's outlying enclaves, the name of St. Oswald, the martyred king of early Northumbria. Two hundred miles south of York, on the northern side of the city of Gloucester, stood the college of secular canons dedicated to St. Oswald and, as was pointed out earlier, subject since 1093 to the jurisdiction of York. The area it commanded was one in which Thurstan was to take a special interest, as he did in all the places under St. Oswald's protection ; but the ecclesiastics in Worcester could hardly be expected to view with equanimity the presence of the northern metropolitan in their midst ; they remembered coldly the days when Worcester had itself been tied to York so as to relieve the poverty of the northern see, and the monks of Worcester were ever ready in their chronicles to put the least favourable interpretation on Thurstan's actions throughout his career.

In fact, it was a monk of Worcester named Nicholas who cuttingly exposed the weakness of Thurstan's position in the province entrusted to him. There is no shadow of justification, he writes[19], for York's pretensions to exercise a primacy over the Scots ; far from Scotland having an obligation towards York, the history of the church in Northumbria shows the reverse to be true : it was the Scots who brought Christianity to York. And look, he says, at how the number of its suffragan bishops has been reduced by the greed and negligence of the archbishops allied to the instabi-lity in religion of a people given to apostacy. Ripon, Beverley, Hexham and Whithorn are only some of the sees that have been swallowed up by the greed of York so that it has scarcely any suffragans left, apart from Durham and the insecurely held church in Cumbria. Nicholas' firm contempt for the confusion over York's boundaries and rights cannot be gainsaid in the light of our own survey, and it underlines the difficult task before Thurstan.

But such troubles were not, in the twelfth century, confined to York. What was peculiar to the northern province, bestowing an unmistakable tang upon its story in the early twelfth century, was the fact that the criss-crossings of ancient boundaries had been

19. Wharton, *Anglia Sacra* II, pp. 234–6. Nicholas is identified by Wharton, p. xiii, as Nicholas the monk of Worcester who had been trained by Lanfranc at Canterbury, where he had been a fellow-monk of Eadmer's.

blurred and re-shaped by so many different types of settlers, conquerors and plunderers. As a result the land had taken on many of the features characteristic of a newly opened up territory in which there was ample scope for land speculation, building booms and careerism. The open spaces left by the Conqueror's devastation of the North acted as a bait to men of enterprise : such men as the land speculator Colswen, who obtained from King William a grant of some waste land outside Lincoln, upon which he built 36 houses, and as a further attraction to intending tenants erected two churches for their spiritual welfare[20]. Rein was given to similar initiative when Thomas I of York allotted some of the waste land of St. Peter's to individual canons so that "each of them might be eager to build on and cultivate his own share for his own sake"[21]. Further evidence of rapid building is given by a writ of William Rufus granting permission to the canons to use the land in front of the church of St. Peter for building lodgings and other needful purposes ; the canons proceeded to build many houses very near to the western end of the Minster[22]. This vogue for building churches seems to have received added stimulus from the founder's hope of not having to pay tithe on the adjacent lands to the mother-church ; to quell such hope, for instance, Henry I issued a writ directing that the church of Pickering should have the parish which it had in the time of King Edward, notwithstanding the erection of any new chapels, and that it should have seisin of the tithes which Ingenulf de Furnellis was withholding from it[23].

The careerism fostered by these shifting conditions is well illustrated by the rise to affluence of that Osbert de Humber who first appears in the Domesday Survey of Lincolnshire as Osbert the priest. Later referred to as Osbert the clerk he became sheriff of Lincoln and subsequently retained that office when he was appointed sheriff of York. Through his high favour with Henry I he had amassed a very sizeable estate which he left to his sons at his death

20. W. Page, Some Remarks on the Churches of The Domesday Survey, *Archaeologia*, 2nd series, 16, 1914–15, p. 89.

21. *H C*, p. 11.

22. *E Y C* I, no. 127.

23. *E Y C* I, no. 399 ; *cf* also *E Y C* VI, no. 9, where Thurstan is protecting the interests of the priory of Holy Trinity, York, in its church of Leeds : Prohibemus etiam ne quisquam vel heremita vel quilibet alius presumat infra territorium ecclesie eiusdem parrochie capellam aut quodlibet oratorium construere absque permissu et spontanea voluntate prioris et capituli predicti monasterii, nec quisquam recipiat parrochianos eiusdem ecclesie vel beneficia eorum.

in 1115[24]. The abandonment of his priestly calling for administrative preferment is interesting and is paralleled by that other
Osbert, Thurstan's nephew, who likewise founded a family that was
to loom large alongside others such as the Nowells, the Chamberlains and the Sottewaines, who all found fortune in Yorkshire[25].
Fortunes at a higher level still were made available by the series of
veritable landslides that had occurred in recent generations; for
the Norman Conquest was not alone in producing a wholesale
change of greater landowners in the North. In 1095 vast estates were
forfeited by Roger de Mowbray, earl of Northumberland, on account
of his rebellion against William Rufus; in 1102 the lands of Roger
the Poitevin went the same way; the Lascy family, already com-
promised in 1095, was once more on the wrong side at Tinchebrai
(1106) as were the Stutevilles, William of Mortain and other northern
landowners. The outstanding beneficiary of these foiled rebellions
was Nigel de Albini, who received most of the Mowbray and Stute-
ville fees; the bulk of the Lascy estates went to Hugh de Laval;
and the net effect was to leave plenty of room for the emergence of
such middling barons as Walter Espec, Eustace FitzJohn, the Bruses
and Balliols. It was simply the latest chapter in a story that told of
shifting populations, of incursions by men of different races and
of many cultures being gradually fused.

Over two centuries ago York itself, once the proud centre of
Anglian power, had fallen first into the hands of Danish invaders
from over the North Sea and then, only a few generations later, into
the power of the Norse kings of Dublin. Yet another generation
later York was the seat of the Norwegian ruler, Eric Blood Axe;
here was imprisoned Eric's enemy, the famous Icelandic warrior
and poet, Egill Skallagrimson, who only saved his head by composing a panegyric to his harsh Norwegian captor. The meeting at
York of two personalities from the extreme limits of the Scandinavian world illustrates how quickly the city had become a centre to

---

24. *E Y C* I, pp. 355–6.
25. Families which did well out of the expanding economy of "Danelaw"
England included the Kimes in Lincolnshire and the Chamberlains in
Yorkshire, to take but two examples. For the Kimes, *cf* Farrer *Honors
and Knights Fees* II, 117, 118; and for the Chamberlains see B. A. Lees,
Records of the Templars in England in the Twelfth Century, 1935, p. ccii;
as Miss Lees remarks, "these families, just below the highest court circle,
but wealthy, capable, and influential, formed the county society of the
twelfth century, a society saved from narrow provincialism by the wide
ramifications of feudal land tenure, inheritance and intermarriage, and
kept from stagnation by the constant demands of public service, central
and local;" her account of the Templars reflects "the amazing vitality
and energy of this great English upper middle class" (*ibid.* p. cxcix).

which traders and adventurers from the whole Scandinavian area resorted regularly, and how readily the north of England had to learn to adapt itself to the ways of strangers. It is these rough lessons of the previous centuries which go far to explain the quite remarkable speed with which the Normans, when they came, were assimilated to the native inhabitants of the land. Even the terrible harrowing of the North by the Conqueror, which might have been expected to instil into the people a bitter hatred of the Normans, does not seem to have left them resentful beyond reconciliation. Indeed, for at least one of them, Ailred of Rievaulx, the Normans were to be thought of as liberators who had freed the country from the Danish yoke[26]. Moreover, those worst hit by the harrowing joined the stream of refugees fleeing southwards out of Yorkshire through the border shires of the western midlands in 1069[27] ; in so doing they left behind them open spaces that could be re-occupied and rendered prosperous in the following half-century. One indication of where the new occupants came from is given by the frequency of Norse-Irish place-names on the eastern slopes of the Pennines ; this points to them as coming from the Lake District, which their ancestors had originally occupied as emigrants from the Norse settlements in Ireland[28]. In its turn the area around Carlisle was itself being colonized by immigrants whom William Rufus sent there as part of a scheme to strengthen his hold upon a border that was contested by the king of the Scots. Amongst them were many Flemings as well as southern English, whilst the feudal lords set over them included several from Bayeux who would be known to Thurstan.

Because of this constant shifting of peoples there was no telling who one might encounter in northern England during these years ; as was discovered to his dismay by the devout Norfolk merchant Godric. One of the most travelled men in the country, Godric had been on pilgrimage to Rome and Compostella and had sailed often to Scotland, Denmark and Flanders ; when he determined to abandon the world and live the life of a solitary he fixed upon the Carlisle district as a place of isolation where he might find peace to live unknown and ignored. Not long after getting there, however, he was recognized by some of the local people who turned

26. So we may infer, I think, from Ailred's language concerning an earlier occasion : Angli Danico jugo quasi ab Aegyptia servitute liberati. P L VI, 195, col. 744.

27. *Chronicon Abbatiae de Evesham* (R S, 1863), pp. 90–91.

28. A. Goodall, *Place-Names of S.W. Yorkshire*, 1914, p. 36.

out to be blood-relatives of his ; they made such a fuss of him that he had to take to the woods to regain his solitude[29]. In pursuit of a different crown was another adventurer whom one might have met, but this time in the streets of Grimsby. This man, Harold Gille-christ, had been begotten by an Orkneyman on an Irishwoman, and these strains in his blood endowed him with a daring and imagination that was now brewing up schemes to seize the crown of Norway for himself. Within a few years he had achieved his aim but had left in his wake a trail of blood, cruelty and deception such as even Nor-wegians found hard to stomach[30].

Grimsby was not such an unlikely place for planning a *coup* in Norway when one remembers that Norway was only forty-eight hours' sailing away from the east coast, and that traffic across the North Sea was frequent and ran easily in both directions. Just how easily and confidently men took the passage over the sea was strikingly illustrated by King Magnus of Norway who went so far as to entrust a great part of his treasure, twenty thousand pounds of silver, to the keeping of a rich citizen of Lincoln[31]. And at a more humble level, the foot-loose young Northumbrian Bartholo-mew attached himself to a Norwegian priest and received the orders of diaconate and priesthood from a bishop there before returning to lead a hermit's life on Farne Island[32]. In the opposite direction came a Dane of noble birth who obtained permission from the prior of Tynemouth to set up as a hermit on Coquet Island ; known in the calendar of saints as St. Henry of Coquet, he died there in 1127[33]. To take ship from one coast to the other cannot have been difficult in view of the normal intercourse of trade which, amongst other things, included the importation of that prized

---

29. *Vita Godrici*, ed. Stevenson (*S S*,)1847, pp. 41–2 : Nam a suis consanguineis cognitus, in pluribus familiaritatis gratia ab eis est honoratus ; quem honorem ipse pro onere habuit, et eorum familiare contubernium sibi fore sensit animae salvandae grave detrimentum.

30. G. M. Gathorne-Hardy, *A Royal Impostor, King Sverre of Norway*, pp. 24–29.

31. On hearing of Magnus's death the Lincoln man seems to have thought that the king's demise gave his banker a right to his money ; but King Henry of England thought otherwise and took the twenty thousand pounds to his own hoard. (Ordericus Vitalis, *Ecclesiasticae Historiae* IV, p. 194).

32. Symeon of Durham *Opera* I, p. 298 : Adolescens itaque, diversarum gentium patriam et mores affectans inquirere, vagus et instabilis ad loca de locis aura ferebatur levitatis, fastidiosus novitatum amator, adeo facilis contemptor ut conspector. In Norwegiam demum evectus cuidam presbytero adhaesit, et ibidem ab episcopo eiusdem loci diaconatus, deinde presbyteratus gradum accepit.

33. *History of Northumberland* V, pp. 316–18 ; *Acta S. Boll.* II, p. 60.

sporting bird, the Norwegian gerfalcon, for the king's mews[34].
Thurstan must soon have been made aware of this circumstance,
for amongst the first things he did, on arriving in his diocese, was to
visit the aged Turgot at Durham ; one of the most vivid episodes
in Turgot's life, and one that he might well have retailed to Thurstan,
had been the occasion when he fled to Norway in order to escape
the clutches of William the Conqueror's henchmen. It was his
Scandinavian name, perhaps, that had prompted the Normans to
seize him at a time when their hold on the country was being
threatened by an alliance of Scandinavian rulers beyond the sea.
In any case, Turgot eluded them ; and we are told that he made
profitable use of his exile at the Norwegian court by teaching
psalmody to Olaf[35], the son of King Harold "Hardrada."

Other influences, stronger by far than the Scandinavian, were
being brought to bear upon the province and more particularly upon
its baronage ; they came in the train of the crusading fervour that
had begun to seize the European nobility and to imbue them with
the new notions of chivalry. Already in 1096 Gerard de Gourney
had made his mark on the crusade to Jerusalem, thus inaugurating
a crusading tradition for which generations of the family were to
become famous. Eight years later he made the pilgrimage to Jerusalem, where he died ; on this second journey he was accompanied
by his wife Edith ; their grandson, Roger de Mowbray, a more
famous crusader still, was also to leave his bones in the Holy Land[36].
Another northern baron to win esteem in crusading circles was the
founder of Whitby Priory, William de Percy ; going to the Holy
Land for the second time, he died on the march to Jerusalem at a
place called *mons gaudium* within sight of the city[37]. In 1106 the
archbishop of York himself, Gerard, was moved to write a letter to
Bohemond saying that he was preparing to join his crusade[38].
Inevitably these travellers brought back with them some knowledge
of the strange manners of the East as well as some of its products ;
a phylastery from Jerusalem containing precious relics was gifted
to the canons of Bridlington by Walter de Gant who had received it

---

34. Auti de Lincoln was a royal dealer in falcons who owed 100 Norwegian
hawks and 100 gerfalcons to the crown in 1130. See *Pipe Roll* 31, *Henry I*,
p. 111 for the details of the types that were acceptable to Henry.
35. R. L. G. Ritchie, *The Normans in Scotland*, p. 44.
36. For an account of the 1096 expedition, see William of Jumièges' *Gesta
Normannorum Ducum*, Bk. VIII, c.8.
37. *The Chartulary of Whitby*, S S, p. lxxx ; and *E Y C* II, p. 198.
38. *Quadripartitus* (ed. F. Liebermann), p. 161.

from his brother-in-law Baldwin[39] ; also the practice of carrying a standard into battle erected on a chariot was borrowed from the East and was to be used effectively by the northern barons[40].

There was a tradition in the border country that Gospatric of Carlisle, the son of Waldef, had brought back with him a bone of St. Paul, and one of St. John the Baptist, two stones of Christ's sepulchre, and a part of the true cross[41]. Whilst it is true that these relics were not sufficient to make Carlisle a rival to the Church of the Holy Rood in Edinburgh where Queen Margaret of Scotland had deposited the celebrated Black Rood and other treasures brought from Hungary, nevertheless it was a sign of how Carlisle was emerging as a centre worthy of attracting to itself the growing cult of chivalry. The day was still to come when the city would be chosen as the site, on Whit Sundays, for the descent of the spirit of chivalry upon the sons of kings, as happened when Henry of Scotland and Henry Plantagenet were each knighted there[42]. But its dawn could have been anticipated, for the district lay within the archdeaconry of Richmond over most of which the great counts from Brittany held sway ; these lords stood somewhat remote and isolated from Yorkshire life[43], but it was through their honour of Richmond that the roads ran northwards into Cumbria, and the Breton *conteurs* who fostered and spread the Arthurian legend were likely to have felt the fascination of Carlisle, that lonely outpost of Roman civilization rumoured to have been founded by Julius Caesar[44].

---

39. *E Y C* II, no. 1136. Another Yorkshire pilgrim to Jerusalem at this time is referred to in the *Pipe Roll* 31 *Henry I*, p. 33, where John de Oburville pays 5 silver marks for the custody of his uncle Peter's land until Peter returns from Jerusalem. Further references to northern travellers to the Holy Land are to be found in *H C Y* I, pp. 315–6, and pp. 318–20 ; in *E Y C* II, no. 1095 ; Richard Maleverer's pilgrimage to Compostella is the subject of *E Y C* II, no. 729.

40. Ordericus Vitalis, *Ecclesiasticae Historiae* (ed. Le Prévost and Delisle), p. 341n.

41. J. Denton. *Cumberland* (Kendal) 1887, p. 99, says of Carlisle priory : "The priory wanted not for reliques of saints for Waldeive the son of Gospatrick Earl of Dunbar brought from Jerusalem and Constantinople a bone of St. Paul and another of St. John the Baptist, two stones of Christ's sepulchre, and part of the holy cross which he gave to the priory . . ." Unfortunately Denton gives no authorities for this statement.

42. R. L. G. Ritchie, *The Normans in Scotland*, p. 296.

43. The two Wapentakes of Gilling and Hang where they were so powerful, are "later additions to the pre-Conquest shire of Yorkshire" (*V C H* Yorks. II, p. 135).

44. R. S. Loomis, *Wales the Arthurian Legend*, pp. 187–9 ; and Ordericus' description of it : . . . validissimum oppidum quod Julius Caesar, ut dicunt, condidit, *Ecclesiasticae Historiae* V, p. 111.

Yet Carlisle was never likely to challenge for the status of leading city in the North ; that position belonged unquestionably to York. *Eboracum* had even more antique claims than *Lugubalium* upon the minds of men beyond the Humber. The city from which Thurstan was to conduct his work still in the twelfth century bore signs of its Roman greatness. Part of the old city wall of Roman construction was plainly to be seen in the north-eastern corner of the city, and was known as the *aldewerk*[45]. That a Roman arch had also withstood the wear of centuries seems likely from the use of the word *steinbowe* to describe one such an arch, whilst the name *Steingate* for one of the streets probably testifies to the durability of Roman paving. Whether these remains made the ordinary citizens conscious of their Roman legacy is, of course, doubtful, but the more learned of them may well have shared Geoffrey of Monmouth's vision of the city as a site of Imperial dignity. And there for all to see stood the church in Fishergate dedicated to St. Helen, the woman whom the Emperor Constantine was thought to have wooed and won in the city of York[46].

Of Scandinavian culture there was less visible evidence in spite of the fact that York had long been regarded as a Danish city[47]. The area known as *Conyngesgarth* must once have been the site of the residence of the Scandinavian kings but was by this time in ruins. In the last years preceding the Norman Conquest the earls of York appear to have lived outside the north-western boundaries of the city, in the area known as Earlsburgh, upon the edge of the great forest of Galtres[48]. And the nearby church of St. Olaf, where its founder Earl Siward lay buried, was a tangible reminder of the family that had held sway in those years. But it was in the traffic of everyday life that the impress of the Scandinavian countries lay most heavily upon the place : in the language spoken there, in the names of the inhabitants and the names that still clung to their streets, but above all in the legal organization of the community. Judgement upon custom, for instance, lay at York in the hands of the lagemen whose presence was so familiar a feature of the towns in England settled by the Danes. When in 1106, therefore, Osbert the

---

45. H. Lindkvist, A Study on Early Mediaeval York, in *Anglia*, 49–50, 1926, pp. 345–394.
46. Angelo Raine, *Mediaeval York*, pp. 118–125 ; *E Y C* VI, nos. 57, 66 ; *V C H* York, p. 382.
47. *H C Y* I, p. 454 (Vita S. Oswaldi) : quae indecibiliter est repleta, et mercatorum gazis locupletata, qui undique adveniunt, maxime ex Danorum gente.
48. Lindkvist, *op. cit.* pp. 352–3.

sheriff was trying to undermine the rights of York Minster in the city, it was the lagemen who were called on to bear witness to those rights and their testimony was written down in a solemn document[49].

From this document we can envisage clearly what a vital role the archbishop and his canons had to play in the legal and commercial transactions of the community. Of the six scyres or wards, one actually belonged to the archbishop ; this was the one to the west of the river Ouse ; and the archbishop administered it with almost regal powers[50]. His land within York, moreover, was "for the archbishop as free from all customs as the king's is to the king." Thus merchants who wished to stay in the archbishop's land were not to be hindered by the royal provost or any other ; much of the merchandise, as well as the meat and fish coming into the city, had to pay custom to the archbishop, whilst all the toll in Clementhorpe and below (as far as the archbishop's lands extends) from all ships lying there, belonged to the archbishop ; and so did the whole custom of the fish from both sides of the water. When we also remember that the archbishop had in his hands two of the mints of York[51], it becomes clear that he was the most prominent personage in the commerce of the city.

Under the immediate supervision of the archbishop and his canons, furthermore, was an object of almost magical potency, the *frithstol* or chair of peace, which stood beside the high altar in the mother church, or minster, of St. Peter. The *frithstol* was the focus

---

49. A. F. Leach, *Visitations and Memorials of Southwell Minster*, Camden Society, 1891, p. 191 ; upon archbishop Gerard's complaining to the King, Henry I sent the following to make inquest on the case : Robert Bloet, bishop of Lincoln, Ralph Basset, Geoffrey Ridel, Ranulf le Meschin, Peter de Valognes (who was probably the Lawman of Lincoln). They convoked the shire-moot and laid responsibility for the verdict upon : Uttreth filium Alwini, Gamellum filium Swartecol, Gamellum filium Grym, Normannum presbyterum, Willellmum filium Ulf, Frengerum presbyterum, Uttreth filium Turkilli Norman filium Basing, Turstinum filium Turmot, Gamellum filium Ormi, Morcar filium Ligulf, Ulvet filium Fornonis, hereditario iure lagaman civitatis.
  We are also told that Ansketil de Bolomer acted on this occasion as interpreter, translating northern English for the benefit, presumably, of both the Normans and the southern English, who were incapable of understanding the Yorkshire dialect (*cf* William of Malmesbury, *Gesta Pontificum*, p. 209).
  For an earlier inquest *cf* Liebermann. An English document of about 1080. *Y A J* 1905, pp. 412–416.

50. In the time of King Edward it contained 189 inhabited houses (Lindkvist. *Anglia*, 1936, p. 349).

51. Liebermann, *Y A J*, 1905, p. 415.

in Yorkshire not so much of justice as of mercy and peace ; criminals and outlaws who fled to it were granted St. Peter's protection for thirty days, in which time they might attempt to make their peace with those whom they had offended, or after which time they might be conducted in safety to another *frithstol*, at Beverley or Ripon, at Durham or Hexham. Anyone daring to seize a criminal who was sitting in the *frithstol* automatically became guilty of sacrilege : he became *boteles*, beyond redemption by any payment of money. Like bands of influence spreading outwards from the *frithstol* with diminishing intensity were the areas of the choir, the church, and the cathedral close, for the sin of seizing an accused man or a criminal in these places was punished by progressively less severe fines. It was not to the archbishop, moreover, that such fines were paid but to the body of the canons. There is indeed a somewhat aggressive note about the section of the customs where this point is made, and in other sections likewise the canons' position is defined by comparison with that of the archbishop. In their houses and lands, for example, they are said to enjoy the same customs as the king enjoys in his, or the archbishop in his. Any infringements of their liberties are to be dealt with at a session outside the porch of St. Peter's church. Here, as always, the canons seek protection for their privileges from St. Peter—much as the burgesses of York themselves sheltered beneath the banner of St. Peter in time of war when it was the custom that at the king's call one man from the whole land of the canons, and one only, was to be equipped with St. Peter's banner and to march in front of the burgesses to battle.

Most of these privileges had their roots in conditions as they were before the Conquest, and it says much for the toughness of Old English institutions that they survived the violence of the first Norman onslaught, an onslaught that had hit York as hard as any place in the country. Of the seven shires existing in 1066 there were now only six ; the area of the lost shire, which had lain in the south-west of the city, had now been cleared for the erection of two castles from which the Normans were in a position to dominate the whole of York. Twenty years after the Conquest the number of inhabited houses within the city had fallen from 1418 to 878[52]. By Thurstan's time, no doubt, the community had made good these losses and in one respect, at least, the Normans had contributed greatly to enhancing York's outward appearance : whereas in 1066 there had

---

52.   *V C H* York, p. 21.

been no monastic communities[53], now there were several impressive foundations, each of them well endowed. Outstanding amongst them was the Benedictine community of St. Mary's Abbey, founded in 1088–9 ; there was also the Priory of Holy Trinity, founded at the same time from Marmoutier, and a small priory established towards the end of the eleventh century by monks from Whitby.

In the wake of the Normans had come another, very different group of people who, though small in numbers, were to make a distinctive contribution to the life of the citizens ; these were the Jews. They came, of course, as money-lenders, but the Jews of the twelfth century were more than mere financiers ; they cherished within their tightly knit ranks a culture that was of special interest to their literate contemporaries, for it preserved the tradition out of which had sprung those very Christian doctrines that gave the twelfth century clerk his whole *raison d'être*. Already before 1108 they were aiding the Christians in their study of Hebrew ; archbishop Gerard had Hebrew copies of certain psalms made and full advantage of them was taken by a Yorkshire boy who spent three years studying Hebrew in the city where he himself tells us that he copied out forty of the psalms in the Hebrew script and that the Jews themselves admired his calligraphy. The boy's name was Maurice and he later became prior of Kirkham, where his considerable knowledge of the Hebrew language enabled him to lay down the law on matters of scriptural exegesis[54].

---

53. Unless one reckons as monastic the "culdees" who manned St. Peter's and supervised the hospital of St. Peter (which was later to become famous as St. Leonard's). For references to these *Colidei* see *Monasticon VI*, ii, pp. 608–9, and W. Reeves, *The Culdees of the British Islands*, pp. 58–61.

54. Bodley. Hatton MS 92 fos. 10/11. On Maurice of Kirkham's knowledge of Hebrew, see the interesting comment of Raphael Loewe (The mediaeval Christian Hebraists of England, *Transactions of the Jewish Historical Society of England*, XVII, 1951–52, p. 234) : "... it transpires that Maurice's Jewish friends gave their word of greeting the slightly inaccurate stress characteristic to-day of the Ashkenazi Jewries of Northern France and the Teutonic and Slavonic lands."

  Other aspects of Maurice's work are dealt with by M. R. James, The Salomites, in the *Journal of Theological Studies*, XXXV, 1934, pp. 287–297.

  The good relations between Christians and Jews evidenced by the works of archbishop Gerard and Maurice were steadily jeopardized as century went on, as we see in E Y C I, no. 300, a grant by Swane, master of the hospital of St. Peter, York, to Adam de Warrum, of land in York : excepto quod non debet eandem terram vel Judeis vendere vel donare, aut excamibium sive aliquod machinamentum collisionis facere quare Judei predictam terram ad usus suas possideant.

  Cf V C H York, p. 47 for the suggestion that the Grento and Benedict of the 1131 Pipe Roll were also Jews.

It can be seen that the community of some eight or nine thousand souls at York [55] which now had Thurstan for its pastor embraced a variety of races and cultures such as few modern communities of a similar size could equal. The range of occupations found there must have both stimulated the curiosity of visitors and satisfied that of its inhabitants. Around the cathedral centred the life of the archbishop's familia and his canons[56], the intellectuals, the music master and the master of the schools ; around the mint dwelt the goldsmiths and metal workers ; along the wharves traders berthed their ships coming from the East Riding, from Ireland and Germany and the shores about the North Sea[57]. The natural meeting point for these traders was at the hansehouse run by the guild merchant where commercial questions were settled. They were no mere hucksters who constituted the membership of this guild merchant, otherwise such a respected man of property as Thomas, son of Ulviet would not have been glad to offer a hunting-horse in order to become an alderman of it[58] ; and already at this early date the guild merchant had probably secured the privilege of farming the tolls and revenues of the city, a long step on the road to self-government. Granted this concentration of peoples at such a strategic point it is not surprising that York should so often have caught the limelight in the political drama nor that it should have become inured to regular scenes of violence, partly occasioned by its cosmopolitan population. As an illustration of such violence one might cite here an incident that took place later in the century, but one that York citizens must often have seen the like of :—A certain man was jealous of his neighbour by reason of the prosperity that his neighbour was blessed with. So empoisoned was he by this

---

55. Tait (*The Mediaeval English Borough*, p. 76) estimates the population of pre-Conquest York at some 8,000.
56. *V C H* York, p. 21, on canons' houses.
57. William of Malmesbury (*Gesta Pontificum*, p. 208) says of York : urbs ampla et metropolis, elegantiae Romanae preferens inditium. A duabus partibus Husae fluminis edificata includit medio sinu sui naves a Germania et Hibernia venientes.
58. *The Pipe Roll of* 31 *Henry I* (1929), p. 34 : Thomas de Everwic filius Ulveti debet. j. fugat ut sit Aldermannus in Gilda Mercatorum de Everwic. This Thomas is the grantee of the charter discussed by Sir C. T. Clay in *A Holderness Charter of William, Count of Aumale* (*Y A J* Vol. 39 (1956–58), pp. 339–342). References to him will also be found in *E Y C* I, nos. 118, 333 ; II nos. 833, 1242 ; III no. 1738 ; V nos. 156, 158 ; and *Fountains Chartulary* II, 486.
    The hansehouse of York is referred to in the famous Beverley charter of 1115–1128 (*E Y C* I, no. 95). Lindkvist, *op. cit.*, pp. 386–7, thought there must have been a gild by 1089 from the use of the term Gildegarde (guild enclosures) ; this is questioned in *V C H* York, p. 32, but without sufficient reason.

bitterness that he hit upon a plan to accuse his neighbour of arson ; he knew that such an accusation would be tested by a combat between himself and his wrongly suspected neighbour. On the day of the combat a great crowd of spectators assembled and saw the unjust accuser prevail ; having overthrown his unfortunate oppo- nent he went on to gouge out his eyes and cut off his sexual parts which he then proceeded to toss into the midst of the horrified spectators. It is gratifying to learn that the victim of this plot went devoutly to the tomb of St. William of York through whose inter- cession the missing organs were miraculously restored ; but even this happy ending to the story cannot dispel the atmosphere of violence around the community that could beget such an incident. No wonder that Henry I reinforced his household troops when going north of the Humber[59].

So far in reviewing the northern scene and the forces that shaped it our eyes have been caught by many different strands, the exotic Jewish and Breton, the less strange Orcadian and Irish, the familiar Scandinavian and the self-confident Norman. But always in the background one is aware of the deep continuity of the Anglian tradition. A main reason for this continuity is the simple fact that many families of old English stock survived at an important level, though not the very highest level, of northern society[60] ; a grant to the monks of Selby, for instance, shows us how a lineal descendant of a pre-Conquest Englishman retained a considerable part of his ancestor's original estate[61] ; another grant informs us how an Englishman of substance obtained for himself a wife of good Norman family[62], whilst a charter to Fountains illustrates the reverse case of a prominent Norman marrying an English woman[63]. Its per- sistence is testified also at the humble level of words for land- divisions such as balk and butt[64] and by the number of field-names that contain Old English personal names as elements[65]. Again,

59. *H C Y* II, pp. 289–90. For a similar illustration of almost casual brutality,
     see the story of the nun of Watton and the vengeance that was wrought
     upon her seducer, as related by St. Ailred of Rievaulx. *P L* Vol. 195,
     Cols. 789–796.
60. *E Y C* III, p. 187.
61. *E Y C* III, no. 1622.
62. *E Y C* III, p. 358.
63. *E Y C* I, no. 64, where Robert de Sartis and his wife make a grant to
     Fountains that is witnessed by a group with a fine array of Anglo-
     Scandinavian names. *Cf* also *Memorials of Fountains*, p. 54.
64. *Chartulary of Whitby* (ed. J. C. Atkinson, *S S*), no. 577, *Place Names of the
     North Riding of Yorkshire*, p. 325.
65. *The Place Names of the West Riding of Yorkshire*, Part VII, p. 70. (See
     also the author's remarks on clough, dene, and -tun and -feld, pp. 271–285).

the traveller in the North met frequent witnesses to the Anglian past in the shape of surviving monuments. Standing high in the cemetery at Durham was the cross erected in the eighth century by bishop Aethelwold in honour of St. Cuthbert[66] ; Hexham was full of such monuments, the outstanding one being the round church of Our Lady erected by St. Wilfrid and lately restored by the hereditary custodians[67] ; and in York Minster were the Gospel Books of St. Wilfrid embellished with gold and silver[68]. The hold which that golden age continued to exercise over the minds of scholars still shines through the works of the Durham and Hexham historians, but the strength of Anglian devotions in the everyday lives of humble people is best illustrated in a story told by Ailred of Rievaulx to demonstrate how the Anglian saints protected the town of Hexham when it was threatened with destruction[69].

It was in the days when Malcolm of Scotland (†1093) was in the habit of cruelly devastating the border country. Remarkably, he always used to spare Hexham out of reverence for the saints who were resting there ; but one day his outriders were attacked, wounded and despoiled by robbers in the neighbourhood of Hexham church. Blame for this crime was laid by Malcolm at the door of the people of Hexham and he alerted his army to prepare to slaughter them. Quickly the news of his intentions reached the ears of the priest of Hexham, Ailred's uncle Aldred, who came to the king to plead for mercy for his people ; he came in vain, since Malcolm assured him that it was only the fall of night that had prevented him from attacking then and there. At the prospect before them the townsfolk were naturally stricken with terror and crowded into the old church in panic to beseech the aid of their saint, Acca[70].

---

66. Symeon of Durham, *Opera* I, p. 39 ; quae etiam usque hodie in huius, id est Dunelmensis ecclesiae coemiterio stans sublimis, utrorumque pontificum intuentibus exhibet monumentum.

67. *Priory of Hexham*, p. 190.

68. *E Y C* III, p. 387.

69. What follows is the story as told by St. Ailred of Rievaulx in his treatise on the Saints of Hexham (*The Priory of Hexham*, pp. 177–181) ; a slightly different version of the same event is given by Symeon of Durham (*Opera* Vol. II, p. 36) and repeated in Anecdota Quaedam Hagustaldensia (*The Priory of Hexham*, pp. 207–8). A similar story of Malcolm being turned back, but this time from Durham, and by St. Cuthbert alone, is related by Symeon (*Opera* II, pp. 339–40).

70. This saint had been a close companion of St. Wilfrid, whom he succeeded as bishop of Hexham in 709 ; in 731 he was expelled from his see for reasons that are obscure ; he died in 740. Bede had a deep regard for Acca, to whom he dedicated many of his works.

Meanwhile, Aldred, who seems to have been rather a cool customer, dozed off and had a dream, or a vision, of his dear church and his flock in their sore predicament with himself standing by the church porch. Suddenly he saw two horsemen galloping up towards him from the south ; they were tonsured, and splendidly dressed in the robes of bishops. Riding up to where Aldred stood they dismounted and said to him, "Here, good man, look after our horses whilst we go into the church to say some prayers." When they returned from their prayers they questioned Aldred about the distressing state of the people in the church, all of them lamenting and wailing ; upon Aldred's explaining to them the threat that lay over Hexham from the king of the Scots they told him not to worry, that everything was going to be all right. Addressing the senior of the two, Aldred then asked, "Who then are you, holy man ? that you come to bring us the necessary help in our distress ?" "My name is Wilfrid," he replied, "and with me here is St. Cuthbert, whom I picked up as I was coming through Durham so that we might come and join our brethren who rest in this church and to save both the place and the people." Comforted by this vision the priest in turn comforted his people in the church, who turned to prayers and psalm-singing. Their confidence was rewarded, for at dawn on the following day as the Scots were preparing their assault a thick mist rolled down the Tyne. It threw the attackers into such confusion that they did not recover their bearings again until they reached Cumberland. That was the manner in which the old Anglian saints drew their faithful servants beneath their protection.

Such, then, was the land and such were the peoples that Thurstan had been called upon to govern in the name of the Lord Christ. For over a quarter of a century he was to exercise this office, and by the end of his days he had come to be recognized as the unquestioned leader of the North ; but before consolidating himself in that position he had to struggle for many years before being able to exercise the full powers of his office. From his predecessors he had inherited a legacy of wrangling as to whether the province of York was subject to the province of Canterbury. He had inherited, also, a battery of advocates in the chapter of his minster who had been schooled to state their church's case against a team of equally hardened advocates of the opposite party in the chapter of Canterbury cathedral. The quarrel between these two chapters is one that later generations have found difficult to sympathize with since it aroused passions that are more easily connected with nationalist or sporting rivalries than with spiritual issues.

The roots of the quarrel reach back over five hundred years into ambiguities in the instructions of Pope Gregory I to St. Augustine (601) and probably into misconceptions in Gregory's own mind about the condition of England. For Gregory seems to have thought that Augustine's mission to England could base itself on the old Roman Imperial organization with the cities of London and York serving as the seats of two archbishops, much as the former Imperial dioceses had provided suitable seats for Christian bishops in Gaul. His instructions do not say this clearly, but they certainly imply that Augustine was to move from Canterbury to London as soon as possible, and from there to organize twelve suffragan bishoprics ; meanwhile he was to send a bishop to York who should consecrate a like number of bishops as suffragans of the northern province. Until Augustine's death, York itself was to be subject to him, but after his death it should become independent ; and after that each metropolitan of York and London was to receive his pallium from the Pope and precedence between them should be determined by which of them had been consecrated first. In the event, of course, the archbishops never transferred themselves from Canterbury to London ; nor did York become an archbishopric until 735 ; and though the southern metropolitan did eventually build up the number of its suffragans to twelve, York never achieved anything like that figure.

A situation had therefore developed that left boundless opportunities for dispute and counter-dispute : whenever the York archbishops defended their position by reference to Gregory's scheme Canterbury countered by reference to what had actually happened ; whatever authority Canterbury produced in favour of its primacy York nullified by quoting Pope Honorius I's decree asserting their equality. With the entry of the legalistic Lanfranc on to the scene in 1070 these opportunities were to be exploited to the full. Immediately he became archbishop of Canterbury he gave warning of his intentions by refusing to consecrate Thomas of Bayeux as archbishop of York unless Thomas made him a written profession of obedience. It was only under protest that Thomas did so, and even then he restricted the application of his profession to Lanfranc personally ; he was not binding himself to Lanfranc's successors. In 1071 the matter was reopened in Rome when the two archbishops were visiting the Pope ; the Pope simply referred the dispute to a council in England. Here in the following year a council ruled in favour of Canterbury, stating that its archbishop was primate of all Britain and that York was by right subject to

Canterbury. Unfortunately for Lanfranc the decision of an English council held in the king's court was not regarded as decisive at Rome, where papal confirmation of privileges was treated as a *sine qua non* of their acceptance. As a result the same complex of issues was brought up time and again in the next forty years, on every occasion in fact when there was a new archbishop in either see.

But though the legal position had not changed in any vital respect between 1072 and 1114 the emotional background and the strategy had in the meantime been transformed. At the earlier date the archbishops had faced each other in almost single combat, well nigh bereft of supporters from their own cathedrals, for the monastic community at Canterbury had become demoralized and disunited under the rule of archbishop Stigand (1052–1070) and York's canons had been reduced to three by the Conquest. But by the year 1114 the monastery of Christ Church, Canterbury, numbered some 130 monks who had been schooled in the rights of their see by Lanfranc and Anselm and were emotionally identified with their archbishops in their claim to the primacy ; in the persons of its nine canons York also had produced a group of vigilantes committed to opposing Canterbury's claims. So whereas in 1072 the archbishops themselves had need to build up enthusiasm in support of their opposing policies, by 1114 it was doubtful whether either archbishop could have dared to accept a compromise ; he would certainly have incurred the wrath and lost the co-operation of his chapter had he done so.

Moreover, the animosity engendered now ran directly from chapter to chapter, as we are able to observe in the comments they passed on each other. Eadmer, for instance, speaking for Christ Church, says that in 1108 the canons of York wrote independently to Anselm to say that they would not stand for Thomas, their archbishop, making the profession of obedience and they were prepared to appeal to Rome if he did so ; they knew full well, says Eadmer, that Anselm was old and worn out by illness and they anticipated that he would soon be departing this life. What sort of reputation these canons had in many circles Eadmer left to be imagined, he himself preferring a charitable silence[71]. Though his own low opinion of them is obvious, Eadmer can hardly be accused of exaggerating the unyielding character of their behaviour since

---

71. Eadmer, *Historia Novorum*, pp. 199–204.

their letters to both Anselm and their own archbishop elect[72] make
it quite clear that they would simply refuse to obey Thomas if he
made the profession and they would then take their case to Rome.
Six years previously their dean had visited Rome where he had
carefully sounded the papal chancellor for Rome's opinion upon the
dispute ; what he had learnt left them confident that they could in
the last resort rely on Rome's support[73]. It is also obvious that
the canons returned Eadmer's contempt in full measure in their
unveiled distaste for the Canterbury monks : "The monks of
Canterbury," wrote Hugh the Chanter, "do not cease to aim at and
shamelessly demand what is unjust ; they think on it while awake
and dream of it in their sleep, and pine away for grief ; nor do they
mind by what means they recover it, as long as they succeed"[74].
And in their letter to Anselm the York canons make it clear whom
they regard as the villains of the piece : "But some counsellors
both clerks and monks, seek prominence rather than service, urging
others to aim at their own goal of preferment for the sake of the
eminence it brings"[75].

Almost every incident, in such an atmosphere of strife, charged
still further the enmity between the two camps. Each year, for
instance, was punctuated by the celebration on October 12th of
St. Wilfrid's feast day, which brought to their minds the Canterbury claim that the bones of St. Wilfrid had been transferred from
Ripon to Canterbury in the tenth century by archbishop Odo. The
most uncompromising assertion of this rather vague story was
made by Eadmer himself in his biography of Wilfrid and in the
sermon he preached to his monastic brethren on the feast of St.
Wilfrid[76]. Naturally the York men rejected the claim and, as
William of Malmesbury says, "this gave rise to a dispute between
Canterbury and York that could never be unravelled"[77]. It could
not be unravelled because almost all the prominent ecclesiastics
were brought into it at one time or another and passions were
multiplied in consequence. These could often take vulgar forms
as was shown in 1102 at the council of Westminster ; when "the
monks had prepared a seat higher than any of the others for their
archbishop (Anselm), Gerard (archbishop of York) felt himself

---

72. *H C* pp. 21 and 19, respectively.
73. *H C* p. 17.
74. *H C* p. 15.
75. *H C* p. 21.
76. *H C Y* I, p. 244.
77. *Gesta Pontificum*, p. 245.

insulted and openly cursing the man who had done this, kicked over the seat and would not sit down until his seat was made as high as the other archbishop's ; plainly showing that he owed him no subjection"[78]. And that some sort of party line should develop in each of the ecclesiastical provinces was only to be expected. Thus although the people of Hexham sometimes indulged in inverted snobbery towards their richer and more powerful brethren at York, even regarding them as a different people[79], the writings of the Hexham historians show them lining up solidly behind the York archbishops in the good old cause against Canterbury[80]. Similarly Durham had reason to be cautious towards York, but the Durham historian of Henry I's reign is unwavering in loyalty towards his metropolitan when recounting the clashes with Canterbury : it is most instructive to see how closely he follows the chronicle of Florence of Worcester for most events, but whenever he comes to a passage unfavourable to the York archbishop he either omits it or inserts sentences in defence of the northern version of events[81].

More important, however, than the growth of emotional solidarity in the opposing camps was the change in their strategic positions. One of the considerations for backing the primacy of Canterbury urged on William I by Lanfranc was that it was essential for the unity of the kingdom ; without a recognized primate "it might happen that some one of the Danes, Norwegians or Scots who used to sail up to York in their attacks on the realm, might be made king by the archbishop of York and the fickle and treacherous Yorkshiremen, and the kingdom disturbed and divided"[82]. But the days when this possibility offered a real threat were now past ; Danes and Norwegians no longer sailed up the Ouse, nor were they likely to do so ; and above all, the Scots were now being ruled by kings who owed their security to the power of the English kings and to whom they were bound by family and feudal ties[83]. If anything the northern metropolitan was a useful agent in maintaining the unity of the realm rather than a danger to it. And outside

---

78. *H C* p. 13.
79. *Priory of Hexham*, p. 202, for the story of how the canons at York wished to acquire relics for their church as Beverley had the relics of St. John, Ripon those of Wilfrid, and Rochester of Paulinus. Having persuaded their archbishop, Thomas, to commandeer those of St. Eata from Hexham, they then fell foul of St. Eata himself and were prevented from achieving their designs.
     The Hexham people who circulated this tale certainly "put on the poor mouth."
80. *Priory of Hexham*, pp. 127-8.

of England, in Rome, strategic moves had been made even more favourable to York. Whereas in 1070 Rome had looked to Canterbury to bring the English church out of its isolation and into the mainstream of European spiritual life the ambitious Popes now realized that the task had virtually been accomplished and Canterbury was no longer indispensable for its plans. Indeed, Canterbury was to be treated with some suspicion, like Rouen and Lyons also, as an institution claiming too much for itself and threatening Rome's direct control over the day to day life of the Church in western Europe. In Europe, as in England, the tide was running in Thurstan's favour so long as he had the patience to ride in on it.

---

81. E.g. Symeon of Durham, *Opera* II, pp. 194 ; 239 ; 249–50 ; 254 ; 257.
82. *H C* p. 3.
83. *Cf* A. A. M. Duncan, The Earliest Scottish Charters, in *Scottish Historical Review*, XXXVII, 1958, pp. 103–135, esp. pp. 131 and 134.

CHAPTER III.

THE SEVEN YEARS OF PROBATION, 1114-1121.

Thurstan entered on his career as archbishop with many advantages. His good standing in ecclesiastical opinion is signalized by the message of personal congratulation and encouragement that he received on his appointment from that great canonist and influential churchmen Ivo, bishop of Chartres. "Blessed be God," Ivo writes, "who is setting you to shed light by your behaviour in the darkness of the barbarous nation over whom you are placed" ; he expresses the hope that the bond of affection between them may be tightened by their praying for each other, and he ends his letter by saying that besides his prayers he also offers Thurstan his services in any affairs for which he is specially equipped[1]. Nor were these idle words since not long afterwards Ivo intervened on Thurstan's behalf with Pope Paschal. He assured the Pope that Thurstan was a man of continent life and good report whose consecration was being deliberately postponed by Canterbury in an attempt to extract from him an unwarranted oath of obedience. He begged Paschal to defend the church of York and its ancient privileges and as a true father to confirm Thurstan in the office to which he had been called[2].

---

1. *P L* Vol. 162, col. 219, Ivo writes : Benedictus Deus qui conversationem vestram lucere facit in tenebris barbarae nationis, quo hiis quibus praeestis, verbo et exemplo prodesse possitis, et bonae opinionis odorem ad nos usque transmittatis. Unde arctius inter nos vinculum dilectionis colligari desiderans, praesentes litteras direxi benignitati vestrae, ut hoc comminitorio discamus invicem mutuis nos consolationibus refovere, et devotis suffragiis orationum relevare. . . . De cetero noverit excellentia vestra parvitatem nostram paratam non tantum ad impendenda orationum suffragia, sed etiam ad omnia charitatis officia, quae impendere valet facultas vel scientia nobis divinitus collata. Vale.

2. *P L* Vol. 162, col. 278. Writing to Pope Paschal, Ivo says : . . . Unde Eboracensis Ecclesia in partibus occidentis posita, diu pastore desolata, tam per filios quam per familiares suos ad aures matris suae pie pulsat, ut in tribulatione posita maternae misericordiae viscera inveniat. Elegit enim praetaxata Ecclesia venerabilem virum, nomine Turstinum in archiepiscopum : qui, quantum ad personam pertinet, continentis est vitae et honestae famae, et utilis, quantum humana conscientia de alterius vita potest iudicare, sanctae Dei Ecclesiae. Huius consecratio studiose dilata est, propter indebitam consuetudinem, et contra eiusdem Ecclesiae privilegia, quae exigit ab eo Cantuariensis Ecclesia. Sed, quia paternae

Continued at foot of next page.

If it was comforting to have such a powerful advocate as Ivo in high ecclesiastical circles it was both comforting and daunting to have as allies nearer home the tough group of canons serving the minster of St. Peter's, York. These had a fund of experience in the moves and counter-moves in the Canterbury/York game and they never missed a trick. They could still recount indignantly how in 1086 the Canterbury monks had tried to pass off a fraudulent charter confirming York's subjection and how William I had refused to be caught by the deceit ; and their instinct for law made them ready to name living witnesses who would verify their story[3]. A similar list of witnesses could be quickly produced to convince any doubter that the defeat of York's claim over Lincoln in 1093 was the result of chicanery and bribery[4]. Men with such vivid memories of their church's struggle could give invaluable aid to a resolute archbishop but they could be holy terrors towards one who wavered in the cause. In 1109, for instance, when pressure was being brought to bear on the newly elected Thomas to make pro-fession of obedience, they virtually took matters out of his hands ; they sent their dean to Rome, they lobbied the king, they wrote directly to Anselm and, most significantly, they won over the papal legate Cardinal Ulric to their side. As for Thomas himself, they were only too well aware of his weakness—"he was full-bodied and fatter than he should have been," says their historian with laconic finality[5]. The wretched man had been brought up amongst them and he in turn knew what stuff they were made of ; had he not lately seen them pursuing their differences with his predecessor Gerard beyond the grave ? The canons had refused to allow Gerard's body to be buried in their church and had grudgingly allowed it to rest in an unworthy mound outside the porch[6]. Ground between upper and nether mill-stones, Thomas eventually made a profession that bound no one but himself.

discretiones est Ecclesiarum contentiones sedare, et pacem inter eos reformare ; quamvis ex abundanti facere videamur, paternitati vestrae tamen supplicamus, ut praedictae Ecclesiae jus suum defendatis, et manentibus in sua stabilitate apostolicis privilegiis electum eiusdem Ecclesiae, in ea dignitate ad quam vocatus est prout dignus est paterne confirmetis.   Valete.

3. *H C* pp. 5–6.
4. *H C* pp. 8–9. Hugh the Dean certainly held his office by this date, for in 1093 he, along with Ranulf the treasurer, Durand the archdeacon, and Gill the precentor, was present when archbishop Thomas I consecrated archbishop Anselm in December, 1093.   By 1114 Ranulf and Durand were dead ; Gill may have been living still, as was Hugh (C. T. Clay, *York Minster Fasti*, 1958, passim).
5. *H C* p. 29.
6. William of Malmesbury, *Gesta Pontificum*, p. 260.

It would be wrong to give the impression that the canons of York, in their provincial backwater, formed a stupidly obstinate or obscurantist body of men. To become a canon of York did not mean being lost in a backwater as had been shown in 1102 when archdeacon William received a call to take over the bishopric of Lisieux[7]. And the canons were shrewd judges of contemporary issues. Their spokesman, Hugh the Chanter, for instance, took a most sensible view of the investitures dispute ; he agreed with Ivo of Chartres that the investiture question was really a secondary one and that it scarcely mattered who did the investing so long as the election itself was free and canonical and no simony was involved. And he laments the fact that there are men in the church who thus tithe mint and anise, and strain out the gnat whilst swallowing the camel, rounding off his judgment with a quotation from Persius, as became a man of culture[8]. And who amongst contemporary chroniclers could match his penetrating and independent comment on King Henry's behaviour when Henry for a time supported the York party: "but whether he was really on our side, or only because he disliked archbishop Anselm for having forbidden investitures, was then uncertain but clear afterwards ? "[9] or how many were prepared to affirm publicly that "the wills of kings and their minds too, are mostly changeable and often contradictory ? "[10]. But neither their bluntness nor the fierce struggle for their rights blinded the canons to the righteousness of certain opponents ; their deep admiration for Anselm is plainly marked even in their letters opposing him. It was simply that they had minds of their own and were ready to express them—as archbishop Gerard sadly realized.

Gerard's exasperation with them is given free rein in a letter which he wrote to Anselm in 1103 after he had been won over by the saint's goodness. He tells Anselm how lucky he is at Canterbury to be dwelling in unity with dependable monks given to prayer and piety compared with himself having to deal with refractory canons. What was particularly worrying him was that he had been guilty personally of the simony so lately condemned (1102) : he had sold a prebend of York to the son of one of his archdeacons and when he became aware of the sinfulness of the sale had tried to give back the money and undo his sin ; but the archdeacon and his son refused to take the money and insisted on sticking to the deal. Other

---

7. *Cf* Ivo of Chartres, Ep. 157 ; *P L* Vol. 162, cols. 162–3.
8. *H C* p. 14.
9. *H C* p. 18.
10. *H C* p. 3.

charges he made against the canons were that some of them remained in minor orders and declined to proceed to major orders in case they were committed thereby to celibacy ; these same people, moreover, accept the revenues of prebends but live away from the Minster, enjoying the fruits of the altar without serving it, putting substitutes in their places. But most disturbing of all, they employed sophistry and chicanery to slip out of obeying the canonical decrees imposing celibacy on the clergy ; they say, "precisely as the Council has laid down, we shall not keep women in our houses ; but there is nothing in the decrees of any general council forbidding us to entertain women alone and without witnesses in the houses of our neighbours "[11].

The canons' response expressed their attitude towards celibacy, which they associated with the deplorable new vogue for monkery and which Gerard was altogether too keen on[12]. Its impudent wittiness, moreover, is paralleled time and again in the work of Hugh the Chanter, an execrable punner[13] ; and perhaps it was his fondness for wit that first drew them to Thurstan[14]. There must have been something striking about a man whom they accepted so readily ; true, he came to them enjoying the reputation of a first-class civil servant with a grasp of foreign and domestic as well as military and legal affairs and a name for generosity, cheerfulness and courtesy, but even so his warm welcome is a striking tribute to his personal magnetism[15].

To both the canons and to Thurstan it was a further advantage that he was not without friends and influence amongst the powerful secular lords of the day. The one he probably knew best from their days together at Henry's court was Nigel de Albini[16], the owner of

---

11. *H C Y* III, pp. 23–25, where Gerard writing to Anselm for advice describes his own canons as *quasi sophistici disputatores*.
12. *H C Y* I, p. 300, and note.
13. E.g. *H C* p. 29 : Nil mirum si torta, que extorta ; p. 43 : E contra noster electus, nunc vero eiectus ; p. 131 : Quod si quis ad vocabulum alludere velit, non iniuria Turstinus nomen habuit, quia contra graves assultus et iacula tanquam turris stetit. And on p. 50 there is a rather ponderous effort to make play with the word *cornu*.
  It is difficult to tell whether his word-jugglery makes Hugh very distinctive or whether it marks him as one of the fashionable intellectuals of North Europe, where a play upon words was almost an essential feature of any polite writer—as anyone who has studied the voluminous *MS Cotton Vitellius A XII* will testify.
14. *H C* p. 44 : Nec gestu tristicie signum dedit, set more solito iocunde et iocose agebat, ac si nichil contrarii contigisset ; quod omnes suos modice consolabatur.
15. *H C* pp. 35–36.
16. *H C* p. 107 : et ipse vero in angaria ista pro ecclesia nostra fideliter stetit.

wide estates in the Midlands as well as of a great fee in Yorkshire which stretched from Thirsk westwards over the plain to Kirkby Malzeard with its outlying castle of Black Burton in Kirkby Lonsdale. Nigel's second wife, Gundreda, and their son Roger likewise proved themselves good friends to Thurstan after Nigel's death. Also at the court of Henry I he had met David, earl of Huntingdon, who was soon to become king of Scotland and open up a glorious chapter in Scottish history; despite the obvious clash of interests between Scotland and York the two of them appear to have preserved respect for each other throughout their lives, and David and his family were generous in their benefactions to the religious houses of their southern neighbours, to Carlisle, Durham and Nostell[17]. Reaching still further back into the past were the ties that linked Thurstan with the family of Ranulf le Meschin, at the time lord of Carlisle and soon to receive the enormous earldom of Chester (1120). Ranulf belonged to the Bricquassard family who were lords over the township near Bayeux where Thurstan was born, and it is hard to believe that Thurstan was not acquainted with this masterful family long before he came to York. Evidence of his co-operation with them is provided in the foundation charter of St. Bees priory on the Cumberland coast (soon after 1120); from which it is obvious that Thurstan acted as adviser to the founder, William, Ranulf's younger brother, in establishing this Bricquassard priory[18]. That he continued to enjoy their confidence and support is shown by his lasting friendship with the founder's wife, Cecily de Rumilly, herself a noted benefactor of religious houses.

The impulse to establish religious houses was another factor already working in Thurstan's favour well before he himself appeared on the northern scene. This fact needs to be emphasized if the splendour of northern monasticism in the mid-twelfth century is not to blind us to the steady recovery being wrought throughout the area in the previous generations, generations to whom credit should be given. It is true that Danes, Norsemen and Normans had each in turn torn at the heart of the region, but they had never entirely wiped out the distinctively northern traditions of spiritu-

---

17. As King of Scots, David informed the managers of his mines at Carlisle that he had granted 3 marks yearly from the mines to the canons of Nostell, circa 1136–1152 (*E Y C* III, no. 1464); his benefactions to the monks of Durham began much earlier, in the days when he was Earl of Lothian (Lawrie, *Early Scottish Charters*, 1905, p. 23; circa 1117) and continued (*ibid.* p. 54, circa 1126, and p. 79, circa 1130–1133).

18. *The Register of the Priory of St. Bees* (ed. J. Wilson), pp. 29, 31, 34, 35.

ality. The Irish evangelization of Northumbria had by no means
been forgotten and interest in their saints and missionaries was to
take a sharp upswing during the course of the century[19]. Parts of
buildings from those early days of the church bore witness to its
austere devotion ; dear memories still clung to the ancient sites
and love for the sternly ascetic, heremitical life of the first founders
had not been quenched[20]. One is struck, for instance, by the
number of famous northern religious houses of the twelfth century
which were raised on sites where hermits were already dwelling.
This was the case at Nostell, at Whitby, Bridlington, Kirkstall,
Kirkstead and Selby[21]. And when Godric came north in search of
a place to lead a hermit's life he teamed up with the hermit Aelric,
hidden in the woods of Northumbria, before himself settling at
Finchale which was in its turn to become a priory[22]. Even after
the spread of settled monastic institutions there were not a few who
turned away from communal life to pursue their solitary calling ;
one of these was that Aelric already mentioned, who had been
trained amongst the brethren at Durham, as had another famous
hermit of that age, Bartholomew, who spent the greater part of his
life on Farne Island[23].

One of the monasteries to be constructed on an old site was
that of Hexham, which is a good example of how the foundations
for Thurstan's achievements were being laid in advance of his

---

19. *Cf* P. Grosjean, The Alleged Irish Origin of St. Cuthbert, pp. 144–154 of
The Relics of St. Cuthbert (ed. C. F. Battiscombe), for the revived interest
at Melrose. *Brit. Mus. Add. MS.* 35110 bears witness to the same revival
at the Newcastle Augustinian house. Laurence of Durham also wrote a
life of the Irish Saint Bridget which he dedicated to Ailred, who was still
a layman at the court of King David (see the interesting remarks of Fr.
Aelred Squire, O.P., Historical Factors in the Formation of Aelred of
Rievaulx in *Collectanea Ord. Cist. Ref.* 1960, pp. 272–4). Like St. Godric
(*Vita Godrici*, pp. 91–2) Ailred exercised the traditional Irish austerity
of immersion in cold water (*Vita Ailredi*, ed. Powicke, p. 25).
        This whole question of the rediscovery of Irish saints by the Anglo-
Normans is one that I hope to treat separately another time.

20. See the story of the Norman knight Reinfrid who was inspired to repair
the desolation of the North by the sight of the ruins of Whitby (*Memorials
of Whitby*, p. 1) ; he and his companions first settled in the ruins of Jarrow.
Durham also must have afforded reminders of its early glory, with the
cross of Aethelwold (bishop of Lindisfarne, 721–739) still standing in the
graveyard there (Symeon of Durham, *Opera* I, p. 39).

21. For hermits at Nostell *cf E Y C* III, p. 133 ; at Whitby, *E Y C* I, nos.
396, 397, 398 ; at Bridlington, *Chartulary of Bridlington Priory* (ed. W. T.
Lancaster, 1912), p. 179 ; at Kirkstall, *Monasticon*, V, p. 530 ; at Selby,
The Coucher Book of Selby (ed. J. T. Fowler, 1891), Vol. I, pp. 6–17.

22. *Vita Godrici* (ed. J. Stevenson).

23. H. H. E. Craster, The Miracles of St. Cuthbert at Farne, *Analecta
Bollandiana*, LXX, 1952, pp. 5–19.

coming[24]. The revival of Hexham as a worthy centre of devotion began when Eilaf (grandfather of St. Ailred) went there in 1085 ; the church was without roof, and grass and shrubs were growing all over the building, whilst the district had so gone to seed that for two years his only way of providing for his family was by hunting with hound and hawk. But eventually he managed to restore at least the chancel of the church to fit it for divine service. When he died about 1090 he was succeeded as priest-in-charge by his son, also named Eilaf ; but the revenues of the area around Hexham were in the hands of a canon of Beverley, Richard de Maton, for whom they served as an endowment to the prebend of Holm, which Richard held in virtue of his stall in York Minster. Things continued in this fashion until Thomas II of York saw the opportunity to make better arrangements ; for though his uncle's efforts to reform the canons at York and Beverley had not been generally successful there were at least two of the canons who had been trained in the regular life and Thomas now decided to send these, one from York and one from Beverley, to accomplish the plan of reform at Hexham. It was on the 1st November, 1113, that the first of them, Eadric, arrived at Hexham, soon followed by his partner. It had only been possible to carry out this plan, of course, by offering some sort of compensation to the clerics being expropriated, Richard de Maton and Eilaf. Richard was fairly easily dealt with ; the canons of York agreed with the archbishop to make provision for him out of their common property and he became a residentiary of the Minster. Eilaf's reactions are more difficult to determine. It is true that his son, Ailred, even credits Eilaf with having taken the initiative in bringing the canons to Hexham ; but this is probably a piece of retrospective family piety, because the historians of the house definitely attribute the initiative to Thomas. And there is some evidence that the change was not entirely welcome to Eilaf's family ; for in Walter Daniel's life of Ailred he recounts that the rumour of archbishop Thomas' death was received by the family with some hilarity and a sharp comment from Eilaf on Thomas' evil ways[25]. And though Eilaf did receive adequate compensation the interference of York seems to have rankled if we are to judge by a story going the rounds at Hexham. The story runs that soon after the canons came the York Minster clergy

---

24. For the account of Hexham's renovation, compare the accounts of Prior Richard (*Priory of Hexham*, pp. 49–56) and Ailred (*ibid.*, pp. 190–195).
25. *Vita Ailredi* (ed. Powicke), p. 72.

began to murmur to themselves that it was not right for the Minster
to have no relics of their own early bishops : Paulinus' remains were
at Rochester, Wilfrid's at Ripon and John's at Beverley, and it
would be impossible for the York clergy to recover any of these
since the local people would prevent them. But the church of
Hexham retained the relics of no less than five saintly bishops, and
so the envious clerks of York put it into their archbishop's head to
go up to Hexham and extract the body of St. Eata from its resting-
place. Being an easy-going man Thomas agreed. When rumours of
their intentions reached Hexham the poor canons there beseeched
St. Eata in prayer not to desert his poverty-stricken resting-place
for the riches of York ; but their prayers seemed vain when the
York party arrived and prepared to remove the saint's remains.
It was the night before the day of removal that decided the issue ;
when archbishop Thomas went to sleep that night he saw in his
dreams a man of severe countenance robed in episcopal vestments ;
to the terrified archbishop this awesome apparition spoke : "Why
have you decided to disturb my peace, and to take me from the
place where I am sleeping contentedly with my brethren and bear
me into foreign parts ? This is not the will of God but your own
presumption for which you will now be punished." At which the
figure raised his pastoral staff, struck Thomas with it twice on his
shoulder, and vanished. The cry of terror with which the archbishop awoke brought his clerks running to him in consternation to
find out the cause of it. This the archbishop quickly explained, at
the same time asking them to pray that he might be forgiven for his
sinful intentions. For three days he lay stricken with illness, but
on the fourth he recovered and went away empty-handed, cured by
the saint whose bones were left to rest in peace at Hexham[26].

This story of how regular religious observance was introduced
at Hexham shows that Thurstan had taken over a diocese which, for
all its disorder and violence, harboured vigour and determination
that promised great things. The North was fortunate to receive
in Thurstan a leader capable of bringing that promise to fruition,
doubly fortunate in that he brought to his office a noble conception
of what it meant to be a bishop. For not all contemporary bishops
could subscribe without blushing to the statements which recur
time and again in Thurstan's charters to characterize his vision of
his duty as archbishop :—"it is the duty of a good pastor," runs
one of his confirmations, "to watch over the flock entrusted to him

---

26.   *Priory of Hexham*, pp. 202-3.

with steadfast devotion and to exercise unceasingly the works of mercy for the benefit of those who have least of life's necessities . . ."[27]. Or, as another one says, "since the burden of pastoral care has been laid upon us by virtue of the recognized authority it is our duty towards those who are subject to us to provide them with whatever is essential for their well-being, both by material aid in their temporal life and proper care for them in their eternal life"[28]. For a bishop with so elevated a conception of his charge the church over which he had been set was in a very profound sense his *sponsa*, his bride to whom he was bound by ties that neither exile nor the wrath of kings could sever. But like another Jacob, Thurstan was to know seven years of exile and labour before he could enter into free possession of his bride. The centuries-old wrangle between Canterbury and York over the primacy was to delay the consummation.

It was obvious to Thurstan that he would have to make a stand on this issue and so he steadily declined in the months after his consecration to allow either the archbishop of Canterbury or his suffragans to ordain him to the priesthood in case the ordination should be construed as giving countenance to Canterbury's claims. Hence he was still only a deacon when in December, 1114, he was enthroned at York by the bishop of Chester, Robert de Limesey[29]. But his oddly indeterminate status did not prevent him from making a preliminary survey of his incoherent diocese, since in the following weeks he visited both Durham and Hexham in the company of the bishop of Durham, Ranulf Flambard. At Durham, Thurstan was able to meet Turgot, the bishop of St. Andrews, now in his last illness yet as well equipped as any man to introduce the new archbishop to the subtleties of Anglo-Scottish relations. Turgot himself accepted Thurstan as his metropolitan and promised him obedience, no doubt explaining to the archbishop how five years previously in the presence of Cardinal Ulric at York he had been consecrated bishop of St. Andrews by Thomas II, and assuring Thurstan that it was no innovation for St. Andrews to be subject to York, as some people maintained. Coming from Scotland Turgot

---

27. *E Y C* VII, no. 8.
28. *E Y C* I, no. 431.
29. Robert de Limesey, who had been a clerk to William the Conqueror, was nominated by him to the bishopric of Chester in 1085 ; he died in 1117, having fifteen years previously removed the see from Chester to Coventry.
    It is worth noting that Hugh the Chantor uses the old title, "Of Chester" (*H C* pp. 35 and 122), though "of Lichfield and Coventry" was the new usage.

would also have been able to fill in the background of the recent arrival at Selkirk of monks from Tiron ; he was in a position to explain to Thurstan whether the introduction of these reforming monks was the work of Earl David himself or of his mentor, John ; and to give Thurstan some notion of who David was planning to set in the empty see of Glasgow, which John was in fact soon detailed to fill[30]. The rest of the story could be pieced together for himself by Thurstan when he continued his journey from Durham up to Hexham, that hub of border intelligence reports. After a few days in Hexham he returned to York to thrash out with his chapter the policy that they should pursue towards Canterbury's demands.

At this point both Thurstan and the York canons behaved with great shrewdness, securing the best of both worlds where they might easily have got the worst of both. If the canons had advised the archbishop elect to refuse the profession downright their property and the lands of the church of York might have come under the hammer of the king's wrath should things have gone badly ; on the other hand, they would have lost all they had been fighting for if they agreed to the profession. Instead they absolved themselves from any decision by leaving the matter in Thurstan's hands, knowing full well what course of action he would take. They knew this because Thurstan had already made his position clear to the king ; he had pointed out to Henry that in no other realm did one metropolitan make profession to another and that it was quite inappropriate for this to be done in England ; besides, were he to make profession to Canterbury he would have no choice but to side with Canterbury if ever that archbishop were to fall out with the king himself (as had lately happened, of course). More penetrating than his predecessors, Thurstan had realized that only the Roman pontiff could undo the knot of discord into which Canterbury and York had by this time twisted themselves. As he explained to the delighted chapter, he would go to Rome and seek advice from the Pope himself ; and he selected several of them to accompany him.

The party set out with the minimum of delay and made their way across the Channel to Normandy on Christmas Day. Unfortunately for them Canterbury had given warning of Thurstan's intentions to the king, who met him with a blank refusal to allow him to proceed to Rome. But Henry was never unreasonable or personally hostile to Thurstan and so asked the advice of Cuno, the

30. *Cf* G. W. S. Barrow, From Queen Margaret to David I, in *The Innes Review*, XI, 1960, p. 33.

papal legate in Northern France, about what he should do in regard to Thurstan. As a result Thurstan was at least permitted to receive priest's orders from one of his own suffragans. It must have been some comfort to Thurstan to receive this sacrament at Whitsun, 1115, in his home town of Bayeux and from the hands of another Bayeux man, the bishop of Durham, Ranulf Flambard[31]. And when one remembers the low estimation in which Flambard was generally held this is worth remarking on : it is not the only evidence that Thurstan and Flambard managed to work together, nor is it the only instance of Thurstan's co-operating with a man whose personal character he can scarcely have found edifying. Perhaps his years at the royal court had taught him how to manage the children of this world and to tap what dregs of loyalty they still possessed. At any rate the bishop of Durham usually stood by him, and was loyal to his archbishop in some very dark days.

Nor were the dark days long in coming, for within a few months the royal entourage was back in England and the two archbishops again found themselves in conflict, this time at the King's Council in Westminster (September, 1115). Again the ritual moves in the game were gone through : Canterbury demands the oath of obedience ; the elect of York refuses it and asks the king's permission to go to Rome ; permission refused, the game is over and the participants prepare for the next round. Repetitious as they were, each of the rounds, nevertheless, brought out the alternating strengths and weaknesses of the opposing sides. Thus at Westminster the Canterbury party was still savouring the elation of having secured the *pallium* from Rome for their archbishop despite the serious canonical doubts about his election[32]. But this elation was tinged with apprehension at the threatening tone of Pope Paschal's letters to

---

31. Ranulf's tortuous character is deftly sketched by *Ordericus Vitalis, Ecclesiasticae Historiae* (Vol. III, p. 310) : Turstini, cuiusdam plebei presbyteri de pago Baiocensis, filius fuit, et a puerilibus annis inter pedissequos curiales cum vilibus parasitis educatus crevit, callidisque tergiversationibus, et argutis verborum machinationibus plus quam arti literatoriae studuit. From his pen also, we learn of the chaos caused by Ranulf at Lisieux where, during his exile from England (1104–1107), he forced into the see first his brother and then his son (*ibid*. IV, pp. 116–117).

His vain attempt to seduce Christina of Markyate, as he had previously seduced her aunt, has lately been brought to the light of ultra-violet ray (*The Life of Christina of Markyate*, C. H. Talbot, 1959, pp. 40–45).

Nevertheless, this consecrated argument in favour of Gregorian reform proved a benefactor to the saintly Godric of Finchale ; and the fruit of one of his escapades, his son Ralph, is singled out by Godric's biographies for his devotion to the hermit (*Vita Godrici*, p. 66).

32. Eadmer, *Historia Novorum*, p. 228.

King Henry. For in those letters Paschal made it clear to Henry that if he continued obstructing the papacy and its legates at work in his dominions severe sanctions would be imposed upon him. Hence the closer Canterbury drew towards the king and the more reliance it placed on his favour the further it drew away from Rome and the more likely it would be to suffer the same censure as the king. Conversely, the more steadily Thurstan refused to accept the king's decision in an ecclesiastical dispute as final the more warmly he was regarded in the final court of appeal at Rome. But Thurstan was being harassed by a more nagging worry and one that struck deep into his scrupulous mind, which was that by continuing as the elect of York, but unconsecrated, he was something of a sham : not only was he unable to protect his church and its property as an archbishop should, but he was receiving an income from it at the same time—it was almost as unacceptable as the sin of simony to a man of delicate conscience[33].

The spiritual torment oppressing Thurstan intensified in the following months and drove him into the most unaccountable act of his career. It was at Salisbury, in March, 1116, when the temporal and spiritual magnates of the realm had been summoned to acknowledge publicly that they would accept Henry's son William as king should Henry himself die. Once the Council had agreed on this measure for the safety of the realm the quarrel between Canterbury and York was again brought up. But this time the ritual of the game was given a different turn because the king openly backed up archbishop Ralph in his demand for the oath of obedience. He accused Thurstan of ingratitude for past favours and threatened that if he did not obey, then others beside himself would suffer : Thurstan's relatives would all be driven out of the king's lands. It was at this moment that Thurstan produced his bombshell : he resigned into the king's hands the archbishopric to which he had been elected almost two years previously. The outburst of astonishment that greeted this announcement spread rapidly throughout England and Normandy ; it was occasioned partly by Thurstan's unyielding behaviour but even more by the unlikely fact that a court cleric such as he was, who owed his advancement to the king, should have taken so independent a line and should not have clung on desperately to his high office.

---

33. *H C* p. 38 : . . . et in periculum magnum anime fructus archiepiscopi recipere, et officium episcopale non facere . . .

Some of his contemporaries took a far from exalted view of Thurstan's action. Eadmer, in particular, the Canterbury spokesman, makes no attempt to disguise his contempt for Thurstan's behaviour ; his very turn of phrase in describing the elect of York, "quidam de clericis regis vocabulo Thurstanus," breathes bitterness[34]. For him Thurstan's resignation was due to his own obstinacy and to the self-seeking of the York clergy who supported him and egged him on. How precipitate and ill-considered his adherence to their counsel was made obvious, according to Eadmer, as soon as the heat of conflict began to die down, when Thurstan came to realize that he was no longer being deferred to and having a fuss made of him ; then he began to get cold feet, and wished to return once more to the centre of the stage. Eadmer's charges against Thurstan would have carried more weight had he not wielded such a flowing pen, which leads him to say more than a trained advocate would. He informs us, for example, that his own archbishop Ralph had himself favoured Thurstan's election, holding a higher opinion of him than he came to take later ; which argues that Thurstan's personal integrity did not get impugned until he ran up against Canterbury bias. Again Eadmer gives himself away when he accuses Thurstan of knowing how to operate the Roman curia to his own ends, but then triumphantly and inconsistently observes that his designs went unfulfilled.

This is not to say, however, that Eadmer's interpretation of the event is entirely implausible. Most gay and high-spirited men have their black and irrational moments, and it may be that Thurstan, after eighteen months of strain and tension, had impulsively tried to force the issue. At the same time there is a more rational and consistent explanation. Just before he went to Salisbury two papal letters arrived at York, one for the York clergy and the other to be delivered by Thurstan to Ralph of Canterbury ; the intention of each of them was the same, to forbid Ralph, in the name of Gregory I and his instructions, to demand the oath of obedience from Thurstan ; and should Ralph refuse to consecrate Thurstan then the suffragans of the northern province were to consecrate him[35]. Armed with such documents Thurstan could hardly lose his fight in the end, but their very force constituted an embarrassment until that day dawned ; for how could he ask his suffragans— Ranulf Flambard, to be precise—to consecrate him in face of the

---

34. *Historia Novorum*, pp. 237–8 ; compare *H C* pp. 41–44.
35. *H C* p. 40.

king's opposition ? All the clergy of the northern province would
have felt the weight of the royal hatred for many a long day after-
ward. It was the king's decisive support for Canterbury in 1116
that made it impossible for Thurstan to deliver the letters received
from Rome ; only by bending the king's will could Rome's intentions be put through without disastrous consequences ; but the
king's will did not bend under the threat of Thurstan's resignation.
Nevertheless, by converting the dispute into one over his own
person and deliberately putting himself into a position of isolation
Thurstan had drawn the burden of displeasure off his dependants
and on to himself ; as Hugh the Chanter says, "our elect had
remained in the chapel with few attendants : he would not have
any of us present, lest, if he opposed the king, he should lay the
blame on our company "[36].

That Thurstan did not act from mere impulse is also suggested
by Symeon of Durham. In his chronicle Symeon normally follows
Eadmer's version (through Florence of Worcester) somewhat
mechanically. But at the point where Eadmer is accusing Thurstan
of breaking with tradition Symeon cuts in upon his text to explain
that Thurstan was in fact following the instructions of Gregory the
Great ; more interesting still, where Eadmer attributes *pervicacia*
to Thurstan, Symeon substitutes the word *sententia*[37], thus transforming an obstinate man into one who sticks to his guns. That
Thurstan was a man of such mettle was proclaimed on this same
occasion by one who knew him well and had every reason to side
with the king, that is Robert of Meulan. When some of those at the
council would not believe that Thurstan meant to resign Robert
curtly commented, "If I know my man he means to do exactly
what he has said"[38]. It was in character, also, that after the
resignation he "showed no sign of sadness, but was as merry and
jocose as usual, as though nothing had happened to him." Or, as
the clergy of York said, in a letter bursting with pride in their elect,
"Viriliter egisti"—"you have played the man." "Nothing," they
go on, "shall separate us from your obedience and the spiritual
fatherhood which you have assumed over us"[39] ; and they triumphantly proclaim that they will have no other but himself as archbishop.

---

36. *H C* p. 42.
37. Symeon of Durham, *Opera* II, p. 250.
38. *H C* p. 43.
39. *H C* p. 46.

Strangely enough, the king seems to have felt much the same, that he wanted no other as archbishop ; accordingly he insisted on his subjects giving Thurstan the title of archbishop in the following months when officially Thurstan had resigned his office. And this respect shown to him offers an instructive contrast to the lack of respect with which even a consecrated archbishop, Thomas Becket, was later to be treated ; the difference is the difference between enjoying the king's good will and incurring his hatred, which in the twelfth century spelled the gulf between prosperity and bankruptcy. Even with the king's good will, however, the next eighteen months must have been a time of great trial for Thurstan as he was trailed around Normandy with the king, almost as though he was a prisoner. It was not long before he began to regret his resignation as ill-advised, even possibly uncanonical ; as he reasoned to himself, he could only resign into the king's hands the dignities which the king had bestowed upon him, not the spiritual office of archbishop in which the Pope had confirmed him. The whole burden of the Gregorian reform was that secular rulers had no right to appoint to spiritual offices ; did it not follow, conversely, that an ecclesiastic who attempted to resign his office into a prince's hands was conceiving at lay investiture ? Troubled by these reflections, Thurstan explained them to the king and asked his permission to visit the Pope in Rome, who might relieve his mind.

At this moment of deadlock one needs to bear in mind the painfully awkward position in which Henry I found himself. As father-in-law to the Emperor Henry V he was bound by mutual ties to the man who stood throughout Europe as a symbol for resistance towards the papacy over the issue of investitures. In the course of his long drawn out quarrel with Pope Paschal, Henry V had endured the humiliation of excommunication, and had suffered the effects of it upon his own dominions where it had given an excuse for rebels to revolt against his authority. Moreover, the spearheads of such attacks by the Church on temporal rulers were the papal legates, a most devastating instrument for chastising recalcitrant temporal rulers in that they superseded the local ecclesiastical heads and brought even distant lands under the direct control of Rome. The instigator of this policy of "thorough" in Germany had been the formidable legate Cuno, and it was the prospect of having him or his likes at the helm of the church in Normandy and England that filled Henry I with dismay. He saw the situation getting almost completely out of hand when in March, 1117, his ally the Emperor marched into Italy with a large force in order to threaten

the Pope ; in order to avoid being taken captive the Pope deemed
it wiser to withdraw from Rome and establish his court at
Benevento.

As if the continental situation had not already heaped troubles
enough on his lap Henry found Canterbury and York piling further
ones upon him. Early in 1117 Rome had tried to insist on sending
a papal legate to England, but Henry would have none of it ; in an
attempt to bring Henry to compliance the papal legate in France,
Cuno, suspended all the Norman bishops and abbots—on the grounds
that they had three times failed to respond to his summons to a
council[40]. The only course left open to Henry, and an unpalatable
one, was to appeal to Rome by sending Ralph of Canterbury to try
if soft words would persuade the Pope to adopt a more conciliatory
policy[41]. The Pope might have been so persuaded, but reading
between the lines of contemporary reports it is easily seen that
Ralph was not the man to do the persuading. To begin with he was
old and sick and hardly fit for the strenuous journey. Nor had he
the necessary diplomatic training, as he sadly proved when he
arrived in Rome, to find that the Pope had fled to Benevento ; he
meekly contented himself with sending messengers backwards and
forwards to the Pope instead of pressing on there himself. Worse
still, he accepted the Emperor's invitation to visit him outside
Rome and stayed for eight days in the imperial camp. Ralph's
defenders assure us that the visit took place with papal approval,
but their very insistence on the point alerts us to the fact that it
constituted a snub to the Pope and aroused papal suspicions that
Ralph was treating with the Emperor on King Henry's behalf.
Ralph's apologists further give the game away by quoting only the
papal letter issued at Benevento on March 24th and not the more
revealing one issued a fortnight later. The earlier one is a completely
formal, non-committal one[42] about Canterbury's claims, which the
York historian rightly describes as a face-saver for Ralph, confirming
him in "things which nobody opposed or claimed"[43] ; but the
second one, issued on April 5th, is a thundering rejection of Canterbury's demands on York[44] : "The more fully we trust in the

---

40.   William of Malmesbury, *Gesta Pontificum*, p. 129.
41.   For the following paragraph compare Eadmer's *Historia Novorum*, pp.
      241–244, William of Malmesbury's *Gesta Pontificum*, pp. 129–131, and
      H C pp. 50–2.
42.   *Jaffé*, no. 6547.
43.   *H C* p. 51.
44.   *Jaffé*, no. 6553.

sincerity of your love," writes Paschal, "the more we marvel that
you should appear to demand what is only appropriate to the church
of Rome." The Pope then orders Ralph to consecrate Thurstan
without any demand for submission ; otherwise York's suffragans
are ordered to do so. In conjunction with Paschal's letter of the
same date and same effect to King Henry[45] this papal directive
underlines the failure of Ralph's mission and the dilemma of the
king.

By the same token it was a feather in the York cap, and a
triumph for that chapter's intelligence service. For it emerges quite
plainly from the years 1116–1118 that the canons of York had kept
constantly in touch with each turn in the course of the contest.
In the summer of 1116 they decided to petition the king to give them
back their archbishop, and chose as their messengers a group meant
to represent the Yorkshire clergy ; there were two archdeacons
from the chapter (one of them being the historian Hugh), one monk
from St. Mary's abbey at York, and a canon of Beverley named
William. A cold reception was given to them in Normandy, and
their petition was listened to impatiently ; but their journey was
not in vain since it gave them the opportunity to discuss the church's
affairs with Thurstan. Also, it seems, they managed to slip William
of Beverley through to Rome with a full account from their viewpoint of the struggle against Canterbury. To judge from Hugh the
Chantor's pages this account was likely to have insinuated at Rome
that Ralph of Canterbury had been boasting of how he would bribe
the curia to make a decision in his favour, as everyone knew how
eminently bribable the Romans were. At the same time York
acquired the backing of the key-figure in the curia, the papal
chancellor, Cardinal John of Gaeta, who was a great help to them in
their battle with Canterbury[46]. It was no wonder that Rome's
attitude to Ralph and King Henry was hardening month by month.

The day was therefore approaching which the king foresaw with
growing dismay, when the world would enjoy the sight of his own
two archbishops openly acknowledging that only the court of Rome,
not of King Henry, could settle the dispute between them. If he
was to put off that evil day Henry had little choice but to accept
Paschal's directions and restore Thurstan to York. Thus in the
early days of 1118, after some eighteen months of exile, the champion
of York's liberty returned to the see where he was welcomed with

---

45. *Jaffé*, no. 6552.
46. *H C* p. 57.

even greater rejoicing than before. It was premature rejoicing :
Thurstan was still not consecrated and, as a result, unable to
exercise any spiritual authority in his diocese or his province. Moreover, Ralph of Canterbury was confident that Thurstan would
remain unconsecrated so long as he himself kept out of England.
By staying in Normandy Ralph was playing for time ; and time
seemed to be on his side, for Pope Paschal died in January, 1118.

To the York clergy the Pope's death was a sad blow. He had
dealt most favourably with them, and his death at the very moment
they appeared to be winning their fight had robbed them of their
most powerful patron. But they were not men to sit down and
weep over their misfortunes ; they had picked up the threads before,
and so they set their information services to work again to devise
appropriate plans. They learnt with deep satisfaction that the papal
chair was now filled by their ally John of Gaeta who had taken the
title of Gelasius II ; through fear of the Emperor the new Pope and
most of the cardinals had left Rome and were journeying towards
France, leaving the Emperor to establish in Rome his anti-Pope,
Burdinus. It was an occasion for quick action ; though there is,
perhaps, a hint of impulsiveness, even desperation, in Thurstan's
next step. In the autumn of 1118 he left England for Normandy
along with his household—but not openly and with the splendour
expected of an archbishop, for his party proceeded with all the
characteristics of men conducting a secret operation, splitting up
in London with one section under Thurstan going by way of Dover
and the other section by way of Hastings, a rendezvous having been
pre-arranged in Normandy. To complete the atmosphere of secrecy
Thurstan himself was disguised as a member of the lower orders[47].

The secrecy was almost certainly necessary because it is fairly
obvious that Thurstan and his advisers were aware that Pope
Gelasius was journeying towards France and they were making a
dash to reach him without King Henry's knowledge. The attempt
was a failure. An informer gave Henry news of Thurstan's expedition and the king came quickly upon the York party to halt them
in Dover. Nevertheless, they did manage to slip a messenger
through to the Pope at Genoa[48] who was able to give Gelasius a
full account of the predicament in which the elect of York found
himself. Already well informed on the background events Gelasius
immediately realized Thurstan's need and was quick to act. He

47. *H C* p. 57.
48. The Pope was at Genoa on the 10th of October ; *cf Jaffé*, p. 778.

despatched three short but pointed letters : to Henry, to Ralph of Canterbury, and to Thurstan himself[49]. To Henry he expressed his sorrow at the treatment accorded to the elect of York and insisted that if Canterbury would not obey previous papal instructions by consecrating Thurstan then the disputants were to present themselves to him for judgment. In his letter to the archbishop of Canterbury, Gelasius did not mince his words : Ralph had been a grave disappointment to Rome on account of his disobedience and neglect of justice ; he must now abandon his hardness of heart and consecrate the elect of York, as he has so often been ordered to do ; and he must present himself along with Thurstan for the Pope to decide the dispute. The tone of his letter to Thurstan is quite different. He refers sympathetically to the injustice Thurstan has endured and says that if he still cannot obtain his rightful demands from the archbishop of Canterbury then he must come to the Pope without him.

Meanwhile the king had been listening to Thurstan's pleadings. And the burden of those pleadings is worth remarking on ; it was that by remaining unconsecrated he was prevented from fulfilling his pastoral duties which were the very justification for his election. Here is but one of the recurring evidences that Thurstan had for ever in mind the essentially pastoral nature of the dignity that had been bestowed upon him ; he remained painfully aware that his flock was defenceless without him. But then Henry himself in these months was equally conscious that by giving way to any external authority at that period he might lay his Norman territories open to waves of rebellion even fiercer than the ones now sweeping it. For Henry at this point was in great danger of losing his grip on his Norman lands. Along his borders were ranged his customary enemies, the count of Flanders and the count of Anjou, for ever under incitement by his main enemy King Louis VI of France. Their incursions were now all the more threatening through the sapping of Norman loyalty from within, where William Clito, the son of Henry's elder brother, was able to make respectable claims to possess the duchy. Louis had lately tied the Clito's own interests tight to his own by marrying him to Jeanne de Montferrat, sister of his own queen Adelaide, and bestowing on him Pontoise, Chaumont, Mante and the Vexin. The Clito's own supporters amongst the turbulent Norman baronage were led moreover by the violent Amaury de Montfort who was related to both Louis and the count

49. *H C* pp. 58–9.

of Anjou ; he was now claiming to be count of Evreux and in pursuit of that claim had brought his auxiliaries against the city. Joining in the anarchy were other nobles such as Hugh de Gourney, Stephen of Aumale and Eustace de Breteuil, as well as scores of lesser fry that numbered mercenaries and brigands[50].

It was this rebellion in Normandy that made Henry acutely sensitive to any papal interference in northern France for the very good reason that in recent years the Popes had turned ever more frequently to the house of Capet for support to resist the threats from the German Emperor. This intimacy with the papacy had even enabled Louis to use ecclesiastical sanctions against his internal enemies. Thus in 1114, for instance, the papal legate Cuno had organized a veritable crusade against that thorn in Louis' side, the marauding Thomas de Marle ; he had gone so far as to promise indulgences and absolution for all who took part in the campaign against him. What was there to prevent Cuno from stirring up a similar crusade against Henry I should the English king fall foul of ecclesiastical authority ?

In fact, Cuno's personality has to be given full weight if one is to understand the diplomatic tensions in northern France and Thurstan's part in them[51]. Cuno is never mentioned by Hugh the Chanter without some accompanying word of praise[52], and it is quite obvious that he stood extremely high in the estimation of Thurstan and his clergy just as they themselves were high in his esteem. Of German origin, Cuno had early shown firm devotion to the religious life. He and his companion Hildemar had founded a house of regular canons at Arrouaise in Picardy ; and the thorough-ness of their work made Arrouaise into a model for the regular canons in the twelfth century. Their efforts to formulate an appro-priate rule for the community had taken them on one occasion to England[53], and it is possible that they had there made Thurstan's acquaintance. But it was not long before Cuno's talents caught the eye of his superiors and in 1107 he was created Cardinal Bishop of

---

50. Ordericus Vitalis, *Historiae Ecclesiasticae*, IV, pp. 313–15.

51. For a study of this striking figure see *Kardinallegat Kuno*, by G. Schoene, published in 1857, of which there is a copy in the British Museum, its pages now cut.

52. *E.g. H C* p. 36, vir venerabilis, verax, et justus, et constans . . . ; p. 77, qui archiepiscopum nostrum multum diligebat ; p. 83, illum etenim erga se quatuor istis, iustitia, et veritate, et fide et dileccione quadratum experti erant.

53. *Acta Sanctorum*, Jan., Vol. II (Jan. 13th) 114A ; quoted by J. C. Dickinson, *The Origins of the Austin Canons*, p. 116.

Praeneste. From then until his death in 1122 he distinguished himself by conducting unceasing warfare against the claims of the Emperor Henry V to control the church in his lands. About the year 1112, whilst returning from the Holy Land, he seized the opportunity to proclaim Henry's excommunication in Greece and Hungary. In 1114, having been made papal legate in northern France, he again proclaimed the Emperor's excommunication, in a council at Beauvais. The following year he threw out a challenge to Henry of England by specifically calling the clergy of the province of Rouen to his council in Chalons ; he had called them in vain on two previous occasions and when they again failed to come he suspended the bishops and abbots of Normandy and excommunicated them. In 1116 he took part in the Lateran Council and spoke so vehemently against any compromise with the Emperor[54] that when returning to France soon afterwards he had to disguise himself as a wandering scholar so as to avoid capture by the imperialist troops. In May, 1118 he was again in the front line, holding a council at Cologne ; and in July of the same year he joined forces with another severe reformer of the regular canons, St. Norbert, at a council in Fritzlar ; at both these councils adherents of the Emperor were excommunicated. Such was Cuno's single-mindedness in the cause of reform that one can well understand how it gave rise to Abelard's mordant observations about his simple-mindedness and *faroucherie*. And one sympathises also with Henry of England as he observed this bane of secular rulers winning the friendship of the elect of York.

A yet worse calamity, from Henry's point of view, was only avoided by a hair's breadth. At Cluny in January, 1119, Pope Gelasius was dying, and as his gaze ran over the assembled cardinals to see which one of them would maintain his own uncompromising stand against lay investiture it fell, not unnaturally, upon Cuno. He uttered the hope that Cuno might succeed him as Pope. Though he turned down the suggestion for himself Cuno showed how well he understood Gelasius' mind by putting forward the name of Gui, archbishop of Vienne, who was indeed elected as Pope, taking the name of Calixtus II[55]. Henry had only narrowly escaped having

---

54. "In 1116 Paschal was forced (by the Curia) to revoke his pledge (to the Emperor) and under pressure of the Curia to ratify Cuno of Palestrina's excommunication of the Emperor" (H. V. White, Pontius of Cluny, the Curia Romana and the end of Gregorianism in Rome, in *Church History*, XXVII, 1958, p. 202).

55. Ulysse Robert, *Histoire du Pape Calixte II*, p. 43.

Cuno pontificating over him ; in his stead was Calixtus, a distant relative of his, from whom he might hope better things, especially when Calixtus declared that the theme of his work as Pope would be peace and reconciliation.

Not that Calixtus was in any sense an irresolute character[56]. As a son of the reigning Burgundian house and a close relative of the German Emperor he had stepped easily and confidently into the high office of archbishop at the age of twenty-eight. For years he had conducted a running quarrel with St. Hugh of Grenoble and the archbishop of Lyons in defence of his see's rights, before diverting his energies against the evils of lay investiture. The concessions over lay investiture wrung from Pope Paschal by Henry V had found in him a stern critic who did not hesitate to arraign the Pope himself for having climbed down. In 1112 he had held a council at Vienne which excommunicated Henry V and declared lay investiture to be a heresy. And in the following years he gave his blessing to the advance guard of reform within the church when he visited Cîteaux and persuaded Stephen Harding to establish a Cistercian house at Bonnevaux in his own diocese. Bent upon peace though he was, Calixtus was not then a man to be trifled with when the Church's ideals and authority were at stake, as Ralph of Canterbury was quick to discover.

Calixtus was soon primed with the York account of the quarrel with Canterbury and immediately he sent Henry, abbot of St. Jean d'Angély, to escort Ralph through France into the Pope's presence for a personal hearing. Ralph was unable to make the journey, partly because of the ill-health which continually dogged him[57] and partly because the king of France would not give him a safe conduct ; instead, he sent a letter of excuse which goes far to explain the troubles that Ralph was for ever bringing down on his head[58]. Like other letters of his, it is a model of how to alienate and enrage one's superior. He began by protesting, somewhat disingenuously, that he had never received prescripts ordering him to consecrate Thurstan. It is, of course, possible that there had been technical defects in the formal procedure of delivering the orders to him which afforded an appearance of legal correctness to his excuse, but he knew quite well that he was hedging and he was

---

56. For Calixtus' personality and career see the work of U. Robert quoted in the previous note.
57. Cf Ordericus Vitalis, *Ecclesiasticae Historiae* IV, pp. 430-1, and William of Malmesbury, *Gesta Pontificum*, p. 129.
58. *H C* pp. 62-3. Passed over by Eadmer in silence, as was the Pope's reply.

foolish to imagine that the Pope could be deceived. Even more fool-ish was the scarcely veiled rebuke he administered to Calixtus for prejudicing the case : he reminded the Pope of the scriptural warrant for the saying : "Blame not till thou has examined." And it can scarcely have improved matters that the messenger to whom he entrusted his letter, and the oral explanation it required, was a mere youth. What sort of reply to his message he expected from Calixtus is difficult to imagine. The one he got was a blistering reprimand[59]. Obviously Calixtus was nettled by the suggestion that he had prejudged the Canterbury/York dispute, and he curtly explained that his predecessor's instructions to Ralph had been quite unambiguous ; he was forwarding them so that the facts of the case could no longer be questioned. The Pope showed, more-over, that he also could boast acquaintance with the scriptures, in token of which he called Ralph's attention to the text : "The disciple is not above his master, nor the servant above his lord."

In contrast to the disorganized and demoralized Canterbury group[60], Thurstan and his household were now looking forward hopefully to their inevitable victory. By means of their efficient intelligence service they were kept informed of the Pope's progress as he moved through Burgundy and France, and they were probably informed, even before its public announcement in May, 1119, of the Pope's intention to hold a general council of the Church at Rheims. Thurstan's supporters were being infiltrated through from Nor-mandy to the papal entourage to make sure that the York case was adequately presented when the day of reckoning came. And there was an air of determined confidence about Thurstan's language when he once more interviewed King Henry with the request to be accorded full power in his see : "My lord," he said, "it is not right and proper either to the church which I should be directing, or to my own person, for me to be there [i.e. in York] and yet be unable to consecrate the chrism when the time for it is due, nor to celebrate the Holy Pasch with the solemnity befitting a metropolitan in his metropolitan church"[61]. When the king tried to insist that Thurstan should in any case return to York after Easter he replied that he placed his trust in the counsel of God and the king ; at which a wag who was present said that he should forget about God's

---

59. *H C* pp. 64–5.
60. Eadmer, *Historia Novorum*, pp. 249–51 ; his own morale was at a low ebb and his protestations indicate murmuring within the cloister at Canterbury.
61. *H C* p. 65.

counsel and stick wholeheartedly to the king's. The comment brought a smile to Thurstan's face. He had reason to smile, because he could see the opposition to his consecration crumbling away. At the level of diplomacy Henry I was in no position to alienate the Pope ; obstinacy on his part could no longer win him the sure support of his son-in-law, the Emperor, who was being slowly forced to come to terms with Calixtus. Henry stood in great danger, therefore, of being left isolated whilst his immediate adversary, Louis VI of France, basked in papal favour. The time was ripe for Henry to cut his losses.

The next move on Thurstan's part has given rise to conflicting stories. The one least favourable to Thurstan maintains that the archbishop elect was now given permission by the king to join the Pope on condition that he promised not to seek consecration from him without the king's assent, a promise which Thurstan was soon to break[62]. Hugh the Chanter's story is, of course, very different. According to him Thurstan refused to make any promise not to accept consecration and bravely told the king : "About this I will make no bargain, but under God's direction I will so act as to render unto Caesar the things that are Caesar's, and unto God the things that are God's"[63]. This version of events is certainly more in keeping with everything else we know of Thurstan's character and, curiously enough, receives confirmation from the hostile Eadmer when he later says of Thurstan's consecration, "Many were of the opinion that he could never have presumed to behave as he did in so great a matter if he had not noticed that the king was a willing party to it"[64]. It is probably also true, as with so many long drawn out quarrels, that the intentions expressed and the very connotations of words had by now become hopelessly tangled. The art of quarrelling revolves round the misunderstanding of subordinate clauses, and there were now plenty such clauses available.

In any case, it is difficult to imagine so hard-headed a character as Henry I having failed to see that once Thurstan had joined the Pope his consecration would not long be delayed. And indeed by September, 1119 Thurstan was at least able to join the Pope at Tours, having first picked up at Chartres the representatives he had sent ahead of him. From that moment on Thurstan became a kind of travelling companion to the Pope, one of the great caravanserai

---

62.   Eadmer, *Historia Novorum*, p. 255.
63.   *H C* p. 68.
64.   *Historia Novorum*, p. 257.

of distinguished ecclesiastics which moved slowly across northern France, through Blois, Orleans, Étampes and Paris, to arrive at Rheims by the 18th of October[65]. Welcomed as one who had suffered long for the sake of ecclesiastical principles Thurstan inevitably struck up friendships with these rulers of the church. Of these friendships more will be said later ; it is enough for the moment to point out that they help to explain how the York chapter came to enjoy exact information upon church leaders and a grasp of the motives that inspired their actions. The advantage of such personal contacts is well seen by comparing the actions of the York party, and its official account of these years, with the actions and account issuing from Canterbury. One is immediately struck with the confidence and sure touch exhibited by York in handling the situation as compared with Canterbury's fumbling efforts to get a grasp of what was happening.

One instance of how deftly the York men were able to seize their opportunities occurred outside the church of St. Martin-des-Champs, in Paris, early in October. As the Pope was coming out from Mass three of them approached him, two archdeacons and the chancellor[66] ; they drew him into a corner on his own where they could talk confidentially, with no one else to overhear them, and explained how overjoyed they were at his election. Especially pleasing to them was the fact that he, a secular clerk, should hold the see of Rome which had long enough been held by monks. Their dig at the monks was obliquely aimed, no doubt, at the monkery of Canterbury, but it was also a shrewd perception of the wind of change blowing throughout the Church. For over fifty years now the papacy had been held by men trained in the ancient monasteries of Cluny and Monte Cassino ; they had done great deeds to liberate the spiritual order from dependence on the temporal order, but the reaction had now set in and the York men were quick to see its implications. They had at this moment to talk fast to the Pope, as Hugh the Chanter drily observes, because the old guard of Roman clerics was rapidly approaching them ; they begged the Pope to do justice to their see and consecrate Thurstan as soon as possible.

---

65. For Calixtus' journey through France, see U. Robert, *Bullaire du Pape Calixte II*, and his *Histoire du Pape Calixte II*.

66. The word used by Hugh the Chanter is *scolasticus*, who may or may not be the same as the *magister* of several lines later (*H C* p. 70) ; this person was responsible for the functions later fulfilled by the chancellor, *cf* The Early Precentors and Chancellors of York, by C. T. Clay in *Y A J* XXXV (1943), pp. 116–138.

The Pope just had time to make a reply which, though guarded, gave them good grounds to believe their request would be granted. And so it proved. On Sunday, the 19th of October, the day before the opening of the General Council, Thurstan was consecrated in the cathedral church at Rheims and in the presence of the innumerable archbishops, bishops and religious who had gathered for the Council[67]. The Pope in person performed the ceremony and was himself deeply moved by the text that was turned up in the gospel-book as it lay on Thurstan's shoulders: "As the Father knows me, even so do I know the Father; and I lay down my life for the sheep." To all it symbolized Thurstan's five years of endurance for his flock, but it seemed particularly significant to his York men and to his suffragan, Ralph of Orkney, who was also present. For them the taste of victory was made all the sweeter, one suspects, by the manifest failure of the Canterbury party. Archbishop Ralph had failed to arrive; so had the English and Norman bishops who had been charged by King Henry to object to Thurstan's consecration[68]. Canterbury's sole representative, in fact, was one solitary archdeacon of Canterbury, Ralph's nephew John; he did at least make a protest against the consecration as the ceremony was proceeding; but it was in vain, for he found himself ejected from the assembly. As a result, when the Norman and English bishops did arrive later in the day there was nothing they could do except show their disapproval by shunning Thurstan—during the Council even his suffragan, Ranulf Flambard, dared not take his seat next to his archbishop, whose only support was Ralph Nowell.

It has not always been appreciated how serious a breach Thurstan and the Pope together had thus driven into the wall of insularity that the Norman kings had thrown up around the ecclesiastics within their territories. But contemporaries were not blind to it. The bishops, for instance, saw straight away that Henry could only close the breach by refusing to allow Thurstan to return

67. H C p. 70.
68. This was only one of their charges; the rest, as reported by Ordericus Vitalis (*Ecclesiasticae Historiae*, Vol. IV, p. 373) show how clearly Henry saw the issues at stake: Omniplenariam rectitudinem conquerenti faciam in terra mea: reditus ab anterioribus constitutos Romanae ecclesiae singulis annis erogo, ac privilegia nihilominus pari modo mihi concessa teneo. Ite, dominum papam de parte mea salutate, ac apostolica tantum praecepta humiliter audite: sed superfluas adinventiones regno meo inferre nolite.
    The impossibility of reconciling the partisan accounts of these events is illustrated by comparing the remark of Symeon of Durham (*Opera* II, p. 254): legati Cantuariensis archiepiscopi praesumptuose calumniati sunt, with the chronicle of Worcester's condemnation of Thurstan s.a. 1119.

to his territories during his lifetime ; and Henry did announce that he would do so, bolstering his refusal with the statement that he had previously taken a solemn oath against Thurstan's return—though Hugh the Chanter shrewdly observes that the oath was probably fictitious, an *ex post facto* justification[69]. That Henry realized the breach to be ominous is shown not only by the order he issued to disseize Thurstan of his archiepiscopal lands but also by his first question to his empty-handed bishops when they returned : Had Thurstan been given the *pallium*, that irrevocable seal of authority ? The bishop of Exeter confidently said not ; but he was mistaken, for Thurstan received the pallium on November 1st.

The breach had doubtless been made, but the wall of insularity behind which Henry sheltered with his bishops was extremely tough ; this is unwittingly demonstrated by both Eadmer and Hugh the Chanter, each of whom in his chronicle blandly ignores the great issues debated at the Rheims Council which concerned the whole of Christendom and proceeds immediately to detail the events of the following month that touched English affairs more closely. It was in this month of November that Calixtus showed his desire for peace and reconciliation to be no mere gesture but a driving purpose. To many of his entourage the solidarity amongst ecclesiastics engendered at Rheims offered a great opportunity for announcing sterner measures against the kingdom of England should a profession of obedience be required from Thurstan. Amongst these extremists was the influential Cuno of Praeneste who was probably responsible for the letter that Calixtus had entrusted to Gilbert of Tours for delivery to Henry I, in which Ralph of Canterbury was suspended and an interdict put on York until Thurstan was restored[70]. These measures may also have received Thurstan's approval since a contemporary assures us that he was emboldened against Canterbury at this moment through knowing Ralph to be stricken with palsy[71] ; in any case, Thurstan had the good sense and tact to keep in the background where he devoted himself to bringing the consolation of religion to an old companion at the royal court, Eudo the dapifer, who was dying nearby in the castle of Préaux[72]. But Calixtus himself did not press for his letters to

---

69. *H C* pp. 74–5.
70. *P L* 163, Col. 1135.
71. *Anglia Sacra*, I, p. 7.
72. *Receuil des Historiens des Gaules et de la France*, ed. M. Bouquet, XII, 791 : ipse vero per aliquas hebdomadas, saepe confessus peccata sua, semper deflens, saepe absolutus, saepe disciplinatus, secundum quod Gaufridus Rotomagensis et Turstanus Eboracensis Archiepiscopi dictabant, rerum omnium fecit divisionem.

be enforced when once they had induced Henry I, late in November, to come to Gisors for parley. Meetings between the king's party and the Pope's took place over several days and an atmosphere of cordiality prevailed throughout despite the differences of policy. The cordiality may have been purchased, as William of Malmesbury hints[73], by the king's presents to the papal party or by the dialectical joust which was put on for their entertainment ; but the blood relationship between Henry and Calixtus also seems to have counted for something. And the net result of the discussions was that the Pope promised to withdraw his legate, Anselm, from Henry's dominions and agreed not to send a legate to England in future except at the king's request[74].

It was an admirable compromise, and the delay of fifteen months which now ensued before Thurstan was permitted to return can fairly be interpreted as a means of allowing the king to give way with good grace. On his own side it is significant that Henry did not vent his spleen on Thurstan for the humiliation he incurred ; of course, he seized Thurstan's estates—the very least he could do to save face—but he left the archbishop's clerics unmolested, a token that no irreparable cleavage was intended[75]. What is more, Henry was to use Thurstan during the year 1120 as a diplomatic agent to secure peace with the king of France and to prevent open conflict with the papacy. Both of these objects were indispensable to Henry if he was to build up a secure position for himself in northern France, and it was fortunate for him that he had in Thurstan a subject who was acceptable to the other parties. Though it was a piece of good fortune which he had to take hold of rather delicately since he could scarcely avoid a suspicion that Thurstan was too warmly regarded by Louis of France and might even be playing for his own hand. Louis' offer to grant Thurstan an archbishopric within his own territories gave grounds for his suspicion ; Thurstan's refusal revealed their emptiness.

For the next few months after leaving Beauvais Thurstan lived like one of the papal entourage as it moved slowly southwards across France ; and all the time he was receiving increasing signs of papal favour towards his own person and his diocese. During this period, for instance, he was allowed the unusual privilege of wearing

---

73.   William of Malmesbury, *Gesta Regum*, Vol. II, p. 482.
74.   Eadmer, *Historia Novorum*, p. 258.
75.   *H C* p. 81 and pp. 81–91 for Thurstan's journey with the Pope.

his pallium though outside his own province. His help was sought by the Pope in consecrating altars and dedicating churches and he assisted the Pope in his crown-wearing processions along the stages of their journey ; and at one stage the Pope presented to him relics of the saints with which Thurstan later enriched the shrines at York[76]. Even allowing for patriotic exaggeration there is truth in the York historian's assertion that Thurstan was treated to all intents as if he were a cardinal. For example, at Gap in March, 1120, just before Thurstan took his leave of the Pope and the cardinals, he was invited by the Pope to bestow minor orders upon the bishop elect of Geneva, Humbert de Grammont, whom Calixtus himself then consecrated. The invitation was a fitting climax to a whole series of favours.

His friendship with the Pope also brought benefits to the province of York. To begin with, Calixtus made it clear to King Henry in messages entrusted to the archbishops of Rouen and Tours that the papal curia had not looked kindly on his gentle treatment of Henry at Gisors, and that England would already have been under interdict had it not been for the pleading of the exile Thurstan ; Henry would do well to remember in whose hands rested the ultimate sanctions. Having these sanctions in mind Calixtus, as he was leaving Thurstan at Gap, provided him with letters of interdict addressed to the king, to the archbishop of Canterbury and to the faithful of York, which he might implement if he were kept out of the country much longer[77]. Thurstan's position within his own province had already been strengthened by papal bulls directed to the bishops of Durham, Orkney and Glasgow, and all the bishops throughout Scotland, whom he treated as unquestionably suffragans of Thurstan, ordering them to render honour and obedience to their metropolitan in York[78]. The faithful Ralph of Orkney likewise had his reward when Calixtus sent a letter to the Scandinavian rulers, Eystein and Siward, admonishing them to help Ralph take over his diocese and maintain him in peace there[79]. Yet another sign that separation from his see had not dulled Thurstan's sense of its needs was given at Tournus when he secured from Calixtus a bull

---

76. *Cf The Fabric Rolls of York Minster* (ed. J. Raine, Surtees Soc., 1859). Item reliquiae quas apportavit Beatus Willelmus, & Henricus Archiepiscopus, et Thurstinus Archiepiscopus, scilicet de ossibus Apostolorum Simonis et Judae.

77. *H C* p. 82. This was on the 20th November, 1119.

78. *Jaffé*, nos. 6785, 6786, 6787.

79. *P L* Vol. 163, col. 1142.

confirming the canons at Nostell in their adherence to the Augustinian rule as well as in their material possessions[80].

Still the greatest advantages that Thurstan derived from his six months of intimacy with the Pope and his curia were the friendships it brought and the insights its gave him into latest currents of European spiritual and political life. Merely to have been present at Rheims for the Council was an education in itself. There he had mingled with the Council's fifteen archbishops and two hundred bishops, as well as with many abbots and secular lords[81]. He had witnessed the marshalling of spiritual might for the excommunication of the Emperor and his supporters ; he had listened to King Louis of France in person accusing both King Henry of usurpation in Normandy and Theobald of Blois for aiding and abetting him. He had heard Amaury de Montfort arraigned before the assembly by his own brother Audouen, who had emphasized his distress by sporting a beard that he had sworn never to shave until justice was done to him. He had watched the countess of Poitou pitifully complaining to the Pope that her husband had deserted her for another woman. Another day had witnessed bishop Urban of Llandaff defending the ancient claims of his diocese before the Pope. Yet another day the archbishop of Lyons and his suffragans bitterly complained against the abbey of Cluny for appropriating churches and ignoring episcopal authority ; their complaints were repulsed when the abbot of Cluny eloquently asserted Cluny's immediate subjection to the see of Peter and Calixtus acknowledged the abbey's uniquely privileged position. And all the time these particular issues were being brought forward the ecclesiastical diplomats such as Gerard of Angoulême and Geoffrey of Chartres and cardinal John of Crema were hammering out the church's policy line regarding simony, lay investiture and clerical concubinage. Truly Rheims was the debating chamber of Europe for a fortnight in late October, 1119.

Scarcely less instructive than Rheims for the head of a remote archbishopric were the dispute and causes brought before Calixtus during the six months Thurstan spent with him. Any twelfth century archbishop, for instance, could count at some time in his career on having to settle a quarrel between monks and canons ;

---

80. *Cf* James Wilson, The Foundation of the Austin Priories of Nostell and Scone, in *The Scottish Historical Review*, VII, 1910, pp. 154 - 5.

81. Ordericus Vitalis, *Ecclesiasticae Historiae* IV, p. 372.
    For a detailed study of the Council of Rheims, see W. Holtzmann Zur Geschichte des Investiturstreites, in *Neues Archiv.*, 50, 1935, pp. 246–319 ; and for the documents, Mansi XXI, cols. 234 ff.

a classic instance of such a dispute, almost perfect in its complexity and intrigue, was provided by the monks of Morigny and the canons of Étampes. The prebends attached to the church of Étampes were bought, sold and inherited like any piece of property and the monks of Morigny got hold of one such prebend ; trouble arose when the monks claimed the right to bury the dead of the parish whom the canons of Étampes regarded as their parishioners. These rival claims were supported by rival parties at the French court, the chancellor Stephen of Garland siding with the canons and the queen favouring the monks, and the presence of Calixtus in France during 1119 gave all these wranglers the chance to pester him on his journey to and from Rheims. Thurstan was present on these occasions[82] and he must have learned from them a good deal about how men lobby the great. Lessons for one in his position were also to be drawn from the success of Bernard, archbishop of Trèves, who came to Calixtus for his own claims to metropolitan jurisdiction over Metz, Toul and Verdun to be recognized and for Mainz's claim over his own province to be repudiated[83]. This was but one of the stream of causes pouring into the papal curia, not all of them fortunately so litigious ; thus Thurstan was privileged to attend several that were great spiritual occasions[84]. He was at Cluny, for example, in January, 1120 at the great festival when Calixtus examined the life and miracles of abbot Hugh, who had died in 1109, and in whose honour he instituted a feast. It is rather ironical to think of these celebrations at Cluny remembering that only a fortnight previously, at Saulieu, Calixtus had given his blessing to a religious upheaval that would shake Cluny when he had confirmed the constitutions of the struggling community at Cîteaux. The two events also meant that Thurstan's knowledge of both Cluny and Cîteaux was anything but second-hand. He had been at the fountain-head of their inspiration.

Of the friends that Thurstan made and the personalities that he met during his exile we have no direct account, but it is beyond doubt that they gave him an insight into policy-making at the highest level[85]. Amongst those to show him special affection was Lambert, cardinal and bishop of Ostia, who was soon to ascend the papal throne as Honorius II. Thurstan also met Honorius' suc-

---

82. Teulfi, *Chronicon Mauriniacense*, *P L* 180, cols. 133–175 ; where his name is curiously spelt : Tostanus.
83. The effect of this case on York's apologia is seen in *H C* p. 105.
84. *Cf* Ulysse Robert, *Histoire du Pape Calixte II*, pp. 98–101.
85. *H C* p. 84.

cessor, Gregory of St. Angelo (who was to take the title of Innocent II) as well as the man who was to become the anti-pope Anacletus, at this time the cardinal-deacon Peter Pierleone. In fact, he came to know well that group of church leaders, the "new men," who between 1123 and 1140 spear-headed the assault of religion upon the world, including John of Crema, Peter Ruffus, Romanus of St. Mary in Porticu and Guy of Pisa. Though it is perhaps significant of Thurstan's large-hearted understanding that he developed particularly warm relations with one of the older school, Peter of Pisa ; for a quarter of a century Peter had been a confidant of Popes, respected for his knowledge of canon and civil law and for his upright character ; in the schism of 1130 he was not swept off his feet by the zeal of the "new men" but supported Anacletus on legal grounds[86]. Peter, in fact, was of the same generation and the same mentality as Thurstan's earliest mentor Cuno.

In a word, Thurstan had now become a man of European status. And it was this achievement that allowed him to play such a vital role as a peacemaker during the rest of the year 1120, for the confidence placed in him by King Henry, King Louis, the legate Cuno and Pope Calixtus also permitted him to moderate their extreme demands. How carefully and skilfully he walked this tight-rope stretched between the points of their confidence is shown by his refusal to attend the French king's Easter court at Senlis ; he was pressed to do so by Louis, who held him in sincere regard, but to have agreed would have lost him the trust of his own king Henry ; so instead Thurstan turned aside to Adela of Blois' castle and busied himself with spiritual concerns. His prudence was justified soon afterwards when he was able to bring Henry and Louis together and persuade them to make a sensible peace : Henry's son William was to do homage to Louis who would then recognize him as the legitimate ruler of Normandy. Much of the credit for this agreement, says Symeon of Durham, must go to Thurstan who thus put himself into King Henry's good books[87]. Yet another ground for Henry's favour was established by Thurstan through his blunting the edge of the Pope's anger against England : papal messengers made it clear to Henry in the summer of 1120 that he was now being given a last chance to allow Thurstan back to his see ; if he did not take the chance then he would be excommunicated and England

86. For a sketch of Peter's career, see F. J. Schmale, *Studien zum Schisma des Jahres 1130*, pp. 62–3.
87. Symeon of Durham, *Opera* II, p. 258.

placed under interdict[88]. A lesser man than Thurstan would have
seen this moment as an opportunity to avenge the running humilia-
tions he had endured for years ; but he did not fall for the tempta-
tion. Already some months previously he had proved not to be
seeking his own ends or personal glory when he had turned down the
Pope's offer to make him papal legate over England[89] ; as papal
legate he would, of course, have been vindicated in the face of
Europe, but the triumph would have brought bitterness upon the
king and his own flock. Hence he had refused the offer just as now he
refused to countenance the hard conditions that the papal agents
were trying to force upon the king. They wished to extract permission for Thurstan to return to England immediately ; he was
content to bide a few months rather than go back under the shadow
of a grudge. Thurstan's policy of conciliation on all sides was most
seriously threatened by the aggressive spirit of his close friend and
adviser, Cuno ; ever ready to use the weapon of excommunication,
Cuno almost wrecked the good work of 1120 when he summoned a
council to meet at Beauvais in October. Those summoned, naturally,
included the bishops and abbots of Normandy ; none of them,
however, turned up, and it was only Thurstan's swift dash to
Beauvais and the influence he had with Cuno that prevented the
council from excommunicating the Norman ecclesiastics. He did
more : he persuaded Cuno to come to Gisors and meet Henry, the
man with thom he had so often crossed swords ; and it must have
been a great satisfaction to Thurstan to see these two rugged
campaigners, who had each befriended him, exchanging compli-
ments and presents and learning to know one another better. Only a
man compounded of interior strength and affable manners could
have brought these two together, and they were qualities that had
stood Thurstan in good stead in 1120.

After the king left Gisors to go to England events moved
quickly. Within a month (25th November) Henry had lost his son
and many of his leading nobles in the wreck of the "White Ship" ;
within three months (29th January, 1121) he had taken to himself
a second wife, Adeliza, daughter of the duke of Louvain. And in
between times he had broken to Ralph of Canterbury and his bishops
the sad news that if they continued to bar Thurstan from England
then beyond a doubt Ralph himself would be suspended and the

88. *H C* p. 95.
89. *H C* p. 89.

country placed under an interdict[90]. This was made so obvious to Ralph that he gave in straight away. With surprisingly little formality after so much bickering, Thurstan was now recalled to England ; he arrived at Windsor on January 31st, not quite in time for Henry's marriage but soon enough to join in the wedding feast, where he took the position his office required.

But it was upon York that Thurstan's eyes were now set, where the citizens were already jubilantly preparing to receive back their father in God. As the historian of York tells us, archbishop Thurstan "set off to meet his bride so long widowed by his absence, that is to say, the church of York. And as he drew near to the city there came out to greet him such a great crowd of clerics, monks, nobles, knights and men and women, on horse and on foot, that certain of those present called to mind what was written about St. John : 'When he was returning from exile St. John was met by the whole population, men and women alike, acclaiming him in the words, "Blessed is he who comes in the name of the Lord." Then on the Sunday when the service begins with the verse *Esto mihi in deum protectorem*[91] he was received in the church in the manner worthy of an archbishop so long exiled for his church's freedom ; he was taken into the bosom of his bride with exultation and rejoicing. In the presence of that great assembly was read out and explained the apostolic privilege confirming the liberty of the church, at which everyone rejoiced and gave thanks to God' "[92].

---

90.   *H C* pp. 99–100.
91.   20 February, 1121.
92.   *H C* p. 100.

CHAPTER IV.

SKIRMISHING ON TWO FRONTS, IN ENGLAND AND SCOTLAND.

It was symbolic that Thurstan should have returned to his church just in time to lead his flock into the cleansing period of Lent. For when he sprinkled Lenten ashes upon the heads of the faithful in the Minster three days later he was foreshadowing the death of the old unredeemed manner of living that had so often characterized English bishops and their dioceses. And what he had foreshadowed on Ash Wednesday he clearly revealed on Holy Thursday, after he had consecrated the chrism that would be distributed throughout his diocese. For "he freely remitted and decreed to be remitted for ever, the six pence from each parish Church and four from every chapel" which they customarily paid for the chrism. He also forbade the exaction of fees for burial, anointing of the sick, or baptism, or the acceptance of them unless freely offered. This action was tremendously important as a signal to the clergy and laity of his diocese that he would not countenance any practices that smacked in the least degree of simony. Thurstan belonged to a generation of ecclesiastical thinkers who had come increasingly to see simony not simply as an offence but as a heresy in that to commit simony was to assert implicitly that the Holy Spirit could be bought. Soon after he had come to England the English court had been ruffled by the declarations of a critical council held in Westminster Abbey under Anselm's presidency. The very first clause in the statutes issued by the council condemned simony as a heresy[1], in virtue of which several leading abbots were deposed who had been guilty of that offence and many English bishops twisted uncomfortably in their episcopal seats at the thought of their own guilt. During the next fifteen years some of the liveliest minds in England and on the continent systematically analyzed the elements of heresy in simony so that by the time of Thurstan's exile a veritable drive against it was under weigh backed by the force of theological argument[2]. This drive was being

---

1. Eadmer, *Historia Novorum*, p. 142.
2. *Cf* J. Leclercq, Simoniaca Heresis, in *Studi Gregoriani* I, 1947, pp. 523–30.

inspired in 1119 by the Pope himself, who in June held a council at Toulouse which forbade fees to be taken for the sacred oil, the chrism and burial[3] ; Calixtus returned to the charge a few months later at Rheims where the prohibition was repeated along with a list of offences that constituted simony, such as taking or giving money for bishoprics, abbacies, deaneries and archdeaneries, ordinations and consecrations ; anyone guilty of such an offence was to be anathema and cut off from the church[4]. Thus Thurstan's first public act in his diocese was one that put into practice the reforming decrees of Rheims.

It must have seemed, in that first Lent after his return, that his seven years' combat had crippled his enemies outside the gates and that he was free now to busy himself with the domestic order of the diocese. When, for instance, on March 20th he presided over the assembly in the chapter house at York the atmosphere was almost that of a cosy family quarrel after the elevated discussion of principles lately engaging him. Sitting beside him were his brother Audouen, of Evreux, and his suffragan of Durham, Ranulf, surrounded by many of the leading notables, as they listened to the claim being put forward by the monks of Durham. Which was that they, rather than the monks of St. Albans, were the true owners of the monastery of Tynemouth. They maintained that Tynemouth had been granted to them in the last century by earl Waltheof when their predecessors had contracted to bring up and educate Waltheof's cherished cousin, Morcar ; they had lost possession of it when Roger de Mowbray expelled the monk in charge and gave it

---

3. *Mansi*, XXI, col. 227.
4. *Ibid.*, col. 234. Testimony to Thurstan's revulsion from simony is contained in Hugh the Chanter's reply to Roger the prior of Durham to say that Thurstan had remitted the six pence which had by ancient custom been paid to the mother church of York by each parish "quia emptio crismatis videbatur" (*H C Y* II, p. xii–xiii). When an attempt was being made to purchase a bishopric or an abbey such simony was in particular a sin against the Holy Spirit since the Holy Spirit is particularly invoked at the consecration of a bishop or abbot ; and as Hugh the Chanter says, "et in celebri et tam sacro officio divino, in quo spiritus sanctus invocari et cooperari debet, falsitas et ficcio abicienda sunt (*H C* p. 111). For similar reasons lay investiture was at this time being analyzed as a heresy (*cf* Geoffrey, abbot of Vendôme's works, *P L* 157, cols. 214–219, 282–290 ; and B. Gigalski, *Bruno von Segni*) and any consecration that was made conditional upon an oath came within the scope of the same principle, and smacked of heresy. Though not made explicit by Hugh the Chanter, this was the intellectual background to Thurstan's own refusal to receive consecration on condition of giving the oath of obedience to Canterbury : it was not simply a question of a sensible compromise such as one might reasonably make in the field of politics, but of theological purity on which there can be no compromise.

to St. Alban's ; but they had also the satisfaction of reminding the assembly that after Paul, the prior of St. Alban's, had taken possession of Tynemouth he was struck down on the return journey as a divine punishment, and died[5]. Whatever the effect of this story upon the listeners at York it does not seem to have moved the king's heart since he issued a writ warning all and sundry not to disturb the Tynemouth monks in their possessions[6]. Nor was he shaken from this attitude a month later when a great gathering of northern magnates at Durham reconsidered the case and were regaled with a dramatic story from one of their number, Alan de Percy, who bore witness that Roger de Mowbray had in fact contritely repented of his misdeed at Tynemouth even before St. Cuthbert finally brought him low[7]. It was an edifying story, but Henry simply repeated his earlier injunction and left the monks of Durham brooding over possible ways of recovering their property[8].

And if Thurstan imagined that the Canterbury party were now content to let him enjoy his domestic bliss in peace, he also was mistaken. There still remained several avenues of skirmishing open to them. Some of their number even resorted to the desperate expedient of forgery in the spring of 1121 when they composed a series of spurious papal letters containing statements to justify Canterbury's claims over York[9]. But there were also legitimate ways of harrying the northerners. The first was to play upon King Henry's irritation with York, knowing that the king was hardly likely to forget the public humiliation he had suffered through being forced to go back on the oath he had sworn never to allow Thurstan to return unless he made a profession of obedience to Canterbury. No such opportunity of rousing Henry was ever lost. Another line that Canterbury pursued with some success was to draw together those prelates who bore grudges against the archbishop of York and to disseminate amongst them an unfavourable view of the archbishop's actions.

To disseminate such unfavourable views can have presented little difficulty since most of the bishops and abbots belonged, of course, to the southern province and owed their advancement to

5. Symeon of Durham, *Opera* I, 124–5 ; II, 260–1, 346.
6. *Regesta*, II, no. 1264.
7. Symeon, *op. cit.* II, 261–2.
8. *Regesta*, II, no. 1331.
9. R. W. Southern, The Canterbury Forgeries, in *English Historical Review*, lxxiii, 193–226 (1958).

the services they had given to the king as clerks and diplomats ;
already most of them were scandalized at Thurstan's independent
stand against the king's wishes. How ready the southerners were
to accept the Canterbury version of events is illustrated in the
chronicles composed during these years at Malmesbury and Worcester, in which Thurstan and his canons are given a very bad press
indeed[10]. The particular antagonists of Thurstan amongst the
bishops are identified by Hugh the Chanter as William Warelwast
of Exeter, Bernard of St. David's and Sieffrid, bishop of Chichester,
who was the nephew of Ralph of Canterbury. Another prelate whom
we frequently find ranged against Thurstan is Alexander of Lincoln ;
nephew to the influential Roger of Salisbury and known as "the
magnificent" on account of his lavish spending, Alexander owed his
elevation to his being a reliable court man and showed himself ready
to fall in with the policies of the king and Canterbury.

But more promising agents for tormenting Thurstan, for
taking him from the rear in fact, were the Scottish bishops. Not
that any persuasion was needed to induce a bishop of Glasgow to
take sides against York since the desire to keep his diocese
independent inevitably drove him to oppose Thurstan. The bishop
at this time was John, who had been appointed about 1114 by his
former pupil, Earl David of Lothian ; he had been trained as a
monk and was clearly a cultured man of considerable personal
charm. Unfortunately he was rather too unstable to make a good
bishop, and not long after his appointment he grew so disgusted
with the brutality and vices of his flock that he abandoned them
and set out for Jerusalem[11]. On his way through Rome (1117) he
was prevented from going further by Pope Paschal II who personally
consecrated John at Thurstan's request[12], thus giving him heart to
return to his diocese and try to win the people from their wild ways.
The fact of having received consecration from the Pope and not
having to seek it at the hands of the York archbishop certainly put
some stiffening into John who realized perfectly well that he could
now avoid taking an oath of obedience to Thurstan ; indeed, not

---

10.   Later historians have often allowed themselves to be swayed by the weight
      of opinion built up by Ralph of Diceto following Florence (*Opera Historica*,
      I, pp. 240–1, 242, 245) and by Gervase of Canterbury taking the same line
      of authorities (*Opera* II, pp. 377–385).
11.   A. C. Lawrie, *Early Scottish Charters*, p. 45   . . . infelicis populi feritate
      et abominabili vitiorum multiplicitate utpote perterritus Jerusalem
      proficisci disposuisset.
12.   *H. & S.*, Vol. II, Pt. I, p. 20 ; *Jaffé*, no. 6944.

even fiercely worded papal letters directing him to do so[13] could drive him to take the oath.

Bishop John was well aware that he could rely both on the Canterbury ecclesiastics and on his king, Alexander, to use their influence against York since each of them was dependent on the other for consolidating their hold over church and society in Scotland. King Alexander, who probably owed his very name to the reforming Pope Alexander II, was a man of deep religious feelings who fully sympathized with the efforts of his mother, St. Margaret, to bring the reformed Benedictine manner of life to Scotland. It was at Margaret's request, in fact, the Benedictine monks from Christ Church, Canterbury, had been sent by Lanfranc to establish another Christ Church at Dunfermline. In their new home they maintained close ties with their original one, from where St. Anselm later sent other monks to join them ; when Alexander succeeded to the Scottish kingdom in 1107 Anselm wrote to him urging him to protect his monks[14]. So it was quite natural for Alexander to employ the prior of Dunfermline, Peter, as his envoy when submitting a request to Ralph of Canterbury that a monk of Christ Church should come and occupy the leading see in Scotland, that of St. Andrews[15]. But when one remembers that the see had already been vacant four years and that it was four years since Alexander had first applied to Canterbury for help one cannot help remarking that Ralph had been very slow off the mark in response and wondering why he and Alexander had so suddenly been jolted into action. The answer is that both of them had been pulled up sharp by the firm backing that Calixtus gave to Thurstan. Alexander, in particular, was bound to make some move when faced with Calixtus' letter from Beauvais of 20th November, 1119 ; in it the Pope upbraided the Scottish bishops for consecrating each other instead of doing what he ordered them to do, which was to seek consecration at the hands of their metropolitan, the archbishop of York[16]. It was under the shadow of Thurstan that Ralph and Alexander drew together, and what better omen for dissipating that shadow than their agreeing on Eadmer as the ideal candidate for the vacant see of St. Andrews ?

13. *Jaffé*, nos. 6944, 6982.
14. Lawrie, *Early Scottish Charters*, p. 20.
15. For a reconstruction of these events, see G. W. S. Barrow, From Queen Margaret to David I, in *The Innes Review*, XI, pp. 22–38 (1960).
16. *Jaffé*, no. 6787.

By this year, 1120, Eadmer had won for himself a reputation as a gifted writer and analyst of ecclesiastical affairs, a reputation enhanced by the friendship he was known to have enjoyed with the great Anselm. He was also known as the skilful propagandist of Canterbury's claims and the unwearying opponent of York's. The bearing of this last point had not escaped Thurstan's observant eye, even though he was at this time abroad in France, for he quickly let King Henry know what a poor opinion he had of these negotiations with the Scottish king and urged him to stop them going further. Henry did intervene to some effect, sending one letter to Ralph of Canterbury forbidding him to consecrate Eadmer, and three letters to King Alexander urging him to prevent Eadmer being consecrated[17]. These letters had the effect of making Eadmer, who was already very sorry for himself, even sorrier. He had found, like Turgot before him, that King Alexander was an awkward person to manage ; scarcely had he arrived in Scotland and been acclaimed as their elect by the clergy and people of St. Andrews (29 June, 1120) before a dispute arose between himself and the king. Alexander wished to invest him with the episcopal staff and ring in best pre-Gregorian fashion whereas Eadmer, not for nothing a pupil of Anselm's, refused to condone such lay investiture just as he refused to pay homage to Alexander. Nor was lay investiture the only issue on which the sophisticated monk from the metropolitan cathedral clashed with the king of this untamed land. They both discovered soon that despite their common abhorrence of York they were themselves at loggerheads over the position of Canterbury : Eadmer was determined to have Canterbury's pre-eminence over all the churches in Britain acknowledged whilst Alexander was equally determined that Canterbury should not be exalted above the church of St. Andrew's. To show Eadmer that he meant business Alexander cut off his revenues and brought back as administrator of the episcopal lands a certain William, a monk of St. Edmund's, who had been running the estates ever since Turgot's departure. For a month there was stalemate until in early August Alexander relented and Eadmer was allowed to take his pastoral staff from the altar as a token that he was receiving it at the hands not of the king but of God ; but Alexander successfully insisted that he himself should set the ring upon Eadmer's finger[18].

17. Eadmer, *Historia Novorum*, p. 283.
18. Eadmer, *Historia Novorum*, pp. 285–6.

It was at this moment that the letters from Henry already mentioned threw Alexander into confusion of mind. They revealed to him his error in supposing that by wooing Canterbury he had automatically been winning the favour of his powerful neighbour the king of England. He decided to cut his losses, the first of these being Eadmer. This could be done without too much difficulty for Eadmer was not of the stuff that martyrs are made of ; indeed he cuts a pathetic, almost comic figure, in these months as he goes about telling virtuous matrons pious stories about his great friend Anselm or complaining that he is not allowed to visit Canterbury for advice where for over fifty years he had made his home[19]. Alexander summed him up well enough when he said quite simply that Eadmer had certainly failed to adapt himself to the Scottish people and to the circumstances of his diocese[20]. Suspecting that this was the king's judgment on him Eadmer sought the advice of John of Glasgow and two Canterbury monks who were with him ; these three sounded out the king for his opinion and then came back to Eadmer with their report : "If, as a son of peace, you desire to live in peace, search for it elsewhere. So long as he reigns here the bond of peace will not be granted to you. We know the man. He wishes to be all in all in his own kingdom, nor will he abide that any one should exercise power in any transactions unless he is the arbiter. He is already incensed against you without having grounds for being so ; nor will he ever be perfectly reconciled to you, even though he should see his way clear to it. Hence you must either abandon your position here entirely or else remain for ever amongst the Scots, conforming to their usages, and lead a wretched life that is a threat to the salvation of your soul"[21]. This speech may represent the substance of what the three mediators had to say, but the form is, of course, the result of its being turned on the lathe of Eadmer's self-justification. In any case, it brings out the weaknesses in the character of those in Scotland who were arrayed against Thurstan ; with their combined intellectual and political gifts Eadmer and John of Glasgow could have built up a formidable threat to York, but each of them was too easily inclined to raise his hands and wail when faced by unpleasant situations. Thurstan was fortunate in his opponents : by the spring of 1121 Eadmer was

19. *Ibid.*, pp. 434–5.
20. *Ibid.*, p. 286 : . . . consuetudinibus terrae moribusque hominum ut res et tempus exigebat, et ut justum et necessarium esset, condescendere noluit.
21. *Ibid.*, p. 285.

thankfully back in Canterbury, having relinquished his staff and ring and abandoned the bishopric of St. Andrew's ; and the Canterbury effort to overwhelm York from the rear had failed ignominiously.

This set-back to Canterbury left the monks in a desperate mood during the first half of 1121 and drove at least one of their number to produce a series of forged papal letters in the hope of snatching victory from York at the eleventh hour. But until these forgeries could be publicly proclaimed a certain amount of desultory skirmishing was kept going with the aid of the king. Thus at Michaelmas, 1121, soon after the king had returned from his Welsh campaign, Thurstan found himself summoned by Henry to a conference of the bishops and barons of the realm. Here the king made a further attempt to save his own face ; alternately cajoling and bullying, he tried to get Thurstan to make at least a personal profession of obedience to Ralph ; this would neither bind Thurstan's successors nor would it bind Thurstan to Ralph's own successors. Henry through his bishops urged Thurstan to accept this arrangement for the sake of peace and even suggested trying to secure the Pope's permission for him to do so. Though he still refused firmly to abandon any of what he had suffered for, Thurstan at this point carefully avoided embarrassing the king. He could have immediately produced the bull of privilege to York issued by Calixtus which would have settled the matter ; but to have shown it first to the bishops would have been a discourtesy to the king. So Thurstan waited until he was in private audience with Henry before producing this master card, the privilege which freed the archbishops of York from making any profession whatsoever to Canterbury. Once he had seen it Henry realized that the game was up ; he simply advised Thurstan to order some of his entourage to come along when the bishops were present and explain the privilege to them ; then the bishops would have to call off their hounding of York. When this was done the bishops tried to shout the York men down and one of them even accused them of having fabricated the privilege, saying the Pope had had nothing to do with it. He was a rash bishop thus to have challenged the well-trained York contingent, for one of them—probably Hugh the Chanter himself—coolly pointed out that, on the contrary, the Pope himself had ordered it to be drawn up and had subscribed to it personally. He had been present when the Pope did so. There was no answer to that, and the York men were able to return home in triumph[22].

---

22. *H C* pp. 105–7.

Back in York once more Thurstan now carried the attack into Scotland by demanding profession of obedience from John of Glasgow and threatening to suspend him if he did not obey. At the same time he wrote to the Pope asking for papal support in his cause. The Pope was not slow in his response which came in a series of letters issued from Tarento in January, 1122, one addressed to King Alexander, one to the Scottish bishops in general, and one to John of Glasgow personally[23], the burden of each being the same : that Thurstan was metropolitan over the Scottish bishops and must be obeyed as such. These letters put Alexander in an awkward position ; he was thinking of paying a visit to England just at this time, possibly to seek advice on his predicament[24] ; nor was his confusion lessened when Eadmer and Ralph of Canterbury made another attempt to force Eadmer back into the see of St. Andrew's ; in the end he decided to play for time by sending a plea to Pope Calixtus begging a respite for bishop John. The good bishop meanwhile made things even more awkward for his king. He left Scotland and went to see the Pope in Rome ; but when he found the Pope to be unflinching in support of Thurstan, John simply departed from Rome without a word to the Pope and made his way to Jerusalem. Here he was given hospitality by the Latin patriarch, Gurmond, with whom he spent several months, helping his host to carry out ecclesiastical functions in the city. It is true that John was persuaded to return to his diocese by 1123[25], but already his cavalier disregard of the papacy's orders had harmed his reputation at Rome and can hardly have enhanced the reputation of his backers, Ralph and Alexander.

Moreover, John had been out of his diocese at a time when his presence could have been useful, that is in October and November 1122, the one occasion in his reign when King Henry visited Cumbria, and when John might have tried a personal approach to bring the king round to his side. Again, whilst Henry was in the North news was brought to him of the death of John's aider and abettor Ralph of Canterbury (20 October 1122). The omens were not good, then, for John, but at least another election at Canterbury would give the successful candidate the opportunity to renew the wearisome dispute with York all over again. And that would happen soon, because already letters had gone out through Christendom summoning its

---

23. *Jaffé*, nos. 6943, 6944, 6945.
24. Eadmer, *Historia Novorum*, p. 301.
25. *H. & S.*, Vol. II, Pt. 1, pp. 21–23.

prelates to a council to be held in Rome on March 18th, 1123, and if the see of Canterbury was to be represented at it then there was an urgent need to fill the vacant see with all speed. Hence Thurstan was summoned to attend a council at Gloucester on February 2nd for the election of a new archbishop.

Thurstan must have set out for Gloucester with mixed feelings. The entourage which went with him did at least provide a comforting contrast to the sparse company he had so often had to be content with previously ; not only had he his own clerks with him but several of his canons and archdeacons, as well as Athelwold the prior of St. Oswald's, Nostell, and Geoffrey abbot of St. Mary's, York. Also the journey would give both himself and Athelwold the opportunity to pay devotion to their revered Saint Oswald by visiting his shrine at Gloucester which came under the archbishop's protection. Any increase in his sense of security that came from his entourage was offset, however, by foreboding of disputes ahead. Thurstan realized that the rest of the English bishops were incensed that, unlike them, he had not made profession of obedience to Canterbury ; perhaps the memory of setting their hands to these professions rankled with them and filled them with envy of Thurstan who had escaped it ; whether through rationalization or not they thought of him as an outsider who had cut himself off from the community of English bishops, as they showed by taking offence when the king consulted him[26]. More menacing than the thunder over York, however, was the storm that was brewing over Canterbury. It had looked to be on the point of breaking some eight years previously, on the occasion of the last election ; at that time there had been disagreement between the two groups who claimed the right to elect, on the one hand the bishops of the country and on the other the monks of Canterbury. The monks, in 1114, had unanimously wished to have Faritius abbot of Abingdon as their archbishop, but the bishops and magnates were set against electing a monk and hoped instead for a cleric, either one of themselves or one from the king's chapel. Neither party got their way in the end because the king imposed a compromise in the person of Ralph who was both a bishop and a monk. In the eight years following animosities between monks and secular clerics throughout the country

---

26. *H C* p. 109 : . . . ideo quod a professione subtractus quasi de illis non esse videbatur.

began to burn more fiercely[27] and broke into open conflagration in
1123 when the anti-monastic party was headed by the doyen of the
curiales, Roger of Salisbury, and Thurstan's old chief, Richard of
London ; the most impressive protest against their stand came
from Henry, the abbot of St. John d'Angély, who was at this
moment acting as Rome's agent for collecting Peter's Pence and
who told the king that it was uncanonical to set a cleric over monks,
and especially when they had previously elected their archbishop
in their chapter canonically. The king was not moved by Henry's
lecture on canon law and preferred to back up his tried civil servants
the bishops, whom he allowed to put forward the names of several
candidates, out of whom the monks were to name the one acceptable
to themselves. In the words of the Anglo-Saxon Chronicle : "When
they were all assembled, the king asked them to choose for themselves an archbishop of Canterbury, whomsoever they wished, and
he would give his consent to the election. Then the bishops discussed this amongst themselves and declared that they would never
again agree to the appointment of a man from one of the monastic
orders to be archbishop over them, but all went in a body to the
king and desired that they might have permission to elect as their
archbishop a man from the secular clergy, whomsoever they wished ;
and this the king granted them. The bishop of Salisbury and the
bishop of Lincoln before his death were originally responsible for
this, for they had never had any love for the monastic rule, but were
ever in opposition to monks and their rule. The prior and the monks
of Canterbury, and all the others there who belonged to a monastic

---

27. *Cf* pp. 181-191 of this work and Ordericus Vitalis, *Ecclesiasticae Historiae,*
   IV, pp. 431-2: Ecce antiquus mos, pro invidia qua clerici contra monachos
   urebantur, deprivatus fuit . . . Angli monachos, quia per eos ad Deum
   conversi sunt, indesinenter diligentes honoraverunt, ipsique clerici reveren-
   ter et benigne sibi monachos praeferri gavisi sunt. Nunc autem mores et
   leges mutatae sunt, et clerici, ut monachos confutent et conculcent, clericos
   extollunt.
   William of Malmesbury, *Gesta Pontificum*, p. 146.n4 : "Ricardo (bishop
   of London) et omnibus episcopis annitentibus, ut spreto antiquo usu non
   monachus sed clericus induceretur sedi primariae, Videbatur enim non
   exiguum gloriae dampnum, si tot clericis unus monachus imperitaret. Sed
   ut palliarent ambitum qui aperte proderetur si secularem ponerent
   clericum, hunc potissimum eligendum putaverunt, cuius reverentiae intuitu
   monachi frontes reverberati, nichil sibi de religione blandirentur. Enimvero
   postea penituere, quod ille, frugalitati deditus, opiniones eorum minus
   implesset, immo penitus evacuasset. Palam enim jam et in triviis cantatur,
   non esse idoneum episcipatui qui nolit vel nesciat pompis abuti seculi in
   exercitiis nemorum, in irritamentis gularum, in vestium apparatu, in
   satellitum strepitu. De animarum lucris cura minor, et prorsus nulla.
   Cumque eis obicitur quondam spectari episcopos solere religione et litteris,
   non ambitione et nummis, respondent, "Nunc aliud tempus, alii pro
   tempore mores." Atrocitatem videlicet rei, lenientes facilitate responsi.

order, held out against it for two whole days to no effect, since the bishop of Salisbury was powerful and ruled all England, and opposed them with all his strength and for all he knew. Then they chose a canon called William of Corbeil : he was a canon from a monastery called St. Osyth's. They presented him to the king, and the king gave him the archbishopric, and although all the bishops accepted him, the monks, earls, and almost all the thanes who were present opposed him"[28].

William of Corbeil, the candidate who emerged successfully from this screening process, was neither a monk nor a secular cleric but a regular canon and prior of the Austin canons' house at St. Osyth. When King Henry had consulted Thurstan as to William's suitability for the see Thurstan was pleased with the choice. For many years William had been a familiar figure in English ecclesiastical circles ; as a young cleric in Ranulf Flambard's household he had been one of the privileged witnesses at the translation of St. Cuthbert's relics in 1004 ; some years later he underwent a conversion from worldly living which led Richard bishop of London to appoint him prior of the Augustinian house he had founded at St. Osyth. This office alone was enough to commend him to such a patron of the Augustinians as Thurstan, but a weightier consideration still in his favour was that William had openly shown approval of the York case in the running quarrel with Canterbury[29].

If, on this account, Thurstan imagined that William would knuckle under to him he was in for a rude shock—as were the bishops also, who had put forward William's name trusting him to be a nonentity from whom they had nothing to fear. The bishops were shocked to discover that William was just as much given to austerity and monkish practices as any candidate who might have emerged from the Canterbury cloister itself, and that he was quite prepared to impose his own notions of strictness upon the clergy throughout the whole country. Thurstan was equally taken aback at discovering that William on election assumed the defence of Canterbury's rights just as wholeheartedly as he himself had taken over York's in 1114.

The issue over which William immediately took up the defence was over who should consecrate him. According to the York advocates, appealing to the custom of alternate consecration

---

28. *Anglo-Saxon Chronicle*, s.a. 1123.
29. *H C* p. 131.

established by Pope Honorius, it was Thurstan's right to do so ;
and Thurstan made it clear to William that he expected to perform
the ceremony, though he was happy to allow that the ceremony
should take place in William's own cathedral of Canterbury. This
offer of Thurstan's was almost certainly meant as a friendly gesture,
for the evidence shows that he felt much more respect and warmth
towards William than he had ever felt for Ralph. But William
would only accept, on the condition impossible to Thurstan of the
consecration embodying an acknowledgement that Canterbury was
primate over the whole of Britain[30]. Even when William rejected
Thurstan's offer, and harsh words passed between their respective
familiae, and when the consecration was carried out by the bishop
of London (18th February, 1123), still no bitter quarrel was stirred
up between them[31]. They did, indeed, travel separately in March
when they both set out for Rome, but amicably enough all the same.

Setting out in mid-March, of course, gave them no chance at
all of reaching Rome in time for the council, but King Henry had
sent messengers ahead of them to explain to the Pope that they had
delayed so that William could be consecrated and would therefore
be in a position to receive the *pallium*. Whether he would get the
pallium, however, even after consecration, seemed rather doubtful
from the chilly reception he received in Rome. There were good
grounds for this chilliness in Roman eyes since William's election
offended against so many of the conditions which advanced Roman
opinion nowadays regarded as essential for canonical validity ;
thus it had taken place in the king's chapel ; it was by the king's
prompting and not through free election ; nor had William been
consecrated by the proper authority, Thurstan ; and so on[32]. No
wonder William was made to wait before he was permitted an
audience with the Pope ; no wonder either if some suspected
Thurstan of having turned the Pope's mind against William when
they saw, by contrast, what a great fuss was made of Thurstan by
the Pope and cardinals, still mindful of the exile they had endured
together a few years previously[33]. In fact these suspicions were
probably unfounded, for the only eye-witness account of these days
comes from Hugh the Chanter and he assures us that Thurstan did

---

30. Symeon of Durham, *Opera* II, p. 269.
31. *H C* pp. 109–10.
32. *H C* p. 112 ; Symeon of Durham, *Opera* II, pp. 272–3.
33. *Anglo-Saxon Chronicle*, s.a. 1123.

everything he could for William[34]. At first the *curia* maintained
adamantly that William certainly could not receive the *pallium*
though by stretching a point he might be given a bishopric. According to Hugh it was Thurstan's intervention at this stage which won
the day when he reminded Calixtus that unless the canonical
irregularities in William's election were overlooked King Henry
might well do what he had done before—keep the see vacant to the
loss of every Christian man[35]. This consideration must have
brought home to the Pope the dangers of obstinacy and certainly
within a fortnight he did grant the *pallium* to William; but a more
likely reason for the grant was the pressure put upon him by the
letters from King Henry and the Emperor Henry which had been
brought along by the Canterbury party[36]. Calixtus could hardly
afford to alienate the Emperor at this moment since he had already
alienated some of the cardinals by his policy of conciliation to
wards the imperialists at Worms and afterwards ; he had paid a
fairly high price for the Emperor's co-operation and there was no
point in throwing it away[37].

Though Hugh the Chanter may have exaggerated the part
played by Thurstan in securing the *pallium* for William his account
of the following days shows that he did not deceive himself about
the way decisions were made in Rome. His account, in fact, breathes
the mischievous delight which someone of Hugh's quick and intriguing mind would find in threading his path down the alleyways of
Roman diplomacy. He tells how no sooner had the *pallium* been
granted than the Canterbury party began to raise once more their
grievances against York. This was the moment they had been
waiting for ever since that day three years ago when those mar-
vellous documents had mysteriously come to light in their library
which supported to the letter all Canterbury's claims to the primacy.
Their day of triumph seemed to have dawned as they were led into

---

34. It is possible to dismiss Hugh's evidence, of course, on the ground that he
    was biased, as historians frequently have done with Hugh's evidence ;
    but since almost all eye-witnesses, in the nature of the case, are biased,
    the strict adherence to such grounds would only permit second-hand
    evidence. The fact is that Hugh cannot be caught out at any point on
    questions of fact that came within his experience. It is customary to quote
    against him the careless explanation he gave of Anselm's quarrel with
    Rufus (*H C* p. 9), but, as we point out, this was not a matter which he
    regarded as of first importance and had taken place before his day.
35. *H C* p. 112.
36. Symeon of Durham, *Opera* II, p. 272.

the Roman *curia* to present their case ; how the day turned out was given to Hugh the Chanter to describe in a paragraph of mordant economy :—

"The said privileges were ordered to be read. They were headed with the names of Popes of Rome, but had no trace of the style of the Roman chancery. When they had been read, ending with the letter of St. Gregory to Augustine about the separation of the two metropolitans of England, some of the Romans asked the Canterbury party whether the privileges had bulls attached. But they said that they had left the originals with their bulls in their church and brought copies of them. And because privileges are not valid evidence unless they have bulls attached or signatures, they were asked whether they would swear that the originals had bulls. They retired and consulting together said that the bulls were wanting. One of them tried to persuade another to swear for the sake of their church. (What sound and canonical advice !). But they were by no means willing, and were afraid to supply the missing bulls by perjury. They made up their minds to come back and say that the bulls had either perished or were lost. When they said this, some smiled, others turned up their noses, and others laughed aloud ; making fun of them and saying that it was a miracle that lead should perish or be lost and parchment survive. Some may think that this story is made up, and the writer trifling with him, but the thing is as true as it seems false. They afterwards suggested that perhaps bulls were not used so early. But the Romans bore witness that there had been bulls in St. Gregory's time, and that some privileges of his with bulls were preserved in the church of Rome. Having no more to say, they retired in disorder ; their privileges were disbelieved, and their speeches neither praised nor kindly received"[38].

Forgery having thus failed the Canterbury advocates turned to "the thing that overcomes all the world . . . gold and silver," as the Anglo-Saxon Chronicle puts it ; and the Pope duly bestowed the *pallium* upon William. Even in Rome, however, gold and silver could not buy everything, as the Canterbury party found out when they tried to get a grant of the primacy for their church by bribing

---

37. F. J. Schmale, *Studien zum Schisma des Jahres, 1130*, p. 44.
38. *H C* pp. 114–115.

the papal chamberlain, a man named Guy[39]. Though they managed
to get him on to their side he was not in good standing with the
nobles of Rome and could only persuade three members of the papal
curia to support him. Meanwhile the York party, aware of the
rivalry between the chamberlain and the *curia*, had made sure that
the cardinals of the *curia* knew all about the plan that the chamberlain was cooking up with the Canterbury monks, and had pricked
them into using strong language about it[40].

The result of their machinations was that the Canterbury
party did manage at least to have Thurstan summoned before the
curia to answer their charges ; but they did not catch him unpre-
pared. He pointed out that the case could not be tried there and
then because he had not been called to Rome for this cause at all
but for the quite different one of the council. Nevertheless he was
perfectly willing that the *curia* for their own satisfaction should
examine certain transcripts of York privileges which he had brought
with him. Once these had been produced and scrutinized by the
curia it became obvious that nothing but desultory squabbling could
emerge from further examination, so it was very sensibly decided
that the archbishops should return to England. After they had
thoroughly prepared their cases they were to come before an English
church council which would meet under the presidency of a papal
legate who would decide the matter once and for all[41].

Though their main business in Rome had in this way dragged
into stalemate one has to remember that journeys to the papal city
were often profitable in other, incidental ways, and this journey of
1123 was no exception. For instance, Thurstan was able to obtain
from the Pope a letter confirming the community of canons at
Bridlington in their adherence to the Augustinian rule and guaran-
teeing their rights as a religious corporation[42] ; it also gave him the
opportunity to express at headquarters his grave dissatisfaction
with John of Glasgow once more and to receive assurance from the
Pope that he would back him to the hilt in whatever measures he
took to bring John to obedience[43]. Over Glasgow, inevitably,

39. *Jaffé*, no. 7056 (*P L* 163, col. 1287) helps to identify this Guy as the
    "cunning and wicked man" whom Hugh the Chantor accuses of being
    open to bribery (*H C* p. 115).
40. *H C* p. 116.
41. Symeon of Durham, *Opera* II, p. 273. Calixtus' letter to the English
    clergy announcing his decision is given by Holtzmann, *Papsturkunden* II,
    pp. 140–1.
42. Holtzmann, *Papsturkunden*, III, p. 135, no. 11.
43. *H C* p. 119.

William of Corbeil had ardently opposed Thurstan, but there were other matters on which even these two antagonists could agree to co-operate ; it was through the good offices of Thurstan and William, for example, that a Durham monk present with them, named Robert, was able to obtain from Calixtus a confirmation of the monks' occupation of Durham cathedral which was justified by the "depraved and incorrigible behaviour of the secular clerics" previously in occupation[44]. It is interesting to see the tension in England between monks and secular clerics reflected here in the petitions at Rome ; and we see it again in the privileges obtained for his monastery at the same time by Anselm, abbot of St. Edmunds, a member of the Canterbury party. These included the assurance that "if the place (i.e. Bury St. Edmunds) were to be transformed into a bishopric no one should be ordained bishop there who was not a monk of St. Edmund's"[45]. Another abbot from the Canterbury party who took advantage of the journey to obtain protection for his monastery was Sieffrid of Glastonbury, Ralph d'Escures' nephew[46], whilst the loquacious spokesman of the group, Bernard of St. David's, obtained a similar papal protection for the lands of his see[47]. These advantages gained at Rome by members both of Thurstan's and of William's entourage are worth noting as illustrations that the toil of travel was often more fruitful than appears from the chronicles.

After the archbishops returned to Normandy to report to the king there were the usual recriminations from each side about the deceitful behaviour of the other side in Rome, but nothing of substance emerged from their wranglings. In any case, both now and for the next eighteen months, Henry had other and more pressing concerns on his mind than tattered ecclesiastical disputes—during the whole of this period he was engaged in fighting on the borders of Normandy against Louis of France and Fulk of Anjou. In the England to which the archbishops had returned the year 1124 was unremarkable for churchmen ; it was in the Rome they had left where events took a dramatic turn that was to alter the direction of Christendom for generations.

---

44. M.S. Eccl. Dun. Cartuarium Vetus fo. 13r.
45. *Jaffé*, no. 7074 (Batteley, *Antiquitates S. Edmundi*, p. 65).
46. *Ibid.*, no. 7071.
47. *Ibid.*, no. 7073.

The change in direction at Rome[48] had already begun,
though imperceptibly, by the 8th of May, 1123 when for the first time
a papal decree was signed by the Burgundian Aimeric, the new papal
chancellor ; because Aimeric was the moving spirit in the group of
high ecclesiastics who felt that the first aims of the Gregorian
reformers had now been achieved and that the main effort of
Christians henceforward should be bent upon reforming the interior
life and organization of the church. This effort was in the next few
years to draw together a brilliant company of men which included
St. Bernard, St. Norbert and Peter the Venerable, and those
especially connected with the new trends of monastic life amongst
the Cistercians and Austin canons. Already in 1122–3 the crop of
fresh cardinals numbered several of these "new men," and with the
forceful Aimeric holding the central position of chancellor they were
quickly welded into a powerful pressure group. They won their first
resounding success in December, 1124, when, in spite of the fact
that a majority of the cardinals had elected cardinal Theobald as
Pope (Celestine) they pushed in their candidate, cardinal Lambert
of Ostia (Honorius II). In fact the ancient cardinal Theobald was
just intoning the *Te Deum* for his election when Honorius stepped
in ; the daring and conviction, not to say *panache*, of the victorious
minority gave warning of how they were to take Christendom by
storm in the following years.

One of the most prominent cardinals supporting Honorius was
John of Crema ; and to him thus fell the task of implementing the
new policies in Normandy and England. Even before the death of
Calixtus, John had been sent as legate to Henry I's dominions but
he had been kept immobile in Normandy by the king who had no
intention of allowing legates to interfere in English affairs. However, John of Crema was every bit as sharp as the king, for by some
means or other he persuaded Henry to let him exercise his legation
in England in 1125. Some observers said that John had bribed his
way through the king's defences, but a more likely explanation is
that John had lately done Henry a very good turn and was now
reaping his reward[49]. The good turn was to have nullified the
marriage of Henry's nephew William to Sybilla (daughter of Henry's

---

48. *Cf* F. J. Schmale, *Studien zum Schisma des Jahres, 1130*, pp. 93–144.
49. Verum, nimia Henrici regis industria praevalente, praescripta copulatio
     penitus interrupta est nimis, precibusque, et auri, argentique, aliarumque
     specierum ponderosa enormitate. Ordericus Vitalis, *Ecclesiasticae His-
     toriae*, IV, p. 294. And William of Malmesbury's comment : Praesertim
     cum non contemnatur eloquentia, quam pretiosa condiunt xenia.

enemy Fulk of Anjou) on grounds of their consanguinity ; whatever the grounds, Henry was grateful since Fulk was hardly likely now to support William in his claims against his uncle. So John of Crema was allowed to cross from Normandy.

A new and significant feature of John's commission from Honorius was that it covered not only England but Scotland as well[50]. It is significant of that Scottish desire to play a larger and more independent role in ecclesiastical affairs which had animated Alexander and moved his successor, David, even more strongly. Shortly before David came to the throne (April, 1124) his elder brother had named an Augustinian, Robert, prior of Scone, as bishop of St. Andrews, and now David himself was urging the Pope to grant the *pallium* to Robert, which would free Scotland from dependence on either York or Canterbury. It was in order to assess the Scottish situation for himself that John of Crema went through to Roxburgh, on the borders of England and Scotland, in the late summer of 1125 and held a conference with King David. In accordance with his instructions from Pope Honorius he made a preliminary survey of the controversy that had been raging between Thurstan and the Scottish bishops for so long, but he gave no public sign of his opinion, nor did he say anything about granting a *pallium*[51]. John was making sure not to prejudice the chances of the council which he was about to hold a little later in the heart of the English kingdom, at Westminster.

The council over which John presided in September of that year was attended by archbishops Thurstan and William as well as by twenty bishops, about forty abbots, and a multitude of other clerics and lay people. It represented a remarkable triumph for Rome's new direction since until now Roman legates had received short shrift from Henry : Anselm of Bury, Peter Petrileone, Henry of St. Angély, all of these had in recent years attempted to break through Henry's guard but had failed. Yet here was John, as legate, promulgating decrees from Westminster in true Gregorian style : prohibiting simony in all its forms whether it was offices, sacraments or consecrations that were being trafficked ; forbidding lay investiture in any church whatsoever ; decreeing that prebends must not be treated as hereditary ; condemning priests living with women ; and so on throughout the whole reforming litany[52]. How unpopular

---

50. Symeon of Durham, *Opera omnia*, II, p. 277.
51. *Ibid.*, p. 278.
52. *Ibid.*, pp. 279–281.

these measures were with the English clergy snugly settled in their
unreformed ways could be easily guessed ; but there is no need to
guess, since we have on record a series of stories about John of
Crema which reflect clearly what many Englishmen thought of this
interfering busybody from Rome. One of these stories, taken from
the Annals of Winchester, will stand for the rest. It tells us that
"Ralph de Passeflabere (i.e. Ranulf Flambard) was accused by the
said John of incontinence, and of many other things that are
unbecoming holy persons : but, though often summoned to undergo
degradation, he met the citations with divers excuses, and did not
make his appearance before the judgment seat. Hereupon the
legate hastened to Durham, and was received with due respect.
After the wine had circled freely, and was beginning to work, the
legate became enamoured of a young lady of eminent personal
charms, the niece of the bishop. He made an assignation with her,
and she, as the bishop had desired her, went to his bed-chamber to
put it in order, according to the Roman custom. When she had lain
down upon the bed, the bishop, with the clerks and attendants,
entered the chamber, bearing goblets and lamps, which with their
radiance illumined the shades of night. Standing round the legate's
couch they shouted aloud, "Benedicite, benedicite." Whereat he,
astounded, said, "By St. Peter, what are ye about ? " "My lord,"
said the bishop, "it is the custom of our country, whenever a nobleman is married, for his friends to pay him this mark of respect and
courtesy. Rise, then, and drink what is in the cup which I hold in
my hand. If you refuse to do so, assuredly you shall instantly drink
of a cup after which you shall thirst no more." Up he rose then,
will he nill he, and naked as he was, he drank to the bride half of
what was in the bishop's goblet. The bishop then retired, no longer
in dread of losing his bishopric. But the legate, before the dawn of
day, making his escape with his disgrace and his concubine, returned
with all possible speed to Rome"[53]. The story was, of course, far-
fetched, and from other sources we learn that John acquired a good
reputation for his work in England. According to these he was aware
how ingrained the old ways were in the land and so refused to try

---

53. *Annales Monastici (R S)*, II, pp. 47-48. A rather different version is given
     by Henry of Huntingdon, *Historia Anglorum (R S)*, p. 246.

to change them by threats and curses but relied instead on sound doctrine and encouragement, and the country reaped the harvest of the blessings he had sown[54].

Certainly his subtle diplomacy is evidenced in the scheme he drafted in the hope of composing the differences between Thurstan and William of Corbeil. According to this scheme the archbishop of Canterbury was to give up to the archbishop of York three bishoprics, Chester, Bangor and the untenanted St. Asaph. In return Thurstan was to accept the archbishop of Canterbury as primate by word of mouth only, though if the Pope were to allow it, his successors were to place their hands in Canterbury's hands and promise to obey him as primate[55]. The scheme was an ingenious one, attractive to each side for what it would gain but ultimately unacceptable to each for what it would lose. That Thurstan should have given even preliminary assent to something he had so strongly opposed for years astonished Hugh the Chanter, and it is difficult for us to understand his motives. Hugh suggests that Thurstan believed Rome would not consent anyway ; and it is probably the case that Thurstan never took John of Crema's scheme altogether seriously, but the king was pressing his archbishops hard to accept some plan for ending the wretched strife. Above all, the king insisted that neither should institute proceedings against the other if Rome did not agree to the scheme ; because whatever else happened Henry did not want this issue to be judged by a court outside England.

When the two archbishops then set out separately for Rome[56] the legate chose to travel with the York company, which also included Thurstan's brother, Audouen of Evreux. Though the legate's presence gave Thurstan and his followers an opportunity

---

54. *Materials for the History of Archbishop Thomas Becket*, Vol. V, p. 539 ; writing to Becket in 1166 Gilbert Foliot suggests to the archbishop that he might profit by the example of John of Crema : Cremensis ille Johannes, diebus nostris in partes has a sancta Romana directus ecclesia, regni consuetudines, in quibus jam senuerat, immutavit ; quod non maledictis aut minis, sed doctrina sana et exhortationibus sanctis, obtinuit. Benedicendo seminavit, de benedictionibus et messem fecit. The enormous difficulty of making a just judgment on the personality of such a controversial figure of bygone centuries is brought home to us by the quite different description of him given in the *Liber Pontificalis Dertusensi* (ed. March, p. 208) : Hic (i.e., Honorius) Johannem Cremensem, hominem litteratum et providum, sed turpis famae magis quam opus sit, suspendit a cardinalatus officio ; sed ipse scit et Deus, qualiter eum postea restituerit. One has to remember, of course, that this author was a supporter of Anacletus and hostile to John.
55. *H C* pp. 122–123.
56. *H C* pp. 123–8 for the events of this Roman journey.

to consolidate his support for their cause it also landed them in considerable hardship because John was taking back with him great sums of money that he had collected on his mission, such as the Romescot traditionally paid by all households in England. As a result the party became the target of robbers along the way and in his efforts to dodge these John of Crema dragged his companions along outlandish, steep and devious routes where on occasion they were captured and held to ransom. They did not finally arrive in Rome until the Canterbury party had been there three weeks. Not only had this given Canterbury three weeks' start in lobbying, it had also enabled them to attach to their cause one of the most powerful advocates of the day, Gilbert the Universalist. Concerning Gilbert, whom he regarded as a money-grubbing dialectician, the York historian has some hard things to say, all the harder no doubt because York had hoped to attach him to their own side and because his presence added further prestige to a side which could already boast Alexander bishop of Lincoln, John of Glasgow, Geoffrey abbot of St. Alban's and Thurstan, abbot of Sherborne. There was one notable absentee from this party— Bernard of St. David's ; whether through a real change of heart or simply for political reasons he had gone to Thurstan earlier in the year and asked forgiveness for the hostility he had previously shown to York and its archbishop.

Bernard's ability to darken counsel was not missed ; there were plenty in attendance who could perform that function. To begin with, the archbishop of Canterbury made it plain that his relinquishing three dioceses was no part of the solution as he understood it. Immediately the legate John of Crema stepped in and declared that William of Corbeil had agreed to this in England. Here, the familiar round of recrimination began again, with some making one proposal and some another, whilst Thurstan sat tight, knowing he was invulnerable. He was invulnerable because William of Corbeil, by refusing to accept the agreement as a package deal, had no hope of making Thurstan acknowledge his subjection to Canterbury except by initiating a case against Thurstan in the Roman *curia* ; and this was precisely what King Henry had both feared and strictly forbidden. If William had disobeyed him Henry would have made his life a misery.

William had the good sense, then, to drop this elaborate scheme and concentrate on the attempt to get himself nominated as legate for England. This latter aim, to have the archbishop of Canterbury appointed legate, had been uppermost in Henry's intentions for the church since at least 1120. By that date he had come to see clearly that the legates were the striking-force of the Roman *curia*, and that his best means of defence against the over-mighty *curia* was to have a legate for himself. It was in February, 1120, that he had entrusted to William Warelwast, bishop of Exeter, the task of persuading the Pope to establish the archbishop of Canterbury as legate over all Britain[57]. And though Warelwast failed, nevertheless Henry returned to the charge in this year 1125 ; irritated by the sight of John of Crema laying down the law for the church in his lands the king resolved never to receive another Roman legate in his kingdom[58]. He therefore charged all his churchmen setting out for Rome to help William in every way possible to secure the legation. According to Hugh the Chanter, Thurstan at least responded loyally to Henry's wishes ; when questioned by Honorius he assured the Pope that William was the ideal man for the job. But throughout Hugh the Chanter's account of these proceedings there is a marked undertone of resentment as though he felt that a triumph for Canterbury was bound to be interpreted by the same token as a defeat for York. That very interpretation, in fact, which prompted the Durham chronicler's laconic observation : "Thurstan of York and William of Canterbury returned from Rome ; William as legate of the apostolic see throughout England, Thurstan however in the same status as he set out"[59]. Yet Thurstan himself seems to have accepted the situation unreservedly and, as one wise in the ways of the world, he probably recognized that the real victor was King Henry ; henceforward it became customary for the archbishops of Canterbury to assume the function of *legatus natus* throughout England, leaving the kings of England with small fear of the men from Rome.

This oblique solution to the friction between York and Canterbury allowed Thurstan to turn his attention to the disobedience within his own province which he saw incarnate in the person of John of Glasgow present amongst the company at Rome. Almost as soon as he arrived in Rome Thurstan complained to the Pope about the flagrant disregard of papal orders on the part of John of Glasgow and the other Scottish bishops. His complaint quickly stirred up a three-cornered argument ; the Scots' supporters maintained that

---

57. *H C* p. 87.
58. *H C* p. 123 : de futuro precavens ne Romanum legatum in regno suo reciperet.
59. Symeon of Durham, *Opera* II, p. 281.

they owed no obedience to York because Scotland, not being part
of England, should have its own archbishop—of St. Andrews—who
should be granted the *pallium* ; Thurstan, for his part, refuted this
claim by showing to the Pope's satisfaction that the Scottish king
owed allegiance to the king of England ; meanwhile the third party,
the archbishop of Canterbury, vigorously pleaded the case of the
Scottish bishops against York but at the same time claimed primacy
for his own see over all Britain, unconcerned at the offence to
Scottish pride that this would eventually entail. Thurstan was the
one who emerged in best order from this rumpus and his designs for
Scotland were underwritten by a series of letters which Pope
Honorius issued on December 9th : one of these ordered Sigurd,
king of Norway, to ensure that Thurstan's suffragan bishop, Ralph,
was established in his see in Orkney[60] ; a second instructed Gilla-
Aldan, the elect of Whithorn, to go to Thurstan for consecration[61].
The one addressed to John of Glasgow and commanding him to
render due obedience to Thurstan[62] would seem to have been
superfluous since John was present in Rome, so the matter could have
been settled there and then. At least Thurstan hoped so, but John
was not to be caught napping, for he rightly asserted that he had
come to Rome as King David's envoy and not to answer Thurstan's
charges ; and so he had a right to be given due warning. Hence
the net result of this wrangling, was that Thurstan and John were
told to present themselves again at Rome, on the 16th January, 1127,
to have their disputes settled.

     Honorius' decision illustrates the disadvantages which both
kings and old-fashioned churchmen felt were inseparable from the
growing practice of frequently appealing to Rome. Here at Rome,
in December, 1125, were Thurstan and John of Glasgow, both of
whom had made the long trek to Rome on an earlier occasion, now
being instructed to make another such journey in another twelve
months. The inconvenience and expense were obviously considerable. Furthermore, the practice initiated a process of inflation by
which more and more journeys to Rome became essential if you
were to protect your rights adequately. Thus on December 9th, also,
Thurstan obtained a papal privilege for the protection of Whitby
Abbey [63] and another one for the abbey of Savigny[64] ; again, a few

---

60. *Jaffé*, no. 7224.
61. *Ibid.*, no. 7225.
62. *Ibid.*, no. 7228.
63. *Ibid.*, no. 7230.
64. *Ibid.*, no. 7223 ; Martène, *Thesaurus Novus* I, p. 361 : ... venerabilis
     fratris nostri Turstini Eboracensis archiepiscopi precibus inclinati.

weeks later he secured confirmations for Durham[65] and Beverley[66] whilst his brother Audouen obtained protection from Honorius for his own diocesan possessions[67]. A like privilege for Lincoln lands was granted to its bishop, Alexander, one of the Canterbury company[68].

The English contingents had stayed about two months in Rome collecting these various privileges before they returned to the king in Normandy. It was Thurstan's last visit to a Pope and marks the end of a period of suffering for his diocese, as is pointed out by Hugh the Chanter who terminates his book at about this time. Not, of course, that all the sources of dispute had now dried up. At Christmas, 1126, for instance, Henry was holding a great court for his ceremonial crown-wearing at Windsor ; and William of Corbeil threatened that he would boycott the court if Thurstan were thus allowed either to have his cross borne before him or to take part in the crowning ceremony. The king was angered by this threat of which he informed Thurstan who, in his turn, won the king's esteem by returning a mild answer ; he said he would not like the king's court to be disturbed on his account and so did not insist on his rights[69]. This mildness on Thurstan's part was especially commendable because he could have shown William to be completely in the wrong ; he could have made it public that twelve months previously Pope Honorius had sent letters to William and King Henry ordering them to allow Thurstan to carry his cross and to help in the coronation, following the ancient custom of the land[70]. As it turned out Thurstan was heaping coals of fire on William's head, for within a few months William received a blistering rebuke for his attitude from the Pope : "We have heard," the papal letter ran, "that when you are in the North, you can bear no superior or

---

65. M S Eccl. Dun. Cartuarium Vetus f. 13r.
66. *E Y C* I, no. 112.
67. *Jaffé*, no. 7240.
68. *Ibid.*, no. 7241.
69. *H C* pp. 129–30. It is interesting to compare Hugh's account of this Christmas gathering with the account by the Worcester chronicler, who paints a picture of everyone's hand being set against Thurstan for trying to insist on having his cross borne before him (*Chronicon ex Chronicis*, II, p. 84) ; Hugh does not mention the bishops' reaction ; the Worcester chronicler does not mention the king's.
70. *Jaffé*, no. 7226 : 9th December, 1125 : G(uillelmo), archiepiscopo Cantuariensi, apostolicae sedis legato, et universis per regnum Angliae constitutis, et H(enrico) Anglorum regi praecipit, ut "Thomae (lege Thurstano) Eboracensi archiepiscopo iuxta antiquam consuetudinem crucem ante se deferri absque contradictione antiqua permittant, et regem more solito coronare" *P L* 166, p. 1242.

equal, you crush those whom you ought to have loved and honoured, and strive to appear more important than anyone else"[71] ; for the rest William was ordered to allow Thurstan his ancient privileges. Perhaps on the strength of this rebuke Thurstan thought himself absolved from attending the legatine council convoked by William a few months later (May, 1127) ; at any rate he did not attend the council, nor does he seem to have been harried for his failure to do so[72]. In general, moreover, William's legatine powers seem hardly to have affected Thurstan at all, and one is left wondering if victory or defeat on these issues was anything like so vital as the disputants reckoned them. Indeed, one is prompted to ask whether it would have made much earthly or heavenly difference if York had even accepted the dreaded primacy of Canterbury. Such a reflexion is, perhaps, a luxury of posterity ; certainly it was not amongst those permitted by Hugh the Chanter who pens a triumphant finale to his account of the struggle when he writes : "This book might somewhat fancifully be christened 'The Freedman' ; because it shows how our church was recalled from the yoke of an unlawful profession to its ancient freedom by Thurstan, the fourth French archbishop"[73].

It is noticeable, though perhaps not surprising, how Hugh, for all his praise of the freedman, seems to have no inkling that as York felt towards Canterbury so Glasgow might feel towards York. In fact he never shows any great interest in the Scottish issue and tells us little about it. This is a pity, because for the next few years his northern neighbours were to bulk large on Thurstan's horizon as they became more self-confident. One of the evidences of their growing self-confidence at this time is the letter which King David wrote to William of Corbeil requesting him to send north a suitable Canterbury monk to become the first abbot of the monastery of Dunfermline, which was now being transformed from a Priory into

---

71. *H C* p. 130.

72. Florence of Worcester and Hugh the Chanter, in the passages cited in note 69, do not agree on the grounds for Thurstan's absence ; Florence says he showed "reasonable cause" for his absence, but Hugh states that Thurstan's messengers back from Rome gave him news which made him not wish to go to the Council, and so he did not.

73. *H C* p. 132.

an Abbey[74]. Similar ambitions were being conceived for other Scottish religious houses at the same time, several of which received abbatial status in the next few years ; along with the demand for a *pallium* for St. Andrews[75] these moves indicate the trend of David's ambitions. These were to be revealed to Thurstan after the Christmas feasting at Windsor in 1126 when Thurstan went from there to London *en route* for Rome, where his dispute with John of Glasgow was to be settled. He was soon joined by King Henry and David of Scotland, each bent upon persuading him to postpone his journey, because the very last thing these two monarchs wanted was to have the Pope acting as arbiter between Thurstan and John[76]. As we have already seen, the argument between Thurstan and John had been made to turn on the question of whether Scotland was subject to England or not ; and should the Pope's verdict on the ecclesiastical issue be accepted there arose in royal minds the disturbing fear that the temporal issue might therefore be treated as coming within his jurisdiction as well. Never entirely banished from Henry's mind were the ghosts of those Emperors whose realms had been thrown into turmoil by analogous papal decisions. Thus Henry and David did persuade Thurstan to seek a postponement from Rome and permission to settle the case out of

---

74. *Regesta Regum Scottorum* I. (ed. G. W. S. Barrow) no. 8. In his letter David insisted that Dunfermline should in no way be subject to Canterbury, though the monks of the Scottish abbey were to be free to choose an abbot from Christ Church, Canterbury, if there were no suitable candidate found amongst themselves. On the significance of these negotiations, Prof. Barrow comments : "It seems to be significant that independent religious houses, having abbatial status, begin to appear in Scotland after 1127, by which time there was a duly consecrated bishop of St. Andrews subject neither to York nor Canterbury and ready to co-operate with the king" (*Scottish Historical Review*, XXXI, p. 26).

75. "The assertion of the York Chronicles that the Church of St. Andrew was even at that period seeking to be made a metropolitan see, and to obtain a pall (*H C* p. 126) is proved to be correct by the Leg. S. Andr. assigned to 1165 (in Ussher, *Antiq. Brit. Eccl.* Op. VI, 189, and Skene, 140)" (*H & S*, Vol. II, Pt. I, p. 212n). Within a few years a number of dioceses were established that might well have justified a *pallium* for St. Andrews ; at Dunkeld, Aberdeen, Brechin, Caithness and Ross. (For Dunkeld, *cf* Anderson, *Early Sources of Scottish History*, II, p. 178 and 267 ; Aberdeen, *cf H.* & *S*, II, p. 210 ; and Anderson, *Early Sources of Scottish History*, II, p. 178. Brechin, *cf Regesta Regum Scottorum*, p. 170. Caithness, *cf* Anderson, *Early Sources*, II, p. 182. Ross, *cf H.* & *S*., II, p. 217). A similar development was taking place at the same time in Ireland, where Malachy was also seeking the *pallium* from Rome (*cf St. Malachy of Armagh*, p. lx, 65 (ed. H. J. Lawlor)).

76. If he was as "clerkly" as tradition would make him, Henry may even have remembered that in the work by Hugh of Fleury dedicated to him there occurs the sentence : regis officium est etiam dissidentes episcopos reconciliare, sicut multis documentis possumus approbare (*Libelli de lite*, Vol. II, p. 489).

the Roman court—though it was "with difficulty", says Hugh the Chantor, that permission was obtained from the Pope, who knew perfectly well what lay behind the request[77].

The fruits of the London conference were gathered in the early months of 1127 when an impressive assembly met at York to witness the consecration of Robert of St. Andrews by Thurstan. Though David himself was not present his kingdom was well represented by John of Glasgow, Nicholas prior of Scone, Herbert of Roxburgh and some half-dozen knights ; others present, such as Ralph of Orkney and Waltheof of Croyland, came from England but by their connections can be reckoned as bridging the two countries ; witnessing for the York province were Ranulf, bishop of Durham, Geoffrey abbot of St. Mary's (York), Athelwold prior of Nostell, Hugh the dean and the whole chapter of St. Peter's, besides such secular notables as Geoffrey Murdac, Eustace FitzJohn, Walter de Gant and Anketill de Bulmer[78]. The decisive feature of this consecration—so decisive that both David and Thurstan had it documented in the form of a solemn charter—was that Robert did not make a profession of obedience to Thurstan. That Robert might be quite ready to give the oath was darkly suspected in some quarters on account of his ties with the diocese of York[79] ; he had been trained as a canon at St. Oswald's, Nostell, before becoming prior at Scone and moving from there to St. Andrews. These suspicions would explain why John of Glasgow and other Scots warned him against taking the oath, though it is clear they were being officious since Thurstan and David had previously agreed that there was to be no oath ; their agreement also underlined that Robert's consecration was not to be taken as in any sense prejudicing Thurstan's claims upon St. Andrews ; David would hear these without ill-will whenever Thurstan chose to raise them. The arrangement, in fact, was a great credit to both the archbishop and the king ; St. Andrew's received its bishop duly consecrated ; nobody lost any rights, and good will between the English and Scots authorities was greatly multiplied.

A little later, on July 17th, the flourishing border town of Roxburgh saw the second instalment of this good-will programme when Robert as bishop of St. Andrews summoned Algar, prior of Durham, to the porch of St. John's church and solemnly freed the

---

77. *H C* p. 129.
78. *H & S*, II, Pt. I, p. 215.
79. Florence of Worcester, *Chronicon ex Chronicis*, II, p. 89.

priory of Coldingham (a cell of Durham's) from paying certain ancient dues which it was accustomed to render to the bishop of St. Andrews. This occasion, the feast of St. Kenelm the martyr, was graced by the presence of King David, Thurstan, Ranulf of Durham, John of Glasgow and Geoffrey of St. Albans along with their retinues[80]. Such a moment of splendour must have convinced the borderers that a new day of peaceful co-existence had now dawned for the kingdoms of England and Scotland.

The unfortunate John of Glasgow, however, was not to be a beneficiary from the changed situation ; he continued to be ground between the royal and episcopal mill-stones. Soon, indeed, the grinding he endured was to get worse, when the papal hand was applied to the wheel after the fateful papal election of 1130. That event was a crucial one for the whole of Europe, but particularly for Scotland, and a word about it is essential.[81]

When in February, 1130, Pope Honorius II lay dying in the monastery of St. Gregory on the Coelian Hill the papal chancellor Aimeric made preparations to carry out an electoral manoeuvre in favour of a successor just as he had operated in Honorius' favour six years earlier. The person Aimeric had resolved to exclude was Cardinal Pierleone, and the person he favoured was Cardinal Gregory of St. Angelo. But as an unintended result of Aimeric's sharp practice each of these cardinals was in fact elected by one section of the electoral college, each could make out a reasonable case for the validity of his own election, and Christendom was consequently thrown into violent schism. Taking the title of Anacletus II, Pierleone rapidly established his position in Rome, where his family was strong, and in southern Italy, where Honorius' policies had alienated other powerful dynasties. Innocent II, as Cardinal Gregory became, had fewer supporters amongst worldly rulers at first but, more important, he was of one mind with the group of spiritual leaders whose visions were to dazzle Christians for over a generation, Aimeric himself, Bernard of Clairvaux, Peter the Venerable and Norbert of Magdeburg in particular. Under the ceaseless urging of such men, Louis of France[82], Lothair of Ger-

---

80. *Liber Vitae Ecclesiae Dunelmensis* (Surtees Society), pp. 67–68 and 59.

81. The best summary of the schism is that given by F. J. Schmale, *Studien zum Schisma des Jahres, 1130.*

82. Council of Étampes. September/October, 1130 ; under the influence of St. Bernard.

many[83] and Henry of England[84] all proclaimed their support for Innocent, and by 1131 his cause was substantially won ; but the schism continued for a full eight years and they were years when Christians were set against Christians. For example, many in France did not follow King Louis' lead : the celebrated scholar Hildebert of Tours adhered to Anacletus and the respected papal legate in the south, Gerard of Angoulême, supported him whilst another of his supporters, Aegidius of Tusculum, commanded so much respect that the Innocentians were constantly trying to detach him from Anacletus. In England also, despite Henry I's decision, a deep current of doubt regarding the validity of Innocent's election is discernible in much contemporary writing[85] ; there was a strong rumour going around that Honorius had, in fact, still been breathing when the Innocentians made their election, which was therefore invalid ; the rumour is enshrined in the chronicle of William of Malmesbury who also gives in full a letter favourable to Anacletus written by the oldest cardinal, the highly respected Peter bishop of Portus[86] ; but perhaps the most remarkable English gloss on the events of 1130 comes in the chronicle of John of Worcester where we are assured that the schism was really brought about by the conflicting ambitions of the Emperor and Roger of Apulia over southern Italy, a conflict in which the rival Popes and cardinals were mere puppets dangled by strings of gold[87]. England, it will be seen, was hardly swept by Innocentian enthusiasm.

Perhaps the very worst feature of the schism was the flood of abuse which was poured out by both sides over their opponents, a flood made more poisonous from the Innocentian side by the salvific fervour accompanying it. The most revolting of the pamphlets in this war of scurrility came from the pen of an Innocentian, Arnulf archdeacon of Séez ; in his *Invectiva* he accused Anacletus of having

---

83. Council of Würzburg. October, 1130 ; under the influence of St. Norbert.

84. 13 January, 1131 ; prompted by St. Bernard, and in spite of the English bishops ; cf Ernaldi, S. Bernardi Abbatis Vita, Bk. II, c. I, 4 : quem vix persuasit Innocentium recipere, ab episcopis Angliae penitus dissuasum.

85. For instance, copies were kept of the letter of February 25, 1131, from the Lateran in which Anacletus announced to the clerics of France and Normandy that a schismatic (i.e. Innocent) had seized the papacy, cf Corpus Christi College (Oxford) M S. E.137, f. 87r—this MS belonged to Worcester Priory ; also B M Royal MS 5. A xiii, f. 199.

86. William of Malmesbury, Gesta Regum, II, pp. 531–533. Also in MS Harley 633 which Levison traces to northern England. Cf W. Levison, Aus Englischen Bibliotheken, in Neues Archiv., 53 (1910), pp. 331–431.

87. Florence of Worcester, Chronicon ex Chronicis, II, pp. 99–100.

committed incest with his sister[88], and he embittered the smear by slighting references to Anacletus' Jewish blood ; throughout his pamphlet there recur several ugly overtones which are echoed in a letter written to the Emperor Lothair by another Innocentian, Bishop Manfred of Mantua ; "The close agreement between the two documents reveals how well the party of Innocent II had organized its propaganda of vilification"[89]. In this propaganda Bernard of Clairvaux played a leading part through his regrettable habit of listening to detractors and then issuing thundering judgments based upon hearsay[90].

The tale is a sorry one, but so much needs to be told of it if we are to understand the genuine confusion that might lead to good men supporting either of the claimants for the papacy. King David was one such man who, along with the church in his realm, adhered to Anacletus[91]. Whilst recognising that good reasons for his decision may be adduced, however, the result was nonetheless detrimental to the schemes for the development of his church that he had been pursuing with great success for several years ; from 1130 onwards the Scottish church again lapses into the isolation out of which David had begun to wean it. Above all, since Anacletus proved to be the wrong horse, Scotland was deprived of papal help and John of Glasgow in particular had to endure the effects of his king and lord's decision. He felt the first effects in 1131 when Innocent from Auxerre issued letters both to John of Glasgow individually and to the Scottish bishops in general ordering them without dissimulation to perform due obedience to Thurstan ;

---

88. Incest seems to have been a favourite form of smear amongst the reformers ; the Cistercians made the same accusation against William FitzHerbert (W. Holtzmann, *Papsturkunden* II, p. 176, no. 32, Pope Innocent II instructing Henry of Winchester to enquire into the charges against William).

89. H. Bloch, The schism of Anacletus II and the Glanfeuil Forgeries of Peter the Deacon of Monte Cassino, in *Traditio*, VII, 1952 (pp. 159–264), p. 167, n.29.

90. *Cf* C. H. Talbot, San Bernardo nelle sue lettere, in *S. Bernardo, Pubblicazione Commemorativa*, 1954, pp. 151–165.
    Perhaps the best comment on St. Bernard's behaviour at the time of the schism came from St. Wulfric of Haselbury. Bernard asked Wulfric to pray for him to be forgiven for his presumptuous speeches during the schism, to which Wulfric mordantly answered : Quid ita sibi voluit usurpare scientiam secretorum Dei ? (*Wulfric of Haselbury* by John, Abbot of Ford, ed. M. Bell, Somerset Record Society, 1933, p. 79).

91. In a letter of about the year 1131 Bernard of Clairvaux numbered the king of Scotland amongst the adherents of Innocent (*The Letters of St. Bernard*, p. 190) ; coming from some other source this statement might lead us to think that David at first hesitated between the two claimants but, as it is, we can dismiss it as a piece of rhetoric.

Innocent reminded John sharply that he was not the first Pope who had found it necessary to call him to order on this matter[92]. However, these papal letters show that Innocent had yet to learn what other Popes also had taken long learning—that Scotland was a long way from the papal *curia* and its power—for the situation was if anything worse when he wrote to Thurstan over two years later. In this letter (2 May, 1134), after commending Thurstan warmly for his constancy in religion and his loyalty to the see of Rome, Innocent goes on to say that he has come to hear of the oppressions and wrongs inflicted upon Thurstan and the see of York by the king of Scotland and John, bishop of Glasgow; he ends by thanking Thurstan for asking after his well-being and promises both help and prayers to right the wrongs he was enduring[93].

By this same year of 1134 the harassed bishop of Glasgow was no longer in the field ; he had wearied of his task entirely and had sought peace for himself by entering the monastery of Tiron. He was not even tempted out of his retirement by the greatest occasion his diocese had seen for many a long year, when on July 7th, 1136, it celebrated the dedication of the church of Glasgow to St. Kentigern. As part of the celebration King David made a grant of land in Partick to St. Kentigern (i.e. to the church of Glasgow) and it is likely enough that the same day saw the presentation of the *Life of St. Kentigern* by an unknown cleric, one who had travelled through many lands and was now providing Glasgow with that *desideratum* of every self-respecting diocesan church, a legend of its founder[94]. It was sad that these diocesan festivities should not have been

---

92. *Jaffé*, no. 7515.
93. *Jaffé*, no. 7650.
94. The land in Partick had once been held by Ailsi and Tocca ; by David's charter the present holder, Ascelinus the archdeacon, is ordered to pay annually to the church of Glasgow the mark of silver which he had hitherto paid to the king and, on his death, the church was to hold this part of Partick free from any duty or service. *Cf* Lawrie, *Early Scottish Charters*, no. CIX, and notes on p. 349, where he rightly observes : "It is strange that the dignitaries of the church, and some of the clergy of the diocese do not attest the grant."
    The Life of St. Kentigern was edited by A. P. Forbes in *The Historians of Scotland*, Vol. V.
    The reorganization of the church at Glasgow, to make it worthy both of St. Kentigern and of its position as the "national" church of the Cumbrians, had been proceeding apace ever since the Inquisition into the lands of the diocese made by David as Earl of Cumbria (Lawrie, No. L and notes, pp. 299–304 ; he gives circa 1124 as the date of the Inquisition, but 1120 or 1121 is more likely for the reasons given by *H. & S.*, II, p. 16). Already by 1128 the church had an archdeacon, Ascelinus, who witnessed a number of David's charters and appears to have been a man of standing in the country (Lawrie, pp. 68, 69, 73, 79, 93, 108, 136, 186, 202 & *Regesta Regum Scottorum*, pp. 179, 193).

crowned with a papal blessing but should rather have taken place under the shadow of a papal curse. For in April of this year Pope Innocent, now confident in his rule over Christendom, issued a clutch of letters from Pisa, to King Stephen of England, to the papal legate William of Corbeil and to Thurstan respectively, each of them aimed at bringing John of Glasgow to acknowledge his subjection to the see of York : William of Corbeil, acting as legate for all Britain, was to give John three months' grace to submit and, in case of his refusal, to excommunicate him ; Thurstan was to do likewise[95]. What marks these letters off from previous papal orders is the new note of great severity towards John personally ; he is referred to as a rebel and a pseudo-bishop who has not only turned his talons against his mother the Holy Roman Church and the church of York but has also seduced others into rebellion. Perhaps King David was the one whom Innocent was choosing to regard as having been misled by John, because his letter to Stephen urges the new king of England to develop the see of Carlisle yet does not name the outstanding obstacle to this development, which was King David. Now in possession of Cumbria, David was making every effort to squeeze out the bishop of Carlisle in favour of Glasgow and he was effectively preventing bishop Athelwold of Carlisle from occupying his see. And the Pope's anathemas produced no effect whatsoever.

In regard to Scotland, then, as in regard to Canterbury, Thurstan could claim that the supreme ecclesiastical authority had vindicated the stand he had made for the rights of his province. But as with his southern, so with his northern, neighbours he was forced in the end to recognize that without the approbation of the secular ruler papal privileges by no means commanded automatic obedience in the remote lands of northern Europe. But of all the English ecclesiastics of his generation Thurstan was the one who did most to make such papal intervention first a possibility and then a factor that had to be reckoned with. His whole career had, in fact, been dominated by the appeals he made to the Popes against King Henry's overbearing hand in his early days as archbishop elect ; it was this which threw him so much into the company of the papal legate Cuno, for whom the legateship was the exciting new weapon in the church's armoury. Thurstan saw this weapon being manipulated with increasing frequency and skill during the years after 1127

95. *Jaffé*, nos. 7765, 7766, 7767.
96. *Mansi* XXI, cols. 357, 378, 375.

when control over the church began to slip away from the local hierarchies and the secular rulers who appointed them, and to be grasped by papal representatives. In 1128, for instance, the papal legate cardinal Matthew of Albano presided over local French councils at Troyes and Rheims as well as over a Norman one at Rouen[96] which, significantly enough, proved to be the last provincial council held in Rouen for over sixty years—so decisively had the initiative in legislation passed from the local ruler and local hierarchy to the papal *curia*[97]. The point was made most effectively by Pope Innocent II three years afterwards when he himself held a council at Rheims to which Henry I and other rulers sent representatives ; at the council they found themselves accepting a canon which wrested from secular rulers one of their main holds upon their hierarchies ; this was canon 7 which laid it down, under pain of excommunication, that after the death of a bishop or priest the treasurer of the church, and he alone, should take charge of the property until a successor was appointed[98]. In other words the custom, known as regalian right, by which secular rulers had taken over bishoprics and exploited them for their own ends, and for which Henry I was notorious, must be stopped forthwith.

Of course, Henry I virtually ignored this canon, as he could afford to[99], but it was a very different story with his successor, Stephen, for Stephen supported his claim to the throne by an appeal to papal judgment and stressed to the country that Pope Innocent had ratified his claim[100]. By 1136, in fact, a habit had taken on yet more powerfully favourable to papal influence than the institution of legates ; this was the habit of appealing to the papal *curia* for settling localized and even secular disputes. Stephen's appeal in 1136 was but a striking instance of the habit which had been fostered during the previous decade by internationally-minded ecclesiastics of whom Thurstan was the outstanding. We have seen how very careful he was at each stage of his disputes with Canterbury and the Scots to secure papal ratification for his every move. No bishop in the land was so energetic as he to secure confirmations for the religious institutions within his province such as Durham, Hexham, Nostell, Kirkham, Bridlington, Guisborough, and the minsters at Beverley, Ripon and Southwell[101]. Nor was he forget-

---

97. The next provincial council for Normandy did not take place until 1190 ;
     cf H. Boehmer, *Kirche und Staat*, p. 320.
98. *Mansi XXI*, col. 457.
99. M. Howell, *Regalian Right in Medieval England*, pp. 20–29.
100. Stubbs, *Select Charters* (1942 ed.), p. 143.

ful of his own ; in December, 1125, he secured from Honorius II a
statement of the privileges of the church of York and obtained a
similar though fuller one from Innocent II in 1131[102]. Since this
latter was issued by the Pope from Auxerre on the same day as he
sent out some fierce letters to the Scots in support of York's claims
upon them, and only a few days after the Council of Rheims, it looks
very much as though Thurstan had managed to push representatives
through to Rheims who had negotiated these privileges for him.
At every turn of the road, then, Thurstan looked to the papacy for
his directions so that any Yorkshire churchman old enough to
remember previous archiepiscopates must have been astonished to
notice how closely the diocese had now been brought into contact
with the Popes and the European mainland.

It was entirely fitting, therefore, that Thurstan should have
been called in by Innocent to help judge the case which, between
1126 and 1135, did more than any other to stimulate traffic between
Rome and England. This was a dispute over diocesan boundaries
between the bishop of Llandaff, Urban, and the bishop of St.
David's, Bernard. The former royal chaplain Bernard, it will be
remembered, had been Thurstan's most inflexible opponent until
the autumn of 1125 when he came to beg Thurstan's forgiveness for
having waxed so hot against the church of York[103]. One does not
have to be unduly cynical to observe that Bernard's change of heart
took place about the time that he was beginning to harbour ambitions for making St. David's into a metropolitan see and to envisage
himself fighting battles against Canterbury on the lines already laid
down by Thurstan. He was led to go digging for the body of St.
David to give substance to his visions[104], and to fabricate some
intensely curious history in support of his claims[105], but the only
result was to complicate further his dispute with the Urban over
their diocesan boundaries. The attempts made by the Popes to
disentangle the disputed lands were always thwarted by their

---

101. W. Holtzmann, *Papsturkunden*, II, p. 138 (Durham) ; II, p. 147 (Hexham,
Beverley, Ripon, Southwell) ; III, p. 145 (Beverley) ; III, pp. 134–5
(Kirkham and Bridlington) ; I, p. 237 (Guisborough) ; and for Nostell
see p. 129 of this present work.
102. W. Holtzmann, *Papsturkunden*, II, nos. 12 and 13. Holtzmann dates the
first of these to 1128 instead of to 1125, as does *Jaffé* ; there is little to be
said in favour of his revised date beyond the fact that R.M.A. gives it,
but this source is frequently unreliable on dating.
103. *H C* p. 121.
104. William of Malmesbury, *Gesta Regum*, I, p. 28.
105. Giraldus Cambrensis' *De Invectionibus* (*Y Cymmrodor*, XXX, pp. 143–6).
Quoted by James Conway Davies in *Episcopal Acts Relating to Welsh Dioceses 1066–1272*, pp. 249–50.

inability to bring the two contending bishops face to face in the papal *curia*, until finally Pope Innocent II decided to entrust the settlement of the dispute to judges delegate. In November, 1131, soon after the council of Rheims, he issued letters instructing the parties to present themselves in London on the 24th of April, 1132, where the case would be tried by William archbishop of Canterbury, Thurstan archbishop of York and Hugh archbishop of Rouen[106]. But even these famous prelates with the bishops of St. David's and Llandaff before them, could not easily untwist the knot of discord ; they made a first attempt at doing so in London during the last week of April, 1132, but had to adjourn for a second trial in London on Ash Wednesday of the following year where once again they had to adjourn, this time to Winchester. It was here in Rogation Tide that judgment was at last made, and apparently in favour of St. David's, because the next that we hear of Bishop Urban is that he died on the Roman road, now an old and weary man who had spent much of his energies in pursuit of this famous case[107]. The last glimpse we get of bishop Bernard and Thurstan together is a happier one ; whilst his case was being examined at Winchester in the spring of 1133 Bernard was asked to witness the confirmation by King Henry of Thurstan's gifts to the recently begotten community at Fountains[108]. As he was making his witness he might well have reflected on the changing relations of the last ten years and of how Thurstan, in the simile beloved of his admirers punning on his name, had stood firm as a tower amidst the changing moods of prelates and princes[109], steadfast in his adherence to the papacy and its policies.

106. *Liber Landavensis* (ed. J. G. Evans), pp. 66–7—*Jaffé*, no. 7511, given at Troyes on the 21st November, 1131.

107. The authorities for these meetings are all given by J. Conway Davies on p. 252 of the volume cited previously, which provides a thorough account of the whole Llandaff v. St. David's controversy.

108. *Regesta*, no. 1834, dated by Cronne and Johnson as 1131–3 but clearly to be dated 1133, and, since Henry was at Winchester during Rogation Tide. can be limited to April 30th to May 3rd.

109. *H C* p. 131 ; and *H C Y* II, p. 261 ; Thurstanus, quasi turris stans contra mala mundi, Exponit nomen per sua facta suum.

CHAPTER V.

THE RE-ORDERING AND EXPANSION OF THE ARCHDIOCESE, 1114-1133.

Having examined the chief occasions of jurisdictional dispute that faced Thurstan outside his diocese we may now turn, as Thurstan himself gladly turned, towards the diocese and its internal development. Here Thurstan was confronted with a double task : firstly he needed to encourage and strengthen the ecclesiastical institutions already in existence and secondly, to found centres of Christian observance whose influence would be felt amongst the scattered population of his wide and untamed territories. Inevitably he found himself involved in wearying feudal disputes and he had to spend much of his time negotiating with the great magnates ; he was even driven, in the final crisis of 1138, to assume both the moral and military leadership of these great magnates. But all his traffic with the secular world was subordinated to the double task referred to : the building up and strengthening of the Christian community in the North.

Obviously the running of such a great province as that of York was only feasible if an adequate revenue was coming in to pay the large staff of officials and bailiffs who were needed to secure the smooth working of the province in both spiritual and secular affairs. This need was one by which the king was able to bring great pressure to bear on Thurstan to act in accordance with his wishes since the archbishop could not enjoy the fruits of his archiepiscopal lands, which he held as tenant-in-chief of the king, until he had been duly consecrated and had done homage for those lands. And as Thurstan well knew through his experience as a courtier, a yet greater danger to any ecclesiastic losing the king's good will was that he thereby bared the church property in his diocese to the incursions of any great baron who wished to take advantage of his helplessness. One great baron who had lately taken advantage of the unprotected ecclesiastics in the North had been the king's confidant, Nigel de Albini ; in the early years of the century he had usurped lands in the dioceses of York and Durham belonging to various religious houses. We learn of this through a series of letters that he wrote later, at the time when he had been struck down with illness and thought his end was near. For dramatic insight into the soul of a twelfth-century baron cleft between awe before his king and terror in the face of his divine Judge these letters are hard to match[1]. "To his dearest lord the King of England," runs the first letter, "Nigel de Albini his faithful servant. I beseech you, dearest lord, in whom, after God, lies all my trust . . . have mercy upon me. Since in the course of your service and in my other works I committed great sins and did little or no good ; trusting in your most sweet goodness I have restored certain lands which I had taken from various churches . . ." Nigel proceeds to explain that illness prevents him from casting himself at his majesty's feet, as he would wish to do, but he nevertheless implores Henry, for his soul's sake, to confirm these decisions of his repentance. He ends by repeating that he is not trusting in any service he might have performed but in the king's goodness. The same note of terror before the Lord is struck by Nigel's letter to the bishop, Ranulf, in which he acknowledges that he has offended St. Cuthbert by his seizure of Durham lands—"because God almighty in his justice and power has stricken me down with bodily infirmity and I lie here, deeply tormented, not knowing what is to become of my soul." Other letters composed at the same time were addressed to his brother William and to Thomas, archbishop of York, who was present at Nigel's side and witnessed some of the letters ; other witnesses ominously include Nigel's doctor, Matthew, and his chaplains and retainers. In fact, Nigel recovered—and, chastened by his experience, behaved more considerately towards Thomas' successor, Thurstan, during the latter's exile[2]. At least, the only hint of oppression by him upon York lands is the writ issued by King Henry to him during this period ordering that carrying service and castle works are not to be demanded from the canons of York, Beverley, Southwell, Ripon and Hexham[3]. The charge of oppression is more justifiably made against Serlo de Burgh, who was directed to make sure that the canons of York received full enjoyment of their property and dues

---

1. The originals are to be found in the manuscripts of the church of Durham, D. & C. Mun. I. 12. Spec. ; No. 23 (addressed to William de Albini), no. 24 (to the king), no. 26 (to archbishop Thomas). The original of the letter to the bishop of Durham appears to be lost, but a copy is to be found in *Cart. Vetus*, fo 64, v–65r. In *H C Y* III, pp. 54–56, Raine prints no. 23, but wrongly dated ; the others are tucked away in a footnote on p. 150 of *Feodarium Prioratus Dunelmensis* (ed. Greenwell, S.S. 58, 1871).
2. A place was found for him in the martyrology of Durham on the 21st November (D. & C. MS. Biv. 24, fo. 37r).
3. *E Y C* I, no. 130.

in Aldborough and warned that if he did not do so others would[4].
We also find Serlo still owing £26/7/3d. (in the 1130 Pipe Roll) from
the time when property of the archbishopric was in his hands ; that
such a large debt was still outstanding suggests that some of
Thurstan's lands had not been given back by the king's ministers
immediately after his return in 1121. Until this date Thurstan had
lived for years in acute financial embarrassment which even drove
him, during his years of exile on the continent, into borrowing
money from the better established ecclesiastics amongst whom he
found himself[5]. He probably took a long time to make up for those
stringent years since he still seems to have been financially embarrassed in 1129 when the king in Normandy had to lend him £10[6].

The extent of the land whose profits were available for the
overall ecclesiastical needs of his archdiocese has been calculated
from the Domesday Survey of 1086 as 1,200 carucates, of which
950 were held by the archbishop as tenant-in-chief[7]. These 950
included the lands of St. Peter, St. Wilfrid and St. John, and at the
time of the Confessor had been worth about £320 ; their value had,
of course, fallen steeply by the time the Survey was made, due to the
ruthless harrowing of the province by the Conqueror, and it was
calculated at some £166 in 1086. Indeed, as we make our mental
journey over the land of Yorkshire by means of the entries in
Domesday our eyes become accustomed to the desolation bleakly
shown up through item after item of the kind : "Patricton. In the
time of King Edward it was worth £30 ; now £10 5s." ; "In Wet-
wangham there are 13½ carucates for geld . . . In the time of King
Edward it was worth £4 ; now it is waste." The monotonous
regularity of these depressing entries, stretching for page after page,
is only occasionally lightened by signs of prosperity—in the area
around Hessle, for instance, the manor had actually increased in
value since the Conquest, due possibly to the iron-working that was
being developed there[8], and it is significant that this area constituted a growing point for Yorkshire's wealth in the coming century.
The important manor of Sherburn in Elmet had likewise managed
to hold its own, still being worth the £34/6/od. in 1086 that it had
been valued at in King Edward's time, but here the significant

---

4. E Y C I, no. 500.
5. H C p. 81.
6. Pipe Roll, 31, Henry I, p. 27.
7. V C H Yorks., 3, p. 10.
8. V C H Yorks., 2, p. 342.

feature is that archbishop Thomas of Bayeux had put more than half of its 96 carucates under enfeoffment to certain knights who would help him fulfil his knight service towards the king.

In fact, the poverty of the diocese had led the king to fix knight service due from the archbishop of York at a very low figure, no more than seven, as compared, for example, with the sixty due from the archbishop of Canterbury (who, of course, had the much higher income of £1,600) or the like sixty due from the wealthy abbey of Glastonbury with its income of £827/18/8d.[9]. On the face of it this low assessment put York in a very favoured position ; but further reflexion suggests that, like many another comfortably low financial assessment, it might well have led to stagnation, leaving the archiepiscopal lands undeveloped. If, that is to say, the archbishops had contented themselves with enfeoffing only seven knights these would not have provided sufficient resourceful management to open up the land again, and what the district needed above all else was an influx of energetic human beings to restore its losses and exploit its potential wealth. In the event such an influx did take place so that by the date of Henry I's death there were some 39 tenants holding of the archbishop by knight service, obliged between them to provide just over 40 knights in aiding the archbishop to fulfil his obligations. These details are known to us through the archbishop of York's reply in 1166 to Henry II's demand for details of the enfeoffments made by his tenants-in-chief ; the reply includes the explanation that "we have indeed more knights enfeoffed than are necessary for that service as you may learn from what follows. For our predecessors enfeoffed more knights than they owed to the king, and they did this, not for the necessities of the royal service, but because they wished to provide for their relatives and friends"[10].

To which of his predecessors archbishop Roger was addressing his retrospective rebuke it is now impossible to determine since the relevant documents simply have not survived. Certainly Thomas the Elder is reputed to have caused distress to his successors through his prodigal distribution of lands[11], and archbishop Gerard was also accused of having impoverished the archbishopric[12]. And it would seem that by the time of Thurstan's election at least those tenants with the greater obligations towards the archbishop had

---

9. D. Knowles, *The Monastic Order in England*, p. 702.
10. *The Red Book of the Exchequer*, p. 412.
11. William of Malmesbury, *Gesta Pontificum*, pp. 257–8.
12. Eadmer, *Historia Novorum*, p. 200.

already been given their lands ; the representatives of the Aumale family, for instance, of the FitzHerberts, and the Lascies and the de Verlies[13]. And we know that the office of provost of the archbishop's lands had already been established in the time of the second Thomas, for we find Nigel the archbishop's provost witnessing one of his grants not long before he himself took the monastic habit at Selby[14]. Nigel's son, Gilbert, succeeded to his father's lands and in 1166 was reckoned as owing two knights' service to the archbishop's quota ; but there is no indication that he succeeded to his father's office of provost. But we do know that Thurstan acknowledged the office and lands of the *dapifer* to be hereditary because a charter of his has survived in which he increased its endowment by granting to William his *dapifer*, and his heirs, some land in Halton (modern Halloughton) in addition to the third of a knight's fee which William already had, there[15]. Though in this case the land did not pass out of archiepiscopal control since after William the *dapifer's* death, in the reign of Henry II, Roger of York took the land and transformed it into a prebend of Southwell Minster[16]. Whether William had died without heirs or whether Roger had cassated Thurstan's grant is not revealed by the documents. Nor do they enable us to name the other officials in charge of the church's lands, though it is possible that the two and a half knights' fee of Thomas de Everingham carried with it the obligation to perform the office of butler on the day of the archbishop's enthronement since his successors held his manor by doing so[17]. The most that can reasonably be supposed about the exploitation of the archiepiscopal lands in Thurstan's day, in fact, is that it contributed to the steep curve of prosperity that marks the increased income from these manors between 1086, when they were valued at £166, and the 1180's, when £1,100 is an approximate figure for their yield in income[18].

---

13. *E Y C* III, pp. 76–78 ; C. Lloyd, *The Origins of Some Anglo-Norman Families*, p. 110 ; *Red Book of the Exchequer*, pp. 398–9.

14. *E Y C* I, nos. 25 and 45.

15. *Cf* Appendix I (a) (x).

16. *Monasticon*, VI, iii, 1314–15, bull of Urban III referring to "Willielmo bonae memoriae, Turstani quondam Eboracensis archiepiscopi dapifero."

17. J. Hunter, *South Yorkshire*, p. 82.

18. *E Y C* I, pp. 46–47 ; Miss Howell (*Regalian Right in Medieval England*, p. 35) points out that "the evidence for York's [Domesday Valuation] is too incomplete for a useful assessment," but *ii* able to show that during the vacancy of the see in Henry II's time it was capable of rendering a profit of approximately £1,000 annually.

However, secular officials were not the only ones who required sustenance from these lands. Thurstan's own household clerks had to be provided for ; we know the names of two of them—Ansfred and Richard[19]—but not what endowments they received. The canons of the Minster likewise could lay claim to their archbishop's beneficence, and these claims had already been well recognized in the form of prebends for their support. How this first happened is best described by Hugh the Chanter, who writes of Thomas I : "The canons had long lived in common, but the archbishop, after taking advice, determined to divide some of the lands of St. Peter's which were still waste into separate prebends, to leave room for a growing number of canons, and so that each of them might be eager to build on and cultivate his own share for his own sake. This was done. He then appointed a dean, treasurer, and precentor, endowing each of them as befitted the church, himself, and their individual dignities"[20]. The list of prebends probably instituted by Thomas I in this way included those of Holme, Grindale, Warthill, Upper Poppleton (later Givendale) and Sherburn[21] ; to this list were added two more by his namesake, the younger Thomas, but their titles are not known[22]. A further prebend founded before Thurstan's time was that of Laughton just on the Yorkshire side of the shire boundary with Nottinghamshire ; Queen Maud was the donor in this case (though it illustrates the chancy nature of some of these gifts that her husband, the king, had already given the very same church to the canons of Blyth ; they had, however, to concede it to York in 1107)[23].

The prebends seemingly added by Thurstan were at Salton, Weighton and Bramham. Salton, situated in the valley of the Rye a few miles below Helmsley, was granted to the canons of Hexham so that they would have a stall in the mother church at York[24] ; it was one of the richer prebends, being assessed in the 1291 valuation at £53/6/8d. The church of Weighton (along with the churches of Wallop and Grately in Hampshire) was granted by King Henry to William FitzHerbert in 1133 at Westminster[25] ; he was to hold it

---

19. *E Y C* I, no. 218 and *E Y C* VI, no. 9.
20. *H C* p. 11.
21. C. T. Clay, *York Minster Fasti*, II, p. 1.
22. *H C* p. 32.
23. *Regesta* II, nos. 598, 675, 704, 720, 807–8. The story remains to be written of the litigation between monastic foundations caused by careless donors ; on Maud's confusing liberality see the subtle observations of William of Malmesbury, *Gesta Regum*, II, pp. 494–5.
24. *E Y C* I, no. 146 ; *Priory of Hexham*, p. 58.
25. *E Y C* I, no. 132 ; *Regesta* II, no. 1759.

for life. Thurstan, who was present on this occasion, may well have crowned this gift by offering a stall in his Minster to the holder of these churches, who was also the treasurer, though this is not certain. It is certain that Thurstan did put such a seal on Robert Fossard's gifts to Nostell priory : in the 1120's Fossard gave to Nostell the churches of Bramham, Wharram-le-Street and Lythe and at his request Thurstan constituted them a prebend for the support of the Nostell canons[26]. If we add these three prebends to those previously mentioned and then recall what slender traces some of them have left from these early days, it is reasonable to put the number of prebends established by 1140 at a long dozen.

The dozen or so canons maintained by the prebends were obliged in return to serve God and St. Peter in the Minster at York, specifically by singing divine service in the choir and more generally by helping the archbishop to maintain the fabric of Christianity in the city and in the diocese. Together they constituted the diocesan chapter and the ablest or best-connected of them were selected to serve as office-holders of the chapter ; that is, the dean, the treasurer and the precentor or chantor. The dean was the senior of them and acted as spokesman for this odd corporation ; the treasurer, obviously, was the one who looked after the finances ; whilst the chanter not only supervised the liturgical offices but also, by a logical extension of his care for the liturgical books, acted as literary adviser-at-large. There was a fourth office, that of master of the schools, which the elder Thomas had established[27] but which did not carry with it the same status as the other three—though the master of the schools was chosen to help lobby the Pope in 1119[28], and his position was given an extra boost when Thurstan assigned to the schools 100/–s. yearly from synodals and the Rome penny[29].

Each of these offices named was filled in Thurstan's time by men of considerable distinction. For the greater part of his episcopacy the dean was Hugh, who had already been serving in that post for twenty-one years before Thurstan's arrival in York ; he had played the dominant role in securing the election of the younger Thomas to York in 1108 and had worked hard both in Rome and at the English court to prevent Canterbury from taking advantage of Thomas' easy-going nature[30]. A man of wealth and learning, Hugh

26. E Y C II, no. 1012.
27. H C p. 11.
28. H C p. 70.
29. E Y C I, no. 144.
30. He went twice to Rome, H C, pp. 17 and 22.

collected for himself a private library of sacred scripture and took a
scholar's interest in the history of the diocese[31]. He played a less
prominent part in affairs during Thurstan's time, and the two of them
had a fundamental disagreement in the 1120's when Hugh was
guilty of non-residence and Thurstan felt obliged both to reprimand
him and to mention his misbehaviour to the Pope[32]. However,
they seem to have achieved reconciliation since Hugh later came to
the rescue of Thurstan's foundation at Fountains by offering both
himself and his wealth to the Cistercian order. After his entry into
the order he was succeeded as dean by a cleric of equal ability,
William of St. Barbara, whose career shows him also to have been a
friend of the Cistercians though no less a friend of moderation[33].

Serving as treasurer throughout the whole of Thurstan's
episcopate was William FitzHerbert, another man of wealth and
standing, whose father was chamberlain to King Henry I ; William
at this time, in fact, appears to owe everything to his family connexions and in his own person makes little mark upon affairs ; few
could have foreseen that his personality would eventually secure
his elevation to the church's altars as St. William of York. Which
of William's colleagues was chanter in 1114 it is not possible to say
definitely but the signs are that he was a man of culture. These
signs take the form of verses written into the Mortuary Roll of
Matilda, daughter of William the Conqueror and abbess of Caen
who had lately died ; following the pious custom of the time clerks
were journeying from one centre of religion to another invoking
prayers for Matilda's soul ; the responses to their petitions, recorded
on the mortuary roll which they bore with them, are accompanied
by sententious verses on the subject of death and vanity which were
usually written by the chantor of the religious institution where they
were staying. The verses that were thus contributed by St. Peter's,
York, lack nothing in vigour and pungency ; they begin :—

> Heu ! Res crudelis, res dirae conditionis !
> Pallida mors regum turres inopumque tabernas
> Sorte pari pulsat, nec eam quis munere placat[34].

---

31. Cf the letter of Symeon to Hugh on the history of York archbishops.
     Symeon of Durham, Opera I, p. 226.
32. H C Y III, p. 48.
33. Cf G. V. Scammell, Hugh du Puiset, p. 20 ; Priory of Hexham (s.a. 1143),
     p. 142 : Erat enim grandaevus, scientia litterarum prudentia animi, et
     honestate conversationis episcopali dignus officio.
34. Rouleaux des Morts (ed. L. Delisle), p. 199.

The skill of these hexameters favours the notion that they were the work of Hugh Sottewain, who was certainly the chanter later in Thurstan's episcopate and who could turn an adroit elegiac composition whenever the occasion demanded. In addition to epitaphs on the York archbishops, Thomas and Gerard, Hugh also wrote a poem on the battle of the Standard and a long discursive one on the theme of true and feigned friendship, riches and poverty, tyranny and just governance, and similar matters dear to the hearts of moralists throughout the ages[35]. He was also the author of the history of the archbishops of York which we have often quoted and which is one of the most skilful pieces of writing to emerge from England in the twelfth century ; so there is plenty of material extant to give us the feel and texture of his personality.

---

35. Wright, *Satirical Poems of the Twelfth Century*, II, pp. 219–229.

It has also come to be accepted that Hugh was the author of a poem attacking the Cluniacs (*cf* Raine, *H C Y* II, p. xxiii ; Cantor, *Church, Kingship and Lay Investiture*, p. 295 ; Johnson, *H C*, p. ix) ; but it is quite clear if one examines the MS where this poem is said to be found that the MS does not justify the attribution. It is Cotton Vitellius A XII, where on fo. 133r occur the verses printed by Wright (as above), but there are other pieces by different authors before one reaches fo. 135r, where the verses are to be found which begin, *Forma fuit quondam Cluniacus religionis*, which there is no reason to think Hugh composed.

According to James Raine (*The Priory of Hexham*, p. 90n), Hugh was also the author of a lamentation for Wulgrinus the organist. Here Raine is following William Camden, the Antiquary, who wrote (W. Camden, *Remains Concerning Britain*, 1674, repr. 1870, p. 402) : "It may be doubtful whether Wulgrine the Organist was so good a Musician as Hugh, Archdeacon of York, was a Poet, which made this epitaph for him ; " followed by eight lines to Wulgrinus. The MS in which these lines occur is Bodleian MS Digby 65 where on fo. 11 are to be found the verses printed by Wright (as above), but the lines on Wulgrinus were from fo. 73v–74r, and again there is no reason to think that Hugh composed them. But since Raine and Camden give only eight lines of the lamentation, I have thought it worthwhile to give the whole of it here :—

Te uulgrine cadente cadunt vox organa cantus
Et quicquid gratum gratia vocis habet
Voce lira modulis sirenes orphea phebum
Tres poteras equiparare tribus
Si tamen illorum non fallit fama locorum
Quod fueras nobis hoc eris eliseis.
Cantor eris qui cantor eras hic carus et illic.
Orpheus alter eras orpheus alter eris
Ergo non cantus dulcis non gratia vocis
Vulgrinum valuere tueri tempore mortis
Gallia quum gaudet gemitum normannia notum
Anglicus auditum totus dolet orbis ademptum
Pan ploravit eum planxit speciosus apollo
In quocunque chori gaudent elicone canoro
Orphea non adeo rodope non orpheus ipse
Orpheus euridicen non plus aphiona thebe
Casu cantoris cantandi cura camensis
Destituit. muse mereret in musica mestare.

Of Hugh we can confidently say that his personality is consistent throughout ; in all his comments and observations one encounters the same calm-eyed steadiness, a Stoic quality that is revealed in his predilection for all that is honest and candid and in his admiration for those who are not blown about by every wind of doctrine. All forms of hypocrisy are repugnant to him whether on the part of monks whose lives belie their name, or of bishops who seek for riches, or of kings who behave like tyrants ; on two occasions he cites the condemnation of the Pharisees who tithe mint and anise and strain out the gnat whilst swallowing the camel[36]. Here we have one of the comparatively rare Scriptural quotations in his work and it is clear that such quotations did not come easily to his mind, which was set more in the mould of the Roman satirist Persius, on whom he seems to model his verse, and with whom he shares a fondness for epigrams. Perhaps it was this strain of scepticism in his nature that prompted his mordant observations on the folly of such contemporary judicial customs as the duel and the trial by water or iron ; in his own lapidary phrase, "the guilty sometimes escape, the innocent sometimes perish"[37]. Hugh's incisive radicalism went hand-in-hand with a professional competence in matters of ecclesiastical law and procedure that cannot abide slovenly habits in others ; one instance amongst many is his scornful note on the fraudulent monks of Canterbury who did not even know "that neither does an abbot make his submission to his bishop by oath, nor a bishop to his metropolitan, but only to the supreme pontiff by customs of the metropolitan church of Rome"[38]. When we add to these traits the fact that Hugh was not in the least inhibited in his judgments on bishops[39] it says much for Thurstan's integrity that Hugh's admiration for him was unreserved.

---

36. *H C* p. 14, and *Satirical Poems of the Twelfth Century* (ed. Wright), p. 225.
37. *Satirical Poems*, II, p. 229.
38. *H C* p. 5. *Cf* also *H C* pp. 103–4. Like the good historian that he was, Hugh is careful to vouch for his authorities by telling us that the original of this letter, and of the two immediately preceding, is to be found with its "bull" attached in the church at York. It was necessary for an advocate to support his case by such evidence in view of the vogue for forgery then in swing ; though the authenticity of the letters stands out when compared, for instance, with the more extreme statements to be found in MS Lansdowne 402, 112b, quoted in *Priory of Hexham*, Illustrative Documents, p. x, of which it is rightly said : nec tabula suspicione caret (*Jaffé*, 6831).
39. *Satirical Poems*, II, p. 222 :
Immerito antistes vel episcopus ille vocatur
Qui vitae merito est quolibet inferior.
Pontificem nisi mentis inops non judicat esse,
Qui pontem populo non facit ad Dominum.

Hugh himself does not seem to have been so successful in all his duties as he was in his literary tasks, for the standard of liturgical performance at York Minster under his supervision cannot have been very high. A contemporary tells us, for instance, that the canons of York were not particularly concerned about what they sang so long as they made plenty of noise[40] ; and we can well believe this, since William of Malmesbury informs us that the elder Thomas, himself a gifted hymn-writer, could not tolerate feminine modes in music and so had deliberately fostered a tradition of virile singing at York[41]. Another complaint about the Minster which reflects on Hugh's work was that the canon of the mass in the service-books was corrupt[42] ; the charge is supported by the fact that later in the century a council at York felt obliged to order all missals throughout the diocese to be corrected from an exemplar type, particularly in respect of the text of the canon[43].

Enough has now been said of the Minster dignitaries to show that by temperament they were protected from the occupational diseases of the cathedral close : narrowness of interests and pre-occupation with internal squabbles. Moreover, they sometimes held archdeaconries in addition to their chapter-offices and this again drove them into scanning more distant horizons than those set by the city of York ; Hugh the Chanter, for example, was also archdeacon of the West Riding and the office of treasurer was united with that of archdeacon for the East Riding ; other canons held the remaining archdeaconries of Cleveland, Richmond and Nottingham. In addition, the two houses of Austin canons at Nostell and Hexham each held a prebend within the minster of St. Peter's itself, as we have seen, and so their interests would also have to be taken into consideration when any decision was to be made that bound them all. In fact, any major issue that arose in the York chapter would have to be considered from a series of widely separate points of view, as widely separated as Hexham is from Nottingham or Nostell from Weaverthorpe[44].

Divergencies of temperament were equally marked amidst the circle around Thurstan. It is clear, for instance, that administrative

40. Maurice of Kirkham, whose work is to be found in Bodley MS Hatton 92, and is discussed by M. R. James in The Salomites, *Journal of Theological Studies*, XXXV (1934), pp. 287–297.
41. William of Malmesbury, *Gesta Pontificum*, p. 258.
42. Bodley MS Hatton. 92. fo. 29.
43. Wilkins, *Concilia* I, p. 501.
44. For the archdeaconries see C. T. Clay, *York Minster Fasti*, I.

burdens in St. Peter's had by no means crushed the highest spiritual aspirations of such men as the cultured dean Hugh, who joined the Cistercians, or of Serlo and Tosti, canons of the minster who followed him to Fountains[45], or of canon Gernagot who entered the Benedictine house of Whitby[46]. On the other hand, spiritual aspirations seem hardly to have touched the soul of another canon of St. Peter's, Osbert of Bayeux, who was Thurstan's own nephew ; far from pursuing the latest idealism of Cîteaux Osbert even fell short of the obligatory norm of celibacy laid down by the Gregorian reform, and eventually he went over to the world entirely. Like Osbert, Thurstan's suffragan bishop, Ralph Nowell, and his collaborator Ranulf Flambard each begot children who were to play their part in northern clerical life[47] ; yet these lapses do not seem to have troubled the careers of any of them or to have brought any memorable rebuke from Thurstan. And one of Thurstan's outstanding achievements was his managing to hold together a team which included such different characters as Hugh the dean and Osbert of Bayeux, the sinewy Hugh the Chanter and the easy-going William FitzHerbert. It was remarkable that he should have managed them all so smoothly when one remembers the peremptory—not to say harsh and rebellious—way the chapter treated archbishops Gerard and Thomas the younger[48]. Nor can it reasonably be argued that Thurstan secured the co-operation of his entourage by over-indulgence towards them ; he was quite prepared to discipline them, as we have seen in the case of the dean. The truth is that a man of Thurstan's intelligence and experience did not prejudice good human relations for the sake of doctrinaire theories ; for example, what he had seen of clerical marriage at St. Paul's in his formative years had taught him that the custom was not the source of iniquity that some reformers imagined, and so he was prepared to keep even the married bishop Ralph Nowell beside him, sparing the weaker brethren a burden that would have overtaxed them.

---

45. *Cf* p. 180 of this present work.
46. *E Y C* I, no. 279.
47. That same Master Paulinus and his brothers, for instance, who were sons of Ralph, bishop of the Orkneys, *cf* the grant to them of Garmondsway in the county of Durham made c. 1133–40 by Geoffrey, who was now bishop of Durham, having served as chancellor to Henry I for a dozen years. (G. V. Scamell, *Hugh de Puiset, Bishop of Durham*, p. 10n & pp. 264–5).
48. Gerard's version of the dispute is given in his letter to Anselm, *H C Y* III, pp. 23–25 ; the canon's successful assertion of their traditional privileges is embodied in Henry I's confirmation of those privileges printed by Raine in *H C Y* III, pp. 34–36. Thomas' treatment is shown in *H C* pp. 15–33.

Indeed, Thurstan's solicitude for his canons was of a kind to win their hearts[49]. As an example of his tact in reconciling conflicting interests amongst them we may cite the arrangements he developed respecting prebends. To someone as versed in continental precedents as Thurstan was there loomed the constant danger that prebends would be treated like any other piece of property that could be disposed of in one's own interests just as one disposed of property in one's last testament. And this was not a long step from their becoming hereditary. The Augustinian house at Étampes, for instance, with which he was acquainted, received a prebend from a canon of Paris who simply gave it to them for the weal of his soul[50]. Hence Thurstan decreed that whenever a canon of St. Peter's died the rest of his prebend for the following year was to be made available for the good of his soul and, if need be, for paying any debts he might owe ; but this was all subject to the discretion of the chapter, with whom the last word remained[51]. A little later Thurstan was prompted to make his decree even more explicit when faced with the departure of several prebendaries into religious houses ; he now laid it down, with the chapter's assent, that any canon of York who took the habit of a monk or a regular canon should be allowed to bequeath two-thirds of his prebend for a whole year to the foundation he had joined, or to his kinsmen or to other needy persons ; or he might use the money to settle his debts. The remaining third was to be devoted to the rebuilding of the minster of St. Peter which had just suffered severely in the great fire of York. In the case of those canons who simply remained canons until death their prebends were to remain in the hands of the chapter for the space of a year[52]. Consequently the minds of the canons were set at rest whilst the prebends remained firmly in the hands of the chapter.

Besides helping to dispel financial ambiguity and embarrassment in the community at St. Peter's these decrees contained a further provision. It was that similar rules were to apply at St. Wilfrid's in Ripon, at St. John's in Beverley, St. Mary's in Southwell and St. Oswald's in Gloucester. The implication behind Thurstan's extending his decrees to these old minsters is that he saw them as extension of his *familia* at York, labourers in different

---

49. *E Y C* I, nos. 143, 144, 154.
50. B. Fleureau, *Les Antiquités de la Ville et du Duché d'Étampes*, p. 298.
51. *E Y C* I, no. 149.
52. *E Y C* I, no. 150. The date of this must be 1139 since William d'Eu witnesses as chantor, and not Hugh.

vineyards but partakers of the common fruits. The implication is confirmed when we consider the signs of his favour towards these old-established minster communities that his episcopate reveals. Thus the town of Beverley was already indebted to him, even before he went into exile, for a most generous grant of liberties he made them which is recorded in one of our earliest surviving town charters. Thurstan in this charter, with the advice and consent of the chapters at York and Beverley, granted to the burgesses of Beverley those same privileges that the men of York enjoy in their own city, including the right to exact certain tolls, as well as freedom for themselves from those tolls which the archbishop and canons of York were entitled to exact on three great feasts, two of St. John the Confessor and one of St. John the Baptist, the patrons of Beverley. They were also to be as free from toll throughout Yorkshire as were the burgesses of York themselves[53]. The added prosperity brought by such a privilege (which the canons naturally shared in) was further increased when Thurstan obtained a grant from King Henry[54] which extended their fair at the time of the nativity of St. John the Baptist from two days to five with a correspondingly extended royal protection for all those coming to buy and sell there. Welcome as these trading privileges were the main source of income for the canons serving St. John in Beverley Minster were the thraves of corn from each ploughland throughout the East Riding which were collected for them annually by their provost[55].

---

53. *E Y C* I, no. 95 : the date for this grant is revised, by Cronne and Johnson, to 1114–1116, *cf Regesta Anglo-Normannorum* II, no. 1137.
   For further benefactions to town and gown at Beverley *cf E Y C* I, nos. 94, 96, 97, 98, 99, 102 and 103.
54. *E Y C* I, no. 94.
55. "The canons of Beverley owned a large amount of land at the time of Domesday. It is probable that they were already seven in number, deriving their income, like the canons at York, from a common fund. Thomas of Bayeux is credited with the foundation of the office of provost at Beverley, as at York. (*Cf* the Provost's Book, fol. 81A (*Chapter Act Book*, Surtees Soc., I, 193) where it is attributed to the existence of quarrels among the canons over their common property). But while at York the increase in the number of canons and the assignment of separate prebends to each led to the discontinuance of the office, the provostry remained a permanent feature at Beverley. The possessions of the canons were regarded as one common prebend in which each canon possessed an annual dividend. The *corpus* of each prebendal share was regarded as consisting in the corrody of daily rations delivered from the Bedern. The most important source of income, however, was the tribute of thraves paid by each parish in the East Riding and, although in the course of time thraves from certain specified parishes were appropriated to some of the canons, the scattered nature of such property prevented the establishment of separate prebends with a fixed area. The duty of the provost was to see to the collection of the thraves, and to divide their annual proceeds. He

Continued at foot of next page

And one of the first things Thurstan did on returning from exile was to secure confirmation of this traditional right for the Beverley canons ; again, some fifteen years later, when Stephen succeeded Henry, he quickly extracted a similar confirmation from the new ruler, intent that his canons should not be left fatherless. The seven canons serving the minster of St. Wilfrid at Ripon were perhaps in greater need than those at Beverley, for Thurstan returned two bovates of archiepiscopal land to them as a supplement to their prebend, and accorded them generous tax reliefs for the benefit of their hospital[56]. He also secured for them the grant of a four days' fair spanning the feast of the translation of St. Wilfrid, with the same royal protection for those attending it as had been conferred at Beverley[57] ; indeed, Beverley seems to have been regarded as a model minster to judge by the way that the charter of privileges later secured by Thurstan from King Stephen for Ripon followed that of Beverley almost word for word[58]. For the canons at Southwell similar guarantees of their minster's privileges had been obtained on several occasions from Henry I[59], who also sanctioned the increase in the number of prebends proposed by Thurstan. The two new prebends were those of Dunham and Beckingham. The first was quite modest, a church previously given to Thurstan by King Henry[60]. The second was much more lavish since it embraced the churches at Beckingham and Larton, a plot of land in Southwell itself, as well as a considerable share in the fruits of the archiepiscopal estate of Southwell[61].

It will be noticed that in none of these cases is there any hint of Thurstan seeking to reform these minsters ; quite the contrary, he did everything he could to strengthen the *status quo* and he was perfectly prepared to work through the ancient establishments. This readiness contrasts strongly with the attitude of his successor Henry Murdac who introduced regular canons at St. Oswald's in Gloucestershire and planned to do likewise at Beverley before death

---

himself held no office in the church in right of his provostry, although he was usually admitted to one of the seven canonries. He was, in fact, the officer in whom the temporalities of the church were vested." *V C H Yorks.*, III, p. 354.

56. *E Y C* I, no. 116 ; *Memorials of Ripon* I, pp. 32–3.
57. *E Y C* I, no. 115.
58. *E Y C* I, no. 117. As at Beverley, there were seven canons also at Ripon (*V C H Yorks.* III, p. 368).
59. Southwell Minster MS. Liber Albus pp. 13, 15, 21.
60. *Ibid.*, p. 21 (*Monasticon* VI, iii, 1314).
61. *Ibid.*, p. 21 (*Monasticon* VI, iii, 1313a).

prevented him[62]. The contrast is worthy of note and its explanation may possibly rest again with Thurstan's continental experience : soon after the Council of Rheims he had seen Geoffrey archbishop of Rouen raise a hornet's nest about his ears by trying to introduce into his cathedral chapter the root and branch reforming programme of Rheims, with its insistence on celibacy, and the common refectory[63]. For an archbishop to have attempted the same reform at Beverley, Ripon or Southwell would inevitably have raised the same hornet's nest, because these places were extremely touchy about their local rights. Archbishop Gerard had made this discovery once when celebrating mass in Beverley Minster. During the course of the service one of his own servants, who had been deaf and dumb since birth, had his speech and hearing restored to him ; whereupon Gerard took the opportunity to deliver a homily about the miracle to the congregation, calling their attention to the power of St. John. However, he was hooked with his own line when one of the congregation, an eloquent man of noble English stock, stood up to assure him that they were not at all surprised by this manifestation of the saint's power, with which they in Beverley were very familiar ; rather it was the archbishop who should take the miracle to heart and stop interfering in the affairs of Beverley ; otherwise he would rue the consequences. Altogether shrewder than Gerard as well as more sensitive to the particular situation, Thurstan did not allow himself to be drawn into fruitless controversy[64].

In fact, we have positive evidence that he was prepared on his own responsibility to temper the severity of the reforming programme in accordance with the particular customs of the locality. Thus when he was leaving Rome in January, 1126 he carried with

---

62. *Priory of Hexham*, p. 166 : Zelo etiam legis ductus, dum esset ibi [i.e. Hexham], canonicis in eadem ecclesia plurimam austeritatem quarundam institutionum superaddere studuit. Idem in praebendis ecclesiae Sancti Oswaldi apud Glauocestrie canonicos regulares induxit, praelato eis priore Unfredo, litterato et religioso de conventu Lantoniae. Qui et de prebendis ecclesiae Sancti Johannis Beverlaci idem propositum animi, mortuo Turstino praeposito, gessit, quod tamen cita morte praeventus consummare non potuit.

63. *Concilia Rotomagensis Provinciae* (ed. G. Bessin) *Pars Posterior*, p. 19.

64. *H C Y* I, pp. 299–300.

him a distinctly peremptory letter from Pope Honorius[65] ordering him to set about reforming the discipline of his churches (i.e. the four minsters) and in particular he must restore the refectory at Southwell to the "good condition" in which it existed in time past. The "good condition" to which the Pope referred was the custom of sharing the fruits of the minster income amongst all its clerics, who were thus to live in common, a regulation which Archbishop Ealdred had introduced some sixty years previously. Yet a generation later we find Pope Alexander III taking it as read that the canons of Southwell may be non-resident so long as they find suitable vicars[66], and we can be sure that Thurstan had made no vigorous attempt to deny them this right.

Possibly Thurstan also recognized that the needs of an increasing population throughout the diocese could not now be met by these ancient churches of secular canons ; apart from anything else, secular canons were men of considerable social prestige and were correspondingly expensive to maintain. Progressive opinion within the church favoured in their stead the rising order of Austin canons whose brilliant success at the English court he had himself witnessed, just as he had been on close terms with the learned expositor of their ideology, Ivo of Chartres. The canons had already struck roots in Hexham, Nostell and Bridlington by the time of Thurstan's

---

65. *H C Y* III, pp. 47–8 : Si igitur decanus tuus a fraternitate tua canonice commonitus, juxta collatum sibi ecclesiasticum beneficium et officium (in) Eboracensi ecclesia assidue Deo servire contempserit, ecclesiam tuam ordinandi secundum institutiones canonicus tuae fraternitati est attributa facultas, militantibus enim non vagantibus de publico donaria conferuntur. In ecclesiis igitur tuis religionem reformare satage ; et refectorium de Suthwella, sicut temporibus (retroactis) extitit, in boni status formam restitue. Ad haec quemadmodum sancta et apostolica mater tua ecclesia personam tuam piis caritatis nexibus amplexatur et diligit, ita Beatum Petrum de beneficio quod habet de regno Angliae, nec ab archidiaconis tuis vel parochianis ulterius fraudari permittas, sed ut quae prave acta sunt corrigantur, et ne de cetero similia proveniant sollerti cautela provideas. De praebendis vero super quibus nos rogasti, si decanus tuus habet concambium, numerum canonicarum diminue. Datum Laterani, nonis Januari.

The last sentence of this papal letter, on the number of prebends, is one more of those tantalizing references which scarcity of evidence prevents us from clarifying.

66. As A. F. Leach has pointed out, "At Southwell, non-residence on the prebends must have been well established by 1170, as the Bull of Alexander III of that date especially insists on the right of the canons "to institute fit vicars, whom they please, in their prebendal churches without interference by anyone" (*Visitations and Memorials of Southwell Minster*, Camden Society, 1891).

arrival at York[67] ; but these tender shoots would have barely survived had he not protected and nourished them, whilst it was through his encouragement that the order in the early years of his episcopate made its striking foundations at Guisborough (1119), Embsay (1120, transferred to Bolton 1153–4), Worksop (1120) and Kirkham (1122) ; he gave advice and backing to Robert de Brus at Guisborough[68]. Cecilly de Rumilly at Embsay[69], William de Luvetot[70] at Worksop and Walter Espec at Kirkham[71]. It is noteworthy, moreover, that all these founders' donations included many churches that were situated on their lands, and it was intended that these churches should in future be supervised by the religious houses to which they had been donated. A field of activity for which the Austin canons were ideally suited was thus opening up before them, since it was their vocation to combine the monastic with the pastoral life ; sharing in the liturgy of their community and secure in the inspiration of their rule they would store up the interior energy to exercise a spiritual care over the souls of layfolk in the surrounding countryside.

Granted the distinctive pastoral aim of the order the ideal scheme would have been for each of these Augustinian houses spread throughout the province to have held a prebend in the mother church, thus bringing them into direct and constant contact with St. Peter's. Whether this was ever Thurstan's intention we cannot tell, but we know that he did at least bring Hexham and Nostell into the immediate family of St. Peter's by presenting to each of them a prebendal stall in the minster, with the consequence that the priors of these houses had a say in the business of the chapter. To the house at Hexham Thurstan granted the prebend of Salton, in Ryedale, and he enhanced the gift by providing for the clothing of the canons an annual rental of 100s. from the arch-

---

67. Of Hexham we have already spoken, and Nostell will be dealt with later ; proof that a religious body had taken over the church of Bridlington by 1114 is afforded by *E Y C* II, no. 1151 (a confirmation by Thurstan of the acquittance made by archbishop Thomas II to the Bridlington church of all episcopal custom). Farrer comments that there is no reason to doubt that these were Austin canons (*ibid*. p. 445). The rapid growth of Brid-lington, especially in its endowment with churches, is shown in *E Y C* I, no. 360 ; II, nos. 1152, 1155, 1222 ; III, no. 1367 ; V, no. 390.

68. *Monasticon* VI, I, p. 267. Robert de Brus speaks of the foundation having been made "consilio et ammonitione Calixti papae secundi, et Turstini Eboracensis archiepiscopi . . ."

69. *E Y C* VIII, nos. 1, 2, 3.

70. *Monasticon* VI, I, p. 118.

71. *Ibid*., p. 208 ; *cf Regesta* II, for comment and date.

deaconry of the West Riding[72]. Hexham from the very beginning had been warm in Thurstan's regard ; he was scarcely enthroned before he brought from the Augustinian house at Huntingdon a learned canon named Asketill to be prior of Hexham[73]. By the time of his death in 1130 Asketill had thoroughly justified Thurstan's choice, having won the affection of every class of people in the borders, and having built a worthy series of conventual buildings for the canons. In all this he was backed up by Thurstan who not only brought relics of the saints, and books, and candlesticks for the adornment of the church but also provided for the material prosperity of the canons by his gift of over 50 messuages in Hexham itself as well as several villages nearby, with free pannage throughout the liberty of Hexham and the tithe of all the animals within it[74]. Thurstan further endeared himself to the canons of Hexham when on two occasions he defended the priory's right to grant sanctuary within an area marked out by four crosses similar to the area around the *frithstol* at York Minster[75]. In the first case Thurstan successfully withstood the sheriff of Northumberland, Odard, who infringed the sanctuary boundaries in pursuit of his quarry ; and in the second place, before a great assembly of nobles and officials, he overwhelmed in argument Walter de Bywell, the chaplain of Bernard de Balliol[76]. No wonder that the pages of the Hexham chronicles glow with affection and praise for their steadfast patron Thurstan.

In order to set up a prebend for Nostell, Thurstan combined into one the revenues of three churches, Bramham, Wharram-le-Street and Lythe[77] ; a consequence of the house being a prebendary in York Minster was that the privilege of nominating the prior came to rest in the hands of the archbishop[78], and thus made it all the easier for Thurstan to call upon the advice and services of the prior. The priory of Nostell, in fact, may be taken to reflect the ideal that Thurstan had in mind for the Augustinian houses he favoured, and may act as a reminder of the shape that Yorkshire monasticism might have assumed had it not been for the Cistercian revolution.

---

72. *Priory of Hexham*, pp. 57–58.
73. *Priory of Hexham*, pp. 192–3.
74. *Priory of Hexham*, p. 58n.
75. *Ibid.*, p. 62.
76. This was probably on the 20th March, 1121, when the dispute over Tynemouth was being heard at York and Odard was present (Symeon of Durham, *Opera* II, pp. 260–1).
77. *E Y C* III, nos. 1466, 1467.
78. J. C. Dickinson, *The Origins of the Austin Canons*, p. 160.

The name of Nostell could so easily have come to awaken in the minds of Englishmen the nostalgic echoes and splendid visions that are instantly evoked in them by mentioning the names of Fountains, Rievaulx, Byland and Roche. Hence it is worthwhile to say a little about its early history[79].

Like many another northern house Nostell began with a group of hermits. About the year 1100 they were granted permission by Robert de Lascy to live beside the fishpond at Nostlay (Nostell) and to take over the adjoining woods, known as the woods of St. Oswald after the king and martyr of early Northumbria to whom the site was dedicated[80]. Other local benefactors were quick to follow the example of Lascy : before 1114 the king's chaplain, Geoffrey FitzPayn, had granted them the church of Tockwith along with a parcel of land, and further stretches of land were given by neighbouring worthies such as Swane son of Ailric, Henry Muschamp, William Foliot and others[81]. They even caught the eye of the distant Simon of Senlis who from the borough revenues of Bedford made an annual grant of forty shillings to the canons, as they were

---

79. Several valiant attempts have been made to clarify the early history of Nostell, e.g. *E Y C* III, pp. 133–136 ; A. Hamilton Thompson, *The Priory of St. Mary, Bolton-in-Wharfedale*, pp. 24–30. But the documents available will not permit an entirely satisfactory story.

80. *E Y C* III, no. 1425. This confirmation shows that the woods had already been granted to them before Robert de Lascy's exile (1106 (?)) ; by the date of this confirmation (1120–22) the canons were starting to assart the woods and get the open spaces tilled by men who were working for them.

81. *Cf* G. C. Ransome, *The Chartulary of Tockwith, alias Scokirk* (Y A S Record Series, LXXX, 1931, pp. 151–206) and *E Y C* III, no. 1430. Mr. Ransome dates the foundation of the cell at Tockwith to the period before 1114 ; though the grounds he gives for this early date are rather insubstantial, no. 1430 does appear to push back the foundation of Tockwith to such an early date ; also the fact that no. 1430 refers to an agreement made by archbishop Thomas II (1108–14) between the monks of Pontefract and the canons of Nostell shows how far back the formative period of Nostell goes ; by this agreement (*E Y C* III, no. 1465) the monks of Pontefract quit-claimed to the canons of St. Oswald their church of St. Oswald and a cemetery for their use and the use of their servants dwelling in Nostell, and the canons quit-claimed to the monks and their church of Featherston all ecclesiastical customs which they had received from West Hardwick.
   It is likely that as with many other religious foundations the traditional founder, Geoffrey FitzPayn, has actually obscured the work of another, the original founder, in this case a certain Everard, who was probably uncle to Geoffrey. This is suggested by Henry I's confirmation of Nostell's possessions (*E Y C* III, no. 1428) which includes in its list : "De Ebrardo unam bovatam terre in Tockwith ; " and by the similar confirmation (*E Y C* III, no. 1430) which refers to "quamdam capellam in bosco de Tocwic cum omni terra et rebus que pertinent feodo Ebrardi qui capellam eis dedit ; " and by the Pipe Roll entry (31 *Henry I*, p. 27), where Robert FitzPayn makes a composition of seven silver marks for the lands of Everard his uncle.

now called[82]. And from the far side of the Pennines came a gift made by Stephen, Count of Mortain, who presented to the canons the church of St. Oswald, at Winwick in Makerfield[83]. They were now wealthy enough to afford a guest-house for the maintenance of which they were given the church of Weaverthorpe by Herbert, son of Herbert the royal chamberlain and brother to William the treasurer of York[84]. Soon they had established the first cell of Nostell—at Hyrst in the Isle of Axholme, on land given to them by the king's confidant Nigel de Albini[85]. This cell, it is true, was only adequate for the support of one canon, but by now Nostell's star was truly in the ascendant when, in 1119, the king's favour lighted upon the canons. In that year King Henry conceded to the canons the right to hold a fair in Nostell during the two days before the feast of St. Oswald (5th August), the day of the feast itself and two days afterwards, with the usual protection for those going and coming to the fair[86]. Up to this time one cannot be sure of what rule the canons observed but the king now issued a privilege to Nostell which refers to its members as "regular canons[87], and this presumably marks their acknowledgment of themselves as Austin canons; the privilege itself promises them the reversion of the wealthy church at Bamburgh whenever its present occupant, the priest Algar, should die.

Bamburgh church, like that of Winwick, was dedicated to St. Oswald and this fact brings home to us how Nostell was borne aloft on the surge of devotion to St. Oswald that had received such tremendous impetus in 1104 when those examining St. Cuthbert's grave at Durham had also found in it the head of St. Oswald[88]. The relics of other saints found at the same time were placed in a common reliquary, but St. Oswald's head was given a special place of honour beside the body of St. Cuthbert himself whilst a separate altar was dedicated to him[89] and a special sequence in his honour was added to the fine Gradual acquired by Durham from Canter-

82. J. Wilson, *Scottish Historical Review*, VII, p. 152 ; *cf* also *Regesta Regum Scottorum*, pp. 111–112.
83. W. Farrer, *Lancashire Pipe Rolls and Early Lancashire Charters*, p. 301.
84. *E Y C* I, no. 26.
85. British Mus. MS Vesp. E. XIX. fo. 131r.
86. *E Y C* III, no. 143 ; a possible date given by Johnson and Cronne (*Regesta* II, no. 1207) is the June of 1119 ; if this is correct, as it seems, then Henry was trying quite hard to show his friendliness towards Thurstan in the lull before Rheims. Curiously, this grant does not occur in the recapitulation of 1122 (*E Y C* III, no. 1428).
87. *E Y C* III, no. 1424.
88. Symeon of Durham, *Opera* I, p. 255.

bury[90]. How profound an impression was made upon contemporaries by St. Oswald's resurrected head may be judged from the way that Reginald of Durham a generation later was able to go into the minutest detail when he was describing it along with the martyr's hand and arm which Durham also claimed[91]. Nevertheless, the events of 1104 are not enough in themselves to account for the devotion to St. Oswald in the twelfth century ; this could hardly have become so widespread as it did within a few years unless traditions about him had been preserved in many scattered places during the centuries between his death and the reign of Henry I. We are told, for instance, that the extremely elaborate description of St. Oswald's physical appearance given by Reginald was retailed to him by the master of the hospital at York, Robert, who had himself found it in some Old English verses ; hence the probability that his memory had been preserved at York[92]. There is no doubt that it was preserved between Ribble and Mersey since the Domesday entry for Winwick records that in 1066 "St. Oswald had two plough-lands exempt from all taxation"[93]. This refers to the church at Winwick in Makerfield which was dedicated to St. Oswald and where, to this day, there remain fragments of a cross that almost certainly commemorates the Northumbrian king and martyr[94]. The Domesday entry is a crucial one since we learn that soon afterwards the church in Winwick was granted to the clerics over fifty miles away across the Pennines at Nostell ; what can have prompted this gift other than the fact that Nostell was already reckoned a centre of devotion to the saint and the place to which Winwick was naturally affiliated ?[95].

---

89.   Reginald of Durham, *De virtutibus beati Cuthberti*, p. 167.
90.   Durham MS Cosin. V.V.6. fo. 5rv. This MS was kindly pointed out to me by Dr. I. Doyle.
91.   Symeon of Durham, *Opera* I (where Reginald's life of Oswald is printed), p. 379.
92.   *Ibid.*, p. 378, where Reginald says he owes the description to Robert, master of the hospital at York, who himself found it in Old English writings : Haec Robertus vir ingenuus de hospitali, quod est in Eboraco, se sic in libris veteribus Anglicis descripta invenisse retulit, cuius etiam genus dictaminis in modernae linguae modulatione rhythmico pedis metro decurrit.
93.   *Domesday Book*, 269b., Newton Hundred.
94.   *V C H Lancs.* I, pp. 262–3.
95.   L. Padgett, *Chronicles of Old Pontefract*, p. 31 : "There is a local tradition that formerly no one could be arrested at St. Oswald's Cross, in Pontefract, and a free way leading to it, with about two yards' width of land round the cross, was long kept unpaved in memory of that ancient privilege." This local tradition naturally leads to the supposition that the hundred in which Pontefract stands, *Osgoldcross*, derives its name from St. Oswald. But the editors of the *Place-Names of the West Riding of Yorkshire* (Pt. II, p. 1) make it clear that this fancy is mistaken ; the name of the hundred derives from the Scandinavian personal name Asgautr.

But these were not the only areas where his memory was held in honour. Bamburgh had long contained parts of his severed limbs, though grown careless in charge of them[96] ; Bardney in Lincolnshire treasured the veriest fragments of his bones, which, for all their smallness, retained their deep healing properties[97]. Amongst the midland English enthusiasm for the saint was sustained by his right arm, which was supposed to have been stolen from Bamburgh by a monk of Peterborough, who thus provided his monastery with its most treasured possession[98]. The miracles wrought by it at Peterborough and yet further afield are proudly described by the Peterborough chronicler, Hugh Candidus, who also tells us that he himself kissed and washed St. Oswald's right arm when in Lent, 1139[99] it was shown for veneration to Bishop Alexander of Lincoln on his coming to reconsecrate Peterborough. According to Reginald of Durham the Welsh border country was similarly favoured, where at Oswestry there still stood "St. Oswald's ash," a potent source of miracles for all who came to seek its shade or to touch and taste its leaves, and a source of peril for any who presumed to damage it[100]. The same author also tells us of the

---

96. Symeon of Durham, *Opera* I, p. 374.
97. The virtue of St. Oswald's bones at Bardney is described on pp. 368–9 of Symeon, *Opera* I : Tria vero ossa de sacro illo corpore in monasterio praefato supersunt, quae parvae tamen quantitatis existunt. Quibus tanta virtus inesse multis experimentis edocetur, quod nemo febricitantium qui aquas in quibus lota fuerint cum fide devotionis exhauserit, qui non infra triduum perfecta sanitate reparetur. Hoc enim contestantur plurimi qui ista viderunt, et quam innumeri de diversis finibus aegroti, qui tali medicamine convaluerunt. Of the church of St. Oswald's in Gloucester, p. 370 : Unde propter innumera pretiosi martyris perpetrata miracula ab indigenis magnificabatur vehementius et diligebatur attentius, quasi civitatis suae mater et domina. In illa etenim non minima pars reliquiarum beati martyris, brachium quoque sinistrum, cum parte capillorum ipsius, in antiquis temporibus honorifice erant recondita ; quae regnante nobilissimo rege Henrico primo, praesidente vero Eboracensis provinciae metropolitano Thoma Secundo, illius devotione sollicitante, de locello ubi prius fuerant in capsellam in qua modo venerantur debita reverentia ab eodem pontifice sunt translata. In qua translatione tantam mirifici odoris fragrantiam sensimus, ut mullius sapientis eloquentia tantae redolentiae vapor ad plenum valeat exprimi.
98. *Ibid.*, p. 374.
99. *Cf The Peterborough Chronicle of Hugh Candidus* (ed. W. T. Mellows), pp. 52, 83–4, 105–8).
100. Symeon of Durham, *Opera* I, p. 356 : Usque hodie etiam eius coma folio ubere et viridante vestitur, frondium copia diffuse et perlate distenditur, corticisque superficies illibata conspicitur et conservatur ; and p. 357 : Unde usque in praesenti a nemine laedi praesumitur, quia pro certo quique probatum habent, quod non sine celeri et gravissima poena expietur. Arborque ipsa sancti Oswaldi fraxinus ab omni populo terrae nominatur, nec est aliquis adeo ferocis pectoris, a quo illius ramus vel folium divelli, vel inde deferri praesumatur. Multi tamen illio languentes confluunt, et vel umbra arboris, seu tactu aut gustu folii eius vel frondis, sanitatis opem beati martyris meritis consequi consuescunt.

veneration for St. Oswald maintained at Gloucester, where the citizens regarded him as protector of their city, and where his left arm and some hairs of his head were given a worthy reliquary during Henry I's reign [101]. Finally, the saint enjoyed a place of honour in the mother church of the capital city, for there was an altar in the crypt of St. Paul's dedicated to St. Oswald which had become a focus of devotion to him[102].

Whether or not St. Oswald is to be numbered amongst the objects of Henry I's numerous devotions it is certainly true that the rise of Nostell was dramatically accelerated when King Henry ventured into the martyr's native territories in the autumn of 1122. For on this journey into the North Henry's chaplain and confessor, named Athelwold, was so captivated by what he saw of the life at Nostell that he joined the community there. In a short space of time he was appointed prior[103]. So besides Thurstan, who had

---

101. *Ibid.*, pp. 369–70.
102. *The Peterborough Chronicles of Hugh Candidus*, p. 108.
103. The close ties between Henry and Athelwold are evidenced by the sentence "cui solitus erat [i.e. Henry] confiteri peccata sua" used by Robert de Torigni in his *Chronique* (ed. Delisle, 1872) I, p. 192.
      The narrative of Athelwold's entry into Nostell is found in a fifteenth century Nostell MS that has been treated with undue suspicion. It is clear from the two bulls embedded in the narrative (*Scottish Hist. Rev.* VII, 1910, pp. 154–6) that the compiler of the fifteenth century account was working from respectable authorities. Once it is recognized, with Hamilton Thompson (*The Priory of St. Mary, Bolton-in-Wharfedale*, Leeds, 1928, p. 25) that the "Ralph Adlave" of the manuscript is probably a conflation of Athelwold with Ralph, the canon to whom Nigel de Albini gave the site of Hyrst in Axholme, then the following paragraph from the manuscript holds our interest : Igitur anno domini millesimo centesimo vicesimo primo, quidam Radulphus cognomine Aldlan', illustrissimi regis Henrici primi capellanus et confessor, dum in comitiva dicti regis versus Scociam cum exercitu properantis pro rebellibus reprimendis profectus esset, apud Pontefractum in egritudinem validam, ita quod ulterius proficisci minime potuisset.   Illic ergo usque ad reditum regis commorabatur qui, cum permittente deo aliqualiter convaluisset, cepit loca vicina recreacionis causa sive venacionis invisere, eo quod ferme multum aut plurimum habundabant et loca silvestria erant. Tandem quadam die cum recreacionis causa vel venacionis interiora silvarum penetrasset, ex instinctu spiritus sancti pervenit ad locum illum ubi capella sancti Oswaldi regis et martiris modo sita est et vocatur le Nostell, ubi invenit quoddam tugurium sive oratorium, in quo latitabant quidam heremite, ieiuniis et oracionibus iugiter insistentes, quorum monitis et alloquiis exhillaratus, dimisit in pace eos, iterum temporibus oportunis revisurus. Estuabat eciam eorum vitam et mores imitari et ex tunc licet in seculo positus vitam duxit heremeticam, distulit tamen cum eis habitare et habitum recipere usque ad reditum regis ut de gracia sua et licencia singulari mundum relinqueret et soli deo militaret. Unde negociis pro quibus rex ierat expeditis in pace cum exercitu suo Angliam ingressus Pontefractum devenit cui nimirum Radulphi propositum ipso referente notificatum est. Et licet rei publice et regi necessarius esset, rege tamen permittente et propositum suum ratificante, habitum suscepit ac ordinem et regulam sancti Augustini servare professus est, atque ex mandato regis magister et rector undecim fratrum effectus est. (*Scottish Hist. Rev.*, 1910, VII, pp. 157–8).

clearly been the moving spirit in these events, Nostell now had the backing of the king and was headed by the man who had lately been his confessor ; in addition the house had recently won the support of that great northern baron, Walter Espec ; on his lands a colony from Nostell was allowed to settle and founded the priory of Kirkham[104]. With the influence of such eminent patrons behind the house it was only to be expected that Nostell would flourish, as it did in full measure during the next ten years. By the year 1130 it had taken over churches in Northumberland, Lancashire, Leicestershire, Warwickshire, Staffordshire, Northamptonshire and Buckinghamshire. In Yorkshire, it controlled a whole complex of churches ; in the East Riding these included the wealthy group of Wharramle-Street, Lyth, Bramham and Weaverthorpe, whilst in the West Riding Nostell enjoyed almost the status of another minster through having under its wing the churches at Ackworth, Featherstone, Warmfield, Felkirk, South Kirby, Woodkirk, Batley, Adwick-on-Dearne, Mexborough, Rothwell, Tockwith and Knaresborough. Indeed the analogy with a minster is by no means far-fetched when one considers that with certain limitations the house was granted the same liberties and customs as the mother-church of St. Peter's ; it was also accorded freedom from the customary exaction of episcopal dues by Thurstan. The king for his part made a gift in perpetuity to the house of twelve pence daily which, as if to emphasize its privileged character, was to be drawn officially from the farm of the shire ; the sum of twelve pence was based upon the assumption that the house would normally contain twelve brethren, that is, the prior and eleven canons. When we add to these benefactions the numerous lands bestowed upon Nostell by leading northern nobles the whole endowment constitutes a strong argument that the development of the house, far from being haphazard, was carefully directed by Thurstan[105]. This argument is further supported by the assumption that the cells to which the houses of canons served as a nucleus would be manned by the canons who were to carry their fervour, like Paschal fire, from the mother church to its outposts[106].

---

104. At least this seems the most probable story, cf Dickinson, *The Origins of the Austin Canons*, p. 123, n.3.
105. *E Y C* III, no. 1428 : this impressive confirmation by Henry I gives one a good picture of the development of the priory.
106. J. C. Dickinson, *The Origins of the Austin Canons*, p. 232, points out that the evidence for Augustinians serving the churches they were given is very slight. But the bull of Pope Alexander III which he quotes (p. 235) assumes a basic pattern of the canons serving their churches ; and such people may well be included amongst the "omnibus fratribus Sancti Oswaldi qui extra domum in cellulis habitant" (*E Y C* III, no. 1473).

It is reinforced by the fact that other Augustinian houses, such as Kirkham, received a series of satellite churches to care for in the manner of Nostell as soon as they were founded. So consistently is the pattern repeated that we can be confident Thurstan saw each of these foundations as a spiritual power-house for his province with Nostell serving as their prototype[107].

The first results of his designs for Nostell began to appear as early as 1120 when King Alexander I of Scotland invited the canons to send a colony to establish an Augustinian house at Scone in Gowrie, the hallowed centre of Scotland's ancient kingdom and site of the ritual inauguration of its kings'. At one step, therefore, the Austin canons of Yorkshire had established themselves in Scotland. Their second step was even more decisive : in 1124 their prior, Robert by name, was promoted by King Alexander to the premier see in Scotland, the bishopric of St. Andrews[109]. For the next thirty-five years Robert was to be close to the king besides conscientiously ruling over his flock. In this pastoral task he eventually acquired the help of his brethren of the Austin canons, when they founded a house at St. Andrews and were established by Robert as the clergy in charge of the cathedral[110]. Inspired by his love for the Augustinian rule Robert also tried to draw into the regular canonical life those *céli dé*, or culdees from nearby Kilrimont whose very name reminded men of that ancient Celtic style of religious life which the Austin canons were replacing and yet renewing—very much as in Yorkshire they had grafted their rule

---

107. I agree, therefore, with Hamilton Thompson, that "the prominence given to the churches among the endowments certainly suggests that the founder had some idea that his priory might become a centre of parochial ministrations to the churches of his fee." (*Thoroton Society Transactions*, xxiii, 1919, p. 43) ; but is it not also true that churches were the things that a lay landowner could give away with least pain to himself, since it must have been awkward for him to exploit them financially ?

108. Canon James Wilson (*Scottish Historical Review*, VII, 1910, pp. 141–159) argues very convincingly for the view that Scone *was* founded by Alexander I of Scotland with the aid of canons from Nostell, though whether so early as 1115, the date given in the *Chronicle of Melrose*, is more doubtful. The foundation charter, printed by Lawrie in his *Early Scottish Charters*, no. XXXVI, is regarded by him as spurious, but Prof. G. W. S. Barrow has given some telling reasons for regarding it as substantially genuine (*Regesta Regum Scottorum*, pp. 36–37).

109. Lawrie, *Early Scottish Charters*, no. XLVIII, a grant to Scone by King Alexander I made shortly before his death in 1124 ; witnessed by " Roberto episcopo electo Sancti Andreae et Herberto cancellario."

110. The first mention of them seems to be in 1138 (Lawrie, no. CXVIII), though the official foundation date given by D. E. Easson, *Mediaeval Religious Houses, Scotland*, p. 82, is 1144 ; and the 1138 date only makes sense if they had been in occupation some time before 1138.

onto the traditional hermit life[111]. At St. Andrews, then, the wheel had come full circle for Thurstan since the days of 1122 when the Canterbury party, in the person of Eadmer, had snatched the initiative from York through having a Canterbury monk as bishop of St. Andrews and chancellor to the Scottish king. Now this position was held by a man who had been trained at Nostell and had himself borne witness to the power of the Northern English saints ; as we have already seen, he was not required to take an oath of obedience when Thurstan in 1128 consecrated him, probably because of the personal regard that existed between the two men.

The personal bonds linking Yorkshire to the Scottish court were further strengthened about this time (c. 1128) when one of the outstanding young men of the court himself joined the Austin canons, entering their priory at Nostell. Waltheof, the young man in question, was the son of Simon de Senlis, the Nostell benefactor, and of Matilda, the daughter of the old English Earl of Northumbria. When Simon died Matilda made a second marriage, to King David of Scotland, who thus became Waltheof's stepfather. David introduced Waltheof to the talented company he had gathered around himself at court which could pride itself on such characters as Henry, his own son, and Ailred of Hexham who later became abbot of Rievaulx. In such a circle, still dominated by the memory of St. Margaret, it is hardly surprising that in his childhood Waltheof should have played at being a priest and as he grew to manhood should have been marked down as a future bishop for Scotland. But it was not to be. The fame of Nostell had already reached Waltheof's ears and he sought admittance there rather than have a bishopric thrust upon him ; and its reputation was sufficient to still any doubts that might have been raised from the side of his parents[112].

Waltheof's welcome at Nostell, and Robert of Nostell's promotion to St. Andrew's only became comprehensible against a background of personal contacts between Scotland and York ; and it is this background which explains why Thurstan's next move in his re-ordering of the province was so surprisingly successful. For

---

111. Easson, D. E., *Mediaeval Religious Houses, Scotland,* p. 191. Just as at Carlisle Athelwold was to combine the offices of prior and bishop so, apparently, did Robert at St. Andrews, to judge by some words of Reginald of Durham. After retailing the story of a miracle performed by St. Cuthbert Reginald continues : Hoc miraculum venerandus vir Rodbertus Prior de Nostle, postmodum Prior Sancti Andreae, fratribus nostris in claustro Dunelmensi retulit. (*De virtutibus beati Cuthberti, S S,* I, p. 56).

it is surprising that neither King David nor his vassal Fergus of
Galloway objected to the revival in 1125 of the ancient see of
Whithorn. This was a see that had gained celebrity in the eighth
century when it was joined in close friendship with the see of
York[113]. Its cathedral was situated in a territory that contained
a fascinating amalgam of races : men of British stock and Roman
tradition had held the area in the sixth century ; their descendants
in the eighth century had fallen under the sway of Northumbria
and in the following generations had absorbed wave after wave of
Norsemen, Irishmen and Scots. Most likely the blood of all these
races ran in the veins of their present ruler Fergus. And this variety
of bloods was almost matched by the range of political overlords
that Fergus might look to for protection or alliance ; King David
was the most obvious protector, but should the two of them quarrel
then Fergus could seek security through allying himself with Olaf,
King of Man, or Somerled lord of Argyll, or even with the king who
claimed lordship over both Man and the Western Isles, the distant
king of Norway.

By what manoeuvre the see of Whithorn was so peaceably
inserted into this kaleidoscopic array of principalities and powers
is not easy to see. It may be significant that it took place in the
very year that John of Crema made his legatine tour through
England, and in the course of which he also visited King David in
Scotland. If it was the legate in consultation with Thurstan and
David who did make the arrangements for a certain Gillae-Alan to
become bishop of Whithorn this would also account for the speed
with which Pope Honorius II acted in support of Thurstan. For in
the December of 1125 Honorius ordered Gillae-Alan, the elect of
Whithorn, to go to his metropolitan Thurstan to receive consecration at his hands and thereby acknowledge the subjection of his see
to York[114]. Not only did Gillae-Alan go to Thurstan, he also
adopted a means of manning his cathedral that Thurstan must

---

112. *Cf Acta Sanctorum*, August, Vol. I (pp. 241–277), p. 254.
113. *Cf* St. Boniface, from Germany, applying to the bishop of Whithorn,
      Pechthelm, for information about the prohibited decrees of marriage
      (*H & S*, III, p. 310) ; and the pupils of Alcuin at York who sent him
      verses in praise of the saint of Whithorn, Ninian (W. Levison, *England and
      the Continent in the Eighth Century*, 1946, p. 147).
114. *H & S*, II, I, p. 24 ; *Jaffé*, no. 7225 ; Honorius . . . etc., Cui alii a Domino
      preesse conceditur, nulla suis digne subesse prelatis superbia convincatur.
      Ideoque per presentia scripta tibi mandamus, ut ad karissimum fratrem
      nostrum T(urstinum) Ebor. Archiepiscopum tanquam ad proprium
      metropolitanum tuum consecrandus accedas ; et ab ipsius manu presente
      Sancti spiritus gratia cum humilitatis devotione consecracionem accipias.

clearly have approved of : he introduced at Whithorn a body of regular canons to serve the needs of an area that could certainly never have afforded to maintain a body of secular clerics in its cathedral. Whether these regular canons were actually Augustinians we cannot say ; all we know for certain is that they were replaced later in the century by Premonstratensians[115].

Yet a further instance of Thurstan extending his jurisdiction westwards into this curious Norse-Celtic complex is found in his dealings with Fergus of Galloway's son-in-law, King Olaf of Man. Possibly Thurstan was already acquainted with Olaf, who had been brought up at the court of Henry the First[116] ; in any case, the opportunity for closer liaison arose about 1130 when Olaf turned away from his alliance with the earls of Orkney and initiated a good-neighbour policy towards Fergus by marrying his daughter Aufrica[117]. Soon afterwards, the fame of the Savigniac monks having spread to Man, Olaf sent messengers to the abbey of Furness on the coast opposite Man offering the monks a stretch of land on the island for the establishment of an abbey[118] ; the offer was accepted. The subsequent agreement was officially ratified in a letter that Olaf sent to Thurstan[119]. Grandiloquently phrased, the

---

115. C. A. R. Radford in *Transactions of the Dumfriesshire and Galloway Nat. Hist. & Antiqu. Society*, XXVII (published 1950), p. 104. Mr. Radford also claims that "the Romanesque Church at Whithorn dates from the time of Gillealdan."
116. *Manx Society*, XXII, p. 61.
117. A. O. Anderson, *Early Sources of Scottish History*, II, p. 226.
118. It is possible that Olaf and Thurstan had already been in negotiation over the land the king was presenting since a note has been preserved in the Coucher Book of Furness to the effect that Olaf had previously offered it to Rievaulx, which was unable to accept. Such negotiations would have gone through the archbishop's hands, who might very well have suggested Furness as an alternative to Rievaulx (*cf Coucher Book*, I, pp. 11-12 : Certa terra in Mannia data fuit Abbathiae de Rievalle ad construendam Abbatiam de Russia. Postea tamen data fuit Abbatiae de Furnesio ad construendam eam de Ordine Cisterciensi ubi modo situata est, et sic non de Rievalle sed de Furnesio exivit). But the note is in a late compilation and is an isolated statement without other backing.
119. *H C Y* III, pp. 58-9 : ... De cetero significamus vobis, quod dominus abbas E. Furnes' coenobii, a cuius finibus non longe per mare distamus, audientibus nobis famam religionis eiusdem loci, tripartita petitione, persuasioneque nostra, iter, quamvis arduum, tamen confidenter ingressus, compensato itaque et itinerandi onere laborioso et labore super ecclesia dilitanda fructuoso, Domino inspirante, ad nos usque pervenit. Denique et nostro decreto, et plebis consultu sancitum est inter nos, ut ex suis pontifex eligeretur, qui Christianitati per insulas gentium propagandae praeficeretur. Quapropter ad vos conclamamus, vestraeque benignitatis gratiam humiliter imploramus, quatenus impositione manuum vestrarum ratum fiat quod de communi diligentia tam provide procuratum est fieri, ad honorem Dei, et salutem animarum nostrarum, scilicet ut episcopus noster ad episcopi gradum sub auctoritatis vestrae signaculo pro Dei

Continued at foot of next page

letter frequently invokes the inspiration of the Almighty, who has
exalted Thurstan above all his neighbours both in dignity and
sanctity, his reputation spanning the earth ; it goes on to explain
that Olaf and Eudo, the abbot of Furness, had come to an arrangement by which Olaf's kingdom was in future to have a bishop, and
that the bishop was always to be chosen from amongst the monks
of Furness. Thurstan's role in the arrangement is made clear when
Olaf asks him to consecrate his new bishop because the abbot of
Furness[120] had stated emphatically that he would entrust the
consecration to Thurstan and to no other. In large measure Olaf's
ambitious plans for the church in his kingdom were realized ; on
the land he had donated to Furness in the south-eastern corner of
the island there arose the impressive new abbey of Rushen ; hence-
forth also the bishops of Man, from their cathedral perched upon
St. Patrick's Islet overlooking Peel harbour, were to be spiritual
governors of both Man and the Isles for the rest of the Middle Ages.
But we do not know the name of the person consecrated bishop by
Thurstan[121], and though his successor likewise went to York for
consecration in 1151, Olaf's hopes of orientating his bishops towards
York were disappointed in the following generations as the bishops
of Man and the Sudreys oscillated in their loyalties between York
and Dublin, and Norway and Scotland.

Intriguing though they may be, however, these successes for
Thurstan's policy at Whithorn and Man remain of secondary interest
when compared with the major stroke of his policy in the north-west :
the establishment of a see at Carlisle. According to the story the
diocese of Carlisle was first conceived in 1122 when King Henry

amore et nostri, quamcitius fieri potest, promoveatur. Narrante nobis
igitur domino abbate tam mira tamque sancta de vobis, dicenteque se
nolle nec posse ad alium quempiem ire nisi ad vos, patrem suum, gaudio
magno repleti, pro universis gratias Deo nostro, prout potuimus, persol-
vimus. Valeat sanctitas vestra in Domino.

120.   His name was Eudo de Sourdeval, and he was the first witness to the
       foundation charter of Rushen (*Manx Society*, VII, p. 3). His surname
       suggests that, like his predecessor, the first abbot of Furness Ewanus de
       Abrincis (i.e. Avraches) Eudo came from the home area of the Savigniacs
       since Sourdeval lies in the hinterland of Avranches. A family of Surdevals
       held an under-tenancy of the Ros fee in Yorkshire (*E Y C* X, p. 149) and
       members of it witnessed Walter Espec's charters to Kirkham (*Monasticon*,
       VI, 209) and Rievaulx (*Rievaulx Chartulary*, no. 42).

121.   If we were to accept Raine's dating of the letter he prints on pp. 59–60 of
       H C Y III, even approximately, we could say that his name was Nicholas.
       But the letter clearly belongs to a later date—to a time when the see of
       York was vacant and the king of Man had therefore to address himself
       to the dean, and at a time when the king of Man was quarrelling with the
       monks of Furness.

was making a survey of his northern borders. In Cumbria he discovered to his great indignation that bishop John of Glasgow was carrying out episcopal functions well to the south of Solway Firth—in areas that Henry regarded as English beyond doubt. As a result Henry devised a plan for a diocese of Carlisle that would block bishop John's incursions into English territory[122].

Though King Henry certainly was in northern England in this year the story just quoted represents a drastic simplification of a more subtle and long-term process by which north-west England was brought more securely into the orbit of York influence. From the York viewpoint it was an initial advantage that the only area of Cumberland recorded in Domesday, the area between the Esk and Duddon Sands, was for the practical purpose of that compilation regarded as part of Yorkshire. This advantage was driven home in the reign of William Rufus by the influx of Normans, Bretons and Flemings to the area whose loyalties and family connexions were not embedded in local dynasties or fixed upon Scotland but stretched towards the south and centre of England[123]. Not that this strengthening of temporal lordship over the area in itself prevented it from remaining in ecclesiastical terms something of a no-man's-land. Strictly speaking the district around Carlisle lay within the jurisdiction of one of the York archdeacons, the archdeacon of Richmond[124] ; yet, as we have seen, the bishops of Glasgow could on occasion exercise episcopal functions there, and it seems even to have been with York's approval that bishop Michael of Glasgow (1109–14) helped to dedicate churches as far south as Westmorland ; and a claim to ecclesiastical jurisdiction over the area could still

122. Fordun, *Scotichronicon* VIII, 3.
123. *Anglo Saxon Chronicle*, s.a. 1092 ; also : "Immigration from the south at this time [1093], or shortly after, is well illustrated by the occurrence of a fair number of names ending in -by to which a Norman, or at least a Continental Germanic personal name is prefixed. The thickest concentration of these -by names is naturally in Carlisle and its immediate vicinity— Botcherley, Etterby, etc. Some of them were Bretons such as the Alein and Wigan who gave their names to Ellonby and Wiggonby, some of them Flemings such as the people who gave their name to Flimby or the individual Lambia after whom Lamonby is called." (*The Place-Names of Cumberland*, Vol. III, pp. xxi–xxii).
124. *The Place-Names of Cumberland*, Vol. III, p. xxxv : The barony of Copeland was not included in the diocese of Carlisle, remaining like Kendal and Kirkby Lonsdale in the archdeaconry of Richmond. (*Cf* C. M. L. Bouch, *Prelates and People of the Lake Counties*).

have been made by the bishops of Durham, since they had years ago inherited the rights of the bishopric of Lindisfarne which itself, centuries before, had stretched as far westwards as Carlisle[125].

It was not episcopal agreements, however, that gave the ecclesiastical development of the north-west its decisive turn but the pressure of monastic growth. A mark of this pressure was the foundation shortly before 1100 of the monastery of Wetheral some four or five miles down the Eden Valley from Carlisle on the road that led south through Appleby to York. The prior and six monks who formed the nucleus of the new community themselves came from the flourishing Benedictine abbey of St. Mary's at York ; their land at Wetheral had been given to them by one of St. Mary's most distinguished patrons, Ranulf le Meschin[126]. In addition, moreover, to the manor of Wetheral and the valuable fish-ponds on the river the priory was granted, through its mother-abbey of St. Mary's, the same rights of sanctuary as were enjoyed by those ancient centres of holiness at St. Peter's, York and St. John's, Beverley[127]. About the year 1120 the priory also received from Ranulf the churches of St. Michael and St. Laurence in Appleby, a town which served as the strongpoint in the screen of defences against Scottish attempts to penetrate into England[128]. Already

---

125. *H C Y* III, p. 37 : Thomas, Dei gratia Eboracensis episcopus, Algari clerico salutem. Ipse tibi ore ad os prohibui, cum per te crisma et oleum ad Glasguensem ecclesiam misi, ne crisma vel oleum illud dares in parrochiam Dunelmensis episcopi ; tu vero illud, contra defensionem meam, in Tevegecdale dedisti, de qua ecclesiam Dunelmensem saisitam inveni. Mando igitur tibi, et episcopali auctoritate prohibeo, et omnibus presbyteris de Tevegecedale, ne de crismate et oleo aliquod ministerium amodo faciatis, nisi per octo dies tantum postquam breve istud videritis, ut interim requirere possitis crisma a Dunelmensi ecclesia, quae vobis illud dare solita est. Quod si post illos octo dies de crismate quod misi aliquam Christianitatem facere praesumpseritis, a divino officio vos suspendo donec diratiocinatum sit ad quam ecclesiam pertineat. This letter is to be dated circa. 1112.
126. Here, as so often in these parts, it was the feminine touch that set the ball of benefaction rolling : Ranulf had married Lucy, daughter of Ivo Taillebois, who had endowed St. Mary's, York, with churches and tithes in what was afterwards the barony of Kendal, which he held immediately to the south of the territory of Ranulf. (*Priory of Wetheral*, p. xiii).
127. *The Register of the Priory of Wetheral* (ed. J. E. Prescott), p. 18.
128. *The Register of Wetheral*, p. 10. Cronne and Johnson suggest that Henry's confirmation of this grant was made at Reading in the spring of 1116 (*Regesta* II, no. 1130).
       Cf M. W. Beresford, Mediaeval Town Plantation in the Carlisle Area, in *The Archaeological Journal*, CXV (1958), pp. 215–217, on Appleby and Church Brough (founded c. 1092–1100 by William II). Of the latter he writes : "The new town was placed outside the castle on the eastern edge of the Roman fort of *Verterae* within whose banks William II's castle had been built as one of a line of defences along the Stainmore Road into Scotland after his acquisition of Westmorland and Cumberland in 1092."

equipped with a formidable Norman castle and with its streets so planned that it could quickly convert itself into a fortress, Appleby's reception of Benedictine monks as patrons of its churches must have made it a striking symbol of Norman ways in the debatable lands ; the castle and the church, the lay lord and the monks were intimately joined in the task of transforming an anarchic society into one that might please the Norman eye for orderliness.

About the same year (1120) two more religious foundations were made by members of the same group that had been so generous to St. Mary's and Wetheral ; these were St. Bees on the Cumberland coast and Embsay, near Skipton, on the road out of Yorkshire into Westmorland. It was Thurstan who inspired William Meschin, brother to the founder of Wetheral, to make a substantial grant of lands and tithes and churches for the erection at St. Bees of a cell dependent upon St. Mary's, York[129]. The new community, like Wetheral, was to have a prior and six monks from the mother house. The other foundation made at this time, Embsay, also owned William Meschin and his wife, Cecily, as its founders, but unlike Wetheral and St. Bees it was not Benedictine but Augustinian. As the land it received in Embsay and the church and chapel it received in Skipton were held by Cecily in her own right we can reasonably infer that it was she and her friend Thurstan who first conceived the notion of establishing a house there[130] ; but husband and wife were united in their devotion to religion and, fittingly, it was through the good offices of Cecily's husband William that Augustinian canons came from Huntingdon to man the house at Embsay[131].

Within the space of a few years, therefore, Thurstan had seen three strongpoints of York influence established in the north west of his diocese. To these three must be added the monastery at Furness, whose early story is full of tantalizing glimpses of Thurstan's influence. The story begins with the holy man Vitalis who had been born near Bayeux and became chaplain to the count of Mortain. At one period Vitalis came on a preaching mission to England (1102)

---

129. *The Register of the Priory of St. Bees* (ed. J. Wilson), pp. 28–33 and p. 107. Thurstan's influence is writ large on every one of these grants ; he was present personally, with his archdeacon William, and his two chaplains Ansfred and Richard, for nos. 2, 3, 5 and 6 ; each of them contains the characteristic formula, Pium est ut sancta Dei ecclesia a filiis et fidelibus suis dilatetur et amplificetur. Eapropter dedi . . ." etc.

130. *E Y C* VII, pp. 53–58.

131. *E Y C* VII, p. 6.

where he had already gained support at the court before he returned
to institute his new order at Savigny. There he laboured until his
death when he was succeeded as abbot at Savigny in 1122 bv
Geoffrey of Bayeux who two years later sent a colony of Savigniac
monks to found Tulketh, near Preston ; the land they took over
had been granted to them by Count Stephen of Mortain and Lancaster, Henry I's favourite nephew, and it was he again who donated
the land they occupied in 1127 when they transferred their house
from Tulketh to Furness[132]. Now Stephen and Thurstan had
known each other for years, probably even before Thurstan in 1120
accompanied Stephen's mother, Adela of Blois, to the convent of
Marcigny when she took the veil. Moreover, Thurstan had proved
himself a good friend to the monastery of Savigny when at Rome in
1125 he had obtained a privilege for them from Pope Honorius.
What more natural than that they should have collaborated in
bringing the Savigniacs first to Tulketh and then to Furness ?
The first abbot of Furness, Ewanus of Avranches, one of Savigny's
most holy and learned monks, came to Thurstan for his blessing at
the beginning of his term of office[133], and we have already seen how
his successor at Furness insisted that Thurstan was the prelate to
whom the bishop of Man should resort for consecration. And a fair
reflection of the credit for the good estate of Furness is given by the
names of those who at Rouen in 1127 first witnessed the confirmation of Stephen's gifts to St. Mary of Furness : King Henry and
Thurstan archbishop of York.

It will have become obvious from the foregoing that Thurstan's
acquaintance with the leading men of the country eased the way
for the spread of religious houses throughout his diocese. Perhaps
a word about the group of families in the north west will bring this
fact home. We have already noted the part played by the Meschin,
or Bricquassard family, who sprang from Thurstan's native
serjeantry of Bricquassard : Ranulf le Meschin establishes Wetheral,
William his brother founds St. Bees and, along with his wife Cecily

---

132. The liberal deeds of the royal circle in September, 1127 at Rouen are
       conveniently shown by nos. 1545, 1546 and 1547 of the *Regesta* Vol. II ;
       they are, respectively, a charter by Stephen to Savigny of the forest of
       Furness ; a confirmatory charter of the above grant to St. Mary in Furness,
       made by Henry I with Thurstan, Audouen, Richard of Bayeux and
       Robert of Gloucester amongst the witnesses ; a confirmation of grants
       made to the abbey of Bec, Thurstan and Audouen again being witnesses.
            The foundation of Furness and the confirmation are printed by
       Atkinson in *Coucher Book of Furness*, I, pp. 122–124.
133. *Gallia Christiana*, XI, col. 544.

de Rumilly, introduces Augustinian canons at Embsay ; the son of William and Cecily, himself called Ranulf, soon brings a colony of monks from Furness to set up another abbey on the Cumberland coast at Calder (1134). William and Cecily's concern for the religious life seems to have been passed on to their children, for one daughter married William Paynel who founded the priory of Drax, whilst another daughter married William le Gros, the founder of Meaux in the East Riding. The Bricquassards, moreover, managed to spread their concern to their feudatories, for amongst the witnesses to the earliest Wetheral charters are names that recur in other donations to the church : one of the witnesses, for instance, Waldef son of Gospatrick, also turns up as a witness to the St. Bees charters as well as making liberal donations from his own lands to St. Mary's, York, and to the priories of Carlisle and Hexham[134]. Another witness along with Waldef was Ketell, whose son married Waldef's sister ; he also occurs as a benefactor in his own right, granting to St. Mary's, York, the important church of Morland as well as the church at Workington, and bestowing land in Kirkby (Kendal) on the York hospital of St. Peter[135]. It was not a house actually in York that benefited from the generosity of a third witness, Forne son of Liulf, but it was a house intimately bound to York, that is, Hexham Priory[136]. An interesting feature about this group under the sway of the Meschins is that their differing racial origins do not seem to have constituted any barrier between them when it came to fostering monastic institutions. Perhaps the outstanding example of an English family from this group collaborating in the pious works of this newly emerging society is the family of Ailric, who at the time of Domesday held several manors in the West Riding ; his son Swane (†1130) received from Henry I an extensive lordship in Cumberland[137] whilst Swane's own son, Henry (†1172), obtained Edenhall and Langwathby from the same monarch. Swane's entourage was fairly solidly Anglo-Scandinavian to judge from the names of witnesses to his gifts—names such as Edwin the priest, Ulf the priest, Dolphin and Saxi—yet his son Adam appears to have married a close kinswoman of one of William Meschin's Norman followers, Godard de Boiville[138] ; and Adam crowned his

134. *Register of St. Bees*, p. 29 ; *Register of Wetheral*, p. 4 & n11 ; *Priory of Hexham*, p. 59.
135. *Register of St. Bees*, p. 29 ; *Register of Wetheral*, p. 6 n13.
136. *Register of Wetheral*, p. 5 n12 ; *Priory of Hexham*, p. 59.
137. *Cf E Y C* III, pp. 318-9 for the genealogy of this family.
138. *E Y C* VII, pp. 178, 183.

family's tradition of generosity towards the monks by founding a priory for the French Cluniacs at Monk Bretton in the West Riding[139]. This did not take place until after Thurstan's death, it is true, but the charter for it bearing the names of Henry, Adam's brother, Rainald prior of Wetheral, and Gospatrick son of Orm, is testimony to the links that were being forged between Cumberland and the West Riding in the early years of the century. The old Roman road between York and Carlisle must have been a very familiar one to the monks of St. Mary's as they journeyed along it to Appleby, Wetheral and St. Bees ; it must have been equally well known to William le Meschin and his wife Cecily as they travelled with their retainers from Skipton up to Millom ; above all it was the means by which intelligence of spiritual needs and temporal schemes was brought to Thurstan, the man to whom lay folk as well as monks were accustomed to turn at moments of decision.

One such moment of decision for Thurstan was reached when he executed what we have described as his "major stroke of policy in the north west," the erection of a see at Carlisle[140]. Not that he acted precipitately over the issue ; events were allowed to take their course for a number of years. The impetus was initially given to these events in 1120 when Ranulf le Meschin succeeded to the earldom of Chester and King Henry himself took over the "land of Carlisle" and reorganized it. He divided the area into the two shrievalties of *Chaerliolum* and *Westmarieland* whilst keeping Carlisle itself and the Forest of Cumberland in his own hands[141]. But quarrels and unrest in the North made it clear to Henry that he would have to make a personal survey of the area if he were to keep its inhabitants loyal. Hence his thorough tour of inspection in 1122 in the course of which he saw the threat from Scotland and so gave orders and money for the walls and castle of Carlisle to be fortified by its serjeants and citizens, who were to be engaged in strengthening their city for many years to come[142]. At the same time the incursions of John of Glasgow made Henry realize how much he

---

139. *E Y C* III, no. 1668.

140. See the clear exposition by J. C. Dickinson, The Origins of Carlisle Cathedral in *Transactions of the Cumberland and Westmorland Antiquarian and Archaeological Society*, XLV, pp. 134–143.

141. *Cf The Place-Names of Cumberland*, Vol. III, p. xxxv.

142. Symeon of Durham, *Opera* II, p. 267 ; *Pipe Roll* 31 *Henry I*, p. 140 : (of Hildreth). In Operibus Civitatis de Caerleolio videlicet in muro circa civitatem faciendo liberavit xiv libras et xvi solidos et vi denarios. Et quietus est : p. 141 : (of Richard the knight) : Et in operatione Muri civitatis de Caerleolio vi libras et ii solidos.

needed a strong diocese for his land of Carlisle ; and it is also possible that he had already fixed upon the canons at the church of St. Mary to serve its cathedral[143]. If so his plans were forwarded by two great strokes of fortune ; for soon after he had granted the manors of Linstoc and Carleton to his chaplain Walter at a cornage rent of 37/4d., Walter asked his master's permission to join the canons of St. Mary's. By granting Walter's request and allowing him to take Linstoc and Carleton along with him as an endowment, free now from cornage and all other customs, but to be held in free alms, Henry added considerably to the wealth and stability of the canons[144]. The second stroke of fortune was Athelwold's joining Nostell and subjecting himself to the Augustinian rule, for this also affected Carlisle ; within two years Athelwold had become prior of Carlisle as well as being prior of Nostell, receiving permission from Pope Calixtus II (✝1124) to double up on these offices[145] ; it was through Athelwold, presumably, that the loose association of canons at St. Mary's was now transformed into a regular community of Austin canons.

The priory at Carlisle could hardly have been in better hands. Athelwold was not only a friend and confidant of Thurstan's, he was also in the counsels of King David of Scotland ; thus we find him in David's company witnessing an acknowledgment by a

---

143. Professor V. H. Galbraith, in the appendix to the Introduction to *The Anonimalle Chronicle*, pp. xlvi–xlix, prints extracts from the Ingilby MS which date the coming of the Austin canons to Carlisle at the year 1100 ; but the MS is centuries later than the event it claims to record and there had been time for retrospective extrapolation, and the probability is that the men living a religious life in community at Carlisle from 1100 to 1122 were of the type to be found at Nostell and other places in the North at this time ; their transformation into regular Austin canons is not therefore without precedent : "Anno domini MoCmo primo ordo canonicorum regularium venit apud Karliolum. Rex Henricus primus per industriam et consilium Matildis reginae constituit canonicos regulares in ecclesia Karleoli. Quidam vero presbiter ad conquestionem Anglie cum Willelmo Bastard veniens hanc ecclesiam et alias plures et aliquas circumiacentes villas pro rebus robustissime actis a rege Willelmo in sua susceperat. Hic ecclesiam sancte Marie Karl[iolensis] fundavit et non multo post in pace quievit. Cuius terras et possessiones rex Henricus dedit canonicis regularibus et priorem eorum Adelwaldum, iuvenem quidem estate sed moribus senilem priorem sancti Oswaldi de Nollis constituit. Hunc autem Adelwaldum postea cor[v]upte Adulphum vocabant.

144. *Book of Fees* I, 199 ; & *Regesta* II, no. 1491 [1127, May-August(?)]. Notification by Henry I to the archbishop of York and all his barons and officials of Cumberland and Westmorland that he has granted to St. Mary and the canons of Carlisle all the land which belonged to Walter the Priest. They are to hold it in alms, free of cornage and all other customs.

145. J. C. Dickinson, *The Origins of the Austin Canons*, p. 249, basing his opinion very reasonably on the coincidence of a passage in the *Historia Fundationis* of Nostell and a note of Burton's in *Monasticon Eboracense*.

former canon of Nostell, Robert now bishop of St. Andrews, that the abbot and monks of the border monastery of Kelso may seek oil and chrism from any bishop they desire—"whether in Scotland or in Cumbria," a phrase that in its very casualness reveals the independent status of Cumbria in their minds[146]. Above all, Athelwold, "the man to whom the king used to confess his sins"[147], remained adviser to Henry I whose charters he continued to witness and whose generosity he continued to attract[148]. The next instalment of royal generosity came when Henry granted to the priory the reversion of a whole string of churches that were held by another of Henry's chaplains, Richard d'Orival ; this meant that on Richard's death the canons would secure control of the churches at Warkworth, Corbridge, Wittingham and Rothbury, as well as those of Newcastle-on-Tyne and Newburn[149]. A year or two later we learn that the king had ordered payment by royal writ of £10 as a gift to the canons of Carlisle so that they might build a worthy church[150].

---

146. Lawrie, *Early Scottish Charters*, No. LXXXII. Confirmation by Robert bishop of St. Andrews, of the right of the Abbey of Kelso to the church of St. Mary in Kelso (circa. 1128) : . . . ut abbas et monachi eiusdem ecclesiae a quocunque episcopo voluerint in Scotia vel in Cumbria crisma suum et oleum et ordinationem ipsius abbatis et monachorum et cetera sanctae ecclesiae sacramenta accipiant.

Testibus eodem Regi David et filio suo Henrico, Matildi Regina, Johanne Glasguensis episcopo, Ascelino Archidiacono, Adelufo Sancti Oswailla priore, Nicholao Sconensi priore, Willelmo Regis nepote, Hugone de Moruilla, Roberto de Unfranvilla et aliis.

147. *Chronique de Robert de Torigni* (ed. Delisle), I, p. 192.

148. *H C* p. 109, on the election of William of Corbeil as archbishop of Canterbury : De quo quis esset, archiepiscopus et Adeboldus prior Sancti Oswaldi, a rege antea interrogati, satis eum de sciencia et honestate et religione laudaverant ; *cf Regesta* II, nos. 1459, 1463.

149. Richard d'Orival may perhaps have been a son of Rainald d'Orival, who in the year 1115 was a benefactor to the abbey of Lessay (*Round Calendar of Docs. France*, 330). Richard was a chaplain of Henry I and held the prebend of Brownswood in the diocese of London (*E Y C* I, p. 353).

E Y C I, no. 457, Grant by Henry I to Richard d'Orival, his chaplain, of the four churches on his four royal manors of Warkworth, Corbridge, Whittingham and Rothbury, with the lands, tithes and men pertaining thereto. Dated by Cronne and Johnson (*Regesta*, no. 572) to June 24, 1102 (?), Cirencester.

E Y C I, no. 458, Henry I notifies the archbishop of York, the bishop of Durham, the sheriff of Northumberland and all his faithful men in Northumberland that he has granted to St. Mary of Carlisle and the canons of that place the churches of Newcastle-on-Tyne and Newburn ; and those churches which Richard d'Orival holds from him, after Richard's death. Richard and the clerks who serve those churches are to acknowledge the canons as their lords, and do to the canons the service which they used to do to the king ; and when they die, the churches are to pass into the hands of the canons ; in such wise that the clerks who serve them are to have a maintenance, and the canons are to have the rest. Dated by Cronne and Johnson (*Regesta*, no. 1431) to October, 1125 (?) at Rouen.

150. *Pipe Roll 31 Henry I*, p. 141.

Altogether Carlisle around the year 1130 must have been a hearten-
ing sight as it was in the process of being rebuilt on the lines of a
Norman military and ecclesiastical stronghold. If this sight
prompted Thurstan to conceive of a bishopric there it was his
familiarity with continental experiments which determined the
shape of the bishopric in his mind ; he was warned by the example
of Rouen that secular canons of the old style were not to be dislodged from the cathedral in favour of the reformed canons without
violence and heart-burning and that it was as well, therefore, to
begin with regular canons. Moreover he had the example of Séez
to encourage him to try something as yet unattempted in England,
an Austin canon cathedral : for in 1131 an old acquaintance of
Thurstan's, John bishop of Séez, had established Austin canons in
his cathedral and Henry I had confirmed the arrangement in the
presence of witnesses who had included his brother Audouen[151].
The situation at Carlisle was, in fact, ripe for the appointment of
Athelwold as bishop of Carlisle in the hope that he would organize
a diocese with the help of the Austin canons from St. Mary's priory.
By this arrangement three objects would be attained at one stroke :
the grasp of the English king and the York archbishop on the area
would be strengthened ; the claim to advancement of an outstanding personality, Athelwold, would be honoured, and the enormous
financial burden of a cathedral would be greatly lightened by
having Austin canons manning it rather than secular canons.

It was a moment of considerable triumph, then, when Thurstan
on the 6th of August, 1133, in his cathedral church of St. Peter at
York consecrated Athelwold as bishop of Carlisle at the same time
as he was consecrating the king's chaplain, Geoffrey Rufus as bishop
of Durham[152]. The fact of having Athelwold as pastor in the north-
western limits of his province must have been a special source of
comfort to him for the new bishop was highly regarded in both
English[153] and Scottish circles, and Thurstan could entrust to
him some of the diplomatic negotiations in which York was involved
with the Scottish king. Indeed there was plenty of reason in 1133
for Thurstan to feel that the major part of his work as archbishop
had already been accomplished. Twenty years previously when he
came to York even his hold upon his own see had been unsteady

---

151. *Gallia Christiana* XI, cols. 686–7 ; *Regesta* II, no. 1698. John of Séez's
uncle, also named John, was bishop of Lisieux ; he tried to do the same at
Lisieux as his nephew had done at Séez, but in vain, *cf Gallia Christiana*
XI, col. 773. The idea was clearly in the air.
152. *Priory of Hexham*, pp. 109–10.
153. *The Letters of Osbert of Clare*, ep. 9.

and upon his suffragans unsteadier still. But now the archbishop of York stood high in esteem among the episcopate and was the outstanding personality in northern England. Where his jurisdiction was questioned towards the border country he had the reliable Geoffrey Rufus stationed in Durham and his friend Athelwold watching over Carlisle. Running along the border, again, was a screen of churches that were in the hands of his associates : Newcastle, as we have seen, had been given to the canons at Carlisle along with Corbridge, whilst Bamburgh, Carham[154] and Hexham were all under the direct control of Thurstan and his circle. He had gone further than any of his predecessors of the last four centuries by reviving the ancient see of Whithorn ; and he was about to initiate the bishops of Man. Though the bishop of St. Andrews had not sworn obedience to him, still the bishop was an old subject of his from Nostell and had at least come to Thurstan to be consecrated. The only point at which his plans had completely broken down had been in the Orkneys where it had proved impossible to install Ralph Nowell ; Thurstan had tried to persuade the kings of Norway to intervene in Ralph's favour, but nothing came of it[155]. It is significant that this one complete failure should have occurred in an area where his demands received no backing from the temporal ruler, because the same explanation holds of his relative failure with bishop John of Glasgow. Thurstan may have thwarted Glasgow's expansionist aims in Cumbria, and he may have driven bishop John so hard that the harassed man went into exile, but he never managed to extract from him the oath of obedience, because Glasgow was too closely protected by King David. But in spite of this Thurstan in 1133 had plenty of cause to feel gratified at the amount of influence he now commanded twenty years after coming north.

---

154. Carham seems to have been granted both to the monks of Durham (by Queen Matilda, *Regesta* II, no. 1143) and, some years later, to the canons of Kirkham (by Walter Espec, *Regesta* II, no. 1459). And although it was the canons who enjoyed effective possession, not until 1263 did Durham finally abandon the attempt to gain something from this imbroglio of pious benefaction (*History of Northumberland*, XI, pp. 12–13).

155. *Monasticon*, Vol. VI, Pt. III, p. 1186 (from York Reg. fol. 49). Honorius II to Sigurd King of Norway : Auribus nostris intimatum est, quod venerabilis frater noster Thomas (recte Turstinus) Eborum archiepiscopus Radulphum Orcheneia ipsum consecravit. Postmodum vero, sicut accepimus, alius est ibidem intrusus. Caeterum episcopalem cathedram aut unus optinebit aut nullus. Ideoque per praesentia scripta nobilitate tuae mandamus, quatinus praenominato Radulpho sedem episcopalem Orcheneiam videlicet, cum parochia et caeteris pertinentiis suis, tanquam proprio illius loci episcopo et pastore restituas, et de caetero sollicitudo custodiat, ne ob hoc iram Dei incurrat (*Jaffé*, 7224, 9th December, 1125).

CHAPTER VI.

THE EXODUS FROM ST. MARY'S TO FOUNTAINS.

The rôle played by Nostell in Thurstan's scheme has been singled out as specially important because in the first eighteen years that he held office in the North, the Augustinians represented the advance-guard of the religious life, and so it was entirely natural for their archbishop to turn to them when arduous work was on hand. As the advance-guard of religion the regular canons attracted to their order the most gifted and generous young men of the day, men such as Waltheof, Athelwold and Maurice of Kirkham. But events now took a turn which was to rob them of their leading position and to divert promising recruits away from them—perhaps even to obscure from later historians the amount of reliance which Thurstan had placed upon them in his efforts to rejuvenate the province. This turn of events came about through the arrival in Yorkshire during 1131 of a group of Cistercians, the new order from Burgundy which had begun to sweep like wildfire throughout Europe.

The group who arrived at York in 1131 were not, in fact, the first Cistercians to settle in England ; already some three years previously, late in the year 1128, a foundation had been made at Waverley in Surrey with the blessing of the Bishop, William Giffard. But the Cistercian mother-house to Waverley was l'Aumône, a community that never attracted the spotlight as did Clairvaux under the genius of St. Bernard ; and it was the presence of St. Bernard with his restless driving spirit behind it which brought the Yorkshire group of 1131 into prominence. Nor is the phrase "the Yorkshire group" an empty one in this connection, for not only was the leader of the band, William, a Yorkshireman, but it is clear that this expedition from Clairvaux represents the gift made by the Clairvaux community in return for all the outstanding recruits it had received from Yorkshire in the preceding fifteen years[1]. Of these recruits, William was the most notable ; before entering

---

1. *Cf* D. Knowles, *The Monastic Order in England*, pp. 228-9, for the Yorkshire group.

religion he had been a master in the schools and this made him
specially qualified to serve as secretary to St. Bernard, which he was
doing as early as 1119[2]. They also included Ivo, who had been a
pupil at York of the prominent teacher, Henry Murdac, himself a
recruit to Clairvaux some years later ; and Richard, a native of
York, who was soon to be made abbot of Vauclair before returning
first to Clairvaux and then to Fountains[3]. From neighbouring
Lincoln there went the prebendary Philip, whose entry into the
Cistercian order was announced to his late master Alexander the
Magnificent of Lincoln by St. Bernard in a letter of a didacticism
that goes far to explain why certain men found St. Bernard hard to
bear[4]. One Yorkshireman who escaped St. Bernard's net was
Thomas the provost of Beverley, a young man of good family and
considerable wealth, of attractive personality and great promise[5] ;
he had been pointed out to St. Bernard as a possible Cistercian
recruit by the Ivo mentioned above and in consequence received two

---

2. He was the scribe of the famous letter of the saint to his nephew, Robert
of Châtillon, who had turned his back upon Cîteaux and returned to
Cluny, *The Letters of St. Bernard* (Translated by Bruno Scott James), p. 1.
And as Mr. C. H. Talbot has pointed out, he was a master in the schools
before entering Rievaulx ; after he became abbot one of his Continental
pupils, Guido Augiensis, dedicated a book to him ; since this was on
music and was later quoted with approval in the famous *Tonale*, it is
possible that William was concerned in the early reform of the Cistercian
chant (*cf P L*, Vol. 183, col. 1166 and C. H. Talbot, The Centum Sententiae
of Walter Daniel, in *Sacris Erudiri* XI, 1960, p. 269).

3. *Memorials of Fountains*, p. 108.

4. *Letters of St. Bernard*, no. 67 : "To the honourable Lord Alexander, by
the grace of God, Bishop of Lincoln, that he may desire honour in Christ
rather than in the world, from Bernard, Abbot of Clairvaux."
    The saint goes on to explain that Philip, a canon of Lincoln, on his
way to Jerusalem, had taken a short cut by joining Clairvaux, which is
another Jerusalem. There follows a request for Alexander to bear cheerfully the financial inconvenience to the diocese of his canon's decision :
"He begs you of your fatherly love, and I unite my prayers with his, that
the arrangements he has made for his creditors to have his prebend may
be allowed to stand, so that he may not become (God forbid) a defaulter
and breaker of his covenant, and his daily sacrifice of a contrite heart be
unacceptable because a brother has something against him. He also begs
that the house which he has built for his mother on Church lands with the
ground which he has assigned to it, may remain here so long as she lives.
So much for Philip.
    And now I turn to yourself. I feel impelled and even inspired by the
Charity of God to exhort you not to regard the passing glory of the world
as if it would never pass away . . ." etc.

5. It was probably in 1122 that Thomas, provost of Beverley, witnessed a
notification by archbishop Thurstan of privileges to the men of Beverley
(*Regesta* II, no. 1332). The transaction which took place in York in the
presence of the whole *familia* of the archbishop, both cleric and lay, was
also witnessed by Geoffrey Murdac, Nigel Fossard, Alan de Perci, Walter
Espec, Eustace FitzJohn, Turstin the archdeacon (of Richmond (?)),
Herbert the canon, William son of Thole, and William of Bayeux.

letters from him, each of them a compound of charm and threat that St. Bernard made peculiarly his own[6]. But though he seems to have made some sort of promise to become a Cistercian he did not follow it through.

Since both Henry Murdac and Thomas of Beverley were well known to Thurstan[7] he must also have known full well that they were being solicited by St. Bernard to join the Cistercians and he presumably took a favourable view of the saint's activities ; otherwise the Cistercian entry into his diocese would not have been attempted, for the early Cistercians took scrupulous care not to offend their diocesans. In any case, it is quite obvious that their arrival at York in 1131 came as no surprise to Thurstan, who must have been conducting negotiations with King Henry, Walter Espec and the Cistercians for some time. We have already seen (p. 71) how Thurstan was brought into contact with Cistercian ideals in the pioneering days of the order, whilst it was supposed to be under the influence of the Cistercian Bernard that King Henry had acknowledged Innocent II as the true Pope in January, 1131[8]. Even so, eyebrows might well have been raised by the tone of the letter in which St. Bernard announced the coming of his brethren to Henry I : "In your land there is an outpost of my Lord and your Lord, an outpost which he has preferred to die for than to lose. I have proposed to occupy it and I am sending men from my army who will, if it is not displeasing to you, claim it, recover it, and restore it with a

---

6. *Cf Letters of St. Bernard* (tr. Scott James), nos. 108, 109. The first of these contains a typical piece of spiritual bullying : "as soon as I had heard what Ivo had to say of you I was compelled by charity to write to you, to exhort you, to pray for you. Whether with any effect or not rests with you."
Thomas vanishes from the scene after 1132 when he is succeeded as provost of Beverley by Turstin (Leach, *Memorials of Beverley Minster*, II, pp. xi, cix).

7. As we have seen in a previous note, Thomas was present with Thurstan at York in 1122 at a grant to the men of Beverley (*Regesta* II, 1332), and it was probably during Thurstan's visit to Rome in January, 1126 that Pope Honorius addressed to "Thomas the provost of Beverley and his canons" a confirmation of their property "at the intervention of Thurstan" and in response to the very reasonable requests of the canons (*E Y C* I, no. 112). Thomas and his archbishop were clearly on the closest of terms. Also Thurstan's duties are bound to have brought him into contact with Henry Murdac, of whom John of Hexham wrote : ante monachatum sub venerabili archiepiscopo Turstino, tam in Eboracensi ecclesia quam in circumiacenti provincia, ex dono parentum honoribus et divitis locupletatum (*Priory of Hexham*, p. 150).

8. Ernaldi, *Vita S. Bernardi*, II, I, 4 : "Of what are you afraid ? " asks the abbot [of the king]. "Are you afraid of sinning by obeying Innocent ? Just consider for how many other sins you have to answer to God. Leave this one to me ; I will answer for it."

strong hand. For this purpose I have sent ahead these men who now stand before you to reconnoitre. They will investigate the situation carefully and report back to me faithfully. Help them as messengers of your Lord and in their persons fulfil your duties as a vassal of their Lord"[9]. The land they were to reconnoitre was situated beside the Rye in North Yorkshire on a fee belonging to Walter Espec ; their object, one gathers, was to make sure that it was suitable as a site for a Cistercian monastery and to assure themselves beyond doubt of the support of the local diocesan[10], Thurstan. The time needed to do so, and to report back to St. Bernard, accounts for the interval between their arrival in 1131 and the official foundation of Rievaulx which took place on the 5th March, 1132. And quite a gathering it was which met on that day to bear witness to Walter Espec's foundation, made "by the advice and permission of Thurstan, archbishop of York ; with the permission and advice of Henry, king of the English ; confirmed by the apostolic authority of the Lord Pope Innocent." Amongst the witnesses, ironically enough, was that very Thomas provost of Beverley whom St. Bernard had tried in vain to draw into the Cistercian order. Others present included Walter's fellow-justiciar in the North, Eustace FitzJohn ; a group of clerics from Warter priory ; the sons of Walter's sister Hawise, the sons of his sister Albrea and of his sister Odelina ; and a body of Walter's tenants and neighbours[11].

Thus it was no haphazard enterprise that the Rievaulx colony had embarked upon, but a well-planned expedition organised from Clairvaux with the detailed precision of a military operation. Totally unexpected, however, was the excitement, the enthusiasm, the opposition and heart-burning which it produced almost at once in the northern province. For as the representatives of the new order were journeying through York their simplicity and single-minded renunciation of the world had touched the hearts of certain monks in the well established, prosperous and busy Benedictine house of St. Mary's, close by the minster. Unwittingly the Cistercians had thrust a sword of division into the bosom of the Benedictine family, and as they passed through on their way northwards to Ryedale they had already split the St. Mary's community into those

---

9. *Letters of St. Bernard,* no. 95.
10. For the care taken by the early Cistercians to secure support from the local diocesan, see the Prologue to the Carta Caritatis, in *Analecta Sacri Ordinis Cisterciensis* (1945), p. 53.
11. *Chartulary of Rievaulx* (S S), pp. 16–21.

who could no longer rest content with the ancient ways and those who still clung to them steadfastly. The same debate was about to take place at St. Mary's as took place at Cluny in the March of this same year, as was indeed taking place over most of Benedictine Europe. Stung by criticism of the ancient ways, Peter the Venerable, as abbot of Cluny, was trying to reform his family of monasteries and so remove the grounds of Bernard's accusations ; in 1130 he had spent several months in England assessing his task ; in 1131 he had sent out a call to all heads of Cluniac houses to assemble at Cluny in the following spring, and two hundred of them with several hundred other interested individuals took part in the meetings of March, 1132. The reforming statutes which Peter promulgated on this occasion may not have been any direct concern of the community at St. Mary's, but disturbing echoes of these debates must have already begun to trouble it[12].

If we are to be just towards all parties in the divisions that reft St. Mary's in the following months it is essential to make a just estimate of the condition of the abbey at the time. This requires at least a glance at the history of the community. Originally dedicated to the Norwegian saint, Olaf, the house had been founded in 1055 by Siward Earl of Northumbria, but after thirty years' existence as a priory it was re-dedicated to St. Mary the mother of Christ. The impulse towards this change of dedication came from the increasing number of Norman benefactors that the house was attracting and the transfer of the house itself to a larger site adjoining the church

---

12. Tunc rigor sanctae conversationis in ecclesiasticis viris admodum crevit, et canonicalis ordo in Francia et Anglia multipliciter adamatus invaluit. Fervor quoque abbatum metas antecessorum suorum transcendere praesumpsit, et priscis institutionibus graviora superadjecit, satisque dura imbecillibus humeris onera imposuit.
Petrus Cluniacensis abbas veredarios et epistolas per omnes cellas suas tunc direxit, et omnes cellarum priores de Anglia et Italia regnisque aliis accersiit, jubens ut dominico Quadragesimae tertio Cluniaci adessent, ut praecepta monasticae conversationis austeriora quam hactenus audirent. Illi nimirum archimandritae sui jussis obsecundaverunt, ac ad statutum terminum CC priores Cluniacum convenerunt. In illa die (28 March 1132) MCC et XII fratres ibi adfuerunt, ecclesiastice ritu canentes processerunt, et, cum jocunditate cordis oculos levantes ad Deum, devote ipsum collaudaverunt. Haec iccirco securus edo, quia gaudens interfui . . . (Ordericus Vitalis, *Ecclesiasticae Historiae*, V, pp. 29–30). Ordericus goes on to describe the stricter regulations imposed by Peter the Venerable, of whom he writes : Austerus autem praeceptor, Salomonis oblitus praecepti : *Ne transgrediaris terminos antiquos quas posuerunt patres tui*, Cistercienses aliosque novorum sectatores aemulatus, rudibus ausis institit, et ab incoeptis desistere ad praesens erubuit. Postmodum tamen emollitus, subditorium arbitrio consensit, memorque discretionis, quae virtutum mater est, invalidisque compatiens subvenit, perplura de gravibus institutis quae proposuerat intermisit.

of St. Olaf. At this date there were few houses so well favoured by powerful patrons as was St. Mary's ; William the Conqueror, William Rufus and Henry I each made generous gifts to the community. The Conqueror's beneficence was largely in the customary form of land[13] ; but his son William not only gave land, he also granted the abbey privileges of jurisdiction comparable to those enjoyed by the neighbouring St. Peter's and by St. John's, Beverley, whilst Henry I went further still, for he accorded St. Mary's the custody of the king's forest on the abbey lands, which meant that the abbey could keep the king's foresters out of its estates. Perhaps as a corollary, St. Mary's was also given a tithe of the king's venison in Yorkshire in flesh and hides taken by anyone at all, and it was the duty of the king's larderers and the sheriff of York to see that the monks got their tithe in full and without trouble[14]. Henry's Queen, Matilda, added to these favours by giving to the monks land that was worth £6 annually[15] ; Henry's leading vassals in the North were not slow to follow the royal lead[16] ; Osbert de Arches, Gilbert de Gant and Ilbert de Lascy, for instance, and even a vassal of David earl of Lothian fell in with the fashion[17]. But it was the Counts of Brittany and Richmond who were the prime patrons of the house after the kings ; in company with their sub-tenants they showered gifts upon the abbey in the high lands of Hang East, Gilling West and Gilling East, where the Pennine hills run down to the Yorkshire plain[18]. The only endowments comparable to those of the Richmond counts were those made, as we have seen, by the Meschins when they offered estates to St. Mary's for the foundation of daughter houses at Wetheral and St. Bees.

---

13. E Y C I, pp. 264–266.
14. E Y C I, nos. 351, 352, 353.
15. Regesta II, no. 571.
16. Cf E Y C I, no. 467 for two Lincolnshire benefactors of the house.
17. E Y C IV, No. 2, by Count Alan II : no. 4 by Count Stephen, who was also the donor in no. 8 with its long list of benefactions and its list of Breton witnesses. E Y C V, no. 128, restoration by Serlo de Burgh of the land of Ellenthorpe, for a payment of 24 li. of silver (this is really a sale) ; no. 138, gift by Wimar the steward, of the chapel of St. Martin, Richmond, etc. ; no. 185, gift by Budes when he became a monk ; no. 218, gift by Enisan Musard of the church of Croft ; no. 279, gift of lands and tithes by Odo the chamberlain ; no. 282, gift by Anschitil de Furneaux of tithes ; no. 347, gift of the church of Hornby by Wigan son of Landric ; no. 351, gift of land by Herman and Brian the Breton ; no. 352, gift by William de la Mare of land ; no. 358, gift of land by Ribald, the count's brother.
18. Lawrie, Early Scottish Charters, p. 47, confirmation by Earl David (of Lothian) of the grant of the vill called Karkarevil and its church to the abbey of St. Mary at York.

What emerges from this summary of its early history is that St. Mary's stood as the premier religious house of the province in the minds of Yorkshiremen—and not only of Yorkshiremen, for its fame had led the ancient abbey of Ramsey in the Fenlands to draw up a confraternity agreement with St. Mary's[19], and the names on the Mortuary Roll of Matilda bear witness to the variety of races gathered there[20]. Most of the leading families in the shire had made benefactions to it and were therefore linked to the house by ties of piety. In addition the abbey was a centre of power, business and influence within the city of York—an advantage, no doubt, to its patrons when they themselves had business to do in York, but equally a source of distraction to the monks who dwelt there[21]. One's imagination, in any case, is not over-taxed to understand how shocked and offended the northern feudatories would be on learning that a group within the abbey wished to turn their backs on its honoured position and tradition so as to bury themselves in the wilds of north Yorkshire. What could have possessed this group that they wished to break the peace of their family, their city and their province ?

For that is how the unrest occasioned in the community of St. Mary's appeared to the older generation both inside and outside the cloister—as an offence against the memory of their predecessors. As a Cistercian later put it who had himself been brought up by them, "they were men of religion walking in the ways of their fathers and conforming without protest to the customs they had received from their elders. They lived according to the manner and tradition of their predecessors, decently enough in their subjection to the rule and the abbot ; " but, he goes on, "they were far from the ideal of the rule, far from the aim of their monastic oath, far from the perfection of the Cistercian's training[22] ". Of Cistercian perfection their abbot Geoffrey had heard little ; nor did he care much, for he was now an old man who had spent his life in the

---

19. B M Add. MS 38816, fo. 37r : Hanc conventionem fecit alduinus abbas Ramesiensis in capitulo Sancte Marie Eboraci. (Aldwin was deposed by St. Anselm for simony (1102–7) but restored later ; he died in 1113).

20. *Rouleaux des Morts.* (ed. L. Delisle), pp. 177 ff., Roll of Matilda, daughter of William the Conqueror, abbess of La Trinité at Caen (+1113), entry no. 41 is that of St. Mary's, and the monks certainly spread themselves in their verses, as if conscious that their house was a most important one ; Benedict inserted 50 lines, Richard 28 and Peter 8.

21. Only an institution running its affairs on the lines of a business, for instance, could possibly have dealt with the organization needed to run the places granted to St. Mary's in *E Y C* IV, no. 8.

22. *Memorials of Fountains Abbey (S S)*, p. 5.

service of the abbey and of Christianity in York. He may well have been the monk of St. Mary's who in 1116 braved the king's anger by crossing into Normandy with other Yorkshire clerics to request the return of Thurstan as their archbishop ; it was certainly he, now abbot, who acted on behalf of Thurstan at the king's Candlemas court in Gloucester in 1123, and he is listed as one of the chief witnesses when Thurstan consecrated Robert as bishop of St. Andrews in 1128[23]. Obviously his reliability, good sense and honesty were widely recognized even though he was simple and, in the scholastic sense, unlearned ; but it is equally clear that an upheaval within the abbey was something he dreaded as a personal affront and as too much for one of his age to bear, especially since he further felt that it was not up to him or to any single person to reject the ancient customs and rites which the whole body of monks throughout the world had agreed to[24].

This stress upon ancient ways which one finds in abbot Geoffrey and his supporters reminds us that a clash between the generations was taking place all over Christendom during these years, and the split at St. Mary's is best understood in this wider perspective. We have already referred to the way the younger generation took over the Roman curia and the Papacy itself through Honorius II and Innocent II ; it was the same group who at Cluny had ousted their senior, abbot Pontius, and won control over the abbey for the party of Peter the Venerable and Cardinal Matthew of Albano ; and similar victories over the older generations were won at Fulda, Farfa and St. Martin-des-Champs[25]. But the most spectacular upheaval had taken place in the heart of Paris ; here in 1113 King Louis had introduced regular canons when he established the new foundation of St. Victor, upon which he bestowed rich prebends carved out of the revenues of many churches ; but even he jibbed a few years later when the bishop of Paris, Stephen, a zealous supporter of Innocent II and close friend of St. Bernard, tried to

---

23.   *H C* p. 47 (*cf* p. 52) ; *H C* p. 109 ; Lawrie, *Early Scottish Charters*, p. 64. He also accompanied Thurstan to Selby in 1123 to effect a change of abbot (*The Coucher Book of Selby*, p. (24)).

24.   *Memorials of Fountains Abbey*, pp. 7 and 13. *Cf* also his condemnation of the attempt to "transferre terminos quos patres ab initio praefixerunt," a formulation almost exactly the same as that of Ordericus Vitalis condemning over-zealous reformers who transgress "terminos antiquos quos posuerunt patres tui" (*cf* p. 155n). Ivo of Chartres had similar remarks to make about over-zealous reformers, "qui, pharisaico fermenti inflati, gloriantur in vilitate ciborum et in non parcendo corpore" (*P L* 162, col. 198).

25.   F. J. Schmale, *Studien zum Schisma des Jahres 1130*, p. 257.

oust the canons of Notre Dame Cathedral and introduce regular
canons in their stead. King Louis opposed this suggestion as also
did two other defenders of the old order, Stephen of Garland and
the prior of Étampes. The tension between the generations eventually reached breaking-point when the prior of St. Victor, Thomas,
was murdered in the arms of the bishop of Paris by the nephews of
a Notre Dame archdeacon, and when the sub-dean of Orleans was
also dispatched[26]. The currents of baffled and incomprehending
animosity of which these murders were the outcome produced a
specially severe shock at St. Mary's because the aged had hitherto
enjoyed the preponderating influence in the community. Abbot
Geoffrey's age was something that everyone commented on, and his
predecessor Stephen had also been singled out for possessing the
wisdom of an ancient[27] whilst there was at least one monk, Gervase,
who had spent thirty-two years following the monastic rule under
the two of them[28]. Of course, one cannot know the comparative
numbers of the aged, but two factors are likely to have pushed up
the average age at St. Mary's. The first is the custom frequently
met with at the time of distinguished men in their later years
retiring to some well-regarded house of religion, gracing it with their
presence and their wealth, and in return receiving comfort and
congenial company for the evening of their lives. One interesting
person to have done this was Arnegrim, an Englishman who
managed to survive the Norman Conquest still in possession of his
lands, and who transferred both himself and his lands to St. Mary's
soon after the Domesday Survey, ending his days as a monk of the
abbey[29]. Another to do the same was Budes, who in the 1120's
granted his chapel of Bolton-upon-Swale to St. Mary's when he
became a monk there[30]. These are two examples suggesting that
St. Mary's was the kind of community to which ageing gentry might
look hopefully as a refuge. And in the 1120's they had a good chance
of finding men of their own generation in it, for there was a second

26. Achille Luchaire, *Louis VI le Gros*, p. cxlv.
27. *The Coucher Book of Selby* has some good words to say of Stephen, pp.
     20–21, whom it describes as *vir sapiens et maturus*. According to the
     Ingilby MS (*The Anonimalle Chronicle*, ed. V. H. Galbraith, p. xlvii) the
     first abbot Stephen ruled the house for 24 years, the second abbot Richard
     for less than a year, and abbot Geoffrey for 29 years. Since Richard was
     abbot in 1116 (*Regesta*, no. 1130) Geoffrey must have been made abbot
     about that year.
28. C. H. Talbot, The Testament of Gervase of Louth Park, in *Analecta Sacri
     Ordinis Cisterciensis*, 1951, p. 34.
29. *E Y C* I, p. 266.
30. *E Y C* V, no. 185.

factor at work to produce a group at St. Mary's advanced in years. This was the need to supply first Wetheral and later the priory of St. Bees with its nucleus of monks ; even though Wetheral's critical period was now past there would always be a tendency to draft the younger and more vigorous of the St. Mary's brethren to it, whilst the exodus of a prior and six monks to St. Bees in 1120 would draw off some of the best talent from the house. Then in 1127 the monk Durandus left to become abbot of Selby ; though no master of the interior life he had a reputation as a skilful and vigorous administrator ; if he had stayed in St. Mary's the events of 1132 might well have been given a different turn by his forceful personality[31].

Granted these tendencies within the community it was only to be expected that a section of the monks should feel little sympathy for reforming ideals. Certainly the elderly do not easily respond to the Cistercian ethos, with its insistence on total and extreme measures of abnegation and poverty ; but the elderly have their own special virtues, amongst them a natural desire for peace that can often act as the basis for supernatural reconciliation. There are signs that such virtues were not altogether wanting at St. Mary's. For after the secession had taken place, and after many hard words had been spoken in the heat of the quarrel, we find Geoffrey the old abbot of St. Mary's working peaceably alongside his former subject, Richard, now abbot of Fountains[32]. That they had become reconciled is a tribute, perhaps, to the peace-making of Thurstan, but it is an even surer tribute to the essentially Christian attitude of Geoffrey. He and his family were the ones who had been wounded, and it was they who needed to exercise the greatest magnanimity in being reconciled ; one is reminded of another and similar dispute in which the dynamic Cistercians were again involved, that between St. Bernard and Cluny, where once again the Cistercians were given an example of Christian magnanimity, this time by Peter the Venerable.

In assessing the condition of St. Mary's in 1132 a further fact needs to be borne in mind, especially by those who see the split as one that separated the sheep from the goats. It is that the spiritual life at the abbey cannot have been entirely dead when it could raise up so many monks, thirteen in all, who were to be outstanding

---

31. *The Coucher Book of Selby*, pp. 27, 28, 31.
32. *E Y C* II, no. 877.

figures amongst the first generation of English Cistercians. True, it was in the Cistercian order that they achieved the realization of their reforming ideals ; but equally certain, it was at the Benedictine house of St. Mary's that their responses to such ideals were quickened ; and thirteen can have been no small proportion of the total complement of the monastery. Nor should we fall in with the common habit of regarding these as the regenerate and the ones who stayed in St. Mary's as the unregenerate. As was remarked of the reforming group a century ago, "few things will be found more instructive than the development of the peculiar characters of its first fathers[33] ".

This observation was prompted by the peculiar behaviour of one of the group in later life, that is Adam the first abbot of Meaux, He had by this time retired from Meaux to become a recluse at Watton ; here he had walled himself up in his cell as a result of which he almost perished there when fire broke out ; after being rescued in the nick of time he was prevailed upon to return to Meaux. Amongst the first white monks Adam's awkwardness had numerous parallels. Thus the second Richard abbot of Fountains turned his house upside down in his determination to resign his office, which he had only held a few years[34] ; then Maurice and Thorold, both from Rievaulx, in quick succession threw in their hands soon after being appointed abbots of Fountains[35]. It may be pleaded in their favour that they were never given a fair chance because the archbishop of York was all the time peering over their shoulders ; but then he was another Cistercian, Henry Murdac, and had himself been abbot of Fountains. As archbishop of York he found it necessary to throw out idols at Fountains, where again the rule of the third Richard witnessed painful dissension and rebellion[36]. Most of these failures are accounted for by contemporaries with the explanation that the men in question were better at religion than at practical affairs ; significantly, the same phrase is used of Robert Biset, who had been appointed prior of Hexham by Thurstan and who abandoned his charge, as soon as he heard of William FitzHerbert's election to York, in order to join the Cis-

---

33. *Memorials of Fountains*, p. 1 (i.e. fifty).
34. *Memorials of Fountains*, pp. 75–8.
35. *Ibid.*, p. 105.
36. *Ibid.*, pp. 85, 111–113.

tercians at Clairvaux[37]. It was as though the new order attracted
misfits, such as Robert abbot of Newminster who was once returning
from a grange when a nobleman met him and asked him where to
find abbot Robert : "When I was at the grange the abbot was
present," replied the deliberately ambiguous Robert and rode on
happy to have escaped some tiresome business[38]. Robert himself
was succeeded by a certain Walter of whom Robert had correctly
predicted that he would be the ruin of the house and scandal of the
order[39]. Another of the first generation, Richard from Rievaulx,
who became the first abbot of Melrose, retired from his abbacy in
dubious circumstances, so much so that the manuscript chronicling
the history of the house has been altered for this year, 1148, to foil
the over-curious enquirer ; and Jocelyn of Furness says that he will
only briefly touch on the retirement of the over-severe Richard so
as not to incite the biting tongues of those who mock at Cistercians
and other religious[40]. When we add to this tale of woe the numerous
instances of Cistercian *conversi* running away and disgracing themselves[41] one can well sympathize with the strictures of both
Jocelyn of Furness and Walter Daniel on the severity of certain
Cistercian abbots[42] ; especially when one reads Jocelyn's story of a
contemporary Cistercian abbot who, on being questioned by a monk,
replied to him in the words of Pilate, "Knowest thou not that I
have power to crucify thee, and have power to release thee ?[43]".

Truly these early Cistercians were not easy men to live with.
They were extremely sensitive, quick to respond to inspired leadership but quick also to turn temperamental differences into issues of
principle. They were for the most part introverts, and it has never
been easy for introverts to live in Yorkshire, amidst a population
largely robust and extrovert. Misunderstandings are bound to arise
that baffle both the minority and the majority. Nor was understanding made any the easier at St. Mary's by the fact that one
group could invoke on their side piety towards the customs of their

37. *Priory of Hexham*, p. 139. Robert Biset was present, along with Ailred,
    at the death-bed of Eilaf, Ailred's father, in 1138 at Durham (*ibid.*, pp.
    55–6) ; he is described by Ailred as "qui magis religioni, quam exteriorium
    administrationi aptus . . . abrenuntiavit curae pastorali" (*ibid.*, p. 193).
38. P. Grosjean, Vita S. Roberti, *Analecta Bollandiana* LVI (1938, pp. 334–360),
    p. 345. See also his odd relations with a noble matron on p. 351.
39. *Ibid.*
40. *Chronicle of Melrose*, s.a. 1148 ; *Acta Sanctorum*, August, Vol. I, p. 258.
41. *Analecta Bollandiana* LVI, pp. 347–8 ; *Vita Godrici (S S)*.
42. *Vita Ailredi* (ed. Powicke), p. 40.
43. *Acta Sanctorum*, August, Vol. I, p. 260.

fathers whilst the other could appeal to the generous vision of the new generation. And in following the story of the split it has to be remembered that neither of the accounts preserved for us gives the conservatives' case. One of the two accounts was related some seventy years later by Serlo, now a monk of Kirkstall and almost a hundred years old, who had known the protagonists intimately[44]. The other is by Thurstan in the form of a letter which he wrote to William, archbishop of Canterbury and papal legate, when the events were still burning in his mind. As this letter is the most revealing testimony to the workings of Thurstan's own heart and judgment, and is far more detailed than Serlo's, this is the account we must concentrate on[45].

Thurstan began by referring to the fact that the good reputation and standing of St. Mary's abbey was known to many. In recent years it had grown very wealthy and the increase had been matched by rising numbers and devotions. Since increasing wealth and virtue rarely go together, however, the result has been that certain of the brethren during the past months have become greatly troubled about their manner of life—"moved, unless I am mistaken," says Thurstan, "by divine prompting." In particular their consciences have kept reminding them of the vows they made to follow the rule of St. Benedict at the time of their conversion to the religious life. They fear the wrath of God for failing to carry out their vows, and they keep hearing the words of the psalmist, "Render to God the vows that you made," and the words of God Himself in the Gospel, "No man who sets his hand to the plough and looks back is worthy of the kingdom of God." It seems to them vain, or rather madness, to bear the rule of St. Benedict not towards the goal of their salvation but towards the seat of their damnation. For they have solemnly professed that they will maintain the rule but are held back from doing so by alien and superfluous customs. And the commendations they are always hearing of voluntary poverty, separation from the world, total humility and evangelical perfection, all this only sharpens their feelings of guilt.

Those who first expressed their fears to each other and their hopes of returning to the strictness of the rule were Richard the sacristan, Ranulf, Gamel, Gregory, Hamo, Thomas, and Walter.

---

44. *Memorials of Fountains*, pp. 3–10.
45. *Memorials of Fountains*, pp. 11–29 ; for the authenticity of the letter, see the discussion in Appendix II.

They entered into a compact with each other to be faithful to these initial graces ; and after much trepidation they decided to ask for the backing of the prior, Richard ; they went to him rather than to abbot Geoffrey because the prior was in fact the effective head of the house. Far from encountering the stern opposition they feared on Richard's side, they discovered to their relief that he would not only help them realize their plans but himself entered into their compact. After discussing the matter with the sub-prior Gervase, a man noted for his religious fervour, Richard decided on the 28th of June (1132) to explain the whole case to the abbot. [Perhaps it would have been wiser on the part of the sacristan and his associates to have gone to Geoffrey in the first place, because it is fairly obvious that the confederacy they had formed cannot have escaped the notice of their brethren, and already suspicions must have been aroused as to what these pretenders to piety were up to ; hostile camps within a community are inevitable once the habit of secrecy is indulged in]. When the abbot heard his prior and sub-prior explain their proposals he was quite stunned and protested that he in the small plot of earth entrusted to him did not intend to change the ancient rites and tried customs which the general body of monks throughout almost the entire world had accepted. His reaction called forth from prior Richard an exposition of the dissidents' point of view which takes up almost half of Thurstan's report on the case ; if it was delivered uninterrupted one can only sympathize with abbot Geoffrey for being addressed as though he were a public meeting, but probably it represents a codification of the points that prior Richard put forward.

It was nothing brash, he explained, that he and his associates were about. On the contrary, they wished once more to take upon themselves the ancient rule of St. Benedict, or rather the most ancient Gospel of Christ which precedes all rules. Their proposals were not meant as a criticism of other monks, for they were well aware that it is the one Lord and King who is served by different people in different places : "Job behaved more valiantly on the dung heap than Adam in Paradise." So they do not doubt that some of the best men have managed to live edifying lives even amongst the customs which they themselves most fear—though one has to remember that such miracles of grace cannot serve as the general norm by which Christians are to live. The rule of St. Benedict, an epitome of the Gospel, is the norm by which they hope to follow Christ, and one of its outstanding features is its dis- cretion ; it sets a time for prayer and reading, and a time for physical work, and the alternation of the two ensures that one is preserved from idleness, that enemy of the soul ; part also of discretion is the moderation in eating which St. Benedict prescribes, for many disturbances of the mind are traceable to excessive eating.

But at St. Mary's they had the overwhelming task, Richard continues, of trying to live without sin amidst so-called customs. Under these it became the norm, a few days excepted, for conversations to take place regularly every day, despite the prohibition of unnecessary talk by the rule. Not only do these gossiping groups stand around in the community rooms, but even in the parlours and the various monastic offices, and sometimes on the footpaths, in twos and threes or more, from morning till night. Permission for talk quickly turns into licence and gravely endangers souls. It would not be so bad if we could maintain that all this is harmless recreation ; but everyone knows that in the end it produces scurrility and back-biting and rumour-mongering. Within the community it leads to quarrels, mutual insults and murmuring against superiors. How, asks Richard, can we go on calling ourselves monks of St. Benedict when we behave in this fashion ? No one who knows the customs of St. Mary's can believe that St. Benedict's rule about silence is being observed there. Even after collation, when some retire to the church, others split up into gossiping groups as though the day were not long enough for their malice but they have to extend it into the night.

The same extravagance, says Richard, is shown over food and clothing. Over and above the allowance laid down by St. Benedict dishes of relish are added, exquisite concoctions of different kinds laced with spices and pepper ; with the cup passing round regularly on feast days. Also contrary to the teaching of St. Bernard—that warmth and not display is to be looked for in clothing—the monks' garments are made of precious and variegated material. Was it not precisely for feasting every day in magnificent robes that the rich man of the Gospels was damned ? And because he was using for his own whims things that could have satisfied the real wants of the needy. For even if he should on many occasions be without his customary ease, nevertheless he will be revealed as a double-dealer when he finds himself standing in their presence. Added together these habits of malicious idling, empty and harmful gossip, splendid meals, regular festive drinking and other innumerable vanities constitute a heap of obscenity. In such circumstances, says Richard, there is a real threat to modesty, and the number of its guardians insufficient, because those of suspect virtue considerably out-number those who are upright. Whether private relations are correct or not God knows and we have learnt by experience. With the greater part of the community spiritually debilitated it is no wonder if individuals become sour and quarrelsome, a threat to themselves and their neighbours and a standing reproach to their superiors ; and how can the disease be remedied except by quickly exposing it to the fresh air ?

Another thing, says Richard, is that whether they like it or not monks are made custodians of estates and fall into vices that make them a laughing-stock. Not undeservedly, either, for when a monk is presumptuous and temerarious enough to seek something con-trary to his rule he falls by the just judgment of God into unbecoming positions. Anyone who bothers to read the rule of St. Benedict will see plainly that monks who have to go out on the monastery's business are to return as quickly as possible and must never be found living away from their monasteries like sarabites. St. Bene-dict only acknowledges as his own those who live in community, subject to the rule and the abbot ; and he always insisted that to desire temporal goods and to be occupied by them leads to a lessen-ing of charity. Nor can the need to defend the rights of the abbey excuse either abbot or monk from obedience towards the rule.

Having touched on the issue of obedience at this juncture the prior was clearly raising a point that might be turned against himself should abbot Geoffrey oppose his schemes and demand his prior's obedience. And one cannot avoid the impression that prior Richard, himself being uncomfortably aware of this fact, did what many another has done at a similar awkward moment : that is, he ran out of his dilemma under a gust of rhetoric—or, at least, his speech begins as rhetoric but is finally transformed into a sincere appeal to evangelical truths that still holds one's attention and moves one's heart even at a distance of eight centuries.

The prior's main defence to himself was to appeal from the abbot to the rule by maintaining that the abbot was only to be obeyed if he followed the rule—otherwise it would be a case of the blind leading the blind and both falling into a ditch. Nor is it any answer, he asserts, to argue that even in a monastery where objec-tionable customs prevail it still remains possible for monks to keep the rule by holy contemplation and by mortifying the flesh ; for an example contravening a law cannot be used to substantiate it. For though King David was able to preserve his integrity in the midst of warfare and the tumult of the world, and though it is theoretically possible for a man to remain chaste whilst staying in a brothel, it would be presumptuous for ordinary mortals to imagine that they can do likewise. So if it is granted to any, by a miracle of grace, to live justly amidst harmful customs, let them give thanks to God ; but those to whom it is not given, let them not behave presumptuously but apply to themselves the saying of the prophet : "Go out from here and do not touch vile things." Whoever touches pitch is defiled by it[46].

Aware, perhaps, that his remarks about brothels and pitch had taken him beyond the point of no return prior Richard in justification of his rhetoric produced a catena of Christ's most shattering demands upon those who claim to follow Him. It is as though the still small voice within prior Richard which had hitherto protested mildly against the hypocrisy at St. Mary's had now become a thundering roar : "Unless your justice abounds more than that of the Scribes and Pharisees you shall not enter into the kingdom of heaven ; " "Whoever looks on a woman to lust after her has already committed adultery with her in his heart ; " "Whoever does not renounce all he possesses cannot be my disciple ; " "If any man will come after me, let him deny himself, and take up his cross, and follow me." One after another the quotations come pouring out with the refrain that against each of these commands of Christ St. Mary's blatantly offends ; in the prior's own words : "We lust after everything ; we are moved to anger, we quarrel, we seize other men's goods, we seek our own ends through litigation, we justify fraud and lying, we follow the flesh and its lusts. We live to ourselves, we please ourselves, we loathe being beaten and glory in beating others ; others we oppress but make sure we are not oppressed ; others we envy but glory in our own advantages ; we laugh and grow fat on the sweat of other men and the whole world is insufficient to gratify our malice"[47].

And now the cutting edge of prior Richard's discontent touched the sorest spot of all : the Gospel truths which seemed dead and impossible in themselves at St. Mary's had been clearly visible and

---

46. Unwittingly prior Richard was making his own those very sentiments that Ivo of Chartres had attributed to the pharisaical reformers of Coulomb in his own diocese : . . . tales qui non putantes pie posse vivere bonos in collegio malorum, attendentes illud Ezechielis : . Recedite, exite inde (Ezech. XIV ; Isa. lii) ; et non attendentes illud quod sequitur : Et immundum ne tetigeritis (ibid., et II Cor. VI), quod intelligendum est contactu cordis non corporis. P L 162, col. 199.

47. Memorials of Fountains, pp. 19–20.

vital in the monks of Savigny, and the monks from Clairvaux, who had lately called upon them. Those monks are not men who try to serve both God and mammon ; content with the minimum of land under the plough and for their flocks they do not try to seize their neighbour's property, nor do they go to law to recover what God has taken away from them ; seeking nothing for themselves they provide nothing for the anger of their neighbour to feed upon. They are almost alone in being able to say, "The world is crucified to us, and we to the world." "It does not seem impossible, then, father," says Richard to Geoffrey finally, "to hold to the rule of St. Benedict since God provides us with these examples who go before us, with such shining virtues so that we might follow them. If indeed, because the city is so close, and because there is so much distraction on account of the citizens, we cannot follow them entirely in their purity, then let us straightway change our manner of life and our possessions to conform to the rule of our profession, apart from which we are not monks but dead men."

We can well believe Thurstan when he assures us that abbot Geoffrey "did not receive these sentiments altogether pleasantly." More surprising is the explanation Thurstan offers, which is revealing about himself ; Geoffrey reacted as he did, says Thurstan, "because it is difficult to transform ingrained habits by new forms of virtue." This is the kind of explanation one expects of a younger man ; coming from a man in his sixties burdened with an archbishopric it reveals a flexibility of mind that one associates with the *avant-garde* rather than with the hierarchy. However, Geoffrey too had his virtues, though not perhaps so novel ; he swallowed his pride, confessed his own slow-wittedness and asked prior Richard to set down on paper how in his position the prior would put his ideals into operation. Responding eagerly, the prior drafted a reforming programme which shows his familiarity with the internal debates that the monastic body was at this time busily engaged upon throughout Christendom, and especially in France. The points he makes are those commonly stressed by monastic reformers ; there must be greater austerity in speech, in food and in clothing, the austerity required by the rule, in fact. But Richard's programme contains a particular and unmistakable stress on not becoming parasites ; thus it is essential to choose a site where regular manual labour can be carried out, and the site must be chosen without unjust ambitions. As regards the practice which has brought so much criticism on the heads of monks, says Thurstan, that of taking over churches and tithes, Richard proposes that St. Mary's endowments in this sphere should become episcopal property for the use of the poor, of pilgrims and for hospitality ; the monks should live on the produce of their lands[48].

The austerity of prior Richard's scheme offered a bleak future indeed for those members of the community who had ensconced themselves comfortably in the customs of the house ; angrily they demanded that Richard and his set should either be sent into exile or put into close custody because—and here the conservatives show themselves at their self-deceiving worst—not only have they besmirched the honour of their own house but also of Cluny, Marmoutier, Canterbury, Winchester, Saint Albans, and all the other monasteries of their order. Upon their attitude Thurstan comments that the recent reform in Cluny has shown that even the customs of Cluny were in need of overhauling ; and he believes confidently that "no Christian man would be so silly and stupid as to maintain that either Cluny itself, or any other monastery of the same order, is in the same class as the Cistercian ones for fidelity to the rule and the Gospels"[49].

Still the dispute might have been peaceably resolved ; for though the abbot and the prior continued to argue at length, the abbot showing himself patient and friendly but unable to get a grip on the situation, the prior displaying his superior knowledge and dialectical skill, they were nonetheless arguing amicably. And it was agreed that the abbot should give his decision on the Feast of the Nativity of Our Lady (8th September). But in the meantime the issue had produced an ever-deepening split within the community ; and, worse still, rumours of it had spread outside the monastery into the streets of York. Some of the reforming group had fallen away from their resolution, especially after a scheme had been hatched to send to Coventry anyone who brought up the question of his oath of profession ; these backsliders were only accepted by their conservative brethren after confessing their fault ; and there might have been an outbreak of real persecution had it not been for the intervention by certain moderating influences amongst the conservatives. It was the possibility of open dissension that now

---

48.   *Ibid.*, p. 21. Once more prior Richard stumbles into Ivo of Chartres' line of
fire when Ivo refers to those . . . subtiles divinorum judiciorum scrutatores
. . . [qui] . . . suadent monachis ut monasteria sua deserant propter abbates
suos et procuratores monasteriorum suorum, qui aliquas decimas, quae
jure pertinent ad dispensationem episcoporum, monasteriis suis acqui-
sierunt. *P L* 162, col. 199.

49.   *Ibid.*, p. 22.

drove prior Richard to sound out the archbishop to discover whether he would hear their case ; as a result Richard and the sub-prior soon afterwards went with the whole story to the archbishop, who was a friend of Richard's[50], and—the phrase is surely formal— "besought the clemency of St. Peter" and Thurstan.

Thurstan's response to their request vibrates with the character of the man : "Therefore I, Thurstan, by the grace of God, archbishop of York, hearing that the servants of Christ in accordance with the precept of St. Benedict were aiming to set the love of Christ above all else, was afraid of countering Christ's grace in them should I not do all in my power to support their just request with the fervour that becomes a bishop ; since the supreme privilege of the episcopal office is to ensure peace for monks in pursuit of their vocations, and to comfort the oppressed in their need"[51]. It is the voice of a man who speaks with authority, confident of his own power to command, but conscious also that power is "but held vicariously and from on high, is of one texture with an eternal economy"[52]. For there was nothing overbearing in Thurstan's character ; he consulted men of tried wisdom before calling to him abbot Geoffrey, prior Richard, and the sub-prior, to hear them state their positions. The reformers passionately re-affirmed their desire to bear the cross of Christ, and the abbot tearfully acknowledged that reforms were necessary, avowing that he would not stand in the way of their holy aspirations but at the same time insisting that he could do nothing without the assent of his chapter. In the circumstances there was nothing that Thurstan could do but fix a date on which he would visit the abbey and go over the issue with the chapter.

The date fixed, the 17th of October, 1132, is one of the most dramatic in Yorkshire history, not only for its eventfulness but also for the gathering of personalities it brought to St. Mary's. A call had gone out from the conservative party in the abbey to their brethren of Holy Trinity (York) and the Cluniacs of Pontefract urging them to rally to the good old cause on this day, and by their presence to brand the revolutionaries as traitors to their common inheritance. News of the dispute had spread throughout the land, and the stage was set for another in the series of clashes that had taken place throughout Christendom between the reformers and the traditionalists. The stage was occupied by the adherents of the

---

50. *Ibid.*, p. 6.
51. *Ibid.*, p. 23.
52. David Jones, *In Parenthesis*, p. 2.

older monasticism who were waiting within the chapter house of
St. Mary's as Thurstan and his party rode up, reined in their horses,
dismounted and moved towards the door of the chapter-house. The
company around the archbishop bristled with personalities who had
been attracted into his circle and whose careers were so strangely
interwoven for good or evil. There was Hugh the dean, for instance,
the wealthy and learned canon who two years later was to become a
Cistercian monk under the abbacy of Richard, now facing him as
the unhappy prior of St. Mary's. Also present was William de Brus,
prior of Guisborough and brother to the Robert de Brus who had
founded the priory; since Guisborough was a centre of reforming ideas
it is probable that the reformers had likewise received a rallying-
call and William had responded by coming to York. There was
William FitzHerbert, the treasurer, who ten years later as archbishop of York was to be subjected to the full fury of Cistercian
righteousness ; the future spokesman of that righteousness against
him now stood a few yards away, a harassed member of the reforming group within the abbey, Richard the sacristan ; and beside
William stood the man whose word was later to decide whether he
remained archbishop or not, William of St. Barbara, now a canon
of York, soon to become dean of York, and then bishop of Durham.
William FitzHerbert, one wryly reflects, the child of a wealthy
family brought up amidst all too many of the good things of this
world, was the one and only member of that distinguished and
high-minded group to receive the seal of canonization[53]. Also
present were Hugh the Chanter, whom we have already met fre-
frequently ; a canon named Serlo who later became a Cistercian ;
Ansfred, Thurstan's own chaplain ; and the vigorous head of St.
Peter's hospital, Robert the priest as he is described, who for the
next quarter of a century was to devote himself to building up his
hospital as the pride of Yorkshire. Altogether they were a formidable company who formed up behind Thurstan.

When Thurstan tried to enter the chapter house he was met
at the door by abbot Geoffrey, whilst inside the monks were milling
around behind their abbot. Emboldened, perhaps, by these supporters Geoffrey asserted that he would only allow Thurstan to enter
if he first dismissed the secular clerics whom he had brought with
him ; it was not lawful, he said, for secular clerics to be privy to the
secrets of the chapter, and there was also the danger that in their

---

53. *H C Y* II, p. 223 : Enutritus est semper in deliciis et divitiis, et raro labori
assuetus, benignitate tamen animi innocentis et liberalitate valde carus.

arrogance they might disturb the good order of the house. Here Geoffrey was not simply inventing excuses ; he had long experience of the tensions that had sprung up between his own abbey and the clerics of St. Peter's in disputes over property. In 1093 the two institutions had been at loggerheads over four acres of land (probably at Bootham) and had gone to the king for a settlement[54] ; within the period of his own abbacy their claims had come into conflict over land in Upper Poppleton[55], so there was good ground for Geoffrey's fear that a meeting of monks and canons now might prove disastrous. In replying to Geoffrey, Thurstan was scarcely able to make himself heard above the noise reverberating through the chapter-house, which was more like a throng of madly drunken carousers than an assembly of monks ; he tried to say that it was only right for him in dealing with the matter in hand to have his clerics at his side, who were good and wise men—and were friends, moreover, of the monks themselves. Thurstan's words failed to mollify the monks, several of whom assumed threatening attitudes whilst all of them cried out that their anger would boil over if Thurstan came in.

Their misbehaviour immediately elicited from Thurstan a gesture that bespeaks the man. With the minimum of words and maximum finality he put an end to this nonsense : "As God is my witness," he said, "I came here as a father, wishing you no harm ; I sought only peace amongst you and Christian fraternity. Now, however, since you are trying to deprive me of the authority that belongs to a bishop by virtue of his office, I in turn deprive you of the thing essential to you. Let your church be suspended"[56].

"We don't mind if our church is suspended for a century," shouted a monk named Simeon. This was the signal for the anger of the abbot's supporters to be turned against prior Richard and his associates : "Grab them," they shouted in frenzy, "grab them." This they promptly did, intending to carry out their pre-arranged plan of either thrusting them into gaol or driving them into exile. But by one means or another all the unhappy minority succeeded in wriggling free and clinging on to Thurstan for protection ; surrounded by them the archbishop somehow managed to retreat to the church without serious harm, but with the malcontents at their

54. *E Y C* I, p. 267. For another dispute see *Monasticon* III, p. 547.
55. *York Minster Fasti* (ed. C. T. Clay) 2, no. 83.
56. *Memorials of Fountains*, p. 25.

heels shouting, "Grab the rebels. Seize the traitors." In the church they sat down for a moment to collect themselves whilst Geoffrey and his monks returned to their chapter-house. Through fear of the irate monks the archbishop's party now bolted the church door on the cloister side and stole out the other way, past the crowds of citizens who had gathered at the scene of trouble, and back without further mishap to St. Peter's.

Within the abbey itself the frenzy of recent events was far from stilled. Abbot Geoffrey, in fact, generated such a burst of activity that one wonders how the old man managed it without collapsing altogether. Besides keeping up a flow of alternately threatening and cajoling messages to his lost charges to return home he launched a nation-wide campaign to waken his contemporaries to the enormity of the revolution at St. Mary's—and one made more scandalous through its having been aided and abetted by the arch-bishop of York himself. He sent messengers to King Henry to explain how Thurstan's interference had contributed to the apostasy of the monks, the undermining of the order and the threat of chaos in religion, all these effects showing what folly it is on the part of monks to contravene the decrees of their superiors and try to be better than their predecessors. He sent similar letters to the neighbouring monasteries and to individual bishops and abbots as well as to men of religion throughout the country. And then, says Thurstan, "the abbot took to the road—with what intention I do not know." A curt enough comment which may well be symptomatic of his exasperation at the panic-stricken activity of the old man over at St. Mary's.

And yet Thurstan never seems to have lost sympathy with Geoffrey ; when about this time he wrote his letter to William of Corbeil warning his fellow-archbishop that the distressed abbot might be heading for Canterbury Thurstan's references to Geoffrey are free from any angry overtones. He simply asks William if he would calm the abbot down when he arrives and warn him not to persist with the campaign against Richard and his associates. Less concerned with past wrongs than with discussing the spirit of God at work, Thurstan closes his letter to William with an exposition of the principles that are fundamental for pronouncing judgment on the case ; unobtrusively and respectfully he instructs his younger superior : "The abbot and his monks should, in this case at least, imitate the Egyptians who allowed the children of Israel to return to the promised land. Similarly when Jacob secretly tried to flee

from Laban's oppression ; after a cruel pursuit Laban allowed him
to go back to his father. Hence these are not to be described as
forsaken but as foresighted who abandon a position where there is
greater opportunity for sinning in the desire to serve God more
securely. Surely they [i.e. the abbot and his followers] should be
deterred by Christ accusing the Pharisees of 'not entering themselves and not allowing others to enter.' As everyone knows, the
rule of St. Benedict is utterly neglected on almost all points by almost all the monastic community throughout the world ; hence one
can never cease to be astonished that people should dare to go on
proclaiming with such solemnity before God and the saints sentiments which they themselves flout every day—or rather, to speak
fairly, are compelled to depart from. To them apply the words of
the prophet, to them particularly : 'This people knows me with its
lips, but its heart is far from me,' and of the apostle : 'With their
voices they confess to God, but by their deeds they deny him.' It
is true, perhaps, that because many do behave in this fashion the
regular habit of it has made them bold. For if it had only been a
few behaving so presumptuously, I would invoke the consciences of
all educated men as sure evidence that such people would be
accounted double-dealers in regard to the rule, and traitors. It is
true, certainly, and I say it with sorrow, that the boldness of the
monks is culpable, clearly culpable ; for the fact that the sinners are
numerous does not confer impurity upon the guilty. So that those
who wish to observe the oath they took to the rule should not be
prevented from doing so ; they should be protected. No blame
attaches to them if this involves shifting their habitation, since one
does not 'go to God for the sake of the place, one goes to the place
for the sake of God.' St. Benedict clearly explains that 'in every
place it is the same God who is served, it is the same king one fights
under.' Again and again in the *Collationes Patrum* Joseph the hermit
fully explains that the person who keeps his oath most faithfully is
the one who has stationed himself in the place where he can most
completely fulfil the precepts of divine faith. Moreover he desires
us to seek out the opportunity for holiness, 'who is our helper in
trouble.' Unless I am mistaken those people are to be treated as
Pharisees or heretics who do not fear, nor permit others to fear,
what the Truth says : 'Unless your justice abounds more than that
of the Scribes and Pharisees you shall not enter into the kingdom of
heaven.' 'If an angel from heaven should preach a message other
than the Gospel, let him be anathema.' A message other than the
Gospel of Christ is being presented by any person who attempts to

obstruct those who are anxious to maintain evangelical peace and the rule of their profession. No matter who he may be, such a one is to be utterly rejected since the Truth says : 'If your eye offends you, pluck it out and cast it away from you.' There is no organ of the body which causes us more trouble when it is harmed than the eye ; none that we look after more carefully ; nevertheless when it offends us, spiritually speaking it must be plucked out. Similarly no doubt the director of souls, or anything held most dear (figuratively described as the 'eye') must be set aside for God's sake if it prevents one serving the truth ; for the essence of prudence is to withdraw one's mind from all illusions which are harmful to the soul. Still, so as to avoid scandalizing the weak who are less acquainted with the truth, we beg your grace—and all who give ear to our request—to strive to re-establish peace between the abbot of York and the previously mentioned brothers. Finally, we must remember that it was a similar exodus by the monks of Molesmes which led to the establishment of the Cistercian life as the acme of perfection which is admired by almost the whole church. Their purity of character was praised with Christian reverence by the lord archbishop of Lyons of holy memory who faithfully fostered the return to the unshakable integrity of the holy rule. And eventually when their enemies' criticisms were brought to the notice of the Holy See, in the pontificate of Urban II, a decretal was issued that only the abbot, who had also taken part in the exodus, must return to rule his abbey, but that no obstacle should be put in the way of any of the others who wished to live in full observation of the rule, nor should any pressure be brought to bear on these. "It is clearer than day how brightly the truth of the whole Gospel shines forth in the excellent manner of their lives"[57].

In many respects this is a revealing and intriguing letter. Intriguing because despite his unstinted praise of the Cistercians and equally uninhibited criticism of the older communities, when Thurstan himself retired to a monastery to die, seven years later, it was not to the Cistercians that he went but to that very Cluniac house at Pontefract which in 1132 had rallied to support abbot Geoffrey. It is revealing for the mind that is displayed here : of a man who could even address his superior in tones of command because he had a firm grasp of the issues at stake and the whole background of recent reforming movements—at Cluny and Cîteaux, and at Savigny and Fontevrault ; of an independence and spontaneity rarely met with in the upper reaches of an hierarchy, springing no doubt from his evangelical fervour—for it is noteworthy how Thurstan goes immediately to the New Testament for the principles that are to resolve issues, not to canon law as one would expect an archbishop at other times to do.

Whether the archbishop of Canterbury ever, in fact, had to face the panic-stricken Geoffrey we do not know. But we do know that Geoffrey's attempts to recover his flock met with some success in the autumn of 1132. Two of the seceders, Gervase and Ralph, returned to St. Mary's. Like the rest of their associates they had been living in accommodation provided for them by Thurstan[58] and his canons, and as this accommodation can scarcely have been lavish and was certainly overcrowded, they must have been struck by the contrast between their present condition, living in a social no-man's land, and their previous dignified status as respected members of the premier monastery in the shire. That they were daunted by the hardships ahead they themselves had the candour to admit, and Cistercian historians have been quick to underline the fact; but one must not overlook either their fears that the scandal accompanying their withdrawal from St. Mary's was a sign that this departure from the ways of their fathers was an offence against God[59]. Eventually Gervase decided that it was not, and made a second exodus from the abbey, this time going forward without hesitation to a distinguished career as a Cistercian; Ralph decided otherwise and remained at St. Mary's. What is quite extraordinary is that during their time of hesitation their abbot Geoffrey had the good grace to write twice on their behalf to Bernard of Clairvaux; Gervase and Ralph were still troubled in conscience and had felt that the abbot of Clairvaux might relieve their distress, so they had asked their own abbot to write for them. That he should have done so—and candidly—says much for the fundamental goodness of Geoffrey; that his two restless subjects should have asked him, with recent wounds still stinging, says even more for him. Especially since he can have been under no illusion as to the

---

58. According to William of Newburgh, Thurstan acted as both a father and a mother to these orphans from St. Mary's (*Historia Rerum Anglicarum*, in *Chronicles of the Reign of Stephen, Henry II and Richard I*), Vol. I, p. 50: Quorum studium zelumque venerabilis Turstinus amplexus, egressos paterne suscepit, maternae pietatis sinu fovit, et in suis penetralibus pro tempore occultatos, donec eis, prout animo conceperat, provideret, tandem in loco pascuae collocavit).

59. *Memorials of Fountains*, p. 42.

sort of answer he would get from Clairvaux : "It is not for me to condemn them," says Bernard, "The Lord knows who are his own and everyone shall bear his own burden. Let everyone judge for himself as leniently as he likes, but I shall say what I think of myself. I, Bernard, if I had in will and in deed passed freely from something good to something better, and from something dangerous to something safer, and then afterwards wilfully returned again to what I had changed for the better, I would very much fear that I had rendered myself not only an apostate, but also unfit for the kingdom of God"[60].

Geoffrey can have been left in no doubt that in the magisterial list of ticks and crosses which St. Bernard drew up for Europe's leading personalities he himself had received a cross. Thurstan was more fortunate ; his favour towards the Cistercians drew from Bernard hearty commendation : "The splendour of your work and your reputation amongst men have combined greatly, as I know, to your credit. Your deeds prove that yours is no undeserved or empty reputation, for facts themselves bear out what hitherto has everywhere been reported of you. How, especially of late, has your zeal for righteousness shone forth, your priestly activity stood out, and been strong in defence of the poor monks who had no helper ! All the church has told of your deeds of mercy and alms-giving, but this you have in common with many others, for it is the duty of all who possess the substance of this world. But this episcopal work, this eminent example of fatherly piety, this truly divine fervour and zeal wherewith he without doubt has inspired and girded you for the protection of his poor, who 'has made his angels like the winds, the servants that wait upon him like a flame of fire,' all this is wholly yours, the ornament of your dignity, the mark of your office, a glorious jewel in your crown. It is one thing to fill the belly of the hungry, and another to have a zeal for poverty"[61].

Certainly in the months following the famous 17th of October the group from St. Mary's owed everything, humanly speaking, to Thurstan. There were now fourteen of them, the loss of Ralph having been more than counterbalanced by the accession of two monks from Whitby ; as the priory there was bound by ties of

---

60. *Letters of St. Bernard*, p. 239. Bernard goes on to say that he will not give an opinion on a particular excommunication Geoffrey wishes to have launched because he does not know enough about the details. Who was Geoffrey wishing to have excommunicated ?
61. *Ibid.*, p. 240.
62. D. Knowles, *The Monastic Order in England*, p. 475.

fraternity with St. Mary's[62] it is probable that the two monks in
question, Robert and Adam, had come to hear of the reforming
visions that were being entertained in York and had set out to
follow them. Robert and Adam were both to achieve fame in the
Cistercian order and their fervour no doubt strengthened the morale
of the group, but it also increased the number of mouths to be filled.
The way in which Thurstan hoped to satisfy their material needs,
after himself sustaining them for these months, was to settle them
on a stretch of his estate near Ripon. Here, at Christmas, 1132, he
endowed them with two hundred acres of land in the woodlands of
Herleshow[63]; he then presided over the election of an abbot and
gave his blessing to the one elected, none other than the Richard
who had been prior at St. Mary's. But generously as Thurstan had
behaved when one remembers the other calls upon his purse, his
open-handedness was not sufficient to protect the newly-founded
community from the chilling blasts of winter and poverty; for the
rest of the winter they huddled together in huts beneath the boughs
of a great elm by the banks of the river Skell and slowly began the
painful business of clearing the ground on which to grow their
food[64].

Thurstan may have anticipated that help would quickly come
from local landowners; but if so he was to be disappointed. The
northern barons were happy to acquire a reputation for piety, but
they had no intention of ruining themselves in the process. Since
it is frequently overlooked this fact is worth particular stress. Thus
the amount of land they granted, even when winning the title of
founder of a monastery, was often quite small; Robert de Lascy,
for instance, is reckoned the founder of Nostell, yet he only gave the
half carucate of land upon which the church was set and the two
oxgangs of land in Hardwick[65]; Walter Espec is honoured as the
founder of Rievaulx, yet his fee of Helmsley had 189 carucates of
which Rievaulx was granted no more than nine[66]. Again the land
they gave was often encumbered by legal disputes or uncertain
ownership; Espec, for instance, granted Carham to his priory of
Kirkham though Queen Matilda had already granted it to Durham[67]; Hugh, earl of Chester put the abbey of Whitby and the

63. *E Y C* I, no. 63.
64. *Memorials of Fountains*, pp. 33–35.
65. *Cf* Farrer, *Early Lancashire Charters and Pipe Rolls*, p. 383.
66. *Cf* R. L. G. Ritchie's comments in *The Normans in Scotland*, p. 335.
67. *Cf Regesta* II, nos. 1143 and 1459.

priory of Guisborough at loggerheads by the ambiguity of his gift of churches[68] ; and William le Meschin confused the canons at Huntingdon and at Embsay by granting Skipton church to both of them[69]. Moreover what seems at first glance to be a gift from a baron to a monastery often turns out on closer scrutiny to be a commercial transaction ; one example of this was soon to occur at Fountains where the chartulary of the abbey shows that some of the grants made by Roger de Mowbray were for money received to enable him to make the journey to Jerusalem[70]. In fact, it was inevitable that the early Cistercians should constantly be making these transactions because their system of sheep-farming forced them to be selective in the kinds of land they undertook to work ; they had to buy and sell to achieve balanced husbandry[71]. But the observation above all others that makes one look twice before being overwhelmed by the evidence of baronial piety is that monastic granges were so very frequently the same lands as are written down as waste in the Domesday Survey ; these lands were an encumbrance to the landowner if he did not have the resources to exploit them ; conversely they were just the kind of lands that monks were searching for, especially the Cistercians, because they were not burdened with those feudal ties from which the Cistercians were trying to liberate themselves[72]. Economic interests and the decencies of religion here coincided beautifully ; but the two are not to be identified.

The local feudatories around Ripon had, in any case, not yet caught on to these features of the Cistercian experiment—which they seem to have regarded with suspicion to judge by the fact that they made no grants whatsoever to the little community by the Skell in its first two years of existence. The brethren were, in fact, near the point of starving at one stage until Eustace FitzJohn from the neighbouring castle of Knaresborough sent along to them a trolley filled with loaves[73]. Grateful as they were for this temporary alleviation the brethren by 1135 had decided that lack of material resources to put their community on a working basis made it im-

---

68. *E Y C* II, no. 873.
69. *Cf* p. 113.
70. *E Y C* I, p. 64.
71. *E Y C* I, pp. 65, 67 ; II, p. 292 ; *Chartulary of Rievaulx*, no. 53.
72. See the very illuminating pages of B. Waites, The Monastic Settlement of North-East Yorkshire, *Yorkshire Archaeological Journal*, CLIX (1961), pp. 478–495.
73. *Memorials of Fountains*, p. 50.

possible to remain in Yorkshire. Indeed, negotiations were already well advanced for them to leave the country altogether and settle near Clairvaux when they were saved by the arrival, in quick succession, of three wealthy recruits[74]. The first of these was Hugh, the dean of York, who not only brought money and lands but also scriptural treatises that formed the beginnings of a monastic library. It was this ready cash of the dean's which spelled the difference between failure and survival for the brethren who, chastened by their experience of poverty, prudently divided it into three parts each to its appropriate use ; these uses were, to help the poor, to build their monastery and to provide for their own maintenance. The other two wealthy recruits were also from York Minster, canons Serlo and Tosti, the former of whom had been present on the day of the dramatic exodus from St. Mary's.

By easing the way for these notable figures to join Fountains, as the monastery was now called, Thurstan had ensured the fruition of the work so hesitantly begun in the early months of 1132. Now that Fountains had been established it was easy to see the working of God's providence in the events of that year ; it was to Thurstan's credit that in the confusion of motives around him he had so clearly seen it from the first and had quickly but firmly removed every obstacle to the work of the spirit.

It seems to be the fate of certain historical figures to act as flash-points for fierce tensions that have long been building up around them. Thurstan had performed this function in the York/Canterbury dispute, and his actions at St. Mary's now led him to switch on a current that produced a similar effect in the dispute about the status of monks as such. Clearly one of the gravest matters troubling the minds of the reforming group within St. Mary's had arisen from the difficulty of reconciling the monastic ideal of poverty with the practices that had become general throughout the monastic body, the practice of receiving tithes, for instance, or of taking over churches and their revenues, or of enjoying far wider acres than was necessary to maintain them in apostolic simplicity. Were they not, they asked themselves, usurping both the functions and revenues that properly belonged to the secular clergy ?

In asking themselves this question the troubled monks of St. Mary's were simply echoing the debate that had swayed backwards

---

74. *Ibid.*, pp. 51–54.

and forwards for several generations around the "crisis in the cenobitical life"[75], which threw up the whole question of what it means to be a monk as opposed to being simply a cleric. Surprisingly violent passions were aroused by this seemingly academic query because ever since the papacy had begun its drive for reform in the second half of the eleventh century the impetus towards reform had come from monks who had striven to impose monkish ideals, including compulsory celibacy and a common refectory, upon secular clerics and cathedral canons. Reaction was inevitable. The secular clerics hit back by criticizing the monks for invading the sphere of the secular clergy ; critics such as Serlo of Bayeux and the canon of Rouen whom we quoted earlier (p. 3) pointed to the accumulating wealth and privileges of the monasteries and asked what did it mean to be a monk if such worldly prosperity went with it. However, the reaction against monkish aggression was not confined to the secular clerics, it also sprang up within the ranks of the monks themselves ; Bernard of Tiron, Robert of Molesme, Bernard of Clairvaux and many more, were convinced that in going beyond its proper sphere the body of monks was in danger of losing its *raison d'être* and forgetting what it means to be a monk ; they wished monasteries to cut themselves free from the feudal ties by which they were necessarily bound if they remained great feudatories with jurisdiction over lands and towns and churches. Thus a curious alignment had been brought about, with the established monastic orders coming under fire from both old-fashioned secular clerics and the *avantgarde* of reformed monasticism. And the critics were intellectually strengthened through the arguments urged by that great canonist, Ivo bishop of Chartres, whose influence is writ so large on the mind of the early twelfth century. On one occasion, for instance, Ivo as bishop had to protest against the attempt by monks of St. Cyprian to intrude themselves in a church that belonged to seculars ; he maintained that it was ruinous pride which prompted monks to lord it over clerics and reminded them of St. Augustine's dictum : "Not even a good monk makes a good cleric" ; or if they preferred the words of a monk, let them remember Jerome's observation, "A monk's function is to repent, not to teach," or again, "Clerics feed the sheep ; I am one who is fed," or again, "If you really wish to be a monk (which means 'alone') what are you doing dwelling in

---

75. We owe the phrase to Dom. G. Morin, Rainaud l'Ermite et Yves de Chartres : Un épisode de la crise du cénobitisme aux XI–XII siècles, in *Revue Bénédictine*, XL (1928), pp. 99–115.

cities ? "[76]. When one considers Ivo's experience with these monks, and even more the trouble he had from two monks of Marmoutier, or his successor's running fight with Geoffrey of Vendôme, abbot of La Trinité[77], and remembers the similar struggles being waged throughout Christendom, one appreciates why the tide of feeling against established monasticism was running so high at this time[78]. All the strikingly different people who shared this feeling, secular clerics, bishops and monastic reformers themselves, contributed to the pressure which led the Lateran Council of 1123 to promulgate a canon in restraint of monks. It is laid down by this canon that abbots and monks are forbidden to give public penances, to visit the sick, to administer extreme unction or celebrate public masses; they must obtain the holy chrism, and holy oils and ordinations from the bishops of the diocese where they live, and have their altars consecrated by them[79]. Caught in the same current of opinion the provincial Council of Rouen in 1128 laid it down that monks and abbots were not to accept either churches or tithes from the hands of lay people[80].

In England, meanwhile, the debate had taken some peculiar turns on account of peculiar circumstances prevailing on the hither side of the Channel. A lasting result of the earlier monastic revival of the tenth century had been that several English cathedrals were actually manned by monks already and this struck the Norman ecclesiastics who followed the Conqueror as anomalous. Even men who were not hostile to monks in themselves[81], such as Walkelin who was made bishop of Winchester in 1070, raised their eyebrows at this odd English institution of the monastic cathedral and resolved

---

76. *P L* Vol. 162, cols. 48–9. In cols. 198–202 of the same volume (p. 192) will be found Ivo's brilliant and magisterial treatment of the related question of monks receiving tithes; if only more of his contemporaries had shared his sensitive, discriminating mentality they could have avoided the subsequent clashes over reform.

77. *Cf* L. Compain, *Geoffrey de Vendôme* (Paris, 1891), pp. 175-182.

78. There are so many cases of struggles between bishops and monks over churches and tithes at this time that one could fill volumes with illustrations, but an impression of the intensity of the struggle may quickly be gained by perusing *Papsturkunden in Frankreich* (ed. J. Ramackers). Vol. II, 1937 & Vol. V, 1956, paying particular attention to the great houses of Marmoutier and Fontevrault.

79. *Mansi* XXI, col. 283. CXVII ; Hefele-Leclercq, *Histoire des Conciles*, V, I, pp. 636–7.

80. *Mansi* XXI, col. 375.

81. D. Knowles, *The Monastic Order in England*, p. 130.

to substitute canons for monks as soon as possible. The substitution never took place at Winchester, or elsewhere, for the very good reason that the metropolitan of England for the next fifty years was in every case a monk himself and ready to withstand any attempt to streamline the monastic cathedrals. But the succession of monks as archbishops of Canterbury, Lanfranc, Anselm and Ralph, shook the kaleidoscope of ecclesiastical forces into some unexpected patterns. So that in 1095, for instance, when Anselm found himself withstanding King William Rufus at Rockingham he also found all the bishops except one ranged against him whereas the lay magnates obstinately stood by him. This odd state of affairs is partly explained of course, by Anselm's attractive personality and the sway which he exercised over the great barons, but other factors proved still more influential. To begin with, almost all the English bishops were secular clerics who had achieved their present eminence through their usefulness to the king as obedient civil servants ; and in their dioceses they had put up with more than enough from the reforms of the previous monkish metropolitan, Lanfranc ; to them Anselm's recalcitrance was yet another symptom of the monk's belief that there was one law for the cleric and another for the monk. They had subjected themselves to the king's will and they saw no reason why Anselm should be spared this obligation. In the second place, the lay magnates had no great opinion of Rufus or his civil servant bishops ; they were the natural rivals to the bishops as advisers to the king and as sharers in the rewards of office, and the opportunity to oppose both king and bishops in the shade of such a holy ally as Anselm was unique and not to be missed. With the aid of Anselm they left the bishops discomfited.

But a further opportunity to torment the monks was given to the bishops some twenty years later when they were summoned for the election of another archbishop in 1114. When they arrived at Windsor in the spring of this year, they discovered to their dismay that Henry and the monks of Canterbury had previously agreed on Faritius, the abbot of Abingdon, as the most suitable candidate for the vacant see. To this arrangement they objected firmly ; those two episcopal schemers, Roger of Salisbury and Robert Bloet of Lincoln, solemnly pointed out that as a medical man Faritius was obliged to examine the urine of females and this would be most unfitting for an archbishop[82]. More seriously, the bishops main-

---

82. *Chronicon Monasterii de Abingdon* (*R S*) II, p. 287.

tained that the next archbishop should certainly not be a monk ;
he should be a secular cleric or a chaplain from the king's chapel—
one of their own kind, in other words. In this claim they were
unsuccessful, for though they managed to exclude Faritius it was
another monk, Ralph, who was elected[83]. But by the next time the
bishops got a chance to air their prejudices, in 1123, the atmosphere
had become charged with sinister designs upon the monks ; it
helped them to get William of Corbeil elected and to break the
succession of monkish archbishops, though the monks, earls and
thegns again stood together against the bishops' candidate[84], as
they had done in 1095.

The truth is that the murmuring against them in the first
quarter of the twelfth century threw the English monks into a
posture of aggressive defence. For instance, a certain abbot named
Richard (of Ely ?) wrote to Herbert de Losinga, bishop of Norwich,
asking him to compose a tract against the clerics and in defence of
the monks, since "Some men of perverse mind, with all the wild
lawlessness of canons, and raving at and bearing a grudge to
monastic devotion, are inflamed with arrogance and pride (enkindled,
as it were, by the fires of malice), and bring to bear all the incite-
ments of mischievous talk to stigmatize and weaken the communities of monks, and disturb by the storm-clouds of their boasting
the security of our secret contemplation"[85]. If Richard imagined
that, as a monk himself, Herbert would compose such a tract against
the clerics he was mistaken ; Herbert, as bishop, had seen the other
side of the coin when he had tried to get control of the abbey of
Bury St. Edmunds and been defeated by the monks ; he more or
less told Richard that the monks were doing very well for themselves and had little to complain about, and that the dispute
between clerics and monks was a vain one. Vain or not, his successor Everard seems to have pursued it, for in 1125 the abbot of
Bury St. Edmunds was in Rome to secure from the Pope a privilege
in virtue of which, if ever the abbey was transformed into the seat
of a bishopric then no one should be elected bishop except a monk[86].
At this very time, on the other side of England, a vacancy in the
monastic see of Worcester had set the monks trembling for what

83.   Eadmer, *Historia Novorum*, pp. 222–3.
84.   *Anglo-Saxon Chronicle*, s.a. 1123.
85.   *The Life, Letters and Sermons of Bishop Herbert de Losinga* (ed. E. M.
      Goulburn and H. Symonds) I, pp. 262–3.
86.   *Cf* p. 91. They had seen what had happened at Ely, where the monastery
      in 1109 was made the seat of a bishopric.

would happen to them if a secular cleric were appointed over them ; in consequence they received an impassioned letter from Eadmer urging them to stand together.   "Every kingdom divided against itself shall be laid waste, " he wrote.   "Just think how great is the envy that certain malicious men aim against the monastic order, and how energetically they are trying to root the monks out of all episcopal sees. Have a care, then, for the sake of your own souls, lest you yourselves should be the first one rooted out." Eadmer, in the rather melodramatic way that had become second nature to him, goes on to point out to them what a thin time they were likely to have if they failed to stand together[87].

Indeed, Eadmer may well have been responsible for raising the temperature all round since he had so readily believed or even embroidered the story about Walkelin of Winchester's hatred for the monks in the time of the Conqueror. According to him Walkelin was so set upon driving out the monks from his cathedral that he had stationed forty clerics waiting in the wings, as it were, and tonsured like canons, all ready to occupy the stage as soon as the monks were bowed off. But the hero of the monks, Lanfranc, dramatically intervened to thwart Walkelin's designs just as he later thwarted similar designs against the monks of Christ Church, Canterbury[88]. The fact that Walkelin in reality was no hater of monks simply goes to show how under the threat of a purge history was being re-written by monastic chroniclers to show that the conspiracy against them was of long standing ; even the normally balanced William of Malmesbury subscribed to this version of past events when he wrote : "then the malice of the bishops grew worse as they schemed to eject the monks from all the cathedrals and put in clerics ; the author of this mischief was Walkelin[89]".

Another feature which may have contributed to the shrillness of the debate was the fact that many of the most ardent defenders

---

87.   Wharton, *Anglia Sacra*, II, p. 238 ; *P L* 169, cols. 301–303.
88.   Eadmer, *Historia Novorum*, pp. 18–19.
89.   *Gesta Pontificum*, p. 71. See also *Annales Monastici* II (Winchester), p. 46 for another instance of a quarrel between monks and a bishop : Hoc anno fuit enormis et non tam narranda quam tacenda discordia inter Willelmum episcopum Wintoniae et monachos suos pro dilapidatione, et praecipue pro novem ecclesiis, quae de maneriis monachorum fuerant, quas eis abstulit. Nescientes igitur quid eis agendum esset, crucium pedes verterunt sursum et capita deorsum, et processionem nudis pedibus contra solis cursum et morem ecclesiasticum fecerunt ; ut sicut episcopus contra decreta canonica victus eis necessaria in ecclesia Deo deservientibus abstulit, sic ipsi ecclesiae contra jus et decreta ecclesiastica deservirent. Fovebat autem partem monachorum rex, episcopi vero partem fovebant omnes fere capitanei Angliae.

of the monastic order and its privileges belonged to that curiously self-conscious group of high-churchmen who were held together by their devotion to the feast of the Conception of the Blessed Virgin Mary. Eadmer was probably the most gifted of them, who wrote a treatise on the Conception ; Anselm of Bury, the nephew of Eadmer's hero, brought to the celebration his knowledge of the Byzantine feast derived from his period at the Greek monastery of St. Sabbas ; he it was who at Bury instituted a daily Mass for King Henry I's intentions and provided for the worthy celebration of the Conception and the feast of St. Sabbas, all in the course of the same charter[90]. This combination of extravagant liturgical interests with personal ties produces overtones of preciosity in the behaviour of the group ; thus another of them, Hugh abbot of Reading, observed the feast in his monastery "at the request of King Henry"[91], and when yet another, Osbert of Clare, was writing to his friend Warin of Worcester, a man renowned for his devotion to the Virgin[92], he explained that he could not say everything that he believes in the accompanying tract on the Conception, "since it is not permitted to scatter heavenly pearls publicly before the multitude who are given to obscuring the clarity of the sun with the dense clouds of their own errors"[93]. The suggestion in this letter of a close circle of intimate friends more sensitive than the vulgar herd amongst whom they find themselves is frequently echoed in the writings issuing from Canterbury, Worcester, Westminster, St. Albans, Bury and Reading, and the ramifications of their friendships must have stretched further still ; Osbert of Clare, for instance, was a relative of Athelwold, king's confessor and then bishop of Carlisle, whose intervention Osbert sought to secure his own return to Westminster after a period of banishment[94] ; his period of banishment had been spent amongst the congenial monks of Ely, the spiritual children of that Richard whose fierce loyalty to the monks against the clerics we have quoted[95]. Osbert remained friendly with them just as he cultivated the friendship of a further exponent of high monasticism, Elmer, prior of Canterbury, a disciple of St. Anselm's, who wrote a whole series of letters to a varied

90.   *Feudal Documents from the Abbey of Bury St. Edmunds* (ed. D. C. Douglas), pp. 112–113.

91.   *The Letters of Osbert of Clare* (ed. Williamson), Ep. 67.

92.   *Chronicle of John of Worcester* (ed. J. H. R. Weaver), p. 41.

93.   *The Letters of Osbert of Clare*, Ep. 13.

94.   *Ibid.*, Ep. 9.

95.   *Ibid.*, Ep. 33.

group of lay and religious correspondents of which the unending theme is the superiority of the monastic life[96]. Granted this concentration of sensitivity, friendship and liturgical and monastic interests in the group it is easily seen how readily they would come to think of themselves as a minority defending precious things against the coarse and uncomprehending spirit of the age. And what more irrefutable confirmation could they have asked for their suspicions than that the chief scorner of their cherished devotion was none other than the notorious opponent of the monks, Roger bishop of Salisbury! This scandalous cleric, along with that other "follower of Satan," Bernard of St. David's, had intervened in December, 1127 (or 1128) to try to prevent the celebration of the Feast of the Conception, a feast which they described as "ridiculous" and "unheard of" and without the sanction of the Roman Church[97].

It is true that an occasional voice can be heard in this strident debate urging moderation, as Herbert de Losinga had done, and as the chanter of Salisbury Cathedral, Godwin, was doing in the 1120's[98] ; but they are isolated voices and much more typical is the ceaseless sniping with which Eadmer, on one side, and Hugh the Chanter, on the other, enraged each other. In any case Herbert de Losinga's statement that "a monk is the very same thing as a cleric"[99], however eirenically intended, could hardly fail to render the situation more confused. As with so many issues, what it required now was that some man of independent and direct mind, and not identified with either faction, should put the simple question that the commentators were skirting around and ducking under : what, precisely, is the status of the monk, as such, within the church ? Thurstan was precisely the man required, and he put the question, probably in the autumn of 1132[100]. But more remarkable than his having done so was the address to which he directed it—not to the Pope or any great prelate of the day, but to Theobald of Étampes, a learned secular cleric then teaching in Oxford.

96. J. Leclercq, in *Studia Anselmiana*, No. 31 (1953), pp. 45–117 ; Écrits Spirituels d'Elmer de Canterbury.

97. *The Letters of Osbert of Clare*, Ep. 7.

98. Bodley MS. Digby. 96 fo. 22.

99. *The Life, Letters and Sermons of Bishop Herbert de Losinga*, I, p. 262.

100. There seems to be no possibility of fixing an exact date, but this is the most probable one ; *cf* Mlle. Foreville and J. Leclercq : Un débat sur le sacerdoce des moines au XII siècle, in *Studia Anselmiana*, 41 (1957), pp. 8–118), pp. 30–33. Theobald's attack on the monks is printed in this volume, pp. 52–3 ; the rest of his works are to be found in *P L* vol. 163, cols. 759–770.

Theobald had been educated at Caen some years before Thurstan himself took to the schools ; they may well have met in
Thurstan's youth since Theobald continued as a teacher at Caen and
seems to have known several Bayeux men well[101]. By about 1092
he had become a Doctor of Caen and his reputation brought him an
offer from Queen Margaret of Scotland that he should take up a post
in her own realm, an offer which Theobald graciously declined.
At about the same time he entered the lists against the redoubtable
Roscellinus to defend the sons of priests from Roscellinus' sneers
and to refute the proposition that they were ineligible for the priesthood on account of their tainted birth. In the first years of the
twelfth century Theobald moved to Oxford, into a diocese ruled by
a Bayeux man, Robert Bloet of Lincoln, and carved out a career for
himself as a highly successful teacher. It was almost certainly under
the patronage of Walter, archdeacon of Oxford, that he worked, and
in the college of St. George's-in-the-Castle. During this period he
crossed swords, friendly but distinctly sharp, with Faritius abbot of
Abingdon over the issue of whether baptism by water was necessary
for salvation, and he also answered officially a theological query
from Robert Bloet regarding confession and repentance[102]. In
each of these theological disquisitions the quality of the man is
evident ; massive common-sense is the keynote to all of them, a
firm grasp of the central Christian teaching and an economy of
argument contrived by a series of quotations from the authorities ;
the work of a born schoolmaster, not to be distracted by over-
subtlety. They were the qualities, no doubt, that led to his being
invoked as a theological consultant and so there need be no surprise
on this score that Thurstan should have brought him into the
debate. But it is worth stressing that Thurstan must have known
fairly well what sort of answer he would receive from Theobald :
an answer brusquely critical of the privileged positions within the
church that the monks had worked themselves into.

This was, indeed, the unmistakable message of Theobald's
little treatise. "The church is one thing," he says, "and the monastery another ; for the church is the assembly of the faithful whereas
a monastery is a place or prison of the condemned, that is to say,
of those who have condemned themselves so that they will avoid
everlasting damnation"[103]. Already in these opening sentences

---

101.   For example, Thurstan, Robert Bloet of Lincoln and Roscellinus.
102.   P L Vol. 163, cols. 763–4, 759–763.
103.   *Studia Anselmiana* 41, p. 52.

he is taking digs at the monks in a way not quite paralleled in his
other controversial works ; he continues in a like manner by asserting that monks have no clerical status, as is shown by the fact that
they wear their hoods set transversely to signify that "they have
stripped themselves of their clergy having already lost their heads
because they are not allowed to preach to the people or to baptize
or to bind and loose penitents or any of the other functions which
are ascribed to the church." By what presumption, then, asks
Theobald, do they take over churches that they are unable to serve ?
For as the tag says : A person should not live by the altar who does
not serve the altar. He proceeds to develop this crucial point with
a series of quotations from St. Jerome and Gregory before coming
out with his unqualified condemnation of monks for taking tithes :
tithes from the beginning, in the Old Covenant, were devised for the
support of the cleric ; the monk is not a cleric ; it is therefore a grave
abuse for monks to take over churches and the tithes that go with
them ; the monk should pay tithes rather than receive them. The
monks should follow the example of their primitive founders and
live off the fruits of their own bodily labour[104].

With all this, of course, the reform party within St. Mary's
abbey would have agreed ; it chimed in with their own ideal programme ; but it called forth a fierce rejoinder from an anonymous
English monk—or from a group of them, because the long and
rambling attack on Theobald's letter, *Rescriptum cuiusdam pro
monachis*[105], bears the marks of having been composed by several
people, all putting forward their favourite debating points. Even
for the story of the debate between clerics and monks the rejoinder
cannot claim much intellectual importance so wildly does it veer
about from quotation to quotation or custom to custom ; its significance for that story lies rather in the complex of emotions it
reveals. But to the biographer of Thurstan the anonymous tract
holds considerable interest for its implicit—and not so implicit—
criticism of the archbishop. Clearly Thurstan had meant to initiate
some public discussion of the monastic ideal by his appeal to
Theobald, and the speed at which Theobald's reply became generally
known bears witness to his having succeeded. This alone was
sufficient to have aroused the anger of the traditionalists, but what
really stuck in their throats was the fact that he had sought the
opinion of Theobald—*tantillum clericellum*, as the anonymous tract

---

104. *Ibid.*, p. 53.
105. *Ibid.*, pp. 55–111.

calls him, "a petty clerk"[106]. And here now was this petty clerk sitting in judgment upon the order of monks ! "Though we cannot be altogether sure," says the anonymous author, with the heavy sarcasm he frequently displays, "whether he [i.e. Thurstan] did this to learn from Theobald or in order to tempt him"[107]. Since it surely cannot have been out of ignorance that so eminent a member of the hierarchy acted, he continues, we can only infer that the second alternative is the correct one. Otherwise, he says with an unmistakable dig at Thurstan, what are we to make of Gregory the Great's dictum that if any spiritual issue is laid before a bishop it would be most ignominious if he then had to start learning the answer which it is his office to provide ? This telling dictum, intended to show Thurstan in a bad light, is repeated once more later in the tract[108], adding to its oblique criticism of the archbishop. And in view of Thurstan's fame as a patron of the regular canons the second line of the anonymous attack seems likewise to be pointed at him : Theobald says that a monastery is a place and prison of the condemned, that is, of monks who have condemned themselves in this world so as to avoid everlasting damnation ; but why, writes the anonymous, does he not include the regular canons in his definition since they also live in a monastery ? Why does he ignore the canons ? Perhaps because the canons might then be condemned like the monks"[109].

York, also, this time in the person of certain canons rather than of the archbishop, must have felt the sting in the anonymous monks' sarcasm. The author protests that of course his criticisms of secular clerics only apply to certain types—"we do not mean to write anything disrespectful about other clerics such as canons and archdeacons. Far be it from us, far be it to presume to attribute anything evil to them, especially when they are attached to bishops and—thank God !—are not bleary-eyed. . . . Nor have we ever seen or heard tell of canons or archdeacons or archpriests—God forbid—taking wives or having them or begetting sons and daughters ; or of their sons, on their fathers' deaths, succeeding them in their archdeaconry or canonry by a sort of hereditary succession"[110]. Even the pious ears of a monk would need to have been tightly

106. *Ibid.*, p. 54.
107. *Idem.*
108. *Ibid.*, p. 97.
109. *Ibid.*, p. 55.
110. *Ibid.*, p. 102.

sealed, at this time, not to have heard of canons and archdeacons behaving in the horrifying way he instances ; but to pretend otherwise was the anonymous monk's mock-innocent way of emphasizing the vulnerability of the secular clerics if people were to start looking for beams in each other's eyes. And the chapter at York was as vulnerable as the next ; it is known that one canon, Thurstan's own nephew, Osbert, begot children[111], that another, Letold, was also a father[112], and that a third canon, Serlo, had a son who claimed an inheritance from his father[113]. Perhaps it was specially vulnerable, since the indignant monk greets a reference in Theobald's tract to the penury of clerics with an outburst of scorn that explodes first upon York : "Oh, penury ! What about York ? What about London ? What about Salisbury ? What about Lincoln . . . "[114].

These shafts of sarcasm must certainly have struck home at York and set the canons speculating on the identity of the anonymous author. And if their eyes had turned in suspicion towards the old enemy at Canterbury they may not have been far out. Not only does the anonymous author act as spokesman for the traditional superiority of the monks over the secular clergy for which Canterbury had become the acknowledged mouthpiece, but internal criticism points to the pupils of St. Anselm as the source of his treatise[115]. The monks of Canterbury, moreover, had particular reasons for disliking Theobald since he had engaged in public dispute with Faritius of Abingdon, whom they had unanimously supported to receive the see of Canterbury in 1114 when some of the English bishops had tried to get a secular cleric elevated to the see in preference to any monk. So if Thurstan, by consulting Theobald, had brought to a head the debate about the monastic life he had also given the monks of Canterbury a golden opportunity to pay off several old scores.

---

111.   *Cf* p. 244.

112.   Letold's son John received the archdeaconry of Cleveland (*Yorkshire Archaeological Journal*, XXXVI, pp. 415–9).

113.   *The Chartulary of Bridlington Priory* (ed. W. T. Lancaster), p. 431.

114.   *Studia Anselmiana*, 41, p. 65.

115.   *Ibid.*, p. 51. Dom Leclercq says of the author : "Bref, celui-ci appartient réellement à la famille des disciples de S. Anselme . . ."

CHAPTER VII.

PROMOTER OF HOLY VOCATIONS.

We have already seen how important it was for a bishop, in Thurstan's view, to protect and foster monastic life in his diocese. His efforts to do so have been frequently referred to, but always as events in some wider issue. Since the uproar over Fountains had pointed up Thurstan's reputation as a patron of monks and spiritual director perhaps this is a good moment at which to pause and recall his achievements in this field.

Already before Thurstan's coming to York the revival of monastic life had begun in the province. Recent years had seen the establishment of Nostell (1106 ?), Whitby (1109), Wetheral (1106-12), Hexham (1113), and Bridlington (1113-14), whilst the houses of St. Mary (1088-89) and Holy Trinity (1093) in York itself were going from strength to strength. By 1132 the formative period of these foundations was over, however ; and the same was even true of the second group which owed so much to Thurstan's personal initiative : Guisborough (1119), Bolton (1120), Worksop (1120), St. Bees (1120), Kirkham (1122), Furness (1127), Carlisle (1129-33). Five out of these seven belonged to the Augustinian order which was now receiving less of the limelight. Indeed it is a distinctly shadowy existence that another cluster of Augustinian houses were committed to when they modestly appeared about the time of the stirring deeds in St. Mary's. These were at Drax, south-east of Selby, Warter, some 15 miles east of York, and Thurgarton, a few miles south of Southwell ; and in most cases Thurstan acted as adviser to their founders. The founder of Drax, William Paynel, acknowledges the archbishop's help[1], as does Ralph d'Aincourt[2], the founder of Thurgarton ; the origins of Warter are so obscure

---

1. *E Y C* VI, p. 87. " . . . monitu et consilio domini Turstini . . . "
2. *Cambridge Historical Journal*, IV (1932-4), p. 296. In his charter Thurstan speaks of the foundation having been made " . . . nostra amonicione et consilio . . . " The charter is there printed by Prof. Galbraith in an appendix to his article, *Monastic Foundation Charters of the XI and XII, Centuries*, pp. 205-222.

that we cannot tell whether its founder, Geoffrey FitzPayne, owed a similar debt to Thurstan[3].

But little is known of these three late children of the Augustinian family ; their careers are undistinguished and no chronicle remains to light up the details of their domestic life. They are all over-shadowed by the brilliant success of the Cistercian communities at Fountains, Rievaulx and Newminster and the dramatic happenings at Calder and Byland, in all of which Thurstan's part was of the first importance. It is essential to an understanding of that part to see it as something different from the conventional patronage of monas-ticism which was characteristic of most twelfth century bishops, even of the worldly ones ; in mere patronage Thurstan, though outstanding, was not exceptional. What makes him exceptional, and gives the stamp of distinction to his patronage is the under-standing he shows of the inspiration behind the call to the cloister. His was no external munificence, but a genuine participation in the interior life of the people he was helping, to which eloquent testi-mony was given by the chronicler of Hexham when he wrote : "to mark the contempt in which he held his rank he dispensed himself from nothing of the discipline of a holy life and a fixed resolution of mind ; for in food and clothing and other features of the dedicated life he exhibited the austerity of a true bishop. In distributing alms and benevolence to the poor throughout the days of his ministry there was rarely found another comparable to him. He was constant in prayer and had from God the grace of tears in the celebration of Mass. This same man wore a shirt of hair-cloth and amid frequent confessions did not spare himself from corporal castigation. His overwhelming preoccupation at all times was the care of souls. He promoted disciplined and learned men to ecclesiastical offices ; he placed the disposal of the churches' affairs in their hands ; by his pastoral zeal he cut down the enticements of the wicked. He was cheerful in entertaining guests, approachable but firm towards reasonable men, severe without inhumanity towards the rebellious. He so ordered his men, his lands and his household in quiet peace, with an abundance of the necessities—so preserved the liberties, dignities and privileges of churches and ecclesiastical persons and inspired them to daily improvement in religion—that I would unhesitatingly assert it was the divine wisdom co-operating with him. There are few these days who nurture religious persons with

---

3.   *Cf* N. Denholm-Young, The Foundation of Warter Priory, in *Y A J*, XXXI, 1934, pp. 208–13.

such regard, promote them to benefices and constantly supply needy places with sumptuous alms"[4]. From this passage alone we could confidently conclude that Thurstan was a trusted and experienced spiritual director. And though it goes without saying that the work of spiritual direction must remain almost entirely hidden, beyond the recovery of the historian, nevertheless sufficient oblique evidence has survived for us to glimpse the skill of Thurstan in this sphere.

The first person whom we know to have sought his advice about the interior life was one of Europe's most prominent personalities, Adela the daughter of William the Conqueror, now Countess of Blois. Her having done so is all the more noteworthy when it is recognized that Adela did not belong to that type of pious female who automatically dances to the tune of her priestly acquaintances. She was not the daughter of William the Conqueror for nothing, and something of her grand manner in things ecclesiastical comes out in her son Henry, the famous bishop of Winchester; and when occasion demanded she had set her face against the great bishop of Chartres, Ivo[5]. But in the autumn of 1119, when she acted as host to the exiled Thurstan at Blois, her mind was turning away from matters of church and state towards the quickening of her own interior life. It seemed providential that at this moment she should be enabled to open her heart to the charming archbishop elect whose tenacious grasp of principle had permitted him to withstand the threats and cajolery of her own brother, Henry, King of England. The fact that Thurstan twice returned to Blois in the following months is enough to suggest the understanding that had grown up between them. Having recognized the touch of God's hand upon the countess he, along with other prelates, had the satisfaction of conducting Adela to the convent of Marcigny, where she took the veil[6].

Thurstan's role in nurturing the countess's vocation must have become widely known fairly soon, but alone it cannot account for the fact that by 1122 he was already noted as a promoter of holy vocations[7]. There were other instances, one assumes, that have escaped record. But his reputation we know through his being called in to aid that remarkable female recluse, Christina of Mark-

---

4. *Priory of Hexham*, pp. 128–9.
5. *P L* Vol. 162, col. 140.
6. *H C* p. 93.
7. *The Life of Christina of Markyate* (ed. C. H. Talbot), p. 110 : " . . . erat enim talium fautor studiorum."

yate. Born about 1096 at Huntingdon of a good Anglo-Saxon family that had branches all over the country, Christina had taken a vow whilst visiting St. Alban's abbey to remain a virgin and in her determination to fulfil that vow she had projected herself and a fair number of distinguished ecclesiastics into a series of comic opera situations. At one point she resisted attempts to seduce her made by the notorious bishop of Durham, Ranulf Flambard ; a little later she was forced by her parents to go through a marriage cere-mony against her will, but managed to prevent her bridegroom from consummating the marriage. In fact, she escaped to Markyate, a place near St. Alban's, where she lived under the protection of a hermit named Roger. Knowing that he was soon to die, and wanting Christina to succeed to his hermitage, so we are told, "Roger was anxious both before God and men to provide a patron and the necessities of life for his successor. At length he bethought himself of archbishop Thurstan of York, for he was a helpful promoter of such holy vocations [as well as being a faithful and devoted friend to Roger on account of his holiness][8]. He sent to him, therefore, to ask what he thought should be done about Christina. Thurstan asked to have a private interview with the maiden . . ." As chaperon to her for the journey Roger chose an old man, Godescalc, who "took Christina from him and led her secretly to the archbishop at Rad-bourn. With her he talked privately for a long time and, learning from her what needed doing, he took her from that time into his keeping, and made a promise which later on he fulfilled : namely, the annulment of her marriage, the confirmation of her vow, and permission for her husband to marry another woman by apostolic indult. Then he sent her back home. Christina remained, therefore, with Roger in his hermitage until his death. But when he had gone to heaven, where he rested in peace after his many tribulations, it was imperative that Christina should go elsewhere to avoid the anger of the bishop of Lincoln. Therefore after she had first taken various hiding-places, the archbishop commended her to the charge of a certain cleric, a close friend of his whose name I am under an obligation not to divulge. He was at once a religious and a man of position in the world ; and relying on this twofold status Christina felt the more safe in staying with him. And certainly at the begin-ning they had no feelings about each other, except chaste and spiritual affection. But the devil, the enemy of chastity, not brook-

---

8. This phrase within square brackets is not from the *Life of Christina* but from the *Gesta Abbatum Albani*, I, p. 100.

ing this for long, took advantage of their close companionship and feeling of security to insinuate himself first stealthily and with guile, then later on, alas, to assault them more openly"[9]. We are happy to learn that though the cleric gave in to these assaults, Christina proved to be of sterner stuff and repulsed him. And then the cleric himself was brought back to virtue by a vision in which St. John the Evangelist, St. Benedict and Mary Magdalen threatened him with dire consequences unless he turned from his wickedness. So all was well in the end.

Although we are sorry to discover that Thurstan's trust had in this way been misplaced it seems that his friendship with Christina was not undermined by these happenings, for a few years later her anonymous biographer has this to say of her : "She had frequent visits from the heads of celebrated monasteries in different parts of England and from across the sea, who wished to take her away with them and by her presence add importance and prestige to their places. Above all, the archbishop of York tried very hard to do her honour and to make her superior over the virgins whom he had gathered together under his name at York, and if not, send her over the sea to Marcigny or at least to Fontevrault. But she preferred our monastery. . . ."[10]. The "our monastery" is, of course, St. Alban's, of which the anonymous biographer was clearly a member ; and it is interesting to notice, both here and in the chronicle, how Thurstan is spoken of in a respectful manner, in spite of the occasions for irritation between the abbey and the archbishop which were not lacking. St. Alban's held land in the diocese of York, at Appleton and Thorpe Bassett, and such an enclave was always likely to cause a squabble with the diocesan[11] ; then in 1120 Thurstan had not given judgment in St. Alban's favour when that abbey was disputing Tynemouth with Durham[12], whilst it cannot have pleased Thurstan

---

9. *The Life of Christina*, pp. 113–115. These passages of the biography are baffling for the historian who would dearly like to know how Thurstan managed to annul her marriage, confirm her vow and obtain papal permission for her husband to marry another woman. He was not her bishop, nor was her bishop within his province ; he must have had to stretch his influence considerably to obtain these ends. But how, we do not know.

10. *Ibid.*, p. 127.

11. "The fee in Yorkshire of the abbot of St. Alban's consisted of the town of Norton Conyers and tithes of Cundall, given by Alured or Alfred, the butler of the count of Mortain, and his wife and children (*Monasticon* II, 220) ; Thorpe Basset and tithe of Settrington given by Berenger de Toeni and Aubreye his wife ; the church of Appleton-le-Street with 1 carucate in Broughton, probably given by Arnulf de Hesdin . . . The church of Amotherby, not far distant from Appleton, was also given to St. Alban's, possibly by Arnulf de Hesdin" (*E Y C* II, p. 282).

12. *Cf* p. 76.

to recall that in 1124 abbot Geoffrey of St. Alban's had been one of
the team that William of Corbeil had taken with him to Rome when
Thurstan and William were at loggerheads over the primacy[13].

The passage quoted from Christina's biographer is also noteworthy for other reasons. On the face of it Thurstan's idea of sending
Christina to Marcigny or Fontevrault seems puzzling. Marcigny, it
will be remembered, was the convent to which Thurstan had led
Adela of Blois, a convent founded in 1080 by St. Hugh of Cluny and
favoured by the upper branches of the feudal hierarchy[14] ; to give
just one instance, Raingard, the mother of Peter the Venerable
retired there to become a nun[15]. Fontevrault likewise was fre-
quented by women of gentle breeding ; the first abbess, Hersinda,
sprang from the Angevin nobility and she was succeeded in 1115 by
that grand dame of religion, Petronilla[16]. Neither place would
seem to be specially suited to Christina with her less refined, more
bucolic Anglo-Saxon background. But Thurstan's proposal becomes
perfectly intelligible when we remember what an intense impression
Christina's defence of her virginity had made upon contemporaries,
so intense that the great St. Alban's Psalter is thought to have been
inspired by her story[17] and to have incorporated within its leaves
that exemplary *Chanson de Alexis* about St. Alexius. Alexius' story
was so similar to Christina's : son of a distinguished Roman citizen,
he fled on the night of his marriage into the desert where for many
years he lived an ascetic life ; he returned to Rome as a beggar and
lived under the stairs of his father's palace unknown to either his
father or his wife. On his death his identity and sanctity were both
revealed.

To a person with Thurstan's knowledge of recent religious life
in Normandy it must have seemed that Christina's case was but the
latest and most remarkable in a whole series of conversions in which
women had been led to the peaks[18]—dangerous but most elevated—
of the spiritual life ; there was the Englishwoman Eva, for instance,

13. *H C* p. 122.
14. *Cf Pipe Roll* 31 *Henry I*, p. 121 : In perdonis . . . Monialibus de Marcineio.
    viii solidos.
15. *Gallia Christiana*, IV, col. 1137.
16. For a convenient summary of the early years of Fontevrault see R. Niderst,
    Robert d'Arbrissel et les Origines de l'Ordre de Fontevrault, 1952 ; and a
    provocative commentary by E. Werner, Robert von Arbrissel : Zur Frauen-
    frage und zum Frauenkult im Mittelalter, in *Forschungen und Fortschritte*,
    1955, pp. 269–76.
17. *The St. Alban's Psalter* (Pächt, Dodwell and Wormald), p. 144.
18. *Cf* the article by Werner cited above, Zur Frauenfrage, etc.

who had lived with the hermit Hervé as his spiritual bride much as Christina had lived with the hermit Roger[19]. Thurstan had made a mistake in taking this pattern as destined for Christina when he placed her under the care of his untrustworthy religious friend. But there were other patterns to look to, that of Fontevrault, for instance, which had been founded by Robert d'Arbrissel in an attempt to provide for abandoned wives, for women who had been forced into marriage, and indeed for every type of wronged woman. Into such a community Christina could have stepped as a living model of the vocation to chastity which was the *raison d'être* of their monastery. And it would have been fitting for Thurstan to send her there, for the force of the word *talium* in the description of him as *amator et fautor talium castorum studiorum*[20] is that Thurstan was specially renowned for protecting those people who were driven to extreme measures in their defence of chastity.

The suggestion that Christina might go abroad also gives us an insight into Thurstan's breadth of vision ; it could only have come from someone whose mind and interests were not trammelled by petty provincial prejudices. The field that Thurstan surveyed in the mind's eye, when thinking of suitable monasteries, stretched over the whole of north-western Europe ; he knew it not as a surveyor knows it, from above and remote, but as a native knows it who is familiar with the persons dwelling there and the places they dwell in, aware of the strengths and weaknesses of each. His good offices were invoked, for instance, by the community at Savigny in 1125 to secure for them a bull of privileges from Pope Honorius II[21] ; Savigny had been founded by Vitalis who had also shown a special talent for the spiritual direction of the gentler sex, having converted prostitutes and led them into the way of righteousness ; it was a foundation close to Thurstan's heart as he showed by his encouragement of its colony at Tulketh in Lancashire. On another occasion his good offices with King Henry I secured for the monastery of St. Evroult the nomination of the abbot the monks desired[22],

---

19. L. Gougaud, Étude sur la reclusion religieuse, in *Revue Mabillon*, 13, 1923, pp. 26–39, 77–102, and his Mulierum Consortia, in *Eriu IX*, 1921, pp. 147–156. Such *consortia* does not seem to have been unknown in England to judge from Ailred of Rievaulx's denunciation of the practice in his letter to his sister, *P L* Vol. 32, cols. 1451–74, C. XXVIII.

20. This phrase is a conflation of *Gesta Abbatum S. Albani*, p. 100 and *The Life of Christina*, p. 110.

21. See p. 98 ; also J. H. Round, *Calendar of Documents*, no. 798, where Thurstan witnesses the considerable grant made by William de Sancto Claro to Savigny.

22. See p. 15n.

whilst Fontevrault showed its gratitude to him by inviting him, along with his brother bishop Audouen, to dedicate their monastic church in 1132[23]. Again his close friendship with his brother kept him abreast of happenings in Normandy and even literally gave him a stake on the continent ; for at a time when Audouen was presumably poverty-stricken through the devastation of Evreux Thurstan out of his own pocket bought a house for him in Rouen[24] so that Audouen should have a place to stay when visiting the Norman capital ; after Audouen's death Thurstan wrote sadly to the canons of Evreux to ensure that his brother's chamberlain, Gilbert, was kept on in the house.

However, though Thurstan had a European breadth of mind he had given his heart to the diocese of York and the fact that he tried to bring Christina to York as prioress of his newly-founded convent of Clementhorpe tells us several things : firstly, the high opinion in which he held Christina ; secondly, the care which he was taking to make sure that he got the best person for head, even if it meant going outside his own diocese ; and, as a corollary to this, the importance he attached to Clementhorpe. For Clementhorpe was not simply a house that he had come to take an interest in after someone else had thought of it, it was his own from the beginning. About 1130 he granted to the nuns the plot of ground on which the priory and its offices were erected, two carucates of land at York, six perches of land at Southwell, twenty shillings per year from his fair at York, and the tithes of several miles in the diocese[25]. The site, on the south side of York, was both pleasant and profitable. It bordered on the river Ouse, where the nuns were later to have a staithe or landing place for the river traffic coming up into York,

---

23. *Gallia Christina*, XI, 575. He had witnessed gifts to Fontevrault made by Henry I at Rouen in 1129 ; *Regesta* nos. 1580, 1581.
24. *Cf Regesta* II, no. 1910 (1135 (?) Rouen) ; J. H. Round, *Calendar of Documents Preserved in France*, p. 100, from the Chartulary of Evreux, Archives de l'Eure : G 122. fo. 41v, which reads as follows : T. dei gratia eboracensis archiepiscopus O. decano et canonicis Sancte marie ebroicensis ecclesie salutem et beneditionem. Non ignorat fraternitas vestra me qui eam propriis denariis meis emi, et episcopum vestrum et fratrem meum, cui illam dederam, dedisse et confirmasse Gilleberto camerario suo domum vestram in Rothomago, tenendam de ecclesia vestra et de episcopo vestro per cartam regis et episcopi confirmatum esse. Unde dilectionem vestram obnixe exoro ut predictum Gillebertum manuteneatis et in recompensationem amoris et beneficiorum vobis ab episcopo collatorum tam ipsius episcopi anime quam suis pro viribus vestris succuratis, nunc manifeste cognosci dabitur, quales filii tam boni patris fueritis et sitis.

    M. Le Pesant, Director of the Eure archives, very kindly supplied me with this version of the letter, which corrects Round's transcription in one or two places.
25. *E Y C* I, p. 278 ; *Monasticon*, IV, p. 323.

and its situation led to the growth around it in the later middle ages of the village suburb of Clementhorpe[26]. Unfortunately we know little about St. Clement's in the remaining years of Thurstan's life. We are even more in the dark about another nunnery where one would expect Thurstan's influence to have been felt ; this was Handale, near Whitby, probably the first Cistercian nunnery in England. Its founder was William de Percy, of the family who founded Whitby Abbey, and we learn that the abbot of Whitby at this time was a certain Nicholas, "the intimate friend of Thurstan"[27]. When one considers the close ties between York and Whitby, and this friendship in particular, and then remembers Thurstan's enthusiasm for the Cistercian ideal one can reasonably surmise that he was not idle in the matter of Handale.

This is the more likely, because of his concern for the spiritual direction of the gentler sex which has been made clear and which also shows through in his friendship with two of the great northern ladies who were his contemporaries, Cecily de Rumilly and Gundreda de Mowbray. Cecily we have already met ; she was the daughter of Robert de Rumilly who sprang originally from Remilly, sixteen kilometres north-west of Saint-Lo in Normandy ; she inherited from him the extensive honour of Skipton, and continued to be known as "Lady of Skipton" even when she married William le Meschin, lord of Copeland. Cecily and William between them maintained a strong tradition of munificence towards religious houses firstly in the founding of St. Bees but, above all, in their Augustinian house of Embsay on her Skipton estates. That Embsay represented a combined operation on the part of husband and wife is proved by the fact that the first prior came from the house at Huntingdon where William held lands, some of which were given to the canons there. At Embsay, also, Thurstan's inspiration is acknowledged in the many charters which Cecily issued in favour of the canons. And Thurstan's friendship for Cecily was well rewarded in the flow of gifts from her circle which continued even after the death of her husband. Soon after she became a widow we learn of her son, Ranulf, founding the Cistercian monastery of Calder, whilst her daughters carried on the good work when they themselves got married ; the Paynels, Percies, and Belmeis, who were Cecily's

26. Angelo Raine, *Mediaeval York*, pp. 316–7.
27. *Monasticon*, I, p. 406 ; L. Charlton, *A History of Whitby* (1779), p. 85.
28. See the genealogical table in *E Y C* VII, facing p. 1, and the relationships outlined on pp. 1–9.

sons-in-law[28] all paid tribute in land to the monastic enthusiasm of the family they had married into. Nor does the enthusiasm appear to have been confined to Cecily's actual relations ; it spread also to those retainers who played such a vital part in the running of an honour ; recorded first as witnesses to the charters of their lord and lady they themselves soon appear in the lists of benefactors to houses of religion[29]. How much one would give for a detailed description of a day in Cecily's household when one of her chaplains was drawing up the announcement of certain of her gifts for some monastic house addressed to her friend Thurstan, in the presence of his chaplains and retainers, and of her own retainers, such as the Flemings, Rainer the dapifer, his son William, also her dapifer, and William's brother Walter[30]. And to hear the archbishop's words of encouragement to this lady of outstanding piety.

As with Cecily, so with Gundreda de Mowbray, the second of these ladies, we are unable to penetrate to the intimacy of their friendship whilst nevertheless being in no doubt as to its reality. She was daughter to Edith de Warenne and Gerard de Gournay— of the crusading Gournays—and herself married Nigel de Albini as his second wife in June, 1118[31] ; by him she had a son Roger who did not, however, take the name of Albini but of Mowbray, the reason being that he was designated heir to the forfeited Mowbray estates. By becoming Nigel's wife Gundreda immediately found herself amongst the leading actors in the events of Henry's reign, for Nigel was one of the king's most trusted servants, constantly being called upon to transact the king's business[32]. She also found herself drawn into northern affairs, for that is where the bulk of Nigel's estates lay, and in this manner she came to know Thurstan. Though Nigel, like most of his equals, was given to taking advantage over his neighbours and even usurping church lands (cf p. 111) he seems to have had an admiration for Thurstan and sympathized with the courageous archbishop at the time of his quarrel with King Henry[33]. After the death of Nigel in 1129 it is likely that Gundreda in her widowhood sought advice from the archbishop. At least close friendship between them is the only reasonable basis

---

29. *E Y C* VII, pp. 195–6.
30. *Cf E Y C* VII, no. 5 : " . . . Hugo capellanus huius carte scriptor ; no. 6 . . . " Reginaldus capellanus scriptor huius carte.
31. *E Y C* VIII, p. 7.
32. For the enormous number of deeds of Henry I witnessed by Nigel between 1101 and 1129 see the Index to the *Regesta* II, p. 415.
33. *H C* p. 107.

upon which to explain their easy co-operation when confronted with the refugee monks from Calder.

This incident of the refugee monks took place in 1137[34] when David of Scotland, leading the undisciplined marauders from Galloway, was bringing devastation to Cumberland. The monks from the recently founded Calder, fearing for their lives, fled for shelter to their mother house at Furness. The reception they received there was cold indeed ; some of those at Furness called them weaklings for leaving their monastery just because of the Scots and, more serious, the abbot of Furness pointed out to the abbot of Calder that there was no room for two abbots in the place, nor were there sufficient rations for two communities. Of course, there must have been deeper reasons for the unbending attitude of the Furness community ; probably it was another case of the conservatives who stayed at home feeling that the high-minded reformers (who in this case had moved off to Calder) should now put up cheerfully with the consequences of their idealism. But the net result was the same : the Calder community on the road walking beside the eight oxen that were drawing a waggon on which were piled their few belongings, mostly liturgical books and vestments. Where were they to go ? Almost inevitably they thought of archbishop Thurstan who six years previously had befriended the refugees from St. Mary's in a similar plight ; they set off to seek him in York.

At this point the story reads like an episode out of romance : the sorry caravanserai of monks was observed going through Thirsk by Gundreda's seneschal ; he took pity on them and invited them to feed at his mistress's castle hard by. Gundreda, meanwhile, forewarned of these unusual guests, was secretly observing them through a window in the high tower where she had stationed herself ; moved by their poverty and simplicity she promised to help them. Since her son Roger was still a ward, and not therefore enjoying the profits of his lands, her liberality was for the moment restricted ; but instead she passed the monks on to a relative of hers, Robert de Alneto, a monk of Whitby who was now living as a hermit at Hood, a mile or two eastwards of Thirsk. Here they went and secured a temporary home before eventually moving on to their permanent one at Byland. But in the meantime their abbot, Gerald, had completed the journey to Thurstan. On hearing of their plight

---

34. See *Monasticon* V, pp. 349–50 for the whole episode.

the archbishop immediately wrote to the young Roger de Mowbray, joining his own requests to those of Gundreda, that Roger might make provision for the upkeep of the refugee monks out of his income[35]. This the young man did. But his arrangements for getting provisions to the monks proved so clumsy and unworkable that within two years Thurstan and Gundreda persuaded him to endow them permanently with land which would serve the same purpose more efficiently. By this first charter they received the vaccary of Cambe, and all the land of Wildon, Scakilden and Erghum, and the way was prepared for the development of the fair Cistercian abbey of Byland. It is not a monastery of which Thurstan could literally be described as founder since the take-over did not occur until after his death ; but if inspiration counts for anything then his friendship with Gundreda must be reckoned as the creative force behind Byland.

As with the Rumillies so with the Mowbrays, the family's devoutness seems to have influenced the retainers. Thus certain of the older knights of Roger de Mowbray's household joined the community at Hood as lay-brothers, amongst them Landric de Agys, Henry de Wasprey and Henry Bugge. And not only did they bring their own wealth to the house, but the fact that men of such good standing should have joined the community induced other people of substance to become patrons of Hood[36]. About the recruitment of such pious laymen to the religious life in northern England we have only the scantiest information, but we do catch a glimpse of one of them who came under the influence of Thurstan. This man, Durand de Butterwick, was father to a numerous family of sons as well as of one step-son ; on the advice of Thurstan and other friends he granted half a carucate of land in Butterwick to the abbey of St. Mary's which was to provide for a priest to celebrate Mass there. Not long afterwards he himself took the habit of a monk at Whitby[37]. In the case of Durand, as in so many other cases[38],

---

35. The word used is "hospicium ; " even as a ward, then, he was allowed an expense account.

36. *Monasticon* V, p. 350 ; *E Y C* III, no. 1833 & p. 445.

37. *E Y C* II, no. 1073, Grant by Durand de Butterwick by the advice of archbishop Thurstan : " . . . de consilio Thome [recte Turstini] archiepiscopi Eboracensis et aliorum amicorum meorum . . ." to the monks of St. Mary's, York, of half a carucate of land in Butterwick, when abbot Geoffrey and the monks consented that a priest should for ever celebrate in the chapel of Butterwick, which belongs to the church of Foxholes. ("The church of Butterwick was originally a chapel of Burton Agnes and, probably as such, was given by Geoffrey Bainard to St. Mary's, York" *ibid.*, p. 379).

38. For example, it is almost by chance that we know of his spiritual ministrations to Eudo the Dapifer ; *cf* p. 67.

Thurstan never quite steps into the foreground, remaining content as a good spiritual director that the work should go on unobtrusively.

This near anonymity on Thurstan's part even holds good of the renaissance of monasticism that took place within his diocese during the last years of his life, the renaissance associated with the names of Fountains, Calder, Rievaulx, Newminster and Byland (or Hood, as it was still known). Enough has been said to illustrate how far this applies at Calder and Byland. It even applies at Fountains ; for although one can hardly doubt that Thurstan continued to watch over the community that he had in effect begotten, his name is found less frequently than his influence during the years that witnessed the astounding growth of Fountains. It is probable, for instance, that the coming of Hugh, Serlo and Tosti from Thurstan's family at York to Fountains owed much to the archbishop, though there is nothing in black and white to prove it. Yet it was their advent which touched off a series of benefactions to the abbey without which Fountains could scarcely have provided for the great numbers beginning to flock there. By 1139 there must have been at least a hundred monks at Fountains, otherwise the house could hardly have sent out the colonies which it did to found daughter houses at Kirkstead (2 December, 1139), Louth Park (2 December, 1139), and Newminster (5 January, 1138)[39]. In the establishment of these Lincolnshire foundations at Louth Park and Kirkstead, Thurstan seems to have played no part directly ; Louth Park owed most to Alexander the bishop of Lincoln, an unlikely patron for monastic purity, whilst Kirkstead was the inspiration of a wealthy landowner Hugh Brito who had been deeply moved by what he had seen of Cistercian life in the course of a visit to Fountains. Still, even the Lincolnshire story underlines how completely decisive was Thurstan's action in October, 1132 : the abbots of these two new houses had both begun their monastic life as members of St. Mary's, York.

The story behind the earliest of the colonies from Fountains, that at Newminster, is not unsimilar. As with FitzEudo later, who founded Louth Park, it was a visit to the community at Fountains and the admiration this awoke in him that led Ralph de Merlay to

---

39. For Kirkstead, see *Monasticon*, V, p. 416 ; it is notable that once again the site chosen was already occupied by a group of hermits. For Louth Park, see *Monasticon*, V, pp. 413–4, and *The Chronicle of Louth Park* (ed. Venables, 1891). For Newminster, *The Chartulary of Newminster* (ed. J. T. Fowler). *S S* Vol. lxvi.

offer land near his castle of Morpeth as the site for a Cistercian abbey[40]. The leader of this colony from Yorkshire was another of that group who in the autumn of 1132 had found protection with Thurstan ; this was the monk Robert. His is an example of the rather surprising career that might open up in Thurstan's days before a Yorkshire boy reared in the backwoods of the county. He was born in the Craven district, in the heart of the Pennines, of humble parents ; after acquiring a rudimentary schooling in his home district—presumably from a local priest—he seems somehow to have made his way to Paris to complete his studies. He then returned to Yorkshire to become priest of the parish he was born in, at Gargrave. Hearing the call to the monastic life he soon afterwards became a monk of Whitby, and it was during this time that the exodus from St. Mary's brought yet another change in the trajectory of his career. He joined the refugees about Thurstan and within a few years had been selected to plant the first seeds of Cistercian life in Northumberland. Then at Newminster, as abbot for twenty years, he had many difficulties to surmount, not least those of his own temperament[41] ; but his holiness was recognized even during his lifetime by men so eminent in things spiritual as St. Bernard, Pope Eugenius and St. Godric[42]. The seal was set upon his life when he found his way into the martyrologies of the English[43].

Even Thurstan's influence on the affairs of the other Cistercian house in Yorkshire, at Rievaulx, cannot be boldly stated but has to be guessed at. We know, for instance, that the original group passed through York on its way from Clairvaux to Rievaulx ; we cannot prove beyond doubt that they took the opportunity to greet Thurstan and obtain his formal permission for their enterprise, but only an unduly sceptical person would doubt this. Likewise the charter of Rievaulx's foundation on the 3rd May, 1132 records simply that Walter Espec had been moved to this act of generosity

---

40. *The Chartulary of Newminster (S S)* p. 1 ; and *The Priory of Hexham,* p. 123 and note. For the life of Robert, see *Analecta Bollandiana,* LVI (1938), pp. 334–360.

41. Putting together *Vita Roberti (Analecta Bollandiana* LVI, p. 351) and *Vita Godrici (S S),* p. 169, it is clear that Robert was not particularly careful in his friendship with Edith de Hastings, and this gave rise to nasty rumours. However, St. Bernard was not inclined to believe that there was anything wrong in the friendship ; nor need we, especially as St. Godric saw their souls winging away towards Heaven at the same time.

42. *Vita Godrici (S S),* pp. 168–173.

43. *Acta Sanctorum, June,* II, p. 47 ; the same source assures us that his relics found their way into the keeping of the Cistercians of Westphalia.

"by the advice of Thurstan, and with his consent"; Thurstan is not even on the list of witnesses which is headed, ironically enough, by that same Thomas, provost of Beverley, whom St. Bernard had vainly tried to draw into the Cistercian order. But to go through the list of witnesses takes one immediately into a circle of people at whose centre stood the archbishop of York, the person with the greatest influence upon them[44].

Scarcely more explicit, yet equally suggestive, is the account of his part in the recruitment to Rievaulx of the most outstanding figure in its whole history, the lovable Ailred. Ailred came of an old English family which had for generations supplied the hereditary priests in charge of the ancient church at Hexham. On this account Ailred and his relatives had little cause to regard York with favour, because in 1113 his father Eilaf had been dislodged from this traditional position by the archbishop of York, Thomas, who had set regular canons in his place. And even though Eilaf received reasonable compensation there was no great sorrow in his household when a year later the news was brought to them of Thomas' death. Ailred himself about this time was put to school with the young Prince Henry, son of David of Scotland, and through the close friendship which developed between them he some years later became steward at David's court[45]. Here he formed a further friendship that was to stand him in good stead for his lifetime with David's step-son Waltheof. As we have already seen, Waltheof went south, first to Thurstan's cherished Augustinian house at Nostell and then, as prior, to the house at Kirkham. He was there in 1134 when Ailred himself came south.

Ailred "was in the neighbourhood of the city of York," says his biographer, "where he had come on business to the archbishop of the diocese. By a happy chance he heard tell, from a close friend of his, how, two years or more before, certain monks had come to England from across the sea"—these were, of course, the Cistercians at Rievaulx, and the close friend was doubtless Waltheof. From his friend Ailred received a description of the Cistercians' manner of life which so inspired him that he exclaimed : "O, how greatly do I desire, how ardently I thirst for the sight of them, and to see for myself what you have told me about that happy place." "Go thither," returned the other, "but seek first the leave of the arch-

---

44. *The Chartulary of Rievaulx* (ed. J. C. Atkinson, *S S*), pp. 16–21.
45. For the nature of Ailred's duties as steward, see G. W. S. Barrow's sensible remarks in *Regesta Regum Scottorum*, pp. 32–33.

bishop and receive his blessing, and, if you wish, God will satisfy your desire before the sun sets." Carried away by eager desire for the things to come he hurries to the prelate, obtains his leave and blessing, rushes back to his lodging, mounts his horse, does not stop to go in, and, with the hastiest of farewells to his hosts, speeds his mount he knows not where"[46].

Despite this hyperbole on the part of his biographer Ailred did arrive at a known place ; it was the castle at Helmsley of Walter Espec, friend of Thurstan, patron of both Kirkham and Rievaulx, and a man well known in the border country around Hexham. From Helmsley Ailred paid a visit to Rievaulx, some three miles away ; what he found there in no way belied his friend's description ; so enraptured was he that within two days he himself had joined the community in the Rye valley, leaving his companions to report back to David.

Thus within a short space of time this future saint had threaded his way from the devout David in Scotland to the holy Thurstan and then on to another future saint, his friend Waltheof, before becoming the guest of that upright Christian gentleman, Walter Espec. Upon these five men so much of the well-being of the land between Humber and Forth depended ; rarely can it have been in such capable and righteous hands or in the keeping of men so closely bound in friendship.

So far little has been said about houses where older ways held sway, Selby, Whitby, Pontefract and Holy Trinity (York), for instance, and it is easy to overlook the fact that they also fell under Thurstan's vigilant scrutiny. Actually the very oldest of the ancient foundations, St. Peter's hospital, did take on such a new lease of life[47] during this period that one almost thinks of it as a twelfth century foundation, especially as its vigorous superior Robert ranged himself on the side of the more modern orders in Yorkshire ; and it is symbolic of this revival that the name of the hospital was eventually changed from the traditional one of St. Peter's to that of St. Leonard's. The great wealth and privileges acquired by the hospital are fully listed in the confirmation made by Pope Adrian IV[48], and the extent of these must have given great satis-

---

46. *Vita Ailredi*, pp. 13–14.
47. Gervase of Canterbury, *Opera* I, p. 100, even refers to this famous hospital as having been founded by Thurstan.
48. *E Y C* I, no. 186.

faction to Thurstan, who was patron of the house and had the chief say in electing the master[49] and who clearly initiated many of the favours[50] recorded in Adrian's confirmation.

The other old established houses in the county share a family likeness that can be strongly sensed but not very clearly articulated. One source of the likeness may be their links abroad ; Selby was initiated by a monk of Auxerre, and Whitby by a knight who came over with the Conqueror, whilst Pontefract was an outpost of the famous Cluniac monastery of La Charité-sur-Loire ; Holy Trinity began as a dependency of the ancient abbey of Marmoutier (near Tours) and, if the style of its entry in the mortuary rolls is anything to go by, remained continental in its ethos[51]. Again, perhaps as a consequence of the first feature, several of them were houses where the patrons and their families played an intimate part in the running of the houses they had founded ; thus at Whitby the priors for a considerable stretch of time were members of the Percy family, whilst Selby was governed for over a quarter of a century by Hugh, one of the Lascies[52]. Similarly, the prior of Holy Trinity in the 1130's was Elias Paynel, son of Ralph Paynel the founder ; and as if to underline the ties between this group of monasteries, he became abbot of Selby in 1143 only to be deposed, expectedly enough, by Henry Murdac, the Cistercian archbishop.

We often find this group of monasteries reacting alike to the stresses of the day, reminding us sometimes of their own aristocratic, spacious, unfanatical background by their distaste for the new arrivals ; and sometimes, as in 1132 when they hurried to the call of St. Mary's, their behaviour recalls the panic that can run through the established order when it sees its sacred conventions being dissolved ; and on occasion they were even capable of concerted action to defend their hallowed ways against the threats of novelty, as they showed by their resistance to the Cistercian take-over bid in the province.

Unfortunately we do not have much evidence about Thurstan's estimate of this group beyond the outstanding fact that he chose

---

49. *H C Y* III, p. 74.

50. *E Y C* I, nos. 167, 168, 169, 176.

51. *Rouleaux des Morts* (ed. L. Delisle), pp. 194, 330. *Rouleau Mortuaire du b. Vital. Abbé de Savigny* (ed. L. Delisle, 1909), pl. xxxix.

52. If he was, in fact, a Lascy ; the family name is a later addition to the simple *Abbas Hugo* of the chronicle ; this matter will be dealt with by Dr. Wightman in his study of the de Lascy family, the subject of his thesis at Leeds University.

Pontefract as his final resting-place. But we do at least get a glimpse of his attitude towards Selby, as well as of the control he exercised there, in the *Historia Selebiensis*[53]. This late document (14th century) gives us a vivid description of the man who was abbot of Selby at the time Thurstan came to York, Hugh de Lascy[54]. Having been provost of the community for a long period, Hugh had endeared himself to men of all ranks by the time he was made abbot ; and in this office he applied himself, as well a practical-minded Norman might, to the development of the abbey lands and the building and adornment of the monastery itself ; it is even possible that the eastern bays of the present Norman nave are the work of his hands[55]—literally so, since he used to don the work-man's cloak and heave up stones and cement along with the labourers, even queueing up with them on Saturdays to receive his wages. Such eccentric behaviour suggests that Hugh was slightly "touched," as does his behaviour after 1123 when he took to wandering around the countryside ; and it may account for Thurs-tan's readiness in 1123 to accept his resignation. The redactor of the *Historia* insinuates that Thurstan behaved out of pique against Hugh for having opposed his election to York, but it is clear from his text that Hugh and Thurstan had already arranged the resigna-tion before it was declared. The occasion that Hugh chose to declare his resignation came when Thurstan was brought to Selby on other business, accompanied by Ranulf of Durham, Ralph bishop of Orkney, and Geoffrey abbot of St. Mary's, as well as by the prior of Pontefract and many others[56]. The succession of abbots who followed Hugh is instructive in showing how the leadership of monasteries tended to oscillate between the poles of deep interior life coupled with incompetence in externals at one time and of business ability joined to spiritual mediocrity at another. The first of his successors, a tried monk of St. Albans recommended by King Henry, was a model of religious observance, always first into choir and last out of it, who spent the rest of his time meditating on the Scriptures ; like Mary, Hubert had chosen the better part, but the Marthas within the community who came to him for practical decisions about running the estates found him no help at all. As a result the monastery began to fall into a state of decay. Well aware of his own shortcomings, Hubert took advantage of John of Crema's

53. *The Coucher Book of Selby* (ed. J. T. Fowler), pp. (17–54).
54. For the life of Hugh, see *Acta Sanctorum Boll.*, July, VII, pp. 290–304.
55. *The Coucher Book of Selby*, Introduction, p. X.
56. *Ibid.*, p. (24).

presence in York (1125) to put his dilemma before him. The upshot was that he resigned only to be replaced by someone with opposite qualities, a monk of St. Mary's, York, named Durandus. Handsome in appearance, well-educated, skilled in legal matters, an expert on management besides being eloquent and open-handed, Durandus spoilt his great gifts by his neglect of any sort of interior life. He kept such shady company as to become a scandal to the laity and a source of shame to the clergy, until in the end (1135) Thurstan had to intervene and persuade him to resign[57]. He was then sent off to Cluny, where he changed his ways and became a good religious.

For two years Selby remained without an abbot, unsettled by the ambitions of all those who wished to enjoy the office, until finally they again sought Thurstan's advice. At his instigation they chose as their superior the prior of Pontefract. This man, Walter, was yet another who imitated Mary rather than Martha, but he had the good sense to delegate practical matters to an experienced administrator named William. Freed from such concerns he was now able to devote his energies to nurturing the spiritual life so dear to his heart, expounding St. Benedict's Rule in chapter each day, preaching the word of God and inciting his flock to even more ardent service of God. His period as abbot seems to have passed into the memory of the brethren as an era of tranquillity, order and goodness ; it is a tribute to Thurstan's choice of him[58].

The watchful eye that Thurstan kept upon Selby never tired of anticipating the needs of the religious houses throughout the province, especially in trying to secure for each of them a worthy superior ; he did the same for Whitby in 1127 when the death of

---

57. *Ibid.*, p. (28). It was presumably Durandus who had occasioned the exchange of letters that took place between Thurstan and the Pope in 1135–6, the nature of which can be guessed from Innocent's reply (22 April, 1135) from Pisa. *Jaffé*, no. 7767 (*H & S*, II, I, p. 219) : De caetero noverit tua fraternitas quam si abbas ille de quo nobis significasti ad nostram praesentiam venerit, quod ad honorem Dei et tuum pertinet superna cooperante clementia sollicite providere curabimus. The abbot referred to is certainly Durandus ; perhaps Thurstan had urged him to go to Rome to straighten his position out before going to Cluny ; perhaps Thurstan feared that Durandus might accuse him before the Pope of high-handed intervention at Selby. In any case Thurstan was making sure of his own position with the Pope just as he had been careful to explain his position to William of Corbeil when abbot Geoffrey went off to him (p.)173.
     In an age when communications were so slow a man's reputation could so easily be destroyed by lying rumour that individuals—especially prelates—had a serious duty to protect their good name. This feature of twelfth century life may account for Thurstan's sensitivity so clearly displayed in the letter to which Hildebert of Le Mans replied ; *cf* p. 11n
58. *Ibid.*, pp. (31)–(32).

William Percy gave him the opportunity to put in his friend Nicholas to succeed him[59], and he rightly earned praise from the monks as one of the very greatest patrons of monastic life in the country's history. But before closing this chapter of his life one might ask whether praise from the monks had not been paid for by other Christians at a rather high price ? Were the monks becoming prosperous because other people were being impoverished ? This, evidently, was what his successor Roger of Pont l'Évêque had in mind (1154–1181) when he said that Thurstan had never committed a graver error than when he built Fountains[60] ; for Roger's attempts to keep his diocese financially stable and to provide for all the clerics needed to run a diocese were constantly being frustrated by the fact that so much of the wealth of the county had passed into monastic hands, and succeeding archbishops simply did not have sufficient funds at their command to maintain the level of the secular clergy. Expressed in the personal terms congenial to his age William of Newborough's version of Roger's policy ascribes to him a hatred for men of religion and a penchant for the secular clergy. In terms more congenial to our own age one would say that the exploitation of Yorkshire's agricultural wealth in the twelfth century could most conveniently be carried out by large-scale communities such as monasteries, that the monasteries needed privileges if they were to do the job, but that these privileges, as is the way of privileges, were maintained when the reason for them had ceased to operate. And one feature of the exploitation of the land was that the planting of churches tended to go hand in hand with the opening up of the land to farming[61] ; so it was inevitable that religious houses having been granted lands then secured control of neighbouring churches and their tithes which might well have supported secular clerics. It was precisely this situation that had made Thurstan's question to Theobald of Étampes an urgent, practical issue, and his having put it shows that Thurstan was aware of the harmful side-effects that might be produced by the spread of monastic houses over the land. The same consideration would lead a diocesan to favour the newer monasticism of the Cistercians, which of set purpose refused to take over churches and tithes, as opposed to the more established houses which found no

59. L. Charlton, *A History of Whitby*, p. 85.
60. William of Newburgh, *Chronicles of the Reigns of Stephen, Henry II and Richard I (R S)*, Vol. I, p. 226. *Cf* also p. 114 of the present work.
61. B. Waites, The Monastic Settlement of North-East Yorkshire in *Yorkshire Archaeological Journal*, CLIX (1961), pp. 478–495.

fault in such appropriations. The magnitude of the problem can be guaged by the following approximate figures : at the time of Thurstan's death the abbey of St. Mary's, York, had under its control some thirty-five churches in the diocese ; the priory of Durham controlled thirteen, the priory of Whitby six, and the Pontefract Cluniacs five ; of the Augustinian houses Nostell controlled eighteen churches, Bridlington twelve, and Guisborough two[62]. Thus a large part of the revenues of over nineety churches were being channeled into the coffers of eight religious houses[63] ; if we take the number of churches in the diocese by 1140 to number, at a rough estimate, five hundred, it will be seen that the secular clergy had grounds for being quizzical about the monastic renaissance. Perhaps the well-being of the monks was purchased at the expense of their even-Christians in the diocese whose spiritual life was never quickened by the ministry of an adequately trained clergy. What the laity thought, or what the secular clergy thought, went unrecorded—our story depends almost entirely on monastic witnesses—but their silence should be remembered when striking a balance of the good and evil effects of Thurstan's care for the monks.

---

62. For St. Mary's, York, *cf E Y C* IV, no. 8, and *Monasticon* III, pp. 529, 547, 548, 549, 550 ; for Durham, *E Y C* II, no. 936 ; for Whitby, *E Y C* II, no. 877 ; for Pontefract, *E Y C* III, nos. 1319, 1469 ; for Nostell, *E Y C* II, no. 1012 and III, nos. 1428, 1466 ; for Bridlington, *E Y C* II, nos. 1152 and 1367 ; for Guisborough, *E Y C* II, no. 687.

63. There is obviously no way of making an estimate of their annual value, but it is worth pointing out that archbishop Roger of Pont l'Evêque regarded the church of Edston as a fair equivalent to 100 shillings (*Priory of Hexham*, p. 58 and n). Edston was probably a rather wealthy church and the average ran nearer to such churches as Ledsham and Darrington in the Pontefract area, the first of which was worth 33 shillings annually and the second (minus certain chapels) was reckoned at 21 shillings per annum (*E Y C* III, p. 181 and p. 163 respectively).

CHAPTER VIII.

DEFENDER OF THE REALM.

Thurstan might well have considered, by the autumn of 1135, that the major tasks of his life lay behind him, that he could now look forward with a tranquil mind to watching over the peaceful growth of Christian institutions within his diocese. After twenty years as leader of the vast northern province he appeared to have achieved good relations not only with his own king but also with the king of Scotland and all the outstanding figures in church and state. Wherever he looked the prospects of peace seemed good. In December, however, all this was changed at once by the death of Henry I; over the whole of England his death turned men's minds, divided, towards the question of his successor; but in Yorkshire the turmoil it caused was immediate and dramatic, precipitating a baronial quarrel that had long been fomenting.

The origins of this quarrel stretched back to about the year 1106 when the lord of Pontefract, Robert de Lascy, had been deprived of his fee in Yorkshire for supporting the rebels against the king[1]. What happened to his fee in the following years illustrates well how much the wrath or good will of the king in the twelfth century could make or break a man—even the highest amongst the barons. Henry gave Robert de Lascy's lordship of Pontefract to one of his own favourites, Hugh de Laval, who continued to enjoy it until the time of his death, about 1129. On Laval's death the royal favour again became the operative factor, when Henry accepted a bid for the honour made by William Maltravers, one of the "new men" who by their managerial skills

---

1. Farrer suggests 1106 as the most likely date since, as he points out, by the time of the Lindsey survey (1114–16) Hugh de Laval was then in possession of Robert de Lascy's estates in that part of Lincolnshire. As he is known to have been in possession of de Lascy's estates of Pontefract, Clitheroe and Bowland at a subsequent date, can it be doubted that he held the latter in 1114–16, and had held them with de Lascy's Lindsey estates by one general grant from the crown of an earlier date than that of the survey? (*Lancashire Pipe Rolls*, pp. 383–4): This reasoning permits of any date from 1106–1114, but 1106 seems the most likely because it was the year of Tinchebrai.

were endearing themselves to King Henry and becoming objects of hatred for the traditional feudatories[2]. Maltravers gave the king 1,000 marks for the reversion of the lordship, and £100 payable to the king's nominee, for the widow of Hugh de Laval and all Hugh's land for the term of fifteen years, and after fifteen years for the lady's dower and marriage portion. An arrangement so favourable to the king goes far to explain the hatred that the likes of Maltravers incurred, for it drove other bidders out of the market. Though Maltravers himself was no doubt pleased with the arrangement and thought he had exercised great acumen in securing it, confident that he could soon recoup himself by squeezing the de Lascy estates, his enjoyment of the profits was short-lived. No sooner did Henry's death become noised abroad than one of the knights of the honour of Pontefract, knowing that Maltravers' royal protector had now been removed, attacked and wounded the interloper. The unfortunate Maltravers was carried to Pontefract priory where, following a pious custom of the age with respect to the dying, he was clothed in the Cluniac habit ; three days later he died. The action of the murderer, a knight named Pain, was probably approved of—perhaps even urged on him—by the knights of the fee whose loyalty towards the Lascy family had remained unbroken[3] ; at least one other knight, Robert de Campeaux, was privy to the murder and so, it seems, was the subsequent lord of the honour, Ilbert de Lascy. Ilbert later obtained King Stephen's pardon for the share his men had in Maltravers' death and for the misdeeds they had committed between the death of King Henry and King Stephen's own coronation[4]. Robert de Campeaux and Ilbert de Lascy also took out other forms of insurance against possible consequences of the deed : the former piously gave 42 acres of land in Cridling to the hospital of St. Peter's, York[5], and the latter entered into an agreement with Thurstan that on the day when he should receive his inheritance he would confirm all previous donations of his ancestors to the monks of Pontefract[6].

Though only of regional impact, this Pontefract violence was symptomatic of the divisions that were to rend the kingdom in the

2. Maltravers' financial interests have left traces on many pages of the *Pipe Roll* 31 *Henry I* : pp. 28, 29, 34, 51, 62, 121, 123, 149. For a convincing description of this type of "new man" see the fine paragraph in *Gesta Stephani* (ed. K. R. Potter), pp. 14–16.
3. *Priory of Hexham*, pp. 64–5.
4. *E Y C* III, no. 1440.
5. *E Y C* III, no. 1456.
6. *Yorkshire Archaeological Journal*, XIV (1898), p. 157.

next few years. Loyalties were stretched tight as bowstrings, even when individuals actually knew where their loyalties were attached. Loyalty oaths tend to be extracted from people when they have good reason for not taking them, and this had been true of the oath extracted by King Henry I in 1126 from the great prelates and barons; Henry dragooned them into recognizing his daughter Matilda as his successor because he realized how little support she could command. And from that moment onwards the barons were searching for excuses to go back on this forced oath, as Henry implicitly acknowledged by insisting on its being renewed at Westminster in 1128 and Northampton in 1131. Roger of Salisbury argued that they were released from the oath on account of Matilda's subsequent marriage to Geoffrey of Anjou, about which they had not been consulted[7]; others believed the rumour that Henry had seen the folly of his actions and rescinded the oath on his death bed[8]. As a result the matter of the oath had little effect beyond heightening the sense of justification on one side and the need for justification on the other. Those barons who had been favourites of the late king tended out of respect for him to accept the Empress Matilda as his legitimate successor; others were linked to the family of Blois which had a powerful claimant to the throne in the person of Stephen, nephew to the late king; yet others were to make up their minds according to the way the wind was blowing.

Thurstan himself does not seem to have wavered as to where his loyalty lay; we have already referred to his friendship with Stephen's mother, Adela, and of his close tie with Stephen through co-operating with his religious foundation at Furness; either of these factors, or the fact that Stephen's rapid seizure of the crown promised stable government, may explain why Thurstan from the first seems to have been a reliable supporter of Stephen. Though he obviously could not have reached London in time for Stephen's coronation on the 23rd of December, 1135, he was present in the Easter of 1136 at Westminster when Stephen issued an elaborate charter to the see of Winchester and a no less solemn grant of the bishopric of Bath to Robert of Lewes which were witnessed by an enormous assembly of clerical and lay magnates who virtually recognized Stephen by doing so[9].

---

7. William of Malmesbury, *Gesta Regum* (*R S*) II, p. 530.
8. *Gesta Stephani* (ed. K. R. Potter), p. 7.
9. *Cf* J. H. Round, *Geoffrey de Mandeville*, pp. 16–28 and 262–66.

What augured most ill for prospects of peace in the North was that David of Scotland showed even less hesitation in supporting the other side, that of his niece, the Empress Matilda. His championship of her was all the more passionate because he had headed the list in 1129 of those who had sworn to be loyal to her ; now that so many were going back on their oaths the chivalrous David was bound to think of himself as leader of the faithful few who were standing out against treachery[10]. More fuel was added to the flames of his ardour by the actions of Pope Innocent ; David's kingdom did not accept Innocent as Pope and so regarded his contravention of the oath as the double-dealing to be expected ; but Innocent made matters worse in April of 1136 by issuing a series of letters to Stephen, William archbishop of Canterbury and Thurstan urging them to press on with the establishment of the diocese of Carlisle and the expulsion of John of Glasgow from the area[11]. By referring to John as a rebel and fomenter of heresy, moreover, Innocent was casting a slur upon his lord, King David, who now found himself fighting against wickedness in the highest places.

Nor was David slow to act, for immediately on hearing of Henry's death he made an incursion into England and seized the towns of Carlisle, Carham, Alnwick, Norham and Newcastle ; he also took hostages from the chief barons of the province as a guarantee of their fidelity to the Empress Matilda[12]. After these initial successes he intended to serve Durham likewise and secure a stranglehold on the north country. But Stephen was no less quick to move. Having been crowned king at London by William archbishop of Canterbury, thereby assuring himself of the south, he moved northwards with his army to confront David. For the moment the two kings avoided open conflict by concluding a treaty which allowed both parties to feel that they had secured substantial gains. By this treaty Stephen had restored to him Newcastle, Carham, Alnwick and Norham, which gave him a hold over Northumbria ; he also

---

10. *Gesta Stephani*, p. 35 : Iste, cum in praesentia regis Henrici, cum ceteris regni summatibus, immo omnium primus iureiurando se constrinxisset, etc. Rex [i.e. David] alte ingemuit, zeloque iustitiae succensus, tum pro communis sanguinis cognatione, tum pro fide mulieri repromissa et debita, regnum Angliae turbare disposuit.

11. *Jaffé*, nos. 7765, 7766, 7767 respectively.

12. *Priory of Hexham*, p. 72 says of David : in provincia Northanhinbrorum quinque oppida, scilicet Lugubalium, quod Anglice Carlel dicitur, et Carrum, quod ab Anglis Werch dicitur, et Alnawic, et Norham, et Novum-Castellum, moxi circa Natale Domini, cum magno exercitu praeoccupavit ac tenuit. Sed Bahanburch minime habere potuit. Fidelitates quoque et obsides de potentioribus et nobilioribus eiusdem regionis, ad conservandam fidem imperatrici nepti suae, accepit.

secured the restoration of the hostages and received the homage of David's son, Henry. For his part, Henry was endowed with Carlisle and Doncaster and the earldom of Huntingdon and seems to have extracted from Stephen a promise that before granting Northumbria to anyone he would first have Henry's own claims to it examined in his court. David had therefore secured much of what he wanted (through the person of his son) without betraying Matilda by himself making the act of homage to Stephen[13].

On his return journey south, accompanied by young Henry of Scotland, Stephen spent some time at York in the company of many of his notables, including Thurstan, his brother Audouen of Evreux, Athelwold of Carlisle, John of Séez, Nigel of Ely, and Alexander of Lincoln, as well as many of the northern barons. Thurstan took advantage of the king's presence, and the presence of so many notables, to get charters witnessed for certain of his churches and religious houses[14]. He was again with Stephen a few weeks later at the king's Easter court in Westminster (March 22) when almost all the greater magnates attended[15]. But for some reason or other Thurstan did not accompany this splendid gathering to Oxford when it adjourned to that city to secure the allegiance of Robert of Gloucester—at least, Thurstan's name does not appear on the list of witnesses to the sweeping charter of ecclesiastical liberties issued by Stephen on that occasion, though a copy of the charter was carefully secured for York, where it was eventually written out twice into the great White Book of the Minster[16]. Thurstan's absence from the Oxford gathering may be a sign that his infirmity was already preventing him from making such hasty journeys as the rest of the magnates made from London to Oxford.

For the twelve months following Stephen's charter of liberties the confusion that envelopes the country in general also surrounds Thurstan's activities. It was a period when men were looking anxiously for omens and when disasters were mingled with miracles. Disaster struck York on Friday the 8th of June, 1137, when fire broke out in the city ; much of the city was burned down, including the minster, and the flames spread outside the walls where they attacked

---

13. *Ibid.*, describing this agreement, says of Stephen : Et, ut quidam aiunt, qui se huic conventioni interfuisse testantur, promisit illi quod si comitatum Northanhymbriae alicui dare vellet, prius calumpniam Henrici, filii regis Scottiae, super eo juste in sua curia judicari faceret.

14. E.g. *E Y C* I, nos. 31, 63, 99, 117, etc.

15. J. H. Round, *Geoffrey de Mandeville*, pp. 262–6.

16. *R M A* Pt. iii f. 73d ; Pt. iv f. 22 ; quoted in *E Y C* I, no. 133.

St. Mary's Abbey and the Hospital[17]. The province was blessed
with a miracle when a grave was being dug at the minster of
Southwell; there were found the relics of certain saints along with
a glass vessel containing most clear water, the vessel being set upon
uprights which were apparently intended to protect it from being
broken. When the water was given to the sick they were healed.
These were some of the happenings that Thurstan had to report
when he and Roger of Salisbury called a council together at Northampton attended by many bishops and nobles. The two of them were
acting for Stephen, who was away on the continent, trying to hold
the magnates together in allegiance to him[18]. Thurstan had
already assumed responsibility for defending Stephen's interests
along the borders in this year when King David's forces began to
ravage Northumbria, intent on seizing that province for young
Henry of Scotland. They were halted by the arrival of a large English
army that based itself on Newcastle while Thurstan, although he
was now far spent with age, went on to Roxburgh to negotiate a
truce with David[19].

The truce that Thurstan had negotiated lasted only a few
months because the Scottish king was still bent on having Northumbria; after a few months he sent ambassadors to present this
demand to Stephen as soon as he returned from the continent, in
November, 1137. On being met with a firm refusal David prepared
for war, and in so doing set the scene for Thurstan's last and most
dramatic appearance on the stage of English public life. The drama
of this last appearance is heightened by the fact that the aged
prelate was now greatly weakened physically; some sort of paralysis
seems to have gripped his lower limbs, which he now found difficulty in controlling[20], and he had to be carried around in a litter;
but in striking contrast to his physical frailty, his fine mind was as
vigorous and trenchant as ever, holding together all the relevant
facts and the dispositions of the protagonists and dominating them
all from his bed of sickness.

17. Florence Worcester, *Chronicon ex Chronicis* II, p. 98; Gervase of Canter-
      bury, *Opera* I, p. 100: ... apud Eboracum combusta est beati Petri
      ecclesia ubi sedes est episcopatus et extra muros ecclesia beatae Mariae
      ubi est abbatia cum egregio Hospitali quod fundavit Turstanus archi-
      episcopus.
18. *Chronicle of Worcester, ibid.*
19. *Priory of Hexham*, p. 115. This source is one of the many used by O.
      Anderson in his *Scottish Annals from English Chronicles, A.D.500–1286*
      (1908) where most of the information on the Battle of the Standard is to
      be found very conveniently set out and translated into English.
20. *Historia Novella* (ed. K. R. Potter), p. 29.

The onslaught began in the early days of January, 1138, when King David and his nephew William FitzDuncan began to besiege the border stronghold of Carham, which was held for Walter Espec by his stout-hearted nephew Jordan de Bussey[21]. So valiantly did Jordan de Bussey and his garrison resist the invaders, in fact, that when FitzDuncan pressed on southwards to Warden in the neighbourhood of Hexham his marauding force was weakened by his having to leave a detachment to keep an eye on the Carham garrison. Perhaps it was his irritation at having to do so which led him to allow the Scots to plunder more cruelly than ever after they had crossed the Tyne and driven through to West Durham ; amongst the places devastated by them was that fresh shoot of Cistercian piety, lately planted from Fountains, the priory of Newminster[22]. Meanwhile, Stephen had not been idle, but in early February came northwards to Carham with his army, not only to quell the Scots but also to run his eye over the northern baronage, many of whom were suspected of leanings towards David[23]. It was these suspicions that led Stephen at this time to relieve Eustace FitzJohn of the fortress at Bamburgh with which he had long been entrusted, an action which drove FitzJohn, one of the outstanding northerners, to throw in his lot soon afterwards with King David. King David apparently hoped that others would do the same, for as Stephen pressed northwards he withdrew into the hills of Roxburghshire and schemed to trap Stephen in Roxburgh itself with the aid of its citizens and of certain English malcontents. His schemes failed because the English king did not turn aside to Roxburgh but rode past to the east and laid waste parts of the Scottish Lowlands.

The first engagements of this year had proved indecisive, and Stephen must have been aware that trouble lay ahead as he rode southwards to Northampton, where he held a council that Easter. Thurstan's presence at the council (in spite of his failing health) and the fact that he presided over it[24], suggest that the urgency of the position in the North had been clearly recognized and his own importance as the focus of loyalties there acknowledged. Certainly the urgency was soon beyond the need of underlining, for even as the council was assembling David was mounting a threat to his

21. *Priory of Hexham*, pp. 77–8.
22. *Ibid.*, p. 79.
23. *Ibid.*, pp. 81, 117.
24. Florence of Worcester, *Chronicon ex Chronicis* II, p. 105.

southern neighbours bigger than any they had faced for generations. With an imposing army of Galwegians, Scots, mercenaries and men of Norman lineage he once more entered luckless Northumbria, but proceeding this time by the coast road and moving with such rapidity that he was soon at the gates of Durham. Here his advance was stayed by a threat of rebellion from his ill-disciplined Galwegians and by the rumour that Stephen's forces were marching against him. If David had nonetheless pushed on into Yorkshire at this moment he might well have dealt Stephen's cause a fatal blow, but instead he turned aside to attack the bishop of Durham's castle of Norham. In contrast with the resolute defenders of Carham the garrison at Norham quickly surrendered, bringing shame upon themselves and on their lord the bishop ; the difference between the defenders at Carham and those at Norham, between Walter Espec and bishop Geoffrey, illustrates rather well how a lord's personality could mould his men, much as a colonel's character is reflected in his battalion. Further shame was soon to fall upon Stephen's cause when Eustace FitzJohn, smarting under his treatment by Stephen, handed over his great castle at Alnwick to David and promised to do the same with the key-castle at Malton on the eastern flank of the Yorkshire plain[25]. Not only was the defection of this respected baron and tried king's servant a blow to the morale of Stephen's supporters, it also contained a strategic threat, for Eustace knew as much about the fortifications of the northern castle as any man alive, and if anyone knew how to take them it was him[26]. With Bamborough also heavily besieged the only bright spot for Stephen's supporters was the spurt of defiance at Carham on May 8th : there certain knights of the garrison rode out of the town, as one of David's provision trains was going past, and seized it and carried it back inside the gates ; their audacity infuriated David and drove him to press the siege with redoubled anger but no more success[27].

Meanwhile David's nephew, William FitzDuncan, had been ravaging at the head of a detachment of the fiercer spirits in his army throughout the districts of Furness, Craven and Clitheroe. On the face of it these were surprising areas for him to choose because he had not long before married Alice, daughter of Cecily de Rumilly, and was therefore spoiling lands that might one day be

---

25. *Ibid.*, p. 84.
26. See the many entries referring to Eustace's repair works in *Pipe Roll* 31 *Henry I* ; and *E Y C* I, no. 500 for his work on the castle of Knaresborough.
27. *Priory of Hexham*, p. 84.

his own—though perhaps this was the very reason for his actions, that he was taking advantage of the national crisis to satisfy some private grievance that had arisen between himself and his wife's family[28]. What lies beyond doubt is that this campaign under William FitzDuncan did much to unite the northern barons in opposition to King David ; not only were they stung in their honour by the defeat of Norman knights at the hands of barbarian Galwegians, but many of the knights defeated at Clitheroe[29] escaped with a burning thirst for revenge ; the honour of Clitheroe, for instance, belonged to Ilbert de Lascy, and the disastrous battle left him no choice but to throw his whole resources into the struggle on Stephen's side. Also the barons were genuinely outraged by the cruelty of the Galwegians towards women and children, and their desecration of holy places. The biographer of St. Godric, for instance, has a lurid tale to tell of how these fierce tribesmen from David's army broke into the hermit's little chapel, scattered its liturgical furnishings and even trampled the holy eucharist beneath their feet, threatening to murder the saint unless he handed over to them the treasure which they imagined him to be hiding. The incident is paralleled in the chronicle of Hexham[30], and one can easily see how such tales spread rapidly throughout the North as the inhabitants of the devastated areas fled here and there for refuge in the same manner that we have seen the monks of Calder trailing over the Pennines to Thirsk, a moving image of the misery that would descend upon the land unless its barons joined together against the oppressor[31].

In the following month of July the position became critical, for in this month an army under David, estimated by the English to number 26,000, set out from Norham towards Durham, but wiser than before, was now quite prepared to by-pass that city, seal it off by siege, and unencumbered to strike into the heart of Yorkshire. This was the crucial moment for Thurstan to go into action. He did so by assembling at York all the greater barons of the North so that together they might work out a concerted plan for their campaign against the Scots. To read through the names of those who fore-

---

28. *Ibid.*, pp. 82–3 and p. 163 and note.
29. The actual battle of Clitheroe took place on the 10th of June.
30. *Vita Godrici (S S)*, pp. 114–6 ; *Priory of Hexham*, p. 116.
31. Having no military protection the religious houses had to throw themselves on David's mercy ; he gave guarantees of protection, for instance, to Hexham (*Priory of Hexham*, pp. 80–81) and, in June, to Tynemouth (Lawrie, *Early Scottish Charters*, p. 92).

gathered at York is like listening to a roll-call not simply of great
barons but also of the men who had eagerly co-operated with
Thurstan in his monastic enterprises : William of Aumale, Walter
de Gant, Robert de Brus and his son Adam, Roger de Mowbray,
Walter Espec, Ilbert de Lascy, William de Percy, Richard de
Courcy, William Fossard, Richard de Estuteville and many
others[32]. It is hard, hearing their names and remembering their
subsequent prowess, to realize that they were still torn by suspicions
of one another and were near to despair at the thought of the defeat
looming up before them, a defeat which some seemed to regard as
inevitable[33]. On account of the troubles in southern England
Stephen was unable to come north himself to lead them and the
barons were troubled by the thought that anyone who committed
himself to the losing side now would find his lands and wealth
snatched away from him, and that Stephen's gave every appearance
of being the losing side. It was a crucial moment, one of those
moments at which the destiny of a whole society hinges on the
resolution of one man of decision ; and that man was Thurstan.
Thurstan was not able at one stroke to dispel their suspicions of each
other but he did the best thing possible to alleviate them. In the
words of a contemporary : "being the shepherd of their souls, he
would not, like a hireling on the approach of the wolf, seek safety
in flight, but rather, pierced with the deepest emotions of pity at
the dispersion and ruin of his flock he applied all his energy and
labours to counteract these great evils. Wherefore, by the authority
of his divine commission, and the royal warrant with which on that
occasion he was provided, he boldly urged them, by their loyalty
and their honour, not to allow themselves through cowardice to be
prostrated at one blow by utter savages ; but that rather they all,
with their dependants, should seek God's favour by true repentance,
and turning with all their heart to Him whose wrath these many
and heavy evils proved that they deserved, they should then act
with the confidence and courage demanded in so pressing an emer-
gency. If they acted thus devotedly, trusting in God's mercy, he

---

32. The friendships between the members of this group could produce ironical
    results. William Fossard's son, also named William, was made ward to
    William of Aumale, and whilst in wardship got his patron's sister with
    child. Even more ironically, when the offender's castle of Montferant was
    destroyed in reprisal, its timbers proved extremely useful for building
    parts of the Cistercian monastery of Meaux (*Chronica Monasterii de Melsa,*
    I, pp. 104–5, *R S,* 1866). The structure must have symbolized very well
    the combination of piety and violence so characteristic of the age.

33. *Ibid.,* p. 86.

assured them of victory ; for that infamous people were directing their hostile endeavours against God and holy church rather than against them, and therefore were fighting in an unrighteous cause— a damned one, in fact. But their own cause was a just and most holy one, inasmuch as they were encountering peril in defence of holy church and of their country ; and if so be it should please God that this contest should not terminate without the loss of some of them, yet, by those who were fighting with such an object, death was not to be feared but rather desired." He promised them also that the priests of his diocese, bearing crosses, should march with them to battle with their parishioners, and that he also, God willing, intended to be present with his men in the engagement[34]. "He followed up this speech by persuading them all to take an oath pledging their loyalty to King Stephen and their opposition to David ; then, whilst the oath was still warm on their lips, he sent them off to their own honours to raise the troops necessary for the coming fight. At the same time he published an edict throughout his whole diocese that all who could proceed to the wars should flock to their leaders from each of his parishes, preceded by the priests with cross and banners and relics of the saints, to defend the church of Christ against the barbarians[35]. On one thing the northerners could now set their minds at rest : in fighting for Stephen they were not being disloyal to their late king, Henry ; on the contrary, they were engaging in a holy war with the blessing of the most venerable and saintly member of the English hierarchy[36]. Stephen added force and encouragement to Thurstan's words by despatching a company of knights to the North under the leadership of Bernard de Balliol[37].

After spending the early part of August on their honours, equipping themselves and their men for battle, the barons returned again to their rendezvous at York. There they first cleansed themselves before the coming trial by each of them making his private confession ; after which the archbishop imposed on them a three days' fast to be accompanied with alms-giving. At the end of this period of purification he solemnly absolved them and gave them God's blessing and his own ; and although illness and old age had so weakened him that he had to be carried on a litter, still he proposed

34. *Ibid.*, pp. 86–7.
35. Ailred of Rievaulx, *Relatio de Standardo* in *Chronicles of the Reigns of Stephen, Henry II and Richard I (R S)* III, p. 182.
36. Did Thurstan, when proclaiming a crusade, have in mind the holy war that his great patron, Cuno of Praeneste, had declared against that social scourge Thomas de Marle in 1114 ? *Cf* p. 60.
37. *Priory of Hexham*, p. 87.

to accompany them to the field of battle and encourage them by his presence. "But they compelled him to stay behind, begging him to occupy himself in interceding for them by prayers and alms, by vigils and fasting and other pious exercises ; meanwhile they (with the help of God and in accordance with their status in society) would gladly go out against the enemy in defence of God's church and of him who was God's minister. So he consigned to them his cross, and the standard of St. Peter, and his retainers, at the same time providing them with spiritual advisers in the person of Bishop Ralph of Orkney, one of his York archdeacons, and other clerics, who were to preach penance to the people and bring them absolution. And they proceeded to the town called Thirsk"[38]. Meanwhile the militia from Ripon and Beverley were converging upon Thirsk, marching under the respective banners of St. Wilfrid and St. John[39].

Now that the Scottish and English armies were approaching each other a desperate, last-minute effort to save the peace was made by two barons from the English side who stood in specially close relationship with David[40]. These two, Bernard de Balliol and Robert de Brus, went to David and begged him to stop the destruction that his army was perpetrating. It must have been specially galling to Brus and Balliol to see such a major rôle in David's counsels being played by the Galwegians whom they themselves had been charged to tame years ago when David granted them lands in southern Scotland. Brus reminded David of these things, how he and other Normans as far back as 1107 had obliged Alexander to yield a part of his kingdom to David ; nor should he forget how it was his Norman knights who had helped him in 1130 and again in 1134 to suppress the rising of the men of Moray. The old alliance of Normans seemed to be broken now, with the erstwhile enemies of 1130 and 1134 standing in the ranks of David's army, but Brus and Balliol hoped that it could be mended and they promised to obtain the earldom of Northumberland from Stephen for David's son Henry, if only David would call off his army. David, however, seems to have momentarily lost control of the situation ;

38. *Ibid.*, pp. 87–8.
39. *Ibid.*, pp. 90–91.
40. *Priory of Hexham*, p. 119 ; Ailred of Rievaulx, *Relatio*, pp. 192–5. See also R. L. G. Ritchie, *The Normans in Scotland*, pp. 262–3, where he evokes with remarkable skill the tension of loyalties produced by the Battle of the Standard, of which Ritchie gives by far the best account available.

and when the wild William FitzDuncan responded to Brus's speech
by calling that aged warrior a traitor Robert abjured the homage
which he owed David for his Scottish lands and Bernard abjured
the fealty which he had sworn to him on an earlier occasion when he
had been taken prisoner by David. When they returned to the
English camp they found that the numbers of their own army had
been swollen by the arrival of barons from further south, William
Peverel and Geoffrey Halsalin from Nottinghamshire, and Robert
de Ferrers from Derbyshire amongst others. Still suspicion of one
another's loyalty was not yet quelled in the English camp and the
arrival of these fresh forces was the occasion for another round of
oath-taking, each promising not to desert but to perish or to conquer
together. But just to make sure that there was no running away it
was agreed amongst them that they would fight on foot and leave
their horses well behind the lines so that victory was the only means
of survival[41].

Before the two armies eventually faced each other on a moor
two miles east of Northallerton on the morning of August 22nd,
there was, in fact, a good deal of such talk as though both sides found
lusty oaths essential for maintaining their spirits. The English
army was treated to one such exhortation by Bishop Ralph Nowell.
It was a speech recalling to his listeners the deeds of their Norman
ancestors and kinsfolk in France, Apulia, Antioch and Jerusalem,
and contrasting these achievements with the madness of their
opponents. But, above all, Ralph Nowell insisted on the holy
character of the task that lay ahead of them ; by their sacrilege and
cruelties the Scots had forfeited all claims to mercy and all who
struck them down were instruments of the divine wrath. Speaking
in the name of Thurstan he absolved all who might die in the battle
from the pains due to their sins, "in the name of the Father, whose
creatures they [i.e. the enemy] have foully and horribly destroyed,
and of the Son, whose altars they have fouled, and of the Holy Spirit,
whose elect they have killed"[42]. As he pronounced his absolution

---

41.   Ailred of Rievaulx, *Relatio*, p. 189.
42.   *Priory of Hexham*, p. 88 and n. Raine explains clearly why there must
      remain some doubt as to who were the main speakers to the English host
      and what exactly they said. Henry of Huntingdon, writing not long after
      the event, makes Ralph Nowell the main speaker (*Historia Anglorum*,
      pp. 262–3) ; Ailred gives the credit to Walter Espec (*Relatio*, pp. 185–189),
      and certainly much of the polish and rhetoric in Walter's words must be
      attributed to Ailred's Ciceronian talent. It may well be, of course, that
      both Ralph and Walter—and others as well—delivered rallying speeches
      of a similar tenour ; it would not be the only time this has happened before
      a battle.

from the high mound on which he stood the soldiers below and
around him beat their breasts in remorse and raised their arms to
heaven beseeching the divine mercy, crying, "Amen, Amen" in
response to his words.

That Ralph Nowell did deliver an address of this tenour we
may be sure ; whether its content has been exactly reported is less
certain, especially as the passage celebrating the Normans and their
deeds is so similar to those supposed to have been delivered by
Walter Espec to the same army. Walter Espec's part in inspiring
the army is celebrated in the tract on the battle composed by Ailred,
who at this moment when so many of his English and Scottish
friends were preparing to slay each other was himself busy at his
prayers in Rievaulx Abbey, less than twenty miles from Northallerton. Ailred's insight into Walter's character certainly comes
through in the dignified sentiments he attributes to him, his recalling
the many stirring events he had lived through, the battles he had
witnessed and the changing kings, all Walter's observations being
permeated by a contagious courage and confidence. A man of
enormous size, black-haired and with a flowing beard, his eyes large
and penetrating, his forehead noble, Walter also owned an eloquent
voice, resonant as a trumpet, which he well knew how to tune to the
ears of soldiers ; there is a soldierly note of humour in the words
with which he began his speech : "And for sure, if all you who are
listening to me only knew and understood, I should prefer to keep
silence and lie down to sleep, or play at dice or battle with chess-
men ; or if these seem hardly suitable occupations for a man of my
age, then I would occupy myself with histories, or, as my habit is,
lend my ear to the story-teller reciting the deeds of our ancestors"[43].
Knowing Walter Espec's interest in the legendary *History of the
Kings* by Geoffrey of Monmouth, a book he borrowed for a friend of
his, it is not difficult to guess at the nature of the stories he would
have listened to by the fireside had not duty called—the tales of
Arthur and his knights whose adventures had so frequently brought
them into these same northern parts[44].

Not that there are many sights in the fictitious Arthurian
legends more moving than the actual scene which Walter was gazing
upon in the dawn hours of August 22nd, as the Yorkshire forces
moved into position on the moor beyond Northallerton. "Some of

---

43. Ailred of Rievaulx, *Relatio*, pp. 183–189.
44. *Vita Ailredi* (ed. Powicke), p. lxxxviii.

them quickly erected, in the centre of the frame which they brought, the mast of a ship to which they gave the name of the Standard. On top of this pole they hung a silver pyx containing the Host, and the banners of St. Peter the Apostle, John of Beverley and Wilfrid of Ripon, confessors and bishops. In doing this, their hope was that our Lord Jesus Christ, by the efficacy of His Body, might be their leader in the contest in which they were engaging in defence of his church and their country. By this means they also provided for their men that, in the event of their being cut off and separated from them they might observe some certain and conspicuous rallying-point by which they might rejoin their comrades, and where they would receive succour"[45].

According to one account of the battle this panoply of saints and relics was not the only means devised by Thurstan to ensure success for the defending forces. He is also said to have hit upon an ingenious plan for striking terror into the enemy ; in the underground caves beside the field of battle he set instruments which can be made to produce horrifying noises, these instruments being known as *petronces* ; when they were sounded they struck panic into the beasts which David was having driven before his army to confuse his enemies, and as a result the beasts turned and spread confusion in his own ranks instead. As the author of this account, however, calmly describes the whole encounter as "a battle between David, King of Scotland, and archbishop Thurstan," and is in other matters prone to exaggeration, perhaps he is here transmitting to us a scrap of folklore that had clung to the event and giving the credit to Thurstan. At the same time there can be no quarrel with his succinct report : "and King David was conquered, and conquered were all the Scots"[46], for within a few hours of the engagement starting the Scots were fleeing pell-mell over Cowton Moor to the road that leads north-west over the fells towards Carlisle, and the English were celebrating their victory by cutting them down in flight. And for a verdict on the battle that doubtless reflects the sentiments of many northerners we may quote the solemn words of the prior of Hexham : "The ground on which the above battle was

---

45. *The Priory of Hexham*, p. 91. Ordericus Vitalis, *Ecclesiasticae Historiae* (ed. Le Prévost and Delisle, 1840–55), Vol. IV, p. 341, in his account of the battle at Andely in 1119, refers to the English battle cry *Regale*. On this M. le Prévost comments : "Nous ne connaissons pas la formule exacte de ce cri de guerre ; mais nous supposons que c'était en français : Royal étendard. L'usage de porter dans les batailles un étendard, placé sur un chariot, avait été emprunté ä l'Orient au retour de la première croisade."

46. *H C Y* II, p. 266.

fought was alone the possession of St. Cuthbert, the whole surrounding district being owned by others ; and this occurred not by
design of the combatants, but by the dispensation of Providence ;
for it may clearly be observed that divine justice would not allow
to go unpunished the iniquity that had been perpetrated in the
territory of this holy and beloved confessor and bishop, but would
speedily visit it with wonted vengeance"[47].

Not until three days after the battle, on the 25th of August,
were the Scots able to regroup their forces ; by that date Henry
had joined David in the friendly city of Carlisle, a city which had
itself provided its contingent to fight for David at the battle on
Cowton Moor. As if to try to save something from the wreckage of
his invasion and his reputation David now assembled his troops for
yet another attempt on the obstinate garrison of Carham. This time
he employed all the latest engines of war and tried every trick in the
military book, but entirely without avail ; his assaults were thrown
back every time, the gallant defenders held out steadfastly, and
David had finally to withdraw whilst leaving some of his troops to
continue the blockade of the town.

After the battle of the Standard there remained a considerable
danger that the area bounded by Carlisle, Newcastle and Durham,
already sadly devastated, would lapse into a condition of complete
anarchy and become a hunting-ground for every sort of brigand.
Notice of such a brigand group has come down to us ; it was led by
Edgar, the illegitimate son of Earl Gospatrick, and Robert and
Uctred, sons of Meldred. They scoured the Tyne valley like a pack
of wolves, seizing whatever they could lay their hands on and
pitilessly murdering any who stood in their way[48]. That there were
other such bands under lesser leadership is hardly to be doubted,
and it is likely that they would have ruined the North for generations
had a providential mission for peace not arrived in the land at almost
the exact moment that the issue of battle was being decided at
Northallerton. The peace that was being proclaimed by the head of

---

47. *The Priory of Hexham*, p. 94. There is a poem on the Battle of the Standard
     written in the jolly roistering vein that comes easily to victors, which is
     printed in *Dialogi Laurentii Dunelmensis Monachi ac Prioris (S S)*, pp.
     74–76, and has rather recklessly been attributed to Serlo, the monk of
     Fountains whose story of the monastery is to be found in *Memorials of
     Fountains (S S)*. The author at least had enough acquaintance with Gaelic
     to tell us that the wives of the defeated Scots forbad them to go fighting
     England again and called down the curse of St. Patrick (*maloht patric*) on
     the English and their standard.

48. *Priory of Hexham*, pp. 95–6, and 121.

this mission, Alberic, cardinal bishop of Ostia, was the peace of the church. It was a peace that the church could proclaim with more assurance now that its own schisms had been healed through the death of the anti-Pope Anacletus in January, 1138 ; and since Scotland had given its allegiance to the anti-Pope, Scotland was in need of reconciliation with the true Pope. Hence the appointment of Alberic, a Frenchman by birth and a Cluniac by profession, to serve as legate for both England and Scotland[49].

Alberic soon made for the north of England[50] because at this time the see of Canterbury was vacant, which left Thurstan of York as the premier ecclesiastic in the country, and because its troubles could only be resolved by someone armed with the extraordinary authority attaching to a papal legate. The first knot he had to un-ravel was the one by which William Cumin, King David's chancellor, was still held a prisoner at Durham, the place which he had been transferred to after being captured at the battle of the Standard. As soon as Alberic arrived in Durham he had Cumin released and restored to his king. For the next stage of his peace-making journey, which took him to the Augustinian house at Hexham, the legate was accompanied by Athelwold of Carlisle and Robert the bishop of Hereford ; like Athelwold, Robert had come to his bishopric via the Augustinian order, for after studying under Anselm of Laon he had been elected prior of the Augustinian house of Llanthony on the Welsh borders ; a man of great saintliness, particularly renowned for his passion for justice, Robert was the ideal adviser for Alberic to have beside him.

The legate's party reached Carlisle on the 26th of September where they were received by King David and the Scottish bishops, abbots and priors as well as by the leading secular lords. Despite initial tensions and difficulties the three-day conference that followed was highly successful. First of all a truce was agreed upon, which was to last until the feast of St. Martin (November 11th)— with the one exception that David was to be free to maintain the siege of Carham, where his failure to take the stronghold rankled most bitterly. Secondly, the Galwegians were made to promise that they would bring to Carlisle all the girls and women whom they had

---

49. *Priory of Hexham*, pp. 96 and 121.

50. The legate's party was at Hereford in June ; *cf* Helene Tillmann. *Die päpstlichen Legaten in England* (Bonn, 1926), pp 37-38.

captured earlier and restore them to freedom[51] ; and that in
future they would behave less barbarously. Thurstan's cause was
strengthened by the restoration of Athelwold to his see of Carlisle,
a move which could only have been achieved with the good will of
David who still, of course, retained possession of Carlisle and
district. Also Thurstan's troublesome subordinate John of Glasgow,
who had been skirmishing against York now for over twenty years,
was recalled to his duties from his refuge amongst the monks of
Tiron. Since he had been summoned to return previously without
effect Alberic this time pressed King David to despatch a royal
messenger to him bearing letters from both the legate and the king
which threatened him with dire penalties if he did not return to his
post. For there and other details of the conference at Carlisle we are
indebted to Richard of Hexham, who then tells us, with a touch of
local concern : "Moreover the king, unsolicited, discussed with the
prior of Hexham, who had come with the legate, concerning the loss
sustained by himself and his brethren, which he [i.e. the king] much
lamented, and for which he promised full indemnification, and also
that he would compel his people to make amends for the injury
done to them and their church, and for the slaughter of their men.
And this he in great measure fulfilled ; for nearly all their property,
and that of their vassals, was restored"[52]. It is pleasing to learn that
David, regarded by the gentle Ailred as a model for pious rulers,
should have made amends unsolicited for having in late years
behaved in a manner that is hard to reconcile with Ailred's picture
of him, violent behaviour that is best regarded as a temporary loss
of judgment due to rash advice.

The fact that Thurstan could not be present at this highly
successful peace conference is further confirmation that he was by
this time so infirm physically as to make it virtually impossible for
him to leave York. Otherwise he would obviously have done all he
could to attend personally at such an occasion, which can be regarded
as crowning his work for the spiritual and temporal well-being of the
borders. Similarly, when the term of the truce was approaching, a
month or so later, he was unable himself to make the journey north

---

51. The numbers of English girls captive in Scotland were very large if we are
   to believe the contemporary Alfred of Beverley, who wrote : Repleta est
   ergo Scocia servis et ancillis Anglici generis, ita ut etiam hodie nulla non
   dico villula, sed nec domuncula sine hiis valeat inveniri. (*Aluredi Beverlacensis Annales*, p. 131).

52. For this quotation and the preceding paragraph see *Priory of Hexham*,
   pp. 99–100, and 122.

to get it prolonged ; in his stead he sent William, abbot of Rievaulx. William was an excellent choice ; as abbot of the house which had brought Scotland its first Cistercian foundation—at Melrose—he was on friendly terms with King David[53], whilst the good will of Rievaulx's own patron, Walter Espec, was indispensible in the negotiations that faced him ; for it was William's task to remove from David's path that rock of offence at Carham where the garrison was still holding out stubbornly ; and Walter was lord of Carham and of its defenders. So William brought with him permission from Walter for his gallant soldiers to surrender Carham to King David, since their position was hopeless. As a salute to their courage David allowed them to march out of the place with full honours, bearing their arms ; after which his own troops took over the town and dismantled its fortifications. But not all the English nobles were so ready as Walter to set aside personal interests for the sake of peace ; the Earl of Chester never reconciled himself to surrendering the Carlisle area to the Scots, and he was supported by others who felt that David in defeat was receiving the rewards that properly belonged to the victors[54]. But their protests proved fruitless because within a few months a treaty had been ratified under which Northumbria was given to David's son Henry, who then set his seal on Norman influence in Scotland by marrying Adeline, daughter of William of Warenne and a niece of the French king.

The settlement of the borders was only part of legate Alberic's mission ; even more important in ecclesiastical eyes was the council of the English Church which the legate summoned to meet at Westminster Abbey in the December of 1138. Once again Thurstan had to plead his infirmity and had to send the dean of the minster, William, as head of the York clergy to represent him[55]. The York delegation cannot have been entirely pleased at the comprehensive series of decrees which were passed at this council ; they were

---

53. There is reason to believe also that Abbot William took Ailred with him on this mission, cf *Vita Ailredi* (ed. Powicke), xlvi, and note.

54. *Priory of Hexham*, p. 104 : Quippe plures de baronibus suis, quibus ex discordia eorum gravia dampna contigerant, sollicite ei persuaserant, ut nullo modo pacem cum rege Scottiae faceret, immo se viriliter de illo vindicaret.

55. *Priory of Hexham*, p. 101. Though not of the first importance for Thurstan's story, this council held by Alberic at Westminster seems to me of far greater importance than is usually acknowledged by historians. It was a vigorous attempt to sweep the board clean of malingerers and make the way smooth for the reformers ; Alberic was sent, says Prior John of Hexham, "ad disponendas regulares observationes praelatus monachis cunctis excellentia virtutis et plenitudine eruditionis instructus" (*ibid.*, p. 121).

directed against those abuses which were ever the target of Gregorian reformers ; clerical marriage, lay investiture, hereditary succession to spiritual offices, and other practices which had certainly not been eschewed in Yorkshire clerical circles[56]. However, if one or two Yorkshire faces went red as these sonorous decrees were being read out in Westminster Abbey they had reason to brighten again on hearing the name of the candidate who was being canvassed for the vacant see of Canterbury. He was Theobald, abbot of Bec, a man well known to the brothers Thurstan and Audouen. It was Audouen whose support in the previous year had led to Theobald's being elevated to the abbacy of Bec[57], and it cannot have escaped Alberic's sharp mind that a new archbishop of Canterbury began his career at an advantage if he commanded the confidence of two such eminent and respected prelates as the archbishop of York and the bishop of Evreux.

For despite his years and infirmity Thurstan could still make his presence felt when it came to questions of ecclesiastical appointment, as he had indeed demonstrated that very year. At his old cathedral of St. Paul's, in London, they had been without a bishop ever since the death in 1134 of Gilbert the Universalist. In 1136 a majority of the canons had elected as their bishop Anselm, the abbot of Bury St. Edmunds, who for two years comported himself as bishop though he had not in fact been consecrated[58]. And he reckoned without the diplomatic skill of the man who had opposed his election and refused to recognise it, dean William. One of the Belmeis dynasty that had run St. Paul's for years[59], William, had protested to Innocent II against Anselm's election, and his protest led Rome to make enquiries of the English bishops as to whether Anselm was a suitable candidate. The replies of the other bishops, though unfavourable, are not precisely known, but the historian of the disputed election has preserved Thurstan's observation as if aware that Thurstan was entitled to take the same sort of interest in St. Paul's and to exert the same sort of pressure on the election that would be the privilege of, say, the most distinguished alumnus of a modern American college. And Thurstan did have a special

---

56. Just how toughly rooted they were in York can be gauged from the letter of Pope Honorius III in 1221 complaining that the clergy there still practise these abuses. *H C Y* III, p. 115.
57. *Gallia Christiana*, XI, col. 575.
58. Ralph de Diceto, *Opera Historica* I (*R S*), pp. 249–50.
59. W. Stubbs, *Historical Introductions to the Rolls Series*, pp. 44–5.

interest, for was Anselm not the favoured child of the Canterbury monks, amongst whom he had been nurtured ?[60]. Was it not Anselm who had secured the pallium for Ralph of Canterbury despite his shady election ?[61]. And had Anselm not in 1117 been deflected from defending Thurstan by the gifts and flattery of King Henry ?[62]. Nor was Anselm's reputation entirely satisfactory in his own monastery[63]. In Thurstan's mind there was no hesitation and no need for circumlocution, so he said quite simply, "He deserves to lose his abbacy rather than to be given a see"[64] ; after which he had the satisfaction of seeing the curia quash the election and send Anselm back to Bury St. Edmunds. The decision of the curia was proclaimed by the legate Alberic, who then went on to show how firmly Rome meant to be mistress over Christendom by coolly deciding to forego a new election and instead putting Henry of Winchester in as diocesan vicar[65].

But by the beginning of 1139 Thurstan's weakness was incapacitating him more and more, and he prepared to withdraw entirely from public life. With the humility that characterizes all his behaviour he turned for advice on this point to a man who for all his brilliant qualities was yet many years his junior, that is Bernard, the abbot of Clairvaux. Unfortunately we do not possess Thurstan's letter to Clairvaux, but the gist of it can be gathered from the reply which it elicited, beginning : "To his reverend father and lord, Thurstan, by the grace of God Archbishop of York, health more of the soul than of the body, from Bernard, styled Abbot of Clairvaux. I praise your desire for quiet and your wish to rest peacefully in the Lord. But the reasons you give do not seem to me in themselves sufficient for abandoning your pastoral care, unless perhaps (which I am sure is not the case) you have committed some grave sin or have obtained the permission of the Holy See, for I am sure you are not ignorant of those words of the Apostle : 'Are you married to a wife ? Then do not go about to free yourself.' No

---

60. Cf R. W. Southern, St. Anselm and his Biographer, pp. 10–11.
61. Eadmer, Historia Novorum, p. 228 ff.
62. H C p. 54.
63. Tunc abbas Anselmus nequaquam domi erat. MS Harl. 1005, f218, quoted by Williamson, Letters of Osbert of Clare, p. 196, as a sign of disapproval from within the abbey. But perhaps this is to hear overtones where there are none.
64. Ralph de Diceto, Opera I, p. 250.
65. H. Boehmer, Kirche und Staat in England und in der Normandie, p. 373, on the significance of this episode : "die erste englische Bischofswahl, in welche die Kurie sich einmischte . . ."

promise such as you say you have made[66] can be binding on a bishop so as to impede the ministry to which he is called. It seems best to me, if I can say so without prejudice to the wiser opinion of wise men, that you should stay where you are and exhibit in a bishop the dress and holy life of a monk. But if there is some secret reason for your resignation or if the Lord Pope has gratified your wish for quiet, my advice, such as it is, is that you should not be put off your joining some house where you may see great purity of observance by fear of any degree of poverty or rough clothes and victuals. Bear in mind that in such homes, although the soul is the first concern, yet due regard is always given to physical weakness and age. I am your servant so as always to pray God fervently for you that he may inspire you to do what is best and grant that you may bear the burden and heat of the day, so as to receive in the evening of your life the meed of your labours in coin that bears his image"[67].

The promise referred to in the letter was that made by Thurstan years before to enter the Cluniac order before his death ; it was the need to still Thurstan's qualms over the promise which provided Bernard with this golden opportunity to conduct this unblushing piece of recruiting for his own Cistercian order. It was ironical that he should be given such an opportunity since at this very time he was directing a skirmishing operation against the Cluniacs in the diocese of Langres ; there a Cluniac had been elected as bishop but was meeting violent and abusive opposition from a party within the chapter that was being backed by Bernard. Through his influence at Rome Bernard had the first election quashed and orders were given to the canons of Langres to take heed of the "men of religion," which in hard terms meant that the canons' choice of a new bishop fell upon Godfrey, the prior of Clairvaux and a kinsman of Bernard's[68]. His advice did not, however, carry the same weight with Thurstan, as the archbishop showed when soon afterwards he sent as his representative to the Lateran Council in Rome (4 April, 1139) the abbot of Fountains, Richard, the one-time prior of St. Mary's Abbey. For well-informed sources were agreed that the private business which Thurstan had commissioned Richard to transact with the Pope was that of securing permission for him to resign his see ; so he was still intent upon laying down his

---

66. It is clear that Thurstan had mentioned to Bernard his youthful vow to assume the Cluniac habit before he died.
67. *Letters of St. Bernard*, pp. 244–5.
68. Giles Constable. The disputed election at Langres in 1138, in *Traditio*, XIII (1957), pp. 119–152.

pastoral care. It was also widely believed that the archbishop
hoped to have his own brother Audouen appointed to succeed
him[69]. But none of these schemes matured, death preventing
them. Abbot Richard died in Rome before he could complete his
task ; Audouen also died, in the house of the Augustinian canons
at Merton in Surrey, where he was clothed in the habit of the
brethren before the end. Death again struck at Thurstan's generation in this year by removing those two heroes of the battle of the
Standard, Walter de Gant and Robert de Ferrers. On the 4th of
July[70] it also took the man who probably knew the archbishop
better than anyone else, that is Hugh the Chanter, the archdeacon
of York, whose history of the archbishops was the major literary
achievement of the cathedral chapter. Some little time before his
death Hugh added to his literary fame by composing a poem in
celebration of the great battle fought in the previous year, at which
he had himself been present. Unfortunately only two lines of it have
been preserved :—

> Dicitur a stando standardum, quod stetit illic
> Militiae probitas vincere sive mori . . .[71].

But if one may venture a guess on the basis of these mere two lines
it seems likely that the York contingent marching behind St. Peter's
banner were given a central part in the poem.

The event that caused the greatest stir in 1139, however, was
the arrest of the bishops of Salisbury and Lincoln by King Stephen,
who wished to get his hands on the castles they controlled. As
legate and therefore defender of the church, Henry, bishop of
Winchester, summoned a council of bishops to meet at Winchester
to consider what reply to make to Stephen's action, but "Thurstan,
the archbishop of York, excused his absence by letter on account of
the ill-health from which he was suffering, for he could scarcely
govern his body by the strength of his mind"[72]. One suspects that
external happenings made less and less impact on Thurstan now,
though no doubt he was pleased to welcome such a visitor to York
as Malachy, the reforming bishop from Ireland, who came there in
November of 1139 on his way to Rome ; the accounts of Malachy's
visit are tantalizingly vague, but they do tell us that he met Waltheof
prior of Kirkham, who came over to York from his own priory to

---

69. *Priory of Hexham*, pp. 104–5.
70. *Liber Vitae Dunelmensis* (*S S*), p. 144.
71. *Priory of Hexham*, p. 90.
72. William of Malmesbury, *Historia Novella* (ed. K. R. Potter), p. 29.

meet Malachy[73]. Yet even though it may have been his own fame
as a religious reformer that brought Malachy to York, for Thurstan
the triumphs and achievements of yesteryear were fading into the
background as he prepared himself for death. After all, death is
not an event to be taken casually, and Thurstan set about the
business of dying with the same thoroughness and determination
that had characterized his living. With an equally typical concern
for the material well-being of his successor he made sure that his
barns on the manor of Ripon and other archiepiscopal estates were
well stocked so that his successor was not embarrassed financially
in the early days of his office[74]. Similarly he straightened up the
affairs of his own episcopal household ; he ensured that the members
of his familia were paid their due wages and made up any losses they
had incurred, going over each item in careful detail[75]. He also
wrote to the dean and canons of Evreux cathedral asking them out
of respect for the memory of his brother Audouen to maintain
Gilbert, Audouen's chamberlain, in the house which their late
bishop had acquired in Rouen for which he, Thurstan, had put up
the money[76]. Then he called together the priests of the church of
York into his chapel, and made a solemn confession of his faults in
their presence ; next he stretched himself naked on the ground
before the altar of St. Andrew and received the discipline of physical
chastisement at their hands, weeping meanwhile from the depths of
a contrite heart. After this act of abasement and renunciation of his
exalted position he set off southwards towards Pontefract, accompanied by the greater dignitaries of the church in York as well as by
many of the laity ; on his last journey Thurstan was fulfilling the
vow he had made in his early days to become a Cluniac monk, and
at Pontefract stood the one Cluniac house in his diocese. It must

---

73. *The Life of St. Malachy of Armagh by St. Bernard* (ed. H. J. Lawlor),
pp. 68–9 ; and *Acta Sanctorum, Aug.*, I, p. 256.
74. *Priory of Hexham*, p. 132.
75. *Ibid.*, p. 129.
   A rather different impression is given by the account in the beautiful
Durham MS Eccl. Dun. B ii 35 (printed in *H C Y* II, pp. 513–530) which
makes use of the Hexham Chronicle but is not completely dependent on it ;
according to this MS Thurstan made an attempt to escape from York
without taking advice with his clerics, and had to be brought back. If this
story is true it looks as though the York clergy had already got out of
hand in Thurstan's last year : Unde dispositis rebus suis, prout ei placuit,
absque spe revertendi ab Eboraco discessit. Sed quia clero et populo suo
inconsulto hoc agere coepit, a clericis suis eum persequentibus ad sedem
suam revocatus est. Reversus igitur cum religiosis et sapientibus viris de
vitae suae emendatione, et quomodo in archiepiscopatu sanius et utilius
conversare posset diligentissime tractavit. (*Ibid.*, p. 529).
76. See p. 199.

have been a hard journey for such an old, frail man, since it was January and the priory was over twenty miles away ; it must also have been a moving journey as he passed places indelibly associated with his ministry, the well-ordered nunnery of Clementhorpe, for instance, just outside the south gate of York, and the episcopal manor of Sherburn, standing half-way along his route and where he might well have rested for a night.

Having eventually arrived amongst the Cluniac brothers he received their habit, thus becoming a monk on the appropriate enough day of the Feast of the Conversion of St. Paul, the 25th January. Twelve days later, on the 6th February, "surrounded by the dignitaries of the church of York and other men of religion, as the hour of his summons drew near, he himself celebrated the Vigils for the departed, none other but himself reading the Nine Lessons. And when he came to the verse of the Response, *Dies illa, dies irae,* he laid significant and aweful emphasis on each word. At the end of Lauds, the monks being all assembled at prayer, he gave up the ghost. He was buried with becoming honour before the high altar in the church of St. John the Evangelist"[77].

A few days after Thurstan's burial one of his archdeacons, Geoffrey Turcople, of Nottingham, a man well known for his scholarly accomplishments—and not a little proud of them—was lost in sleep when Thurstan appeared before him, duly arrayed in his pontifical robes. Surprised, no doubt, that Thurstan had not detached himself utterly from earthly surroundings Geoffrey enquired of him, "Surely there is hope of your salvation, my father ? " To which Thurstan answered :—

"Life in the flesh was death ; but being freed
From fleshly trammels, blest I live indeed"[78].

In other words, the appearance of Thurstan to the archdeacon was hardly a sign that he was still not loosed from the world but rather that he was, with the saints ; for Geoffrey's account of this incident, as well as the turgid verses he wrote about Thurstan, make it clear that he was hoping for Thurstan's name to be enrolled on the Church's calendar of saints—hence the words set at the end of his verses, *Explicit vita Beati Thurstini, archiepiscopi Eboracensis*[79]. The monks of Pontefract entertained similar hopes,

---

77. *Priory of Hexham*, pp. 129–131.
78. *Ibid.*
79. *H C Y* II, p. 269.

when a year or two after Thurstan's death someone queried whether
his burial spot before the high altar was correctly marked[80] ; upon
the tombstone being lifted up his body was discovered beneath,
untouched by decay and sweet-smelling, unfailing signs of true
sanctity. Word of God's favour towards their late archbishop
spread quickly throughout the province and the story of his incorrupt body was faithfully recorded in the chronicles at Hexham
and Meaux[81], as well as at Pontefract. But hopes for Thurstan's
canonization were never fulfilled ; Ailred, Waltheof, William Fitz-
Herbert, Robert of Newminster, Godric of Finchale, all these subjects
of his were to be raised to the altars of the church, but not Thurstan
himself. He was, however, remembered with gratitude not only
within the province of York but also further afield ; at Evreux the
canons of the cathedral naturally coupled his name with that of
Audouen and remembered them together in their prayers on the 4th
of July each year[82] ; and in London the canons of St. Paul's showed
their admiration for the most distinguished of their old comrades
when they arranged for prayers to be said every year on his anni-
versary in the church of St. Helen, in Bishopsgate Ward[83]. Normandy, London and York all showed themselves aware of their loss.

80. *Priory of Hexham*, p. 131.
81. *Chronica de Melsa* (*R S*) I, p. 115.
82. *Receuil des Historiens des Gaules*, XXIII, p. 463.
83. St. Paul's MS. Reg. Dec. & Cap. W.D.4. fo. 31.

CHAPTER IX

EPILOGUE.

"After his death lawlessness was let loose, disputes were allowed to run on without restraint, open contempt was shown for the clergy, and lay people behaved with shameless disrespect towards church laws and dignitaries. The unity of the Kingdom was broken because everyone did as he pleased"[1]. These words of the Hexham chronicler, though true of the kingdom as a whole, apply with particular force to Thurstan's own province : Ranulf of Chester, for instance, could no longer contain his anger at seeing Carlisle in the hands of young Henry of Scotland and he smote Henry's supporters hip and thigh ; Alan, Earl of Richmond, a constant trouble-maker, set up a castle on the bishop of Durham's land at Hutton-Conyers from which he terrorized the citizens of Ripon and raided the stocks that Thurstan had carefully left for his successor on his Ripon manors[2]. But it was in the chapter of Thurstan's own church of St. Peter's, at York, that the dissolution of standards was most marked ; for in the course of the next fifteen years the controversy over who should succeed Thurstan drove some of the canons of York into the most extreme and frenzied hostility towards each other, a hostility so keenly infectious that it swept most of the prominent northern clergy into one camp or the other.

The reasons for these divisions are not far to seek. As we have seen time and again, the occupant of the see of York inevitably exerted great influence upon political events in the lands between Humber and Forth, an area spanning the territories of the English and the Scottish kings ; hence at such a time, when the English king's hold upon his throne was being challenged by Matilda, supported by her uncle the king of Scotland, it became vital to both parties to secure control of the territory north of the Humber—or, at least, to prevent any protégé of the opposing party from gaining control of it. This conflict of royal interests came to its climax

---

1. *Priory of Hexham*, p. 131.
2. *Ibid.*, pp. 131–2.

when King David's stepson, Waltheof, was proposed as Thurstan's successor but was firmly vetoed by King Stephen on the ground of his kinship with the Scottish ruler. There was, in fact, almost a third king involved in this particular dispute, for William of Aumale, the great Yorkshire landowner, struck contemporaries as being a further king between David and Stephen[3] ; and it was he who promised to support Waltheof's candidature if only that saintly man would make him a favourable lease of certain archiepiscopal estates. As one would have anticipated, Waltheof rejected this suggestion of bribery with great indignation[4].

But in addition to the political sources of discord a new factor had come into play during recent years. The movement within the church that favoured drastic reform measures had suddenly been swept to power in the north of England. Hardly discernible in the early years of Thurstan's rule it had been able to seize the initiative in church affairs through the backing he gave it. Scores of churches throughout the province were in the hands of Austin canons, whilst they and the Cistercians had begun to accumulate considerable wealth ; friendships between them were consolidating their common outlook, that between Waltheof of Kirkham and Ailred of Rievaulx, for instance, or between Robert the Scribe, of Bridlington, and Gervase of Fountains[5] ; and in Athelwold of Carlisle they had an outstanding personality from their ranks ruling a key diocese. Never again was the reforming party likely to have such an opportunity of winning a trial of strength as it was now given ; for in the previous year the Lateran Council had laid it down that episcopal chapters were not to exclude "men of religion" from helping them to elect a successor whenever their see became vacant ; and if the canons did exclude them, then the election would automatically become null and void[6]. As we have seen from the case of the diocese of Langres the Cistercians on the continent were poised to

---

3. William of Newburgh, *Chronicles of the Reigns of Stephen, Henry II and Richard I* (*R S*) I, p. 103 : . . . qui ibidem sub Stephano rex verior fuerat.

4. Life of Waltheof, *Acta Sanctorum, August 3rd*. Vol. I, cols. 1–2.

5. Robert the Scribe, Prior of Bridlington 1150(?)–1160(?), dedicated his commentary on the minor prophets to Gervase (who had been sub-prior at St. Mary's, York, and then stayed at Fountains until he became abbot of Louth Park), *St. John's College, Oxford MS.* XLVI. prol.

6. Lateran Council, 1139 c. XXVIII : Obeuntibus sane episcopis, quoniam ultra tres menses vacare ecclesias prohibent patrum sanctiones sub anathemata interdicimus, ne canonici de sede episcopali ab electione episcoporum excludant religiosos viros, sed eorum consilio honesta et idonea persona in episcopum eligatur. Quod si exclusis eisden religiosis electio fuerat celebrata ; quod absque eorum assensu et convenientia factum fuerit, irritum habeatur et vacuum. (*Mansi*, XXI, p. 523).

grasp this opportunity to make the ideals of their order into the norm for Christendom ; nor were the English Cistercians any less zealous.

Though these events only concern us for the light they throw on the reactions of Thurstan's collaborators to the crisis, and the reflection this may throw on him during his later years, it will be useful to present a brief outline of his chapter's attempts to agree upon his successor[7]. The well-informed chronicler of Hexham assures us that "the clergy or York were for a whole year, according to the impulses of their heart, driven about in various and unsettled opinions as to whom they should elect"[8]. It was during this period, presumably, that the claims of Waltheof, prior of Kirkham, were unsuccessfully canvassed and possibly others of whom we know nothing. Eventually their indecision was resolved by the pressure of Henry of Blois, bishop of Winchester. He persuaded them to nominate yet another member of the Blois family, King Stephen's nephew Henry de Sully. But as this nominee was already abbot of Caen the Pope refused to allow him to become archbishop of York unless he first resigned his Norman abbacy ; when Henry de Sully decline to accept this condition the York chapter had to begin again. Once more, in January, 1141, it was external pressure that led to a decision, the pressure this time coming from the same scheming member of the Blois dynasty who had earlier tried to bribe Waltheof, that is, William of Aumale. This time he maintained that he was speaking in the king's name when proposing a representative of the Blois connexion—though of the illegitimate branch—that William FitzHerbert who had for a number of years been treasurer of the York chapter, and on whom Stephen had bestowed the title of royal chaplain[9].

William was duly chosen. And no severer blow could have been struck at the reforming group in the North since it represented a clear-cut victory for that secular intervention in ecclesiastical affairs which they so bitterly opposed. Indeed, for Robert Biset, the prior of Hexham who had been appointed by Thurstan in 1130,

---

7. The story is fairly well known now, thanks to three historians and their work : D. Knowles, The Case of St. William of York, in *Cambridge Historical Journal*, V (1936), pp. 162–77, 212–14 ; C. H. Talbot, New Documents in the Case of St. William of York, *ibid.*, X (1950), pp. 1–15 ; G. V. Scammell, *Hugh du Puiset*, pp. 5–21.
8. *Priory of Hexham*, p. 133.
9. *E Y C* I, no. 31.

it signified the end of an era ; to the indignation of his brethren he promptly abandoned them and went to join Bernard as a Cistercian at Clairvaux[10].

But there were tougher characters in this group, whose spokesmen included William, abbot of Rievaulx, the abbot of Fountains, the priors of Kirkham and Gisborough, and Robert, the custodian of the famous hospital in York ; they also had the support of a party within the York chapter headed by Walter of London, the archdeacon, with William the precentor and the other archdeacons standing beside him. A dedicated and resourceful company, they were not slow to respond to the challenge but quickly sent off a mission to Rome to protest against the irregularities in William FitzHerbert's election. Their journey in 1142 was but the first in a long series of such journeys undertaken by both sides to and from Rome in the next dozen years. But this first was not an entirely fruitless one since the reformers did at least manage to arouse doubts in the Roman curia regarding the validity of FitzHerbert's election ; and these doubts were never sufficiently stilled over the next few years to allow the consecration of FitzHerbert. During this period he was kept out of full enjoyment of the see until eventually a Cistercian became Pope in the person of Eugenius III. At once William's cause was lost, for Eugenius in 1147 ordered a fresh election and in December of that year had the satisfaction of himself consecrating as archbishop of York Henry Murdac, the very fiercest of the Yorkshire Cistercians.

For six troubled years Murdac presided over his see, never wholly accepted in the city of York itself, where the hostility of its citizens drove him to reside in other centres of the diocese, at Ripon and Beverley, for instance. His was an unsatisfactory episcopate, especially as contemporaries were bound to take it as an illustration of how sadly the Cistercian reformers failed once they were given the opportunity to put their ideals into practice[11]. Moreover, the anti-climax of Murdac's career is underlined through

---

10. *Priory of Hexham*, p. 139 : Rodbertus quoque Biseth, Prior Hagustaldensis, audita electione eius statim domum suam exposuit et fratres, et sub Bernardo abbate Clarae Vallis monachatui se contradidit.

11. *The Coucher Book of Selby*, I, p. 44 : Cum igitur novem annis Abbas Helias praefuisset Ecclesiae de iure regiminis Henricus eum Archiepiscopus callida machinatione deiecit. . . . The unmistakable resentment in this entry was widespread throughout the North during Henry Murdac's episcopate. *Cf* also *H C Y* II, pp. 273-4 : Scripsit vero adversus eum [i.e. William] Bernardus abbas Claraevallensis, cui Apostolicus quasi peccatum ariolandi reputavit repugnare vel contradicere, et quasi scelus idolatriae nolle acquiescere.

its coinciding with a similar anti-climax in Cistercian leadership throughout Europe ; in particular, this was the period of the disastrous Second Crusade, preached with such ardour by St. Bernard and backed to the hilt by the Cistercian Pope Eugenius. It was a rather sad curtain that drew down upon the lives of these three in 1153, Eugenius dying in the July of that year, St. Bernard in the August and Murdac in October. Eugenius and Murdac were removed by the good God, according to the Pontefract biographer of St. William, for opposing his hero[12].

Thus in the space of months the power situation within the Church had changed entirely, and nowhere more than in northern England. For by May of 1154 William FitzHerbert was once more in occupation of his see ; his case had again been reviewed in Rome, this time by a supporter of his cause, Pope Anastasius IV ; the new Pope had personally consecrated him and removed all obstacles from the path of his return[13]. In the early months of 1154 it seemed as though this was to be the *annus mirabilis* for the Blois family in northern parts now that the advanced reformers had suffered such heavy blows. But in this conflict between the ancient and the new death proved an impartial arbiter, since in this very year both King Stephen and his son died, leaving possession of the English throne to the rival house of Anjou in the person of the young Henry II. Moreover, King Henry from the first showed that he was going to stand no nonsense from the Blois connexion—he simply refused, for instance, to recognize William of Aumale's title to the earldom of York which William had enjoyed since the day of his great deeds at the Battle of the Standard. Whether at a hint from Henry or at the prompting of his own prudence the arch-schemer, the bishop of Winchester, similarly shifted out of the limelight by leaving the county for four years. How William FitzHerbert, as archbishop of York, would have fared at the hands of the young Angevin ruler we cannot say since William himself only enjoyed for a few months the position he had sought so long ; he died in June, 1154, and rumour had it that his death was caused by a poison administered in the chalice at Mass by none other than Osbert of Bayeux, one of his archdeacons.

---

12. Videns igitur bonus Deus nobile vasculum thesaurarii ad unctionis nobilem thesaurum septenae lavacro poenitudinis ad unguem emundatum, majora ei adversantia delevit e medio. *H C Y* II, pp. 273–4.

13. *H C Y* II, p. 396.

Whether these suspicions were justified or not, the mere fact that such black suspicions were broadcast publicly and that Osbert found it impossible to clear himself of them even by compurgation, reveals the deplorable condition into which the York chapter had sunk in the fifteen years since Thurstan's death. We should like to know whether the deterioration had already set in during his last years, when sickness and old age may have weakened his grip on affairs. Or whether, on the contrary, the York chapter had contained these irascible and mutually hostile characters all the time, but that they had been held in check by the firm hand and dominating personality of Thurstan ? And which of them represented the true Thurstan tradition ?

Certainly those who opposed William FitzHerbert were men whom Thurstan himself had chosen, Walter of London and Osbert of Bayeux. Osbert was, in fact, Thurstan's nephew and at least had sufficient respect for his uncle to make a grant of land to the monks of Pontefract for the sake of Thurstan's soul[14]. But before assuming that Walter and Osbert were his true legatees we need to remind ourselves that Thurstan's choice of men was not always unerring, as we have seen in his unhappy choice of a protector for Christina of Markyate. Nor is blood relationship any guarantee of spiritual affinity, for Osbert of Bayeux hardly sheds lustre on the family to which both he and the archbishop belonged. We cannot ignore the fact that so judicious a man as John of Salisbury gave some credence to the story that Osbert had poisoned his archbishop in a peculiarly foul manner[15], nor does Osbert's reply to the accusation carry the immediate ring of innocence[16]. It is obvious, moreover, that his dedication to the work of the church was not complete and whole-hearted since we find that by the 1160's he had returned to the secular life. But even before that, before resigning his archdeaconry, he had already begotten a child ; and now he married and begot further children, took over land in the honour of Skipton[17], and acted as steward to Hugh de Tilly[18], the latter being one of the

14. *E Y C* III, no. 1718.
15. *The Letters of John of Salisbury* (ed. Miller, Butler, Brooke, 1955).
16. *Ibid.*, p. 27.
17. C. T. Clay, Early Archdeacons in the Church of York (*Y A J*, XXXVI), p. 279. A. Morey, Canonist Evidence in the Case of St. William of York, *Cambridge Historical Journal*, X, pp. 352-353. *E Y C* VI, pp. 158-9, *E Y C* VII, pp. 216-7.
18. *E Y C* III, no. 1527. In 1174 a Ralph de Tilly was constable of the household of the archbishop of York. (Roger de Howden, *Chronica*, II, p. 60).

family from Tilly-sur-Seulles, hard by Thurstan's birth-place, which
provided officials to serve the archbishops of York. Perhaps from
the beginning Osbert would have done better as a knight or administrator of an honour than in the spiritual office for which the zeal
of his uncle had cast him.

Still, there can be no doubt that William FitzHerbert's opponents from outside the chapter were the very ones upon whom
Thurstan had relied for backing in the effort to reform his diocese ;
the Cistercians from Rievaulx and Fountains, the Austin canons
from Kirkham and Gisburn, and Robert of the Hospital. More
impressive still, however, is the steady opposition to FitzHerbert
on the part of Thurstan's old and intimate collaborator, Athelwold
bishop of Carlisle. Since he had played an increasingly important
role in the royal councils during the latter years of Henry and the
early years of Stephen[19] it must have counted for a good deal that
Athelwold should have given his vote for Henry Murdac in 1147[20],
when FitzHerbert was being ousted from York ; he remained
favourable to Murdac, and in 1149 when Murdac was unable to take
up his office in York, Athelwold received him with due reverence
at Carlisle[21]. By contrast, when in 1153 William FitzHerbert
returned, Athelwold lost no time in resigning his charge as prior of
Nostell, an office he had continued to hold for about thirty years
and even after having been made bishop ; the reasons he gave were
that he was now old and weak and preparing for death[22] ; but since
he did not relinquish his pastoral care, and since he was sufficiently
strong to travel to Henry II's coronation in the following year[23],
it is likely that these reasons were diplomatic.

When compared with these Israelites who ranged themselves
behind Henry those who sided with FitzHerbert qualify, it must be
acknowledged, for the name of Egyptians[24]. His most fervent
and least respectable supporter, clearly, was William of Aumale,

---

19.   *Regesta*, II, Index : *Priory of Hexham*, p. 98, for his role in the pacification
       of the North after the Battle of the Standard.
20.   *Priory of Hexham*, p. 155.
21.   *Ibid.*, p. 158.
22.   *E Y C* III, no. 1473 :   pro timore mortis et anime mee.
23.   Robert de Torigni, *Chronicles of the Reigns of Stephen, Henry II and
       Richard I*, IV, p. 182.
24.   Perhaps it would be as well here to insert a caution against seeing the
       whole of the northern clergy as divided into antagonistic and mutually
       exclusive groups ; for instance, one of the York archdeacons closest to
       archbishop William not long afterwards became a Cistercian at Rievaulx
       and clearly regarded some of the partisan stories as malicious propaganda.
       Cf William of Newburgh, *Chronicles of the Reigns of Stephen, Henry II and
       Richard I (R S)*, Vol. I, p. 81.

who took it upon himself to cajole, bribe or threaten at almost every episcopal election in this area ; his offer to Waltheof, and his straight order to elect FitzHerbert we have already noted ; he also seized the York archdeacon, Walter of London, on one occasion and shut him up in his castle of Biham, and he may well have been the instigator of the party that later castrated Walter[25]. Again, he frightened away William de St. Barbara, bishop of Durham, so that he could not take part in the election of 1147. But amongst Fitz-Herbert's supporters William was by no means the only one given to violence ; another group of them made an armed raid upon a grange of the Cistercian abbey of Fountains[26] ; and the leader of FitzHerbert's party in York, Hugh de Puiset, kept the population of the city in a state of perpetual readiness to resist Henry Murdac by force[27]—though once again it would be unfair to impute to a man the misdeeds of his associates. It was FitzHerbert, it is true, who had nominated Hugh de Puiset, a distant relative of his, to succeed him as treasurer of York, but then it is equally true that de Puiset eventually came to terms with Henry Murdac—as, for that matter, did even that scourge of the Cistercians, William of Aumale.

As well as those who favoured FitzHerbert for political or dynastic motives there were others who simply by their offices and persons represented a tradition that he and they equally shared and one which Murdac and the reformers equally detested. These men included Thurstan's faithful suffragan bishop, Ralph Nowell, the abbot of St. Mary's, Severinus, the abbot of Whitby, Benedict, and the abbots of Selby and Pontefract. Ralph, Benedict, and Elias of Selby, for instance, all acted as witnesses for a charter issued by FitzHerbert to the monks of Shrewsbury[28], whilst Ralph, Benedict and Severinus all travelled south to Winchester in September, 1143, for FitzHerbert's consecration at the hands of Henry bishop of Winchester, who was to perform the ceremony in virtue of his office as legate[29]. Their presence at Winchester completed a group stalwart in the old ways ; the legate himself a magnificent, lavish, self-confident character whose high-born family and Cluniac training combined to make him at once a knight and a monk of feudal Europe ; his relative William FitzHerbert, who found himself archbishop of York less through personal bril-

25. *Priory of Hexham*, pp. 133–4 ; William of Newburgh, I, p. 56.
26. G. V. Scammell, *Hugh du Puiset*, p. 11 and the authorities cited there.
27. William of Newburgh, *op. cit.*, p. 56.
28. Farrer, *Early Lancashire Charters and Pipe Rolls*, pp. 280–1.

liance or striking achievements than through steady loyalty to his
powerful family ; Ralph Nowell, the bishop who had never managed
to get within striking distance of his see, sufficiently pre-Gregorian
to have begotten children ; Severinus and Benedict, the representatives of established Benedictine communities now being harried by
avant-garde Cisterians and Austin canons.

As one's mind's eye travels over these opposing concentrations
of personalities one is driven to wonder which of them would have
found favour in Thurstan's sight—that supporting William Fitz-
Herbert who had rendered him long if undistinguished service in
the chapter of his cathedral, or the one supporting Henry Murdac
who had been something of a favourite son of his before rising to
great heights on the wave of enthusiasm emanating from Cîteaux ?
Perhaps the nearest answer is to suppose that so long as Thurstan
was alive then the clash between these two concepts of ecclesiastical
life was prevented from developing into open warfare, since he, in
his own person, had managed to reconcile the strains between them
both ; the tension between them had, in fact, enriched his own
personality and enabled him to fulfil the best ideals within each of
them. Born into the old, pre-Gregorian world of family attach-
ments, lay influence and the easy assumption of power, he had taken
a leading place within the new world of spiritual radicals without
ever growing away from the older one. He had been able to achieve
this seemingly impossible ideal through his genius for friendship
which had won for him the confidence of every sort of person from
the unworldly Christina of Markyate to the very worldly bishop of
Durham who had tried to seduce her, from the Popes at one end of
Europe to the semi-barbaric king of the little Isle of Man at the
other. Thurstan's biographers are fond of comparing him to a
strong tower ; perhaps he is better thought of as a bridge over
dividing gulfs, as one who could truly say with Bran the Blessed :
"He who is chief, let him be a bridge"[30].

---

29.   *H C Y* II, p. 222.
30   "A vo penn, bit bont," as the original mediaeval Welsh has it. The incident
      is to be found on p. 34 of *The Mabinogion* (ed. Gwyn Jones and Thomas
      Jones, Everyman Edition). See also Hugh the Chanter's verses in which
      he visualizes the bishop as one who is a bridge between God and His
      people (p. 120.n.)

Appendix I.

THURSTAN'S ACTS.

Since I have only come across one of Thurstan's *acta* not already published, i.e. (*a*) (x) below, I have thought it unnecessary to quote the original MS, and sufficient to refer to the publications where they are to be found.

(*a*) ORIGINAL GRANTS.

(i) to St. Peter's, York ; *E Y C* I, no. 125[1] ; *E Y C* I, no. 143 ; *E Y C* I, no. 144 ; *E Y C* I, no. 149.

(ii) to St. Wilfrid's, Ripon ; *E Y C* I, no. 116.

(iii) to Fountains Abbey ; *E Y C* I, no. 62.

(iv) to St. Clement's Nunnery, York ; *E Y C* I, no. 357.

(v) to St. Peter's, Whitby ; *E Y C* II, no. 876.

(vi) to St. Mary's, Bridlington ; *E Y C* II, no. 1151.

(vii) to Hexham Priory ; *The Priory of Hexham*, I, pp. 57–58, contains a description of Thurstan's gifts to the priory, the originals of which were lost in the fire of 1296 ; the gifts were recorded in The Regesta of Archbishop Melton 426 b. (*cf The Priory of Hexham*, II, p. 134).

(viii) to the churches of his diocese ; *H C*, p. 101.

(ix) to the city of Beverley ; *E Y C* I, no. 95.

(x) to William, his dapifer ; on p. 26 of the *Liber Albus* of Southwell, the compilation of which was begun c. 1335. It reads, extended : Turstinus dei gratia Eboracensis Archiepiscopus omnibus successoribus suis et omnibus hominibus suis de Notinghamscira clericis et laicis Francis et Anglis salutem. Sciatis me dedisse et presentis cartule testimonio confirmasse Willelmo dapifero et heredibus suis et feodo et hereditate fruc-

---

1. This is attributed by Farrer to Geoffrey Plantagenet, a later archbisohp of York, but Professor Cheney gives good reason for believing it to be Thurstan's (see his *English Bishops' Canceries 1100–1250*, p. 66).

tetum quoddam apud Halton in crementum terre sue pro eodem servitio pro quo aliam terram suam tenet videlicet pro servitio tertie partis militis. Hiis testibus Hugone decano Eboracensis, Hugone Sottavagina cantore, Willelmo filius Tole archidiacono, Willelmo preposito, Rogero de Suthwella canonico, Willelmo elemosinario, et aliis. Since Hugh the dean retired to Fountains in 1135, and since William FitzTole's period as archdeacon is probably 1125 to 1135 (*cf Y A J*, XXXVI, p. 284) we can date this charter to 1125/1135.

(*b*) CONFIRMATIONS.

(i) to the deanery of York, of churches given by Henry I ; *E Y C* I, no. 431.

(ii) to the hospital at Ripon, of land for its maintenance ; *Memorials of Ripon*, I, pp. 322–3.

(iii) to St. Cuthbert's, Durham, of its churches in Yorkshire ; *E Y C* II, no. 936[2].

(iv) to Holy Trinity, York, of gifts by the Paynel family ; *E Y C* VI, no. 9.

(v) to the Cluniac Priory, Pontefract, of lands and churches ; *E Y C* III, nos. 1319, 1468, 1469.

(vi) to Nostell Priory, of the church of Weaverthorpe ; *E Y C* I, no. 27.

(vii) to Bridlington Priory, of churches ; *E Y C* II, no. 1152.

(viii) to Bridlington Priory and Beverley Minster of their agreement respecting thraves ; *E Y C* I, no. 103.

(ix) to Bridlington Priory and Whitby Abbey, of their agreement respecting the tithes of Filey fishermen ; *E Y C* II, no. 875.

---

2. Appended to this confirmation (MS Durham D.C. 1.1 Archiep. no. 7a) is the only certain surviving Seal of Thurstan ; to quote the description by C. H. Hunter Blair (Durham Seals, in *Archaeologia Aeliana* XIV (1917), p. 279, Seal no. 3218) : "Oval, $3\frac{1}{2}$" x $2\frac{2}{3}$" (greatly decayed) the archbishop vested in alb. dalmatic, chasuble and a low plain mitre. His right hand is blessing and his left holds a crozier : . . . GILLUM TURSTINI . . . DEI . . . SIS. ARCHIEPISCOPI. Oddly enough, Thurstan's seal was used on one occasion by his successor, William, to seal a grant to Beverley (*E Y C* I, pp. 100–1) ; odder yet, the legend on the seal gives a variant spelling for his name : . . . (SI)GILLUM . . . (T)HURSTINI . . . Naturally I considered the possibility that the "Thurstan" of this seal was Thurstan the provost of Beverley ; but I do not think there can be any doubt that it is the seal of archbishop Thurstan, with a crozier in his left hand and his right raised in blessing.

(x) to the canons of Embsay (Skipton), of churches ; *E Y C* VII, nos. 3 and 8.

(xi) to Guisborough Priory, of churches ; *E Y C* II, no. 687[3].

(xii) to Fountains Abbey, of gift by Robert de Sarz and his wife ; *E Y C* I, no. 66.

(xiii) to Thurgarton Priory, of gifts by Ralph D'Aincourt, *Cambridge Historical Journal*, IV (1934), p. 296.

(c) NOTIFICATIONS.

(i) of provisions respecting the prebends of the canons of York ; *E Y C* I, nos. 150, 154.

(ii) of gift to the canons of Nostell ; *E Y C* III, nos. 1466, 1467.

(iii) of gift by Lambert and Emma de Fossegate to the Hospital of St. Peter ; *E Y C* I, no. 218.

(iv) of agreement between the monks of Pontefract and Robert the Chaplain ; *E Y C* III, no. 1470.

(v) of an agreement between the monks of St. Mary's, York, and the monks of Selby regarding the church of Snaith ; Drake, *Eboracum*, p. 618.

(vi) of churches granted to the canons of Bridlington ; *E Y C* III, no. 1367 ; *The Chartulary of Bridlington Priory*, p. 429.

(vii) of churches and liberties granted to the monks of Whitby ; *E Y C* II, no. 877.

(viii) of Thurstan's consecrating Robert as bishop of St. Andrews without profession of obedience, saving the claims of York ; Lawrie, *Early Scottish Charters*, no. LXXVI.

(ix) of his establishing the prebend of Beckingham at Southwell ; *Monasticon, VI, III,* 1313a.

---

3. *The Chartulary of Guisborough* (Surtees Soc., ed. W. Brown), nos. III, IV, V, supposed to be confirmations by Thurstan, are clearly spurious.

THURSTAN'S LETTER TO WILLIAM OF CORBEIL, ARCHBISHOP OF CANTERBURY AND PAPAL LEGATE.

It has been asked whether there are not grounds for doubting the authenticity of the letter, either in whole or in part. The answer, clearly, is that there are some grounds, and in order to examine them one needs to list the manuscripts in which the letter occurs.

These are :—

A. Oxford Bodleian. Western MSS. Corpus MS. CCIX (folio 98b) ; this manuscript was written in the late twelfth century, probably at Fountains Abbey, to whom it belonged before finding its way into the library of Corpus Christi College, Oxford, and from there to the Bodleian Library.

B. Oxford. MS. Bodley 39. (Summary Catalogue no. 1892) ; a fourteenth century manuscript formerly at St. Mary's, York.

C. Cambridge. Corpus Christi College. MS. 139. fos. 153r–158r ; the MS. in which this copy occurs has been very thoroughly described by Mr. P. Hunter Blair ("Some observations on the 'Historia Regum' attributed to Symeon of Durham", in *Celt and Saxon*, edited by N. K. Chadwick, 1963, pp. 63–118), who argues that it was compiled at the Cistercian abbey of Sawley about 1170. I think it would, perhaps, be safer simply to date it to the last quarter of the twelfth century.

D. London. British Museum. MS. Cotton. Otho. C. XIV. F.90^{v} ; a fragment to be dated mid-thirteenth century.

E. The letter also occurs in Serlo's *Narracio* of the foundation of Fountains, of which there are copies in :

    (i) Cambridge, Trinity College MS. Gale. O.1.79, dating from the early fifteenth century.

    (ii) London. British Museum MS. Lansdown. 404 ; a copy on paper to be dated circa 1600.

(iii)   London. British Museum MS. Arundel 51 ; to be
        dated 1600.

(iv)   Oxford. Bodleian. Dodsworth MS. 26 ; first half of the
        seventeenth century.

Of these manuscripts A, B, C and D, separate copies of the
letter, are in substance identical, as they are also with the corres-
ponding section of E(i). E(ii), (iii) and (iv) all contain the main
points of the letter but omit its elaborations ; for our present
purposes these differences are adequately shown in Walbran's
edition of the letter (*Memorials of Fountains*, pp. 11–29).

The grounds for doubting the authenticity of the letter are as
follows :

(i)   The earliest manuscript of the letter is dated to the period
       1170–1200, over half a century after the exodus from St.
       Mary's. Is this not a period when the Cistercian order is
       under attack, and therefore beset by the temptation to forge
       documents of self-justification ? And is it not suspicious
       that each of the two early copies of the letter (A and C) is
       of Cistercian origin ?

(ii)   The letter itself contains several strange features :

       (*a*) It is unnecessarily long if Thurstan is simply writing
              to William as papal legate to cover himself in case
              abbot Geoffrey appeals to the legate. All it needed
              was for Thurstan to notify William that Geoffrey
              might appeal and to ask William to abstain from any
              action until both sides could be heard.

       (*b*) The sweeping criticisms of the black monks contained
              in the letter are hardly in keeping with Thurstan's
              usual moderation, and were certainly not calculated
              to please William of Corbeil, who as archbishop was
              titular head of Christ Church, Canterbury, one of the
              greatest black monk houses.

       (*c*) The reform programme put forward by prior Richard
              was far more explicit than anything that even the
              Cistercians could have formulated by 1132.

Taking each of these doubts separately the relevant comments
would appear to be :

(i)   There are two complete manuscripts of the letter to be
       dated 1180–1200, and one fragment of it to be dated

c. 1250 ; far from being a meagre support for the authenticity of a letter of 1132 this is unusually abundant manuscript evidence. The earliest surviving MS. of the *Narracio*
itself, for instance, was written three centuries after the
the events it describes, in the early fifteenth century.
Again certain of St. Bernard's letters, including two quoted
in the *Narracio* (*Memorials*, pp. 40, 44) depend on a smaller
manuscript basis than Thurstan's letter does. In fact, the
17 letters dealing with St. Bernard's attack on St. William
of York are found in only one MS.

Also, it is what one would expect that the letter being
of supreme interest to the abbey of Fountains, in particular, and to the Cistercians in general, should have been
preserved in Cistercian manuscripts.

But it does raise one's suspicions that the two earliest
manuscripts were each written about 1190–1210 ; a word
will be said about this below.

(ii) (a) This objection would hold if Thurstan had simply been
writing a routine letter to the legate about one of the
endless jurisdictional disputes that troubled the life of
every prelate at this time. But he was not. The events
in St. Mary's were unprecedented and revolutionary ;
they produced the same sort of tremors in twelfth
century ecclesiastical circles that Newman's conversion touched off in Victorian churchmen. And just
as Newman's conversion was transformed into a public
issue so was the exodus from St. Mary's—in the first
instance through abbot Geoffrey's action in sending
messengers to various monasteries throughout England
to present his case, and summoning them to York to
stand by the good old cause. After this Thurstan
scarcely had any choice but to write an "open letter"
on the recent discontents at York which would put
before the public, in satisfying detail, a true account
of the background to his own actions regarding St.
Mary's. He could not safely have done less than compose such a "small book" since his own reputation was
at stake. Just how much Thurstan's own reputation
was at stake is often forgotten since we now know that
the twelfth century Church was to be characterized
by the astounding success of the Cistercian movement ;

but in 1132 the Cistercians were still innovators, still
on the fringe of church life, and as far as any reasonable observer could tell, the weight of tradition and
influence held the black monks firmly established at
the centre of church life. Anyone lending his name to
the Cistercians, as Thurstan was doing, risked his
name. Hence the "small book" in the form of a letter.
It was a device with numerous parallels in the twelfth
century ; for instance, when Nicholas of Worcester
was issuing an attack upon the metropolitan claims of
York he composed such a "small book," but put it in
the form of a letter to Eadmer ; when St. Bernard
composed his *Apologia* against the Cluniacs he chose
to do so in the form of a letter ; and many of the
Letters of Ivo of Chartres are really statements on
public issues (e.g. *P L* 162, cols. 238–242).

(*b*)　This objection to the authenticity of the letter is quite
the most powerful. It is true, of course, that the most
violent criticism of the black monks and unrestrained
praise for the Cistercians occurs in the passages of
which prior Richard, and not Thurstan, is the author.
Nevertheless, the letter as a whole does constitute a
most severe critique of the standards of black monk
life, often harshly expressed.

　　If the letter, or even its severest paragraphs, were
forged, however, there arises a grave difficulty. Anyone who knew enough to doctor a genuine letter of
Thurstan's must equally have known that Thurstan
had chosen a Cluniac house as his final resting-place ;
surely such a one would have toned down the reflections on the Cluniacs ? Or at least generalized his
criticisms by referring them simply to the black
monks without specifically naming the Cluniacs ?
He must have realized that these passages would
puzzle all readers of the letter who knew of Thurstan's
entry into Pontefract, as indeed they have done ever
since. We are left with the hypothesis of an imaginative forger who was not very imaginative.

　　As to the point that William of Corbeil, being
titular head of Christ Church, Canterbury, was hardly
likely to be sweetened by such criticisms of the black

monks, one need only observe that an archbishop of
Canterbury did not necessarily identify himself with
the black monks, especially if he were an "outsider"
like the canon that William was, the secular clerk that
Becket was, or the Cistercian that was Archbishop
Baldwin.

(c) Commenting on this objection I would say that the
programme sketched by prior Richard is not surprisingly articulate. For ten years now the debate with
Cluny had enabled the Cistercians to hammer out their
own principles *vis à vis* the older monasticism ; each
of prior Richard's individual criticisms of current
monastic practice had already been made time and
again in the debate aroused by the "crisis in the
cenobitical life" which had been in full swing for longer
yet.

Indeed, the programme would be much more
surprising if it came from a Cistercian forger of about
1170–1200. By this date the Cistercian houses themselves were noted for their wealth and extensive
properties ; they had now transformed themselves
into targets for exactly the sort of criticism that prior
Richard was urging against the black monks in 1132.
And if the Cistercians had reasons by this later period
for being embarrassed by appeals to poverty there is
one particular passage in prior Richard's programme
the very transcribing of which must have grated on
the nerves of the Cistercian scribe as his pen flowed
over the vellum ; this is the sentence in which he
speaks of the black monks as highly reprehensible for
living on incomes from churches and tithes. It cannot
have failed to cross the scribe's mind that appropriating churches and living off tithes were exactly the
sins attributed to the Cistercians by their late-twelfth
tentury critics. Moreover, Fountains itself had been
thrown into dispute with Archbishop Roger of Pont
l'Évêque regarding the circumstances in which the
Cistercians themselves should pay tithes ; the year
1190 had, in fact, seen the Chapter General forbidding
any further buying of lands so as not to become
involved in the question of tithes[1]. One would have

expected any Cistercian forger working at this date to
have slipped in a remark or two to justify Cistercian
behaviour in the past half-century, behaviour that was
at odds with their initial programme.

Turning now from the specific reasons for suspecting the letter
to a more general consideration there are numerous features of the
letter that are difficult to square with the suggestion that it is a
forgery.

To begin with, the criticisms contained in the letter are frequently referred directly to the Cluniacs, yet in the period 1170–1200
the Cistercians had no particular quarrel with the Cluniacs whereas
they had in the eleven-thirties. Moreover, the whole of prior
Richard's spiritual agony is a reflection of the agony of self-examina-
tion and reform that the Cluniac family was imposing upon itself
in the great meeting of 1132. Another pointer to the eleven-thirties
is that the letter attributes the heart-searching at St. Mary's to the
sight of the holiness not only of the Cistercians but also of the
Savigniacs, who had lately travelled through York—indeed, it is the
Savigniacs who are given first mention[2]. In the eleven-thirties, the
Savigniac order was still a name to conjure with, but after its
absorption by the Cistercians in 1147 it became of interest only to
historians ; what possible reason could a Cistercian in the eleven-
nineties have for calling attention to the monks of a defunct order ?
And why should he speak of the St. Mary's monks as having seen
them when a visit of Savigniacs to York is otherwise unrecorded in
surviving sources ?

A further aspect of the letter difficult to reconcile with the
forgery hypothesis is that the figure of abbot Geoffrey that emerges,
even indirectly, is too full of human tensions to be simply a paper
creation. Anyone composing a later justification of the Cistercians
would have made him into something of a villain, whereas the letter
shows him to have been an amiable, tired old man, on occasion
driven to desperation. There are similar touches of detail in the letter
which bespeak its authenticity, such as mentioning the name of the
monk of St. Mary's who spoke openly in defiance of Thurstan during
the visitation ; the letter at this point reads : "Then one of the
monks, Symeon by name, said . . ." Again, what forger would have

---

1. J. B. Mahn, *L'ordre Cistercien et son gouvernement* (1945), pp. 110–112.
2. Perhaps it is also significant that the letter does not speak of *Cistercienses*
but of *monachos Clarevallis*, a phrase much more consonant with the early
modes of the order's terminology.

known enough about Thurstan's household, fifty years gone, to have the archbishop refer by name to *Ansfredus, capellanus meus et canonicus* ?

Anyone adhering to the forgery hypothesis has a further difficulty to face : the monk Hugh, writing down the *Narracio* in 1208–9, almost certainly thought that the letter was genuine ; if he had doubted it in any way he would never have allowed the minor differences between Serlo's account and Thurstan's account to pass into public view. Thus Serlo does not refer to the part played by the monk Symeon, and he puts into Thurstan's mouth quite different phrases from the ones that occur in the letter itself ; the intention of the phrases is the same, but certainly if Hugh had suspected the letter of being doctored he would have brought its phraseology into line with that of Serlo. Forgery is like a false alibi in that its minutiae are just a bit too consistent to be real ; the opposite is the case with Serlo's narrative and Thurstan's letter—they record just such a variation in emphasis as one finds in real life.

There remains one point about the letter that may still seem odd, which is that the two earliest MS. both appear at about the same time. The most likely reason for this is not that the Cistercians had taken to forgery to justify themselves in face of contemporary criticism but that such criticism had driven the Cistercians of the late twelfth century to take stock of their situation and to interest themselves in the early days of their order. The *Narracio* of Fountains is not the only instance of this ; over at Rievaulx the precentor Mathew was at the same time composing his verses on leading personalities from the order's past[3], whilst at the very same time the abbeys of Byland and Jervaulx were piecing together the story of their own foundations[4]. Had circumstances proved more favourable the Cistercians might well have developed a historical school comparable to that of the black monks.

What, then, can we envisage as most likely to have happened in the case of Thurstan's letter ? It is clear that Thurstan had to act quickly after the fracas in St. Mary's and to issue some explanation of his action ; the visitation that he had prepared, which might have led to a long and carefully articulated judgment on the reform group within St. Mary's, had now been swept aside by the impetuosity of the black monks ; he, in reply, had suspended the community.

---

3. A. Wilmart, Les mélanges de Mathieu préchantre de Rievaulx, in *Revue Bénédictine*, Vol. 52 (1940), pp. 15–84.

4. *Monasticon*, Vol. V, 349–54 and 568–74.

In the statement of his case there was not time enough for the calm taking of evidence that he had earlier hoped for, and he had to use what evidence was available to him ; most of this came from prior Richard, and above all from the memorandum on the need for, and the manner of, reform within St. Mary's that Richard had compiled at the request of his abbot. This memorandum is obviously the basis of Thurstan's letter, a fact which accounts for some of the abruptness of the letter and the difficulty of knowing sometimes whether Thurstan is speaking *in propria persona* or quoting prior Richard. After composing the letter Thurstan presumably sent one copy to Canterbury, deposited one at York and gave another to prior Richard as leader of the little breakaway community at Fountains. The Canterbury one may not have survived because after a few years there was no one in that place specially interested in what had happened in an obscure northern house ; the York copy probably went the way of most York documents at this time, going up in one of the numerous fires that hit the city. At Fountains they had every reason to preserve their copy : they did so.

BIBLIOGRAPHY.

I. Manuscript Sources.

Since almost all the documents that throw light on Thurstan's career are already in print it is only rarely that manuscripts examined proved to have any relevance, and so many examined are not cited. But I have thought it worthwhile to cite some whose list of contents would seem to workers in this same field to indicate relevant material, and to comment on some of them briefly.

(a) British Museum.

Additional MS. 38816. (In addition to charters in favour of St. Mary's, York, and an account of the founding of that house, printed by Dugdale, it contains a most detailed confraternity agreement of St. Mary's fos. 37–39^v).

Cotton, Cleo. C. iv. fos. 4–19. (A late compilation giving accounts in verse of the foundation of York and the succession of its archbishops. *H C Y* II, p. 446 ff).

Cotton, Otho. C. XIV. fo. 90^v. (Fragment of Thurstan's letter to William of Corbeil).

Cotton, Otho. C. XVI. fos. 65–102. (Transcripts of Folcard's Life of St. John of Beverley, followed by privileges to the Minster pre-1380 ; *cf* G. R. C. Davis, *Mediaeval Cartularies of Great Britain* (1958), p. 8).

Cotton, Tiberius. A. VII, fo. 167. (No more than excerpts from William of Malmesbury's *Gesta Pontificum* on the archbishops of York).

Cotton, Titus. A. XIX. (This fifteenth century paper compilation includes the *Vita Turstini* by Hugh of Pontefract and Geoffrey Turcople printed in *H C Y* II, pp. 259–269, and various derivative notices of York history by Nicolas Walkington of Kirkham and the York historian Thomas Stubbs, who flourished in the middle of the fourteenth century. Also the verse history of York archbishops found likewise in Cotton, Cleo, C. IV).

Cotton, Vespasian. E. XIX. (Chartulary of Nostell).

Cotton, Vitellius. A. II, fos. 94–118. (Contains miscellaneous administrative descriptions of the offices in the diocese of York, tithes, taxation, excommunications, and numerous statutes of York Councils in the later middle ages).

Cotton, Vitellius. A. XII. (This well-known volume, in which some of Hugh the Chanter's verses are to be found, is described by A. Boutémy in *Latomus* I (1957), pp. 278–313).

Harley. 1808. Fos. 47–54. (This XIV MS. records bulls of several Popes in favour of York, Calixtus II and Honorius II amongst them ; in addition there are apologies for York's primacy and the archbishop's right to carry his cross outside his province, as well as a verse history of the see of York almost identical with that in Cotton, Cleo, C. IV).

Lansdowne. 402. (Compiled in 1399, it contains many charters and privileges relating to York).

(b) Cambridge.

University Library MS. KKiv.

Corpus Christi MS. 139. (Contains Thurstan's Epistle to William of Corbeil, printed by Walbran in *Memorials of Fountains*).

Peterhouse 74, p. 217. (Thurstan's declaration at consecration of Robert of St. Andrews).

(c) DURHAM.

D.C. 1.12.Spec. nos. 23, 24, 26 (cf p. 112).

D.C. 1.1.Archiep. nos. 7a. (Thurstan's seal is attached to this confirmation of Durham privileges), 7b, 8, 10, 11, 12, 14a.

D.C. Cart. Vetus.

Eccl. Dun. B.iv.24. (The Calendar enters Thurstan's death on the 8th of February ; the Martyrology enters Hugh the Chanter on the 5th of July).

Eccl. Dun. B.ii.35. (Item 11, fos. 265–281, is a finely written compilation from the third quarter of the twelfth century of short biographies of English bishops with longer accounts of York and Durham ; it is a good representative of the York–Durham–Hexham triangle of historical writing. The section on the York archbishops is to be found in *H C Y* II, pp. 513–530).

(d) OXFORD.

Bodley MS. 561.

Bodley. Digby. 65. (Some of these verses have been printed by Wright, *Satirical Poets*, II, pp. 208–12 and 219–229, but not all ; cf p. 119n).

Bodley. Digby. 96.

Bodley. Digby. 140. (A thirteenth century MS. in which ff. 3–17 are occupied by an account of the archbishops of York ending with Thurstan's death and heavily dependent on Hugh the Chanter ; printed in *H C Y* II, pp. 312–387).

Hatton 92.

(e) SOUTHWELL : Liber Albus.

Thurgarton MS. 3. Chartulary of Thurgarton.

(f) YORK.

D.C. Registrum Magnum Album. (The source for Hugh the Chanter's *Lives of the Archbishops*, as well as of many of the other items printed by Raine in *H C Y*).

(g) P.R.O.

Catalogues of Ancient Deeds (Series 3), no. 6, relating to Carlisle, York, etc.

II. CONTEMPORARY SOURCES.

Abingdon, Chronicon Monasterii de, ed. J. Stevenson (R.S. 2, 2 vols. 1858).

Ailredi, Vita, ed. and tr. F. M. Powicke (1950).

Albani, Gesta Abbatum S., ed. H. T. Riley (R.S. Vol. I (1867)).

Aluredi, Beverlacensis Annales, ed. T. Hearne (1716).

Anglo Saxon Chronicle, The, ed. D. Whitelock, D. C. Douglas, S. T. Tucker (1961).

Annales Monastici, ed. H. R. Luard (R.S. 36, 5 vols., 1864–69).

Anonimalle Chronicle, The, ed. V. H. Galbraith (1927).

Anselmi, *Opera Omnia* S., ed. F. S. Schmitt. 6 vols. (1946–61).

Becket, Materials for the History of, ed. J. C. Robertson and J. B. Sheppard (R.S. 67, 7 vols. 1875–85).

Bees, The Register of the Priory of St., ed. J. Wilson (S.S., 126, 1915).

Bernard, The Letters of St. ed. and tr. B. Scott-James (1953).

Bernardi Abbatis Vita I, in Bernardi *Opera Omnia*, ed. J. Mabillon. 2 vols. (1839), cols. 2089–2398.

Beverley Minster, Memorials of, ed. A. F. Leach (S.S. 2 vols. 98, 108, 1898–1903).

Bridlington Priory, The Chartulary of, ed. W. T. Lancaster (1912).

Brunonis, Vita S , in *Acta SS. October*. Vol. III.

Calixte II. Bullaire du pape, ed. U. Robert. 2 vols. (1891).

Canterbury, The Domesday Monachorum of Christ Church, ed. D. C. Douglas (1944).

Carta Caritatis, — in *Analecta Sacri Ordinis Cisterciensis* I, pp. 53–56.

Christina of Markyate, The Life of, — ed. and tr. C. H. Talbot (1959).

Chronicles of the Reigns of Stephen, Henry II and Richard I, — ed. R. Howlett (R.S. 82, 4 vols., 1884–90).

Concilia Magnae Britanniae et Hiberniae, — ed. D. Wilkins (4 vols. 1737).

Concilia Rotomagensis Provinciae, — ed. G. Bessin (1717).

Councils and Ecclesiastical Documents Relating to Great Britain and Ireland, — ed. A. W. Haddan and W. Stubbs. 3 vols. (1869–71).

Diceto, Ralph of, *Opera Historica*, — ed. W. Stubbs (R.S. 68, 2 vols. 1876).

Domesday Book, — printed in 1783 by the Record Commission.

Dunelmensis, Feodarium Prioratus, — ed. W. Greenwell (S.S. 58, 1871).

Dunelmensis, Liber Vita Ecclesiae, — ed. J. Stevenson (S.S. 13, 1841).

Eadmer, *Historia Novorum*, — ed. M. Rule (R.S., 81, 1884).

Evesham, Chronicon Abbatiae de, — ed. W. D. MacRay (R.S., 29, 1863).

Fees, The Book of, — ed. H. C. Maxwll-Lyte (3 vols., 1920–31).

Fountains, Memorials of the Abbey of S. Mary of, — ed. J. S. Walbran (S.S. 42, 1863).

Furness Abbey, The Coucher Book of, — ed. J. C. Atkinson (Cheetham Soc. 3 vols., IX, XI, XIV, 1886–1888).

Giraldus Cambrensis, *De Invectionibus*, — ed. W. S. Davies, Y Cymmrodor, XXX, 1920.

Gervase of Canterbury, *Opera*, — ed. W. Stubbs (R.S. 73, 2 vols., 1879–80).

Godrici, Vita, — ed. J. Stevenson (S.S., 20, 1845).

Guisborough, The Cartulary of, — ed. W. Brown, S.S. lxxxvi, lxxxix, 1889, 1894, 2 vols.).

Henry of Coquet, — Vita *Acta Sanctorum. Jan.* II. pp. 424–6.

Herbert de Losinga, The Life, Letters and Sermons of, — ed. E. M. Goulburn and H. Symonds, 2 vols. (1878).

Hexham, The Priory of, — ed. J. Raine (S.S., XLIV, 1865).

Hildebert of Le Mans, *Opera* — (1708).

Honors and Knights' Fees, — ed. W. Farrer, 3 vols. (1923–25).

Howden, Roger of, *Chronica.*, — ed. W. Stubbs (R.S. 51, 4 vols., 1868–71).

Hugh the Chantor, *The History of the Church of York*, 1066–1127, — ed. C. Johnson, 1961.

Huntingdon, Henry of, *Historia Anglorum*, — ed. T. Arnold (R.S. 1879).

Jaffé, P., *Regesta Pontificum Romanorum*, — ed. P. Jaffé, 2 vols. (1885–88).

John of Salisbury, The Letters of, — ed. W. J. Millor, H. E. Butler (1955).

Jumièges, William of, *Gesta Normannorum Ducum.*, — ed. J. Marx (1914).

Kentigern, The Life of St., — ed. A. P. Forbes (*The Historians of Scotland*, V., pp. 243–52) and tr. *ibid.* pp. 123–33).

Lancashire Pipe Rolls and Early Lancashire Charters, — ed. W. Farrer (1902).

Laurentii Dunelmensis Monachi, Dialogi., — ed. J. Raine (S.S., 70, 1878).

Libelli de Lite, — Monumenta Germaniae Historiae, 3 vols. (1892–97).

Liber Pontificalis Dertusensis, — ed. J. M. March (1925).

Louth Park, The Chronicle of, — ed. Venables (Lincoln Record Socciety I, 1891).

Mailros, Chronica de., — ed. J. Stevenson (Bannatyne Club no. 49, 1835).

Malachy of Armagh, The Life of St., ed. H. J. Lawlor (1920).
Malmesbury, William of,
Gesta Pontificum, ed. N. E. S. A. Hamilton (R.S. 52, 1870).

Gesta Regum, ed. W. Stubbs (R.S. 90, 1887–9).
Historia Novella, ed. K. R. Potter, 1955.
Man, Monumenta de Insula Manniae, tr. and ed. J. R. Oliver (Manx Soc-
or a Collection of National Docu- iety VII, 1861).
ments Relating to the Isle of,
Man and the Sudreys, Chronicles of, ed. and tr. Goss (Manx Society
XXII, XXIII, 1874).
Mansi, J., ed. Sacrorum Conciliorum Nova
Collectio (1757–1798).
Melsa, Chronica Monasterii de., ed. E. A. Bond (R.S. 43. 3 vols.
1866–68).
Monasticon Anglicanum, ed. W. Dugdale. 6 vols. (1817–30).
Newminster, The Chartulary of, ed. J. T. Fowler (S.S. 66, 1878).
Ordericus Vitalis, Ecclesiasticae His- ed. A. le Prévost and L. Delisle.
toriae, 5 vols. 1838–55).
Osbert of Clare, The Letters of, ed. E. W. Williamson (1929).
Patrologiae Latinae Cursus Completus, ed. J. P. Migne, 222 vols. (1844–64).
Peterborough Chronicles of Hugh ed. W. T. Mellows (1949).
Candidus, The,
Pipe Roll 31. Henry I, The, ed. J. Hunter–C. Johnson (1929).
Pontefract, The Chartulary of ed. R. Holmes (Y.A.J. Record Series
XXV and XXX, 1899 –1902).
Quadripartitus., ed. F. Liebermann (1892).
Receuil des Historiens des Gaules et ed. M. Bouquet. 24 vols. (1840–
de la France, 1904).
Red Book of the Exchequer, The, ed. H. Hare (R.S. 3 vols, 1886).
Regesta Regum Anglo-Normannorum I, ed. H. W. C. Davis (1913).
Regesta Regum Anglo-Normannorum II, ed. C. Johnson and H. A. Cronne
(1956).
Regesta Regum Scottorum I, ed. G. W. S. Barrow (1960).
Reginald of Durham, De virtutibus, beati Cuthberti (S.S.,
I, 1835).
Rievaulx, The Chartulary of, ed. J. C. Atkinson (S.S., 83, 1887).
Rouleaux des Morts du IXe au XVe ed. L. Delisle (1866).
siècle,
Satirical Poems and Epigrammatists ed. T. Wright (R.S., 59, 2 vols., 1872).
of the Twelfth Century,
Scotichronicon, John of Fordun's, (1759).
Scottish Charters, Early, ed. A. O. Lawrie (1905).
Scottish History, Early Sources of, ed. A. O. Anderson. 2 vols. (1922).
Selby, The Coucher Book of, ed. J. T. Fowler. 2 vols. (Yorkshire
Archaeological Association, Record
Series X, XIII, 1891, 1893).
Southwell Minster, Visitations and ed. A. F. Leach (Camden Society,
Memorials of, 1891).
Stephani, Gesta, ed. K. R. Potter (1955).
Symeon of Durham, Opera, ed. T. Arnold (R.S., 75. 2 vols.
1882–85).
Templars in England in the Twelfth ed. B. A. Lees (1935).
Century, Records of the,
Thesaurus Novus anecdotorum, ed. Martène and Durand. 5 vols.
(1717).
Tiron, Vita S. Bernardi abb., in Acta S.S. April, Vol. II.
Tockwith, alias Scokirk, The Char- ed. G. C. Ransome (Yorkshire
tulary of, Archaeological Society, Record
Series, LXXX, 1931, pp. 151–206).
Torigni, Robert de, Chronique, ed. L. Delisle (1872).
Waltheof, The Life of St., by Jocelin of Furness in Acta
Sanctorum, 3 Aug. I. 249–278.

Wetheral, The Registry of the Priory of,	ed. J. E. Prescott (1897).
Whitby, The Chartulary of,	ed. J. C. Atkinson (S.S. 69, 1879).
Worcester, Florence of, *Chronicon ex Chronicis*,	ed. B. Thorpe. 2 vols. 1848–9.
Worcester, The Chronicle of John of,	ed. J. R. H. Weaver (*Anecdota Oxomiensia*, 1908).
Wulfric of Haselbury, The Life of,	ed. M. Bell (Somerset Record Society, 1933).
Yorkshire Charters, Early,	10 vols. 1914–55, ed. W. Farrer. (Vols. I–III) and C. T. Clay (Vols. IV–IX).
York, Historians of the Church of,	ed. J. Raine (R.S. 71. 3 vols. 1879–94).
York Minster, The Fabric Rolls of,	ed. J. Raine (S.S. 35, 1859).

III. MODERN WORKS.

BARLOW, F.,	Durham Jurisdictional Peculiars (1950).
BARROW, G. W. S.,	A Scottish Collection at Canterbury in *Scottish Historical Review*. XXXI (1952), pp. 16–28).
BARROW, G. W. S.,	Scottish Rulers and the Religious Orders, in *Transactions of the Royal Historical Society* (1953), pp. 77–100).
BARROW, G. W. S.,	From Queen Margaret to David I., in *The Innes Review* XI (1960), pp. 22–38.
BATTELY, J.,	Antiquitatus Sancti Edmundi Burgis (1745).
BATTISCOMBE, C. F.,	ed. The Relics of St. Cuthbert (1956).
BERESFORD, M. W.,	Mediaeval Town Plantation in the Carlisle Area, in *The Archaeological Journal* CXV (1958), pp. 215–217).
BERNHARDI, W.,	Lothar von Supplinburg (1879).
BLOCH, H.,	The schism of Anacletus II and the Glanfeuil Forgeries of Peter the Deacon of Monte Cassino, in *Traditio* VII (1952), pp. 159–264.
BOEHMER, HENRICH,	Der Sogenannte Serlo von Bayeux, in *Neues Archiv*. Vol. 22 (1897), pp. 703–738.
BOEHMER, HEINRICH,	Kirche und Staat in England und in der Normandie im. XI und XII. Jahrhundert (1899).
BOUCH, C. M. L.,	Prelates and People of the Lake Counties (1948).
BOUTEMY, A.,	Deux poèmes inconnus de Serlon de Bayeux, in *Le Moyen Age*, 3rd Series. Vol. IX (1938), pp. 241–269.
BRØGGER, A. W.	Ancient Emigrants (1929).
BROOKE, C. N. L.,	The composition of the chapter of St. Paul's, 1086–1163, in *Cambridge Historical Journal*, X (1951), pp. 111–132.
BURTON, J.,	Monasticon Eboracense (1758).
CERTAIN, M. DE.,	Raoul Tortuaire, in *Bibliothèque de l'Ecole des Chartres* 1855, pp. 489–521.
CHENEY, C. R.,	English Bishops Chanceries 1100–1250 (1950).
CLAY, Sir CHARLES T.,	York Minster Fasti , 2 vols. (*Y A J* Record Series, CXXIII, CXXIV, 1958, 1959).
CLAY, Sir CHARLES T.,	*Y A J* XXXVI (1944–47), pp. 269–87, and 409–34.
CLAY, Sir CHARLES T.,	The Early Precentors and Chancellors of York, in *Y A J* XXXV (1943), pp. 116–138.
CLAY, Sir CHARLES T.,	A Holderness Charter of William Count of Aumale, in *Yorkshire Archaeological Journal* 39 (1956–58), pp. 339–342.
COMPAIN, L.,	Geoffrey de Vendôme (1891).
CONSTABLE, GILES,	The disputed election at Langres in 1138, in *Traditio* XIII (1957), pp. 119–152.

CRASTER, H. H. E.,   A Contemporary Record of the Pontificate of Ranulf Flambard, in *Archaeologia Aeliana* VII (1930), pp. 33–56.

CRASTER, H. H. E.,   The miracles of St. Cuthbert at Farne, in *Analecta Bollandiana* LXX (1952), pp. 5–19.

DAVIES, J. C.   Episcopal Acts Relating to Welsh Dioceses 1066–1272 (vol. I in the publications of the Historical Society of the Church in Wales, 1946).

DENHOLM-YOUNG, N.,   The Foundation of Warter Priory, in *Y A J* XXXI (1934), pp. 208–13.

DENTON, J.,   Cumberland (1887).

DICKINSON, J. C.,   The origins of the Austin Canons (1950).

DICKINSON, J. C.,   The origins of Carlisle Cathedral, in *Transactions of the Cumberland and Westmorland Antiquarian and Archaeological Society*, XLV (1946), pp. 134–143.

DRAKE, F.,   Eboracum (1736).

DUNCAN, A. A. M.,   The Earliest Scottish Charters, in *Scottish Historical Review* XXXVII (1958), pp. 103–135.

EASSON, D. E.,   Mediaeval Religious Houses Scotland (1957).

FLEUREAU, B.,   Les antiquités de la ville et du duché d'Étampes (1683).

FOREVILLE, R.,   L'école de Caen au XI siècle et les origines normandes de l'université d'Oxford, in *Études médiévales offertes a m. le doyen Augustin Fliche* (1952), pp. 81–100.

FOREVILLE, R. and LECLERCQ, J.,   Un débat sur le sacerdoce des moines au XIIe siècle, in *Studia Anselmiana* 41 (1957), pp. 8–118.

GALBRAITH, V. H.,   Monastic Foundation Charters of the Eleventh and Twelfth Centuries, in the *Cambridge Historical Journal*, IV (1934), pp. 205–22, 296–8.

GALLIA CHRISTIANA,   16 vols. (1716–1745).

GATHORNE-HARDY, G. M.,   A Royal Impostor, King Sverre of Norway (1956).

GIGALSKI, B.,   Bruno von Segni (1898).

GLAISNER, H.,   Raoul de Caen. Historien et écrivain, in *Revue d'histoire écclésiastique* XLVI (1951), pp. 5–21.

GOODALL, A.,   Place Names of South West Yorkshire (1914).

GOUGAUD, L.,   Étude sur la réclusion religieuse, in *Revue Mabillon* 13 (1923), pp. 26–39, 77–102).

GOUGAUD, L.,   Mulierum Consortia, in *Eriu* IX (1921), pp. 147–156.

GROSJEAN, P.,   Vita Roberti, in *Analecta Bollandiana* LVI (1938), pp. 334–60.

HAMILTON THOMPSON, A.,   The Priory of St. Mary, Bolton-in-Wharfedale (Thoresby Society, XXX, 1928).

HARDY, G. LE,   Mémoires pour servir a l'état historique et géographique du diocèse de Bayeux. 2 vols. 1895–96.

HEFELE-LECLERCQ,   Histoire des Conciles V. I. (1912).

HOLMES, R.,   The foundation of St. Clement's in the Castle of Pontefract, in *Y A J* XIV (1898), pp. 147–57.

HOLTZMANN, W.,   Papsturkunden in England. 3 vols. (1932–1952).

HOLTZMANN, W.,   Zur Geschichte des Investiturstreites, in *Neues Archiv.* 50 (1935), pp. 246–319.

HOWELL, M.,   Regalian Right in Medieval England (1962).

HUNTER, J.,   South Yorkshire (1869).

JAMES, M. R.,   The Salomites, in *Journal of Theological Studies* XXXV (1934), pp. 287–297).

KNOWLES, D.,   The Monastic Order in England (1950).

KNOWLES, D.,   The case of St. William of York, in the *Cambridge Historical Journal* V (1936), pp. 162–77, 212–4.

LECLERCQ, J.,   Simoniaca Heresis, in *Studi Gregoriana* I (1947), pp. 523–30.

LECLERCQ, J.,   Écrits Spirituels d'Elmer de Cantorbéry, in *Studia Anselmiana* 31 (1953), pp. 45–117.

LEVISON, W.,   Aus Englischen Bibliotheken, in *Neues Archiv*. 53 (1910), pp. 331–431.

LEVISON, W.,   England and the Continent in the Eighth Century (1946).

LEYSER, K.,   England and the Empire in the early twelfth century, in *Transactions of the Royal Historical Society*, 10 (1960), pp. 61–83.

LIEBERMANN, F.,   An English Document of about 1080, in *Yorkshire Archaeological Journal*, XVIII (1905), pp. 412–16.

LINDKVIST, H.,   A study on early mediaeval York, in *Anglia* 49–50 (1926), pp. 345–394.

LOEWE, RAPHAEL,   The Mediaeval Christian Hebraists of England, in *Transactions of the Jewish Historical Society of England* XVII (1951–52), pp. 225–249.

LOOMIS, R. S.,   Wales and the Arthurian Legend (1956).

LOYD, L. C.,   The origins of some Anglo-Norman Families (The Publications of the Harleian Society Vol. 103, 1951).

LUCHAIRE, ACHILLE,   Louis VI le Gros (1890).

MANITIUS, M.,   Geschichte der Lateinischen Literatur des Mittelalters Vol. 3, 1931.

MOREY, D.,   Canonist Evidence in the case of St. William of York, in the *Cambridge Historical Journal* X (1950), pp. 352–3.

MORIN, G.,   Rainaud l'Ermite et Yves de Chartres : un épisode de la crise du cénobitisme aux XIᵉ–XII siècles, in *Revue Bénédictine* XL (1928), pp. 99–115.

MUSSET, LUCIEN,   A-t-il existé en Normandie au XIᵉ siècle une aristocratie d'argent ? in *Annales de Normandie* (1959), pp. 285–299.

NEWPORT, R.,   Repertorium Ecclesiasticum parochiale Londinense, 2 vols., 1708–10.

NIDERST, R.,   Robert d'Arbrissel et les origines de l'ordre de Fontevrault (1952).

NORTHUMBERLAND, A   15 vols. (1893–1940).
 HISTORY OF,

PÄCHT, O., DODWELL, G.R. The St. Alban's Psalter (1960).
 WORMALD, F.,

PADGETT, L.,   Chronicles of Old Pontefract (1905).

PAGE, W.,   Some remarks on the churches of the Domesday Survey, in *Archaeologia* 2nd series 66 (1914–15), pp. 61–102.

PEERAGE, THE COMPLETE.

PLACE NAMES SOCIETY,   Publications (Cumberland, vols. XX–XXII,
 ENGLISH,   Yorkshire, vols. V, XIV and XXX–XXXVI).

RADFORD, C. A. R.,   The Excavations at Whithorn, 1949, in *Transactions of the Dumfries and Galloway Natural History and Antiquarian Society*, XXVII (1950), pp. 85–126.

RAINE, ANGELO,   Mediaeval York (1955).

RAMACKERS, J.,   Papsturkunden in Frankreich, 6 vols. (Vol. I ed. H. Meinert) (1932—58).

RASHDALL, HASTINGS,   The Universities of Europe in the Middle Ages (ed. T. M. Powicke and A. B. Emden, 3 vols., 1936).

REEVES, W.,   The Culdees of the British Islands (1864).

RITCHIE, R. L. G.,   The Normans in Scotland (1954).

ROBERT, ULYSSE,   Bullaire du Pope Calixte II (1891).

ROBERT, ULYSSE,   Histoire du Pope Calixte II (1891).

ROUND, J. H.,   Geoffrey de Mandeville (1892).

ROUND, J. H.,   The Commune of London (1899).

ROUND, J. H., — Calendar of Documents preserved in France (1899).

SCAMMELL, G. V., — Hugh de Puiset (1956).

SCHMALE, F. J., — Studien zum Schisma des Jahres 1130 (1961).

SCHOENE, G., — Kardinallegat Kuno (1857).

SOUTHERN, R. W., — The Canterbury Forgeries, in *English Historical Review* lxxiii (1958), pp. 193–226.

SOUTHERN, R. W., — St. Anselm and his biographer (1963).

SQUIRE, AELRED, — Historical Factors in the Formation of Aelred of Rievaulx, in *Collectanea Ord. Cist. Ref.* (1960), pp. 262–282.

STUBBS, W., — Historical Introductions to the Rolls Series (1902).

STUBBS, W., — Select Charters (1942).

TAIT, J., — The Mediaeval English Borough (1936).

TALBOT, C. H., — New Documents in the case of St. William of York, in the *Cambridge Historical Journal* X (1950), pp. 1–15.

TALBOT, C. H., — The testament of Gervase of Louth Park, in *Analecta Sacri Ordinis Cisterciensis* VII (1951), pp. 32–45.

TALBOT, C. H., — The Centum Sententiae of Walter Daniel, in *Sacris Erudiri* XI (1960), pp. 266–383.

TILLMANN, HELENE, — Die päpstlichen Legaten in England (1926).

WAITES, B., — The Monastic Settlement of North-East Yorkshire, in *Y A J* CLIX (1961), pp. 478–495.

WERNER, E., — Robert von Arbrissel: Zur Fraeunfrage und zum Frauenkult im Mittelalter, in *Forschungen und Fortschritte* (1953), pp. 269–76.

WHARTON, H., — Anglia Sacra (2 vols.) (1691).

WHITE, H. V., — Pontius of Cluny, the Curia Romana and the end of Gregorianism in Rome, in *Church History* XXVII (1958), pp. 195–219.

WILLIAMS, G. H., — The Norman Anonymous of 1100 A.D. (1951).

WILSON, JAMES, — The Foundation of the Austin Priories of Nostell and Scone, in *The Scottish Historical Review* VII (1910), pp. 141–159.

INDEX